MW01101050

THE
HANDKERCHIEF
DRAWER

⮜⮞

إنشاء الدبد

THE HANDKERCHIEF DRAWER

an autobiography
in
three parts

by

Thelma Ruck Keene

Trafford Publishing
Victoria, B.C., Canada

© Copyright 2002 Thelma Ruck Keene. All rights reserved.

No part of this publication may be reproduced, stored in a retrieval system, or transmitted, in any form or by any means, electronic, mechanical, photocopying, recording, or otherwise, without the written prior permission of the author.

Printed in Victoria, Canada

National Library of Canada
Cataloguing in Publication

Keene, Thelma Ruck, 1916-
 The handkerchief drawer / Thelma Ruck Keene.
ISBN 1-55369-135-0
 1. Keene, Thelma Ruck, 1916- 2. British Canadians--Biography.
3. Vancouver (B.C.)--Biography. I. Title.
FC3847.26.K43A3 2002   971.1'3304'092 C2002-901735-1
F1089.5.V22K43 2002

TRAFFORD

This book was published *on-demand* in cooperation with Trafford Publishing.
On-demand publishing is a unique process and service of making a book available for retail sale to the public taking advantage of on-demand manufacturing and Internet marketing.
On-demand publishing includes promotions, retail sales, manufacturing, order fulfilment, accounting and collecting royalties on behalf of the author.

Suite 6E, 2333 Government St., Victoria, B.C. V8T 4P4, CANADA

Phone	250-383-6864	Toll-free	1-888-232-4444 (Canada & US)
Fax	250-383-6804	E-mail	sales@trafford.com
Web site	www.trafford.com	TRAFFORD PUBLISHING IS A DIVISION OF TRAFFORD HOLDINGS LTD.
Trafford Catalogue #01-0537		www.trafford.com/robots/01-0537.html

10   9   8   7   6

For Leo,
with love
and thanks for being there.

Also special thanks for giving me a word processor
and telling me to get on with writing
this story.

What's the meaning of a flower?...There's no meaning. What's the meaning of the universe? What's the meaning of a flea? It's just there. That's it. And your own meaning is that you're there.

We're so engaged in doing things to achieve purposes of outer value that we forget that the inner value, the rapture that is associated with being alive, is what it's all about.

Joseph Campbell, 1904-1987

Grateful acknowledgements

To

Richard (Dick) Usborne
who told me I could write.

To

Peter McWhirter
(my brother-in-law) whose patient research finally revealed the undreamed-of origins of the Garsia family.

To

Pam Swanigan and Betty Taylor for professional editing.
Also *Suzin Schiff* for final proofreading.

To

Rupert Clark, Geina Fournier, Laurie Grant, and *Cynthia Lyman* who gave their time to read and edit the final versions of my story. In addition *Rupert Clark* prepared the book for publication; and *Cynthia Lyman* scanned the old photographs into the text.

To

Libby Davies, Bruce Eriksen, Heather Graham, Barbara Lambert, Elizabeth & Howard Leach, Mary Mackie, Ron & Ursule Tribe, and *Linda Willoughby.* These friends listened to or read ongoing versions of the script, giving a medley of support, stringent advice and always laughter.

To

Circle Crafts Executive Director, Paul Yard, who has given unfailing help in many ways. Also to the *Board Members* who, more than once, presented me with unexpected and timely funds. Also to my sister *Felicity Pocock,* who generously contributed to the cost of a reader which shows an enlarged copy of my typescript on the monitor.

Without these gifts of time and money my typescript would have been a manifold of errors, as I am 'legally blind'. This doesn't mean I can't see anything, but I miss a lot of detail. Most of all I am thankful for friendship, discussion, and laughter.

Chapter Headings

PART ONE: 1916 - 1940   page 1
1.   *The Garsias and bits of my father.*
2.   *The Ruck Keenes, with Abbie, Emma, Oophats, and everyone.*
3.   *Turning over old letters and family bones.*
4.   *A marriage, a birth, and a letter from a ghost.*
5.   *The prayer book is adamant, so off to the New World.*
6.   *Life, Liberty and Chiropractic in San Antonio, Texas.*
7.   *Paradise 'was'. 'Now' is mostly one thing after another.*
8.   *So many changes, but Copford is forever.*
9.   *Encountering phenomena from the very good to the truly awful.*
10. *About music, words, and being 'possessed'.*
11. *Family, and belonging.*
12. *Confirmation, Copford, sex and sin lists.*
13. *Confession. Saved by books and music, but beware the Jubjub bird!*
14. *More music, more sex, and that's it for school.*
15. *Freedom! And what is love?*
16. *Freedom sounds good, but it's hard work.*
17. *London! And new aspects of freedom.*
18. *The Foreign Office, a room of my own, and soul muddle.*
19. *Marriage.*
20. *The chemistry of impending war. War, and Budapest.*

PART TWO: 1940 - 1944   page 175
21. *Beautiful Budapest, bedbugs and other problems.*
22. *'Belinda'. A new name, and much else new.*
23. *Three full months, then farewell, Budapest.*
24. *Journey with incidents. Athens, Alexis, and war at closer quarters.*
25. *The Kalanthe makes her last voyage.*
26. *Kimolos. Santorini, and a priest's blessing.*
27. *The Heraklion villa, escape from Canea, and the truth in Cairo.*
28. *Major Wintle's toys, and a spot of spying.*
29. *The Cedars of Lebanon, and a decision.*
30. *Beirut. General Spears, Kassab, and lighthouse territory.*
31. *A river of blood, and war in the Middle Eastern briar patch.*
32. *The Cedars, Christmas 1941, New Year in Damascus. A marriage.*
33. *The Spears Mission clerks. Also a potter, a poem, and a Princess.*
34. *Comings, goings, decisions, and a happiness.*
35. *David coins a phrase. The Press Attaché, and Palestine.*
36. *Changes. I shake on a deal.*
37. *Adieu Beirut. Palermo and the Sicilian circus.*
38. *Unanswered questions. England.*
39. *Sandy and London. David. D-day, Doodle-bugs, and Dartmoor.*
40. *David.*

PART THREE: 1944 - 1966   page 351
41. *The end of World War Two. Marriage. Alexis tells his story.*
42. *Contentious issues, a lunch in Milan, and post-war Germany.*
43. *Krupp's and unmapped territories. A decision.*
44. *"Of the greatest moment...a distant journey into unknown lands."*
45. *Oh! Peter Pumpkin Eater. O Canada!*
    Epilogue.
    Bibliography.

Photographs

Grouped at the end of PART ONE   pages 163-174
    My father, 2nd Lieutenant, 1914.
    Me, 1918.
    My mother, *ca.* 1920.
    My grandmother, Minna de la Paz Garsia.
    Birdie and Ted Ruck Keene and family, April 15, 1891.
    Copford Rectory, Eight Ash Green, Essex.
    Abbie and Emma.
    Junior and me, San Antonio, Texas, 1922.
    Willoughby and my mother with Diplomas in Chiropractic, 1923.
    Wedding photograph of Phil and Dick Ruck Keene, Dec., 1923.
    Me with Oophats, Lymington, 1928.
    Hogs Hill, my cottage in Albury, Hertfordshire.
    Arthur Lyons and me, 1938.
    Engagement photograph for the *Tatler*, 1936
    "Positively the Popsiest Picture I ever Produced."
    Kalanthe survivors. The hospital party on Kimolos, April, 1941.
    Me with Kassab, 1941.
    Me on the balcony of the Spears Mission, 1942.
    Dinner in Beirut, 1942.
    Leo, 1954.
    Leo and me on our first visit to Canada, 1965.
    Leo and me in Vancouver, 1997.

PART ONE

Spiders' webs can tie up lions.

African proverb

1916 – 1940

England, Texas, England

The Garsias and bits of my father.

My father was always quite dead. This meant he wasn't there, though that didn't stop him being there, coming and going un-expectedly like a whisper or a breath. Anyway, that's how he was to me when I was around three years old, and lived with my mother in grandmother Minna's house. In the little room next to the conservatory there were bits of my father under glass, and my mother had a photograph of him on the table by her bed. He sat cross-legged in soldier's uniform, laughing. He looked very happy.

One day I asked my grandmother why he was happy to go off and be dead. She said, "He didn't mean to be dead. He went to fight for you and your Mummy, to keep you safe from harm."

There wasn't much left of him, just some bits laid out on a table like a glass-topped box on legs. There was a shiny button and a sort of big knife, a letter ("From the King," Minna explained) and money on ribbons of different colours. "Medals, not money," Minna said. "The King gave the medals to your father because he was brave." Only the button shone, kept bright with Brasso. The knife was dulled by something that looked like rusty-red earth.

The room where these bits lay was chilly until the door to the conservatory was opened and warmth came in with the bold smell of geraniums. The box table had spindly legs, slightly curved outwards as if about to bend so I could more easily see the bits of my father. As they stayed unbent a footstool was set for me and from this height I could stare through the spotless glass at all the things carefully arranged on royal blue velvet. They lay very still in the quiet room.

"Did my father ever see me?"

"No, pet, but he did know you were born, and that made him very happy."

"Did he only have *one* button?"

"Of course not, darling. They just wanted us to have something that was his, besides the ring Mummy wears." That ring had a black stone on which were carved pictures of two animals. When the stone was pressed on melty sealing wax, there were the two animals. Minna said it was a signet ring, and the lion and doe belonged to my name, Ruck Keene. "The lion is a Ruck," she said, "and the doe is a Keene - unless...oh dear! Maybe it's the other way round."

"Uncle Marston's ring is bigger and has feathers."

Minna said in a happy voice. "Your dear grandfather always wore it. He was very proud of his ring."

I didn't like the knife Minna called a bayonet. "Can't we wash that red stuff off? It's ugly." Minna didn't answer. "Won't it wash off?"

"No...no, it won't wash off."

"Why?"

Did she really say, "That's the blood of a Boche"? Maybe not, but I knew it was blood, even though the Boche in my head looked more like a fat toadstool than a man.

"Is the Boche dead?"

"Yes," Minna said, "yes, poor soul."

Shadows chilled the room, and the geraniums were silent. But Minna gave me a hug and said, "There now, child! Let's see if there's a juicy plum on the tree just ripe for your lunch." Then we walked together through the conservatory, which was warm as a hug, and the bright red geraniums shouted about being alive.

Minna's house was called Woodford. It was in Clarence Park, Weston-super-Mare, which meant Weston-by-the-sea. Later Minna bought a house in Quantock Road for my mother and me to live in. I didn't like that house; it had ugly brown linoleum in the entrance hall. In Minna's house the hall floor was covered by a big red carpet with pictures; it came from India, where she was born. There was also a large, carved chair with a red velvet seat and broad arms. You would never know that there were little boxes in each arm, and some of the littlest spirits lived in these boxes. If you lifted the lids very quietly it was possible to hear a rustle, soft as a whisper: it was the spirits slipping out of sight.

My uncle Marston said the chair was old and had been made for a Spanish grandee. I felt very grand indeed, sitting on the chair with my legs stuck straight out and the red velvet purring soft under my bare skin. The chair was Spanish because my grandfather, Dr. Willoughby Marston de la Paz Garsia, was Spanish. My other uncle, Willoughby, had painted a picture of him - only the top half because there wasn't room to get all of him in. He was dressed like a Spanish soldier of long ago, with a white frill called a ruff round his neck. He had a black beard and dark brown eyes which looked straight at you.

Marston wore the gold ring with three big feathers carved in the centre. He said it could only be worn by the eldest son of the family. "I am really Count Marston de la Paz Garsia," he explained, standing up very tall, adding that somewhere in Spain there was a de la Paz Garsia castle.

"Can't we live in the castle?"

"We haven't found it yet."

"Why? Is it a very little castle?"

"No, no - we've just lost the address." So for the time being we lived here in Weston-by-the-sea.

Besides Minna, my mother, and me, there was my aunt Freda. She laughed a lot, sometimes too much, and Minna would say, "Quieten down now, dear," as if she was a child like me. My two uncles were much more important, though we only saw them when they came on visits from London. Marston was very tall with a big nose and a deep voice; Willoughby was quiet and painted pictures. I loved Willoughby; he had magic hands. One time I woke and heard a terrible wailing "E-e-h! a-a-h! e-e-h! a-a-h!" as if everyone in the whole world was sad. I cried too and couldn't stop until Willoughby came and held my hand, and stroked my forehead. I asked why everyone was so sad. He said, "Everyone is sometimes happy and sometimes sad. But what you heard was just your friend, the donkey."

"Poor donkey! Why is he sad?"

"He was lonely. But he's all right now he's had a good cry."

Quite often my mother had a good cry, and when she played her violin she made the violin cry so sadly it made me cry. In the end she gave up the violin and stuck to the piano. My uncle Marston said she played the piano with lots of dash. Sometimes she got the notes wrong, but that didn't matter. She played nursery rhymes and songs like "There was an old man called Michael Finnigan, He had whiskers on his chinigan" which we sang together, or I danced around the room while the spirits rustled happily above the curtain rails.

My mother cried because she was a widow. In Minna's house there were two marble pillars at the bottom of the stairs, and on each pillar was a marble bust (just the top half), one of a Widow, the other a Bride. The Bride was young and laughing and had flowers in her curly marble hair. The Widow was, of course, very sad. Her curls were covered by a marble veil, her head was bowed and marble tears were frozen on her white cheeks. Halfway up the stairs there was a landing with a big window made of different coloured glass: when sunshine poured through the colours the Bride had a warm band of gold across her curls, and the Widow's white cheeks grew rosy.

"Look, Mummy, she's happy now!" Then my mother would smile, and we were all happy.

Those sunny days were good for flying downstairs. I didn't fly often, just on a good, sunny day. I flew light as a feather, my hair lifting in the breath of my bird flight. One day I told my mother," I just flew downstairs."

"How lovely, darling," she said as if she was thinking about something else, and told me it was time for my milk. She gave me the milk in a silver mug with my name on it, but I didn't want milk after flying downstairs and threw the mug, milk and all, into the fireplace. The fire wasn't lit, but the milk made a mess under the fire-irons.

My mother was angry and cried to Minna, "Look what this bad little girl has done with her christening mug!" No reply from Minna. But later she looked at me with her sky blue eyes, and said:

There was a little girl
Who had a little curl
Right in the middle of her forehead.
When she was good
She was very, very good,

And when she was bad she was horrid.

Being good was something you had to be. Even the cat in "I love little pussy" wouldn't love me if I was bad. So I sang:
> I will sit by her side
> And give her some food,
> And pussy will love me
> If I'm gentle and good.

Being good wasn't easy: there were so many ways of being bad, like not doing as I was told, or not eating up my food. If I didn't eat everything the whole plateful came back at the next meal, more horrible than ever. Sometimes I was sent upstairs with the plate of food and shut in my room until every scrap was eaten.

One day I'd eaten all the vegetables but not the slice of nasty pink ham. "Really Thelma!" cried my mother, and pushed back her chair so hard it nearly fell over. "I'm sick and tired of your naughtiness, if you don't eat your ham, I'll..." Her face was flushed, her brown eyes crunched in a frown and some hairpins fell from the bun of her thick black hair. If her hair fell right down she would be really cross. It didn't, but she went on "...If you don't eat up I'll speak to Miss Blott. She must be told that you are too naughty to be a fairy in the ballet next week."

How could this be? My mother *wanted* me to be in the ballet and wear the dress she'd spent hours making on the Singer sewing machine. But she said, "And I'll give your dress to another little girl who knows how to behave." In my bedroom upstairs she said, "I shall expect to see a nice clean plate when I come back," and shut the door.

I threw the ham out of my window, but it fell on the roof of the bay window below, and my mother saw it there. I didn't dance in the ballet and the green gauzy dress with silver wings disappeared. Probably it went to a little girl who did what she was told and ate up every scrap of her food every day.

At least the Thursday afternoon dancing classes went on as usual. Every Wednesday evening began with my mother lighting the gas in the bathroom geyser to make the water hot. She was frightened of the geyser. Sometimes it went wrong, giving a roar like a lion. She'd start all over again, muttering, "I hate this thing," and to me, "Go outside like I told you, and *stay there*. It might blow up." It never did. After my bath Minna brought out the strips of cloth which she rolled my hair on to make it curl. Each roll was tied up tightly so it wouldn't come undone when I was asleep. Sometimes she tied them extra tight.

"Ouch, ouch! You're hurting!"

"Don't be such a little goose. It won't hurt if you keep your head still."

It did hurt, but was worth it. The next afternoon I put on my silk dancing frock with a wide satin sash. It was tied in a bow at the back, and in the front had a nice slippery feel. In winter I was bundled into warm wraps for the walk to the Assembly Hall. There I put on bronze leather dancing slippers, each with a fat bronze pom-pom, and bronze elastic was looped round my ankles to keep the slippers on my feet. Out on the dancing floor we waited for Miss Prince at the piano to nod to Miss Blott, who cried, "And a *one*-two-three and *one*-two-three."

One day Miss Blott chose me, for the first time, to be her partner for the polka. I felt very proud, but when I placed my hand lightly on her back, I made a terrible discovery.

"Are we all ready? Yes, Miss Prince! And *one*-two-three-four..."

At the end of the polka Miss Blott remarked that today I was, perhaps, a little out of sorts? I hung my head. She was shapely and bendy, but now I knew her terrible secret: she had to live supported in a metal cage, for without it, all her bones would fall out of her skin.

I kept her secret to myself. Then one day I saw my mother taking long bony strips from a new pair of corsets: she said they were bits of whalebone. "They make me feel I'm in a cage. Ugh! horrid things!" So much for Miss Blott's cage.

Dancing class was the best winter treat; in summer the best treat was going to the beach. We took the tram, the bell tinkling at each stop, and soon I could cry, "There's the sea, Mummy!" just in case she hadn't noticed. I got out with bucket and spade, my mother with what she called "all my paraphernalia" - towel, a spare pair of knickers for me, a book for her, Digestive biscuits in case we felt peckish, and a thermos of milky tea.

On beach days my mother usually made sure the tide would be high because at low tide the sandy beach stopped and became a mucky brown stretch of rather smelly mud. Sometimes she got the tides wrong and failed to notice that the sea was slowly gliding away. My dress was tucked into my knickers so I could paddle and for a while I squelched about in the mud. It was soft and warm and oozed like thick brown chocolate sauce between my toes. This never lasted long.

"Whatever are you doing, Thelma! Just look at you, mud all over your knickers."

We always took time to hear the men called 'nigger minstrels' strumming their banjos and singing familiar songs like "De Camptown ladies sing dis song, Doo-dah! Doo-dah! De Camptown race track five miles long, Oh-oh doo-dah day!" Their faces were blackened, leaving white circles round their eyes, their lips were painted to make their mouths look big, and on their curly black hair each minstrel wore a stiff straw hat with a small brim called a boater.

Except for the boaters the minstrels were the spitten image of Golliwog, made by my mother. Golliwog's round eyes were white linen buttons, his hair was a strip of black rabbit fur from an old pair of my mittens, and his big mouth, cut from a remnant of red flannel nightdress, curved in a friendly grin. I knew nigger minstrels were white people with black faces. Real black people were only in books, like

Little Black Sambo whose clothes were stolen by the yellow tigers but he got them back when they chased each other round and round a palm tree and turned into *ghee*, meaning butter. So a 'nigger' was a minstrel, a grown-up who liked making his face black.

Whatever day we went to the beach the sandcastle men would be making turreted castles or dragons or sea monsters, and always there was a British Lion (big enough to sit on if only he wasn't sand) with a Union Jack draped across his back.

"May I give him a penny, Mummy?" If I got a penny I put it carefully in a hat lying between the lion's huge paws. That was a treat. So was a donkey ride. An even rarer treat was being allowed a cone of pink spun sugar on a stick. My mother was against spun sugar. Sometimes I tried wheedling with "Today, just for once...?" but usually she was firm: "No, Thelma. You get covered in sticky and all that sugar's bad for your teeth."

Some days we went on the pier. There were little machines on the pier that had pictures in them. If you put money in and turned a handle the pictures moved. One was called 'What the butler saw', but my mother said it wasn't interesting so I never did know what he saw. But the pier was a fine place. Wooden planks, scrubbed white by wind and weather, stretched far out to sea. Between the planks you could see waves splashing against the pier's iron legs, which at low tide were covered with a crust of shells and seaweed. From above it seemed the seaweed waved long fingers searching for something to grasp, and the water made sucking sounds. But we were safe, high above the sucking water and weedy fingers. The fresh breeze blew my hair into tangles and my mother's brown eyes laughed as she said, "The breeze has blown roses into your cheeks!" And we were happy.

My mother and I were happy doing things together, but not when she tried teaching me to read. I enjoyed being read to or told stories, but hated the book she said she had learnt to read from. *Reading Without Tears* (which wasn't true) was printed on the ugly dark red cover; inside were little black-and-white drawings to show what the words meant. 'The cat sat on the mat. I see the cat. I see the dog.' The alphabet was just as stupid: A is for apple, B is for bat, C is for cat, and not a word about what the cat was thinking or what the bat was for.

My mother said, "I could read *Little Black Sambo* when I was three years old," and in a cross voice to Minna, "If Thelma doesn't want to do something wild horses won't drag her." So Minna said she'd have a try.

We sat down with *Reading Without Tears* and I said for the umpteenth time, "This is a stupid book" - and Minna suddenly laughed. Then she gave me a sugared almond (she always had sugared almonds handy), told me to wait a moment and came back with another, quite old book. When we were both comfortable she read, "A was an Archer and shot at a frog, B was a Butcher and had a great dog, C was a Captain all covered with lace, D was a Drummer and had a red face."

That was much better. I didn't learn to read but soon knew Minna's alphabet by heart.

In wintertime the house on Quantock Road grew more friendly. A fire burned in the grate and often my mother settled down to make another frock for me or a new one for herself. Then I squeezed into the upturned wooden lid of the Singer sewing machine and, holding on tightly (the handle made the lid unsteady), I sailed through rough seas to faraway places.

There was lots to do on winter days - plasticine to fashion into people and creatures, and bright coloured crayons for colouring books ("That's lovely, darling, but try to keep the colour *inside* the lines." I tried, but not for long). My mother stitched sheets of brown paper together to make scrapbooks where I could stick in pictures chopped from magazines and catalogues - dogs and cats, bicycles and beds, natty gents and elegant ladies, and bright flowers from the seed catalogues. When I put a lady in a corset beside a natty gent in a top hat and white spats, my mother laughed. "You're a nut!" she said, and started a 'He said to Her' game.

"The gent in the natty suiting said to the lady in the corsets, 'You must be a trifle chilly, madam.'"

"And *she* said to *him*, 'You are very rude.'"

"And he said to her, 'Dear lady, let us walk to the dairy and eat some delicious ice cream.'"

"And *she* said to *him*, 'I will put on my best dress and then we will get married.'"

When Marston came on a visit from London there would be dressing-up games and charades. Minna told me Marston was training to be something called a barrister but he really wanted to go on the stage. He usually brought what my mother called 'ribald songs from the music halls' and "Come on, Christina," he'd cry, "let's give them a show!" Then they disappeared to learn the words and work out dance steps. When they were ready Minna and I bought tickets from Golliwog, sat on the chairs made ready for the audience, and the show began. "Oh-Oh/Jolly Old Pot/ninety-nine in the shade/What, what!"

Minna and I clapped and cried "Encore!" After the 'Jolly Old Pot' song I couldn't sit still and jumped up and down shouting "What, what!" Minna laughed, and the spirits were merry up amongst the curtain frills.

Naturally we had a dressing-up box with all kinds of clothes. The grandest of all was a Spanish gypsy dress. The full skirt was stitched with dozens of gold coins which rattled when you moved. "I wore this when I was young," my mother said. I was afraid she was going to be sad, but she gave me a kiss and draped my head with some black lace called a mantilla. She showed me how to hold the fat round castanets, saying they were difficult to play properly but their clatter made good effects. The box also held Minna's bits and pieces - a feather boa ("The height of elegance," my mother said), a big hat with feathers, and Minna's tiny shoes (size 3) were only a *little* too big.

After tea we always played games of Halma or Snakes and Ladders ("You *must* roll the dice on the board, Thelma, or it doesn't count") or card games like Beggar My Neighbour which was easy to play because I could count. At first I had to be helped with the Happy Families cards because of the names, but it was easy to remember their faces. They had big faces and small bodies and were rather bad-dream people. Hook-nosed Mrs. Dip the Dyer's wife had blue hands which she held out as if she was just going to do something wicked; poor Miss Mug the Milkman's Daughter had her head entirely hidden by an enormous bonnet.

"Has something happened to her face?"

Minna said no, a big bonnet had been bought for her to grow into. As for Master Bun the Baker's Son he had no proper head at all, only an outsize cottage loaf. Very few of them looked like the sort of people you would choose to live with. Even Mrs. Dose the Doctor's Wife, though stepping forward with a sweetish smile, held out a large bottle which we all agreed could only be very nasty medicine.

I rather liked feeling frightened. One of my favourite books, *The English Struwwelpeter*, was full of threats and disasters. My mother complained she couldn't get her tongue round the word *Struwwelpeter* but Minna said it right because she went to school in Germany and it was a German word.

"Like Boche?"

"No, that's French."

"But the Boches were bad Germans."

"Well yes, in a manner of speaking. But the poems were written long, long ago when the Germans were our friends."

"How...?"

"Yes dear. *Struwwelpeter* means Shock-headed Peter." His picture was printed on the cover. He stood with feet apart, arms spread wide, his uncut nails long and curly like roots. "Look at his hair, like a bush, and those awful fingernails - what a terrible boy!"

The children's clothes could be puzzling, like the boy who wore skirts but must be a boy because he carried a whip.

"Why is the boy in a frock? He looks silly."

"He lived a long time ago, when Victoria was Queen of England and little boys dressed like that."

"Was she nice?"

"Who? Oh, Queen Victoria. Well, I didn't know her *personally*, but I expect she was nice. Why?"

"The naughty children get awful bad punishments. Maybe the Queen didn't know."

Punishments in *Struwwelpeter* were no joke, whether given by a grown-up or brought on simply by being bad. Augustus, for instance, would not eat his soup. He didn't live long:

> Look at him, now the fourth day's come!
> He scarcely weighs a sugar plum!
> He's like a little bit of thread;
> And on the fifth day, he was dead!

The last picture showed a grassy graveyard. Beside a nameless wooden cross lay a very large soup tureen, a warning to all children who would not eat up. There were an awful lot of things children were not supposed to do.

The only person in *Struwwelpeter* I didn't like was the Great Tall Tailor in *The Story of Little Suck-a-Thumb*. In one picture the Tailor runs lightly across the page on long thin legs, so fast his hat blows off. He carries huge scissors ready to chop off Conrad's sucked thumbs, who doesn't even try to get away, just stands there with his thumbs sticking out. I didn't suck my thumb, but I sometimes had nightmares about the Great Tall Tailor who chased me down the lane bordering the allotments. I ran away, fast as I could, but it was never fast enough. What made the dream Tailor extra awful was that his long thin legs were bare and covered with black, spiky hairs. Under one arm he carried a pot of Dundee marmalade, and the other arm was always stretched out, nearly, oh nearly! touching me. I woke howling for my mother.

Not all my books were frightening. The most beautiful were two nursery song books with pictures drawn and painted by someone called Henriette Willebeek le Mair.

"Was she born in Weston-super-Mare?"

Apparently not. You could get right into her pictures. The one for Dickory, Dickory Dock! had a staircase curving up to a landing with a big window. In the picture a boy and girl lean over the banisters to look at a mouse running up a grandfather clock. There was a grandfather clock in the entrance hall at Copford Rectory, where my Ruck Keene grandparents lived. It was here, in the hall at Copford, that Abbie came out of the kitchen and saw my father, walking up the staircase after he was dead.

The Ruck Keenes, with Abbie, Emma,
Oophats and everyone.

It took a long time to reach Copford. We sat for hours in the train to Colchester, and then changed to another train with wooden seats. This one stopped at every little station, all with beds of bright flowers. My mother said a prize was given every year for the station with the most beautiful flowerbeds. The station-masters were very friendly, and at each stop they had a good chat with the engine driver about his family and how *his* garden was doing. When they finished chatting the station-master blew his whistle, waved his green flag and off we went again, chuff-chuffing across the flat fen country where nothing got in the way of the sky.

My mother always said, "We must have some fresh air", and at once opened the window, pulling at a big leather strap on the door. I wanted to pull the strap but she said, "No, Thelma, your hands are too little."

Sometimes smuts from engine smoke flew into my eyes, but my mother knew what to do. She took a clean hanky, and after making one corner wet and stiff with spit, poked out the smut. "Hold still, Thelma, try and keep your eye *open*. There! Is that better?" It usually was.

At last we came to Marks Tey, Birdie's station. All our bags were ready but my mother fussed, "Don't leave Golliwog behind, you know what happened last time."

As the train slowed down we saw my grandmother looking for us, and when it was safe to open the door there she was, arms open to lift me down, crying "There's my darling little gel! Give your Granny a big kiss!" and over my head, "Dickie darling," (my mother was really Christina but at Copford she was called Dickie), "how was the journey, you must be tired, and was my little gel good, of course she was. Here's Benty, he'll take your bags."

Outside it wasn't at all like Weston. No trams, no streets, just country and Oophats, wagging his tail by the pony trap. If it was cool Benty put a rug over my knees saying, "That'll keep you warm, little Missy." It was rough and had a nice smell of horse, like Benty. As we clip-clopped along the lanes my grandmother, Birdie, talked and talked about Phillie and Jackie and everyone, and the air tasted of trees and earth, wild flowers and leather harness. Oophats padded beside us, his tongue hanging out.

"Granny, won't Oophats get tired?"

"Oh no, not Oophats! He's half foxhound, and they can run for hours with the hunt. Dear me, he would be very put out not to come and meet you and your Mummy."

"Darling Oophats." My uncle Phil said they called him Oophats because he had fat 'ooves'. He did have very big paws. I stared down at Oophats, wondering which half of him (the part with the head, or the tail) was foxhound.

The next morning I went walking with Oophats in the water meadows beyond the house. When I came back my mother was in a fuss and cried, "Wherever have you been" but Birdie laughed, and said, "Oophats is as good as a nursemaid. When your dear daddy was no bigger than you, he used to go off with Punch, our hound. Ralphie would put his little arm round the old dog's neck, just like you, my darling, and never came to harm. We could always find them by looking for Punch's tail waving above the long grass."

When I walked with Oophats his ears were silky-soft against my cheek. In the water meadows we looked in the yellow faces of white daisies where sometimes a bee was looking for pollen and had yellow dust on his wings; or we lay down to watch little creatures scuttling about while butterflies fluttered overhead. There were no rabbits in the water meadows, so Oophats didn't want to chase anything.

I loved everything at Copford, especially Abbie and Emma who looked after the kitchen, and Benty who looked after the garden and the pony. When he groomed the pony he whistled through his teeth, "to keep the dust out of me lungs," he explained. Watching Benty brush the pony was just one of many things to do; but best of all was to sit on the rag mat in front of the kitchen range while Abbie told stories. Abbie said she was just a girl when she came to look after my father, after he was born, and Emma soon joined her. Now Abbie was the cook and Emma the housemaid. They knew a lot of stories, but first I asked for the one about Abbie seeing my father when he was dead.

"I was on my way to the dining-room," she began. "My hands were full and I pushed open the green baize door with my shoulder, thinking how I must get after Emma to clean the silver candlesticks. Never a thought in my head about your dear daddy. The door swung behind me and I was hurrying across the hall when, and I don't know why, I stopped and looked up the staircase. I tell you no lie, Thelma - there was Ralphie, his back to me, walking up the stairs, just as real as you are now."

This story was always the same. "There he was, wearing the old blue jersey he loved and your Granny said was a disgrace." Here she stopped and shook her head. "He was large as life against the light from the landing window, and without thinking I cried out 'Why, Ralphie, so you are back at last!' That's what I said, easy in meself, and he turned, gave me such a beautiful smile, and then went on up the stairs and out of my sight."

In our heads we saw Abbie at the bottom of the stairs, and my father gone. "Out of my sight he was," she said, "before I cried right out loud, 'But you're dead and gone!' and believe you me, I stood there, stiff as a statue."

None of us moved until Abbie smiled. "But when I got over my fright I just knew your daddy had come home because you and your Mummy were here with us."

And *I* was here with Abbie and Emma, Oophats and Benty, Granny, Grandpa uncles, aunts, and everyone, all of us at Copford Rectory, which would be forever.

Every morning I scrambled into my mother's bed to share her early morning tea. Emma put the silver tray on a bedside table, drew the curtains and told us what sort of a day it was. The bed was warm as a nest. I was allowed a sip of the sweet, milky tea and one slice of paper-thin bread-and-butter with the crusts cut off. Then I'd go out on the balcony.

The balcony had a low wall of carved stone around it and something called wisteria twisted in and out of the open bits so it was difficult to tell which were stems and which was stone. The papery purple flowers had an escaping scent, and hung like bunches of grapes. Between the stems and flowers I could peer out beyond the garden to the water-meadows and see if the windmill was turning; then I looked the other way to where the dell of beech trees began at the far end of the lawn.

When I was very little I wasn't allowed in the dell alone. The tree roots stuck out from the earth like a ladder, and my mother would tell me to be careful as we clambered down to where the brown leaves were rustly and thick as a carpet.

But one day Oophats and I went to the dell by ourselves. My mother was playing croquet on the lawn with Phil and my aunt Margie. As we climbed down the higgledy-piggledy tree roots the sounds of their laughter, the click of mallets on the wooden croquet balls, and the rooks cawing in the elms gradually faded. On the leaf carpet the earth smell was sweet and strong sunlight speckled between the roof of leafy branches; all around was a breathing quietness, and I was everything and everywhere on the other side of time.

When my mother found me she said I shouldn't go off alone like that, I was too little. But I didn't mind, I was full of happiness.

As we walked back across the lawn my aunt Margie came out of the house with my uncle Hugh who called, "Come on, Oophats, we're going for a walk."

Margie cried, "We've got visitors for tea, Hugh." But off he went and Margie laughed. "Aren't the boys hopeless, Dickie!" and added, "The visitors will want to see the brat."

My mother disliked me being called a brat, but it was all right; Margie said what she meant and didn't fuss. Both she and Hugh had red-gold hair and bright blue eyes. My other aunt, Doshie, had brown hair and big brown eyes, and sometimes when I wasn't expecting it, she'd put her arms round me, her brown eyes filling with tears. She was nicest when she played the piano and sang, her voice warm and soft like the cooing doves.

Visitors meant tea was in the drawing-room, a big, comfortable room with glass doors opening to the garden, and the garden flowers seemed to have walked in and planted themselves all over the chintz-covered sofa and chairs. Tea in the drawing-room was always the same, beginning with the clink of teacups, the sound of tea being poured and my grandmother asking "Sugar? One or two lumps? Milk? Say when." A little spirit lamp kept the water simmering in the silver urn until no-one needed a refill and I was allowed to blow out the lamp through a long silver tube.

For drawing-room tea Emma brought thin white bread and butter, cucumber sandwiches with the crusts cut off, and one or two kinds of cake - fruit or a plain Madeira, perhaps a chocolate cake or Abbie's delicious sponge which was so light it was like eating a cloud tasting of eggs and spread with home-made strawberry jam. I had a glass of milk and one of Abbie's chewy ginger biscuits (the best in the world). I'd have sponge cake for supper later, when it didn't matter if I got sticky.

In my clean frock with a sailor collar I leant against Birdie while she talked to the visitors, who were women from the parish, wearing hats. Most of them had known my father, and a photograph of him when he was as young as me was passed round. Like the little boy in *Struwwelpeter* he wore a skirt and carried a whip. His blouse had a sailor collar, just like mine, and his hair was long and blonde, like mine.

"Like two peas in a pod!" Birdie said, stroking my newly brushed hair. One of the visitors wiped her eyes, and just for a minute came the breath of absence. But not for long: as always the breath slipped away between all the uncles and aunts, Abbie, Emma and Benty, and, of course, my grandfather.

During tea Birdie said, "Run and see if Grandpa wants another cup of tea, there's my good little gel!" As I left the room I heard Birdie explain that he was busy in his study writing the Sunday sermon and would come in later.

I knocked on the door. "Come in! come in!" he said in his growly voice. He sat in his leather armchair, a pipe between his teeth and said, "Having tea with the old puds, eh Thelma!" and gave the sharp bark that was his laugh. His eyes sparked through the shaggy hairs of his eyebrows and, "Think I'm going to bite?" he said. "Well, I'm not. Come here, let's take a look at you." We stared at one another in silence. "H'm. You'll do, you'll do." He didn't say anything else so I delivered my message. "No thanks, I don't want any more tea. Run along now." So I ran along, wondering if sitting in an armchair and smoking a pipe was how sermons were written.

At Copford Rectory the person called God seemed part of the household, but he liked everyone to behave well. When God came to church on Sunday my grandfather kept a sharp eye on the children, especially when he was in his pulpit and had a good view of everyone. Once he made me jump. "Tom Brook!" he roared, "stop pulling your sister's hair." I twisted round, trying to see Tom, but my mother said fiercely, *"Sit still."*

We didn't go to church in Weston and though Minna taught me to say, "God bless Mummy and my Grannies and Grandpa and my daddy" that was about the only time God came up, except when someone said "Thank God!" I asked Minna about God and she said he was great and kind and lived in heaven and looked after us.

As well as church on Sunday there were family prayers every morning in a room at the top of the house. It hadn't any furniture and we stood or knelt on bare floorboards while Grandpa talked to God and sometimes we joined in. I said "Amen" with everyone else and when the grown-ups stood or knelt I did the same. Birdie taught me a prayer she called 'Our Father' and when we got to that I was pleased not to be left out any more. I couldn't say it as fast as everyone else so they slowed up a bit; I didn't know what 'Our Father, which art in heaven' meant, but the words had a nice sound. From time to time water gurgled in the water pipes, sounding like an old man swallowing jugs and jugs of water. Abbie and Emma stood with their hands folded across their aprons, their eyes looking at the floor. There were no laughs when God was around, but we thanked him a lot.

Family prayers always began the day. Tea, at half-past four, meant my day was coming to an end. When there were no visitors we had it in the dining-room, but if Birdie and my mother were out to tea I had mine at the long, scrubbed kitchen table with Abbie and Emma.

Birdie once said that Abbie had been "just a slip of a gel" when she came to look after my father. That seemed funny. Abbie was now tall and slender, and somehow important. She had a laughing way of talking, but I had to mind what she said. Emma was round, her eyes like black boot buttons, rather wide open as if someone had just stuck a pin in her bottom. In a way Abbie-and-Emma were one person, though only Emma called snails 'hodmedods', and her mice were 'they meezen'.

After tea I sat on the rag mat in front of the kitchen range (very black, with steel fittings polished till they shone) and in the big iron kettle water simmered away, always ready to boil up for a nice cup of tea. Abbie leaned back in her rocking chair on one side of the range, Emma in her ordinary chair on the other side, and it was time for stories about the family, especially the boys being naughty.

Emma had a story about my father and Ben hiding from her in the churchyard (Ben was also dead like my father). Emma said, "Your Granny was most particular I was to be back sharp in time for tea, but the boys jumped over the churchyard wall and hid behind the grave-

16

stones. I couldn't climb over the wall in my long skirts, and the lych-gate was the other side of the church. 'Come back here this minute!' I cried, but they laughed and kept calling, 'Come and get us! come and get us!'"

Here Emma got quite flustered. "I didn't know what to do, and was in a taking that Abbie would scold me - she used to scold me something terrible, yes you did!"

Abbie said, "I'd have given them whatfor. Little rascals."

"Did you cry, Emma?"

"Yes, I did and all, and then they came and said they were sorry and took my hands and promised they wouldn't tease me again. But of course they did."

Emma wasn't any good at giving whatfor, but when Abbie caught me with my hands in the big wooden scullery bins - powdery-soft flour in one, interesting gritty oats in another - she'd say, "Take those grubby little puddies out of my flour, Miss, or I'll give you whatfor," and I'd take them out, quick.

"What did Abbie say when she scolded you?"

"She said I was a scatterbrain and she didn't know if she'd ever make a housemaid of me," but they both laughed.

"Well and all," Abbie said, "we've had some good laughs."

There were always stories in the rag mat. "What's this from?" I asked, and Abbie knew at once.

"That's from one of your Granny's winter nightdresses and those snippets were Ralphie's tennis flannels. They'd been washed so many times they weren't white any more." Emma added, "But he wouldn't part with them, not till he tore them so bad they couldn't be mended."

"What are the red bits?"

"Those were the boys' flannel nightshirts when they were quite young. There, Emma! Do you remember when Phillie got hold of a strip of that flannel and tied it to a stick. 'Whatever are you doing?' I asked and he said he wanted to see if a red rag would make the bull mad, but your Grandpa overheard him and told him not to be a young fool."

Then I asked, "Tell the story about Phil and the bee's nest," and added "please," after a look from Abbie.

"Well now, what's the time?" We all looked up at the kitchen clock tick-tocking on the wall beside the big dresser, which had beautiful blue-and-white willow-pattern plates standing flat along the shelves. "Just enough time," Abbie said, and began to tell how Phillie went out one day before breakfast to look at a bee's nest.

"He thought the nest was empty," Abbie said, "and wanted to find out how thick it was. But when he poked the stick into the nest some bees flew out and startled him. Well, you know Phillie, how he sticks his tongue out when he's busy, and when he jerked in fright, the sharp end of the stick went in his tongue."

"Right in?"

"Quite enough to make a proper mess. He came back for breakfast, his face stung and blood all over his shirt. Your Granny was in a great way and your Grandpa went striding off, shouting for Benty to get the pony harnessed to take Phillie to the doctor. But believe you me, that boy would *not* leave until he had eaten his porridge and cream! 'Don't fuss, Mother' he said, though you could hardly understand a word, his tongue was that swollen."

Abbie and Emma shook their heads and "Those boys," Emma said, "always up to something nobody in their right minds would think of doing."

But I was sure there was no-one in the world like my uncle. "Phillie was very brave, wasn't he, Abbie?"

"Oh very brave, in a manner of speaking," Abbie said. "But what about your poor Granny, worriting herself while he sat, cool as cucumber, eating his porridge." It was a lovely story.

I could have sat there on the rag mat for hours, but the green baize door squeaked on its hinges and in came my mother and grandmother. "How's my little gel?" Birdie said, giving me a hug, and began talking about the Women's Institute babies, "such bonnie babies, aren't they Dickie?" (my mother said they were, politely) and Birdie went on until she told Emma to get the hot water jugs, and the last happening of my day began.

At Copford I always had a bath in a big room upstairs which once was the nursery for my father and my uncles and aunts. The bath was called a hip-bath and was rather like a boat; it stood in front of the fire, and towels hung over the shiny brass rail of the tall fender to keep warm. There was a proper bath upstairs with two taps, but only cold water, so a lot of jugs of hot water had to be brought from the kitchen to fill it. This bath was ugly because one day my youngest uncle Jack had given the bath a coat of white paint on the inside; but Hugh had a bath before the paint was dry. A lot of paint came off on his bottom, leaving black patches where his bottom had been.

When I was clean and dry I was wrapped in the biggest towel, now toasted by the fire, and snuggled onto Birdie's lap. It was soft as a cushion and interesting brooches were pinned on the front of her frock. Some brooches had little chains "for safety, darling. These are precious stones." The precious stones and their gold or silver frames sparkled in the firelight. "What's that blue one called?"

"That's a sapphire. It's my birthstone and your dear daddy gave it to me before he went to fight in the war." We sat by the nursery fire, my mother on a low chair, Birdie on a bigger one. Her voice ran on and on. Sometimes my mother spoke, but the sound of Birdie talking was like water tinkling over stones. Now and again she sang a song:

> There was a little woman as I've heard tell,
> Fol lol diddle diddle dol.
> She went to market her eggs for to sell,

18

Fol lol diddle diddle dol...
or
Fiddle de dee, Fiddle de dee,
The fly has married the humble bee.

Usually she told my mother long, long stories about people I didn't know. Sometimes, especially after talking of my father, we sat quietly, listening to the wood burn and watching the flames dance. At last Birdie said, "Time for bed my sleepy-head!" and sang her good-night song:

Past six o'clock and it's bedtime for dolly,
Past six o'clock and it's bedtime for me.

It was the end of another day that was, like all the other days here, forever and ever.

The night before we went back to Weston, Birdie kissed the palm of each hand and, folding my fingers over the palms said, "Those are kisses for you to take home, darling, one for you and one for your other Granny."

"Can't we stay here with you?"

"That would be lovely, wouldn't it? But your other Granny would miss you."

"Oophats will miss me."

"We'll all be here when you come again, darling." She gave me a goodnight kiss, said "Bless you, my precious" and then "Goodnight, sleep tight, angels guard you 'til the light."

Then my mother kissed me and said, "We'll see Minna tomorrow, won't that be lovely!"

But back at the empty house on Quantock Road, even though Minna was there to give me a big hug, I began to cry and went on and on.

"What is it, my pet? Tell your old Minna!"

"She's tired, Mother, I'll put her to bed," and together we went upstairs, slowly, slowly, as if our hearts would break.

❧ 3 ❧

Turning over old letters and family bones.

As I never knew my father it's lucky for me that the Ruck Keenes wrote prolifically to one another, and when my uncle Phil retired from the navy he wrote a memoir. In it he breezily recorded many family sagas, including the monumental row in 1910 between Ralph (my father), and his father. Phil begins:

> *My eldest brother Ralph was a most lovable, good-looking chap, frivolously inclined and who attracted girls like bees to a honeypot, but he had been sent to Jesus College, Cambridge with the express purpose of taking holy orders. My father believed that the only professions suitable for a gentleman were the army, the navy or the church, in fact he turned down flat many suggestions from rich uncles on my mother's side for one of his numerous sons to be given a start in their flourishing business concerns. Any more unlikely candidate for 'the cloth' than my wild and adventurous eldest brother was hard to imagine and after a short and erratic career at Jesus he came home to announce that he considered himself to be totally unsuited for the priesthood and couldn't go on with it.*
>
> *I can't imagine why, but he chose to break the news of his decision very early one morning. My two young brothers and I were awakened by a terrible commotion on the landing outside my parents' room, and rushing out to see what was happening we found my father and Ralph having a furious argument which ended in fisticuffs.*

At this point I draw on Abbie's account for more interesting details. She and Emma heard the shouts as they came through the green baize-covered door which shut off the kitchen noises from the house (and *vice versa*). Abbie was carrying a tray of early morning tea and thin slices of bread and butter for my grandparents, Emma trotting behind with a jug of hot water for their washbasin.

"Ructions!" Abbie said. Tray and jug were abandoned and they flew upstairs just as Birdie ran out on the landing in her dressing-gown crying, "Ted, for goodness sake!" and tried to pull Ralph away from his father. At once Abbie and Emma pitched in behind her, and the younger boys took hold of their father and hung on like limpets. Ted kept shouting, "Let go, you brats!" until he roared, "Stop!" And they did.

A miserable week or so later Ralph was told he was to be dispatched to the colony of Canada. There was no discussion; the accepted thing to do with a rebellious son was send him away, preferably as far away as possible so the disgrace could be kept in the family. In 1910 agents in England did a brisk trade in selling land where disobedient boys could till the soil, prove their worth and earn forgiveness. Phil's description of this period has all the right details:

> As a treat I was allowed to accompany my father to Eastbourne of all places and a plot of land in British Columbia was bought from what turned out to be a phony agent.
> A suitable outfit was ordered for Ralph from the Army & Navy Stores in London and I distinctly remember a packer coming down to the Rectory with all the gear which contained among other items an axe, a tin hip bath, a tent and folding washing bowl.

Birdie insisted on purchasing this interesting outfit, and when telling the story always had a good word for the Army & Navy. "Such a reliable store, darling, and the shop assistants so polite and helpful."

But neither the land nor the outfit were much good to my father. In a letter from British Columbia he described his plot of land as "a useless strip of desert." Maybe the agent was indeed 'phony', but the British tended to imagine Canada vaguely as a huge mass of land (pink on the map) where Eskimos lived in snow houses called igloos, Indians lived in tents called tepees, grizzly bears roamed the forests, fish crowded sea and lakes and on the rest of the land grew miles and miles of golden wheat - why else call Canada "the world's bread-basket"? Very likely the 'useless strip of desert' was an unpromising area where, in 1910, little flourished except a colony of young British gentry, the men funded by regular remittances from home. They pretended to live like gentlemen (hunting, shooting, fishing and entertaining in style), but Ralph wasn't interested in fooling around with the remittance men. Instead he sold his land to the first buyer and went off to Vancouver in search of adventure.

Ralph had been banished from what Phil called 'a paradise for children', and that wasn't a sentimental exaggeration. The grey stone Rectory was a fine old Victorian house with thirteen bedrooms which accommodated the seven children and a constant supply of visiting relatives. The wisteria festooning the back of the house grew nearly to the roof, and was so strong the boys often climbed it to their rooms - strictly forbidden, but they did it anyway. Phil's memoir spells out a litany of delights - the windmill in the water meadows, the pond where moorhens raised their young, the stables, barn and outbuildings, the orchard of gnarled apple trees weighted every year with fruit. Phil adds, with a touch of poetry, "And there was an almost impenetrable wood." 'Almost...' What more could a child want? He concludes:

> ...even when we were all grown up we spent all our leaves there rather than go for exciting holidays elsewhere in

England or abroad. The family possessed a lusty vitality
which sometimes had its drawbacks but bred in us all a zest
for life and love of living which more than compensated for its
occasional disadvantages.

The disadvantages were something Abbie became adept at handling. She was fifteen when brought from the village to help Birdie with her firstborn, my father, and she served the Ruck Keenes for fifty years. Phil wrote:

Abbie and Emma were like members of our family.
They took part in every drama and crisis yet always
maintained an attitude of deep respect for my parents. Abbie,
who lived to be over eighty, corresponded with all of us and
never forgot our birthdays and later those of our children. She
scolded us if we didn't write home regularly or were remiss in
churchgoing, and when a beautiful niece of mine was divorced
she reprimanded her severely and never wrote to her or
mentioned her name again.

Abbie had several marriage proposals from village hopefuls, but her invariable reply was, "The Ruck Keenes need me." Indeed they did, as Phil disarmingly explains:

My father was a strict disciplinarian and would have
made a fine general or an admiral or medieval bishop. A very
impressive man and very handsome. We all adored him. My
mother spoilt us all outrageously and whenever he gave any
order to curb our activities she at once countermanded it
which made life complicated but colourful. But in spite of their
warring temperaments, my mother's teasing ways and my
father's quick temper, my parents were devoted to each other
and were very happy together. He always called her 'Lass'
even when she was an old lady.

One thing my grandparents shared was pride in the ancestry of their families. Birdie was a Corrie: her father's lineage dated from Saxon times, and her mother was a direct descendant of the redoubtable Elizabethan seaman (and slave trader) Sir John Hawkins. Ted's family tree included Oliver Cromwell, but the main branch dated only from 1066 when they came to England from France with William the Conqueror. 'Only' is pertinent. When Ted sought permission to court Birdie, her father, the Reverend Edgar Corrie, observed gravely to his wife, Eliza, "The Ruck Keenes are upstart Norman stock. I don't like it. Foreign blood. You don't know where you are with that sort of thing."

Despite these misgivings the courtship was accepted, and Phil describes Ted rowing Birdie on the Squire's pond at Eight Ash Green:

She sat at one end of the boat and he at the other
reading aloud to her from books on theology. She was

*funloving and lively and found this form of courtship
unsatisfactory. However they did somehow contrive to get
engaged and married and produced eight children.*

The eight children were Ralph, Benjamin, Margery and Dorothy, followed by Philip, Hugh, Jack and poor little Tom who died when he was two. The cause was vaguely referred to as 'a convulsion', but cousin Muriel told me drily that the rambunctious antics in the nursery were enough to send any small child into a fit.

A photograph, dated 1892, shows Birdie and Ted with my father (aged three, in a skirt, holding a whip), Ben nearly two, and Baby Margie. Birdie stares quizzically at Ted whose expression is uneasy - probably for good reason, since this year was for him a crucial one.

Ted was a graduate of Theology from Oxford University where he became part of the Oxford-based Anglo-Catholic movement, a breakaway from the dry Protestant Church of England. A notable Anglo-Catholic project was Oxford House in Bethnal Green, a base for the clergy to work directly in this poorest part of London's East End. One day Ted informed Birdie that he had been invited to work at Oxford House, and his heart was set on it.

Birdie told me she cried at once, "Whatever has got into you, Ted? D'you mean to say our darlings should play in the gutter with little barefoot cockneys?" Ted undoubtedly pointed out that other clerics brought up their children in Bethnal Green and no harm done, but Birdie swept away this nonsense. "Don't you believe it! In no time Ralphie and Ben will be dropping their aitches and up to all kinds of dreadful tricks. And think of their health. Here the air is wholesome, and what about your bronchitis? The London fogs would be the death of you."

That was just the opening round. Many years afterwards Abbie told Phil a story about this troubled time.

"I was serving the two of them lunch," Abbie said, "and put a plate of soup in front of your father - mulligatawny soup it was, his favourite. Well, they'd been at it, hammer and tongs - you know what they were. Your father sat staring at the soup while your mother went on needling him until, without a word, he picked up his plate and threw it, soup and all, right at her...No dear, he missed, but what a mess! The plate hit the wall and I had to move a picture to cover up the stain. Luckily nobody noticed, and," this was firmly added, "I never said a word about it, Phillie dear, not until now."

Dear Abbie. There was nothing servile in her devotion to my grandparents: she loved them as fallible human beings, and probably was not surprised when Birdie defeated Ted's dream of work amongst London's poor. Over the next eight years she presented him with five more children who, apart from little Tom, grew strong and healthy in the little paradise of Eight Ash Green. Unfortunately the damp mists of Essex gave Ted chronic bronchitis which was, at last, the death of him.

I once asked my uncle Philip how my grandfather reconciled his outbursts of fury with Christian forbearance.

"Father had a good healthy temper," Phil retorted. "He had strong principles and believed they should not be monkeyed with. I remember one time when a number of rowdy village boys started making a commotion outside the church while he was preaching. He stopped in full flight, marched down the aisle and once outside knocked down two of the troublemakers - Da was all of six foot two. Then he marched back to the pulpit to finish his sermon."

"What did the parishioners think of all that bashing?"

"They loved him. He kept them lively, plenty to talk about."

This led to a story about the Squire's runaway wife. The Squire lived in a beautiful William-and-Mary manor which was once a Trappist monastery. The monks had bred carp in the pond where Ted had rowed Birdie, and as the church was originally the monks' chapel, a door connected the manor with the church.

Phil said, "One Sunday Da was just about to go down on his knees when the Squire poked his head through his private door and beckoned urgently. Da stopped whatever he was going to do, and after a brief whisper from the Squire, they disappeared. A moment later the congregation heard the pony trap rattle away down the road. Everyone stayed put, and before long Da returned and started praying where he'd left off."

"Everyone must have been bursting to know what happened!"

"Of course, and it wouldn't have been kept quiet for long, though Da would never have said anything. What happened was that the Squire's wife, who was beautiful but flighty, had absconded with her lover while everyone was safely in church. But the Squire was suspicious, had stayed to spy on them, and when they left the house he rushed for help. Da leapt into the pony trap and drove like the wind to the local railway station. Sure enough, wife and lover were waiting for the train."

I asked if he'd knocked the lover down. Phil said, "Very likely, Da disapproved of that sort of thing."

"What sort of thing?"

"Marriages were made in heaven. A lover was one thing, but you had to stick to your marriage. So he brought the flighty wife back to the Squire." When I asked if she was happy Phil said, "Probably not. The squire was a funny old chap."

As for Birdie, she had everything to make her happy. In 1911 she wrote to her beloved sister Edie in Tasmania, describing - with a bland disregard of punctuation or paragraphs - the "great success" of the annual village Concert (with a capital C). It's a long letter, vigorous and confident in the little world of a country parish in England before World War One - Shakespeare's 'demi-paradise' which was soon to change forever.

All the performers are delightedly praised, the family with uncritical warmth. Ben, aged twenty-one, had been cajoled into taking part, as had Margery (eighteen), Dorothy (sixteen), and Jackie, aged nine, who has first mention as Mr. Golliwog...*in red trousers, blue coat, white waistcoat, black calico mask and hair from Emma's mother's old hearthrug stitched all over it. Stockings on feet and hands and big white cardboard rims round his eyes, a red bow round his neck. He is a born little actor.* He turns up also as an old woman, with 8 little choirboys, each supposed to be a man waiting to be hired at the fair, carter, haymaker, cowman, etc...*Jackie stood in the middle with a wig on his head and an old-fashioned black silk poke bonnet, a little old plaid shawl pinned over his chest, and a skirt on. Specs on nose and stick in hand.* He was splendid.

After this child prodigy come Ben and Dorothy (Doll). Ben has been persuaded to dress as an old English gentleman...*with a powdered wig and big black bow behind, one of Dolls coats with lace and ruffles and black stockings and buckle shoes. Doll with big side curls just like our Granny on the stairs and a white straw hat with pink roses and pink ribbon under her chin, really she did look a sweet dear and I could have eaten her. They did 'Madam will you walk' and the people went quite wild over them.* Margery follows getting a rather terse mention for singing...'*No John' and 'Going to market', sweetly.*

Finally Birdie's letter records that...*John Pettitt recited, and Chas Pettitt papered the parlour, Mr. Tripton sang a very witty little song bringing in the coronation and all the 8-Ash Green worthies, from Ruck Keene and Duncan to the Parsonage donkey. It was a delightfully successful concert, a packed room and we took three pounds five shilling.*

There's no mention of my father in this letter. He was presumed to be tilling the soil in Canada. In fact by this time he was a cattleman on a ship sailing to Panama. Later he drove a tram in San Francisco, and from there wrote home explaining about the miserable strip of desert and his changed plans. Before long a letter from Birdie changed his plans again. Ben had announced that he wished to take holy orders and everyone, especially Ted, was overjoyed. Birdie's letter urged Ralph to come home, and thoughtfully enclosed a bank draft for the passage to England.

I always loved hearing how Birdie met my father's ship at Tilbury. "I stood on the dockside," she said, "straining my eyes to pick out his dear figure. Then I saw him! He was wearing the one good suit he'd taken with him and, believe me, darling, he walked down that gangway looking every inch the gentleman!" This was her ultimate accolade.

Oddly enough, despite the English obsession with gentleman-liness, there was no real definition of a gentleman, only John Burke's *Heraldic and Genealogical History of the Landed Gentry*. It was published in the mid-nineteenth century, and a later edition, simply known as Burke's *Landed Gentry*, was Birdie's secular bible. There she could check whether or not any new acquaintances were "people who matter," or reckon if they were "out of the handkerchief drawer, darling" (her version of the common-or-garden 'top' drawer). She meant no harm, the English drew many precepts from the land, and every farmer knew the importance of breeding dogs and horses, chickens, pigs and so on; so it was logical for human beings to pay similar attention to their own breeding.

But ethnic purity ignored history. For thousands of years the Celts and Iberians living along England's east coast were plagued by sea-going adventurers from Europe and Scandinavia, until they settled down with the locals to till the soil and breed the race of Anglo-Saxons. Some 700 years later the Normans turned up.

In 1085 William the Conqueror's Domesday Book lumped Norman and Saxon together, Volume I recording details of the half a million souls scattered along what became Norfolk, Suffolk and Essex. Two hundred landowning magnates were listed, plus 7,000 tenants, the remaining citizens going by a variety of intriguing names such as freemen, drengs, radmen and sokemen, indicating fine distinctions of land tenure. It was from those first 200 landowners that the term 'landed gentry' evolved.

From that time on, land was not only their criterion of being gentry, but was their passion. They hung on to their land for centuries despite debts and disasters. As late as mid-Victorian times there were still some 20,000 families in England who had maintained an unbroken association with their land since 1066, and some even before then.

The connections went deep, and pride in them was very real. Their debts were also very real. The property and its income always went to the eldest son. If the property was in trouble an heiress with a good dowry was sought, even if her family failed to make Burke's inventory. So intermarriages of various kinds were not infrequent, particularly for the younger sons in their perennial plight of scrambling to maintain a gentlemanly existence on little or no income.

So, in their pragmatic fashion, the English muddled along making and breaking their own rules, and talking vaguely about someone "living like a gentleman." All this was confusing for foreigners, like the French, who had more clear-cut social guidelines. The confusion became greater when new industrial magnates bought land and sought acceptance as landed gentry. This alarmed the old-established gentry and unwritten codes or tests grew up by which gentry impostors could be identified. The tests embraced a right jumble of unreasonable taboos and requirements including subtleties of speech

- "a deplorable accent, darling," behaviour - "the man's a cad, sir!" and Birdie had her own curious myths, such as - "Ladies always have sloping shoulders," and - "Only a gentleman has lobes to his ears." These statements confused my mother, as did Birdie's approbation of some young woman as "Such a nice gel, darling, doesn't care *what* she wears!" My mother wanted to do the right Ruck Keene thing, but she made her own pretty clothes and saw no reason to be a frump. An added embarrassment was the admiration of my aunts who wore lumpish garments, often run up by a 'little woman' in the village.

In time I got used to the contradictions; they had a kind of mad charm, a quintessential eccentricity which gave zest to stories about relatives like Ted's cousin, Jack Berners. He inherited Wolverstone Park, a great pile of a house in Suffolk which had been in the family for 200 years. Every morning Jack mounted a horse and trotted round his considerable estate to check the well-being of his tenants and livestock, ending happily with the gamekeeper to discuss the welfare of his pheasants. The estate had a notable shoot, and King George V sometimes stopped off at Wolverstone for a spot of bird slaughter. One day the King's limousine drew up to the front door. Possibly the visit was unexpected, for though Jack bounded down the steps with outstretched hand, he stumbled, and fell flat on his face. He was drunk. Rigid with disapproval the King ordered the chauffeur to drive on - *and never came again.*

Here my uncles roared with laughter. This puzzled me until I worked out that though Jack was a staunch conservative and loyal subject of the King, he was also lord of Wolverstone Park, and if the King didn't like him, that was the King's problem.

Gentry eccentricities, though colourful, had the drawback of outdated convictions, such as Ted's aversion to trade. A gentleman's profession was either the army, the navy or the church: but not trade. This complicated discussions about my father's future after his return from Canada. But Birdie had Corrie relatives with trade interests in the Straits Settlements (now Malaysia), and Ted couldn't dismiss the Corries as non-gents. In the end he gave way, and Ralph was posted to a rubber plantation in Penang.

In 1913 Birdie wrote to her sister Edie:

My Ralph has got a rise in salary £315 a year now and wrote such a bright letter about the work. He loves the little natives and makes them run handicap races on their way home from work and he says it is funny to see them fighting yelling and tripping each other up all for 10 cents.

Ralph's buoyant prospects amongst the dear little natives lasted until August, 1914. In November my aunt Dorothy wrote to her cousin (also called Ralph), who was the only son of Birdie's sister, Edie:

My best congratulations in the world, how simply splendid to get into such a regt. you must be feeling awfully bucked about it, I am so glad. I expect Mother has told you that Ralph is on his way home and is due on the 6th at Tilbury, I can think of nothing else, it will be like nothing else to see him again. I knew he would do all in his power to get home when the war broke out....You must be photoed in your uniform now don't forget.
Ever your affectionate cousin Doshie.

This curiously chipper letter was written not long after the first battles at Ypres which had been a close call for England's professional army. New posters were everywhere showing Lord Kitchener (heavily mustachioed) pointing forcefully under the caption of 'BRITONS JOIN YOUR COUNTRY'S ARMY.'

Back in England Ralph joined up. Before long he received a letter which began, "Greetings from King George V to our Trusty and well-beloved Ralph Edgar Ruck Keene..." From this Ralph learnt he had been appointed a lieutenant in the Temporary Land Forces. Before long he was accepted as a second lieutenant in the Ninth Battalion of the Royal Welsh Fusiliers, and was sent for front line training in Somerset, near the seaside town of Weston-super-Mare.

Early in the new year of 1915 a dance was arranged at the Weston Assembly Rooms, and the officers at the camp were invited. Ralph went cheerfully off in the hope of meeting a pretty girl who would flirt with him, and take his mind off the mounting toll of casualties in France.

✀ 4 ✀

A marriage, a birth, and a letter from a ghost.

My mother told me that my father came into the Assembly Rooms and stood talking and laughing with the other young officers. "He stood out amongst the others," she said. "He was so handsome, and had a kind of happy confidence, as if life delighted him. He caught my eye and I blushed and looked away, but a moment later he introduced himself and asked for my dance programme. It had a little pencil hanging from a silk cord so prospective partners could write their names against the dances. The first half of my programme was full, but he smiled, asked, 'May I?' and without waiting for an answer wrote his name right across all the dances after supper."

A month after Ralph met Christina he went hotfoot to Copford Rectory and announced that he was engaged to be married.

Birdie cried, "My darling boy, how wonderful, and who is she?"

"Her name is Christina de la Paz Garsia - isn't that beautiful! She's beautiful too, you'll love her!"

"Garsia? Who are they, dear boy? Are they *Spanish?*"

"The father was, of course, he was a Count and a doctor and everybody loved him."

"Is he dead?"

"Five years ago. It was very sad. But he was much older than Mrs. Garsia. She showed me his obituary in a local newspaper. It said he was the best known and most highly esteemed member of their church, and that he'd been their honorary treasurer. Wasn't that good? He was quite a scholar and left a fine library; Da would have liked him. Mrs. Garsia had a lectern put up in the church for him; I wrote down the words for you: 'In loving memory of Dr. Willoughby Marston Garsia' from his wife and children.'"

"That was nice, dear. A *doctor!* And how many children?"

Ralph gave not entirely reassuring pictures of the two eldest, Marston (studying law and vaguely in uniform), and Willoughby (somewhat deaf, so not in uniform, and at a college of art in London). Christina was a year younger than Willoughby; and Freda, the youngest, was still a child.

"Are they very Spanish, dear?"

"Freda's fair, like Mrs. Garsia. The others have black hair. Christina's is very long and glossy," Ralph added dreamily. "She has a lovely oval face and brown eyes and she's a jolly good mimic." Then he launched into a confusing story of Dr. Garsia's adventurous past as a young doctor in South America. "He was often paid in precious stones and chunks of gold," Ralph said, "and once he was taken by two masked men to save the life of a boy with a gunshot wound. Dr. Garsia was blindfolded and taken to a great big house where the boy lay on a four-poster, white as a sheet with a dreadful wound in his side. Dr. Garsia operated without anaesthetic, but the boy never cried out." Ralph smiled and said, "Mrs. Garsia is a wonderful story-teller."

Birdie said, "Dear boy, how romantic, but what was Dr. Garsia doing in South America? And who are the Garsias?"

Ralph was exasperatingly vague. "The family had a castle in Spain but left ages ago, something to do with religion. Probably they were Protestant; must have been, being so involved with the church in Weston. The newspaper obituary said he came from one of the most ancient Spanish families."

"And the mother, dear?"

Ralph was on firmer ground here. "She's Welsh," he replied cheerfully. "She says her father's family is descended from the Welsh kings. She was born in India. Her father, Thomas Williams, was in the army and did very well. He was nicknamed Tiger Tom, was in the Crimea and at the siege of Sebastopol and ended as a Major-General with a CB and all kinds of decorations."

"*Was*, dear?"

"Oh yes, he's dead too. But you'll like Mrs. Garsia. She was educated in Heidelberg, where you went, but she spent all her schooldays there. She was about six when she was sent off from India to Heidelberg - can you imagine what that was like? Christina says she was a splendid horsewoman, and Mrs. Garsia told me how she got mixed up in a big tattoo in honour of the German Emperor, and the Kaiser, before he was the Kaiser," Ralph added hastily. "Anyway, she persuaded her riding-master to ride near the back of the arena where the horses and gun-carriages and soldiers were gathering for the parade. Then, just as the parade started her horse took fright, galloped off in front of the whole parade and Mrs. Garsia went flying all alone round the arena." Ralph laughed and exclaimed, "She said, 'Oh, what a ride that was! I never rode like that again.' She said her hat came off and her golden hair tumbled down round her waist, and as she came up to the royal box the young Kaiser got up and bowed to her. Of course," Ralph added quickly, "that was when she was very young and nobody thought we'd be at war with Germany. After all, you were in Heidelberg too and liked the Germans."

Birdie said Mrs. Garsia must be a remarkable woman and asked how she met her husband. Ralph said vaguely, "He was a friend of her parents, and visited her in Heidelberg several times." Then he smiled and went on, "It happened that he visited her just when she was being punished for getting mixed up in the tattoo. But she was allowed to see him, and ran downstairs straight into his arms crying, 'Take me away from here, oh, take me away!' which, of course he did, though not at once. Tiger Tom was dead when they married but her mother was alive, though she's dead too now."

"Of course," Birdie said faintly, by now quite bemused by this helter-skelter of a story, in which the adventurous Spanish doctor and hard-riding Welsh woman did not seem quite believable. Without much conviction she consulted Burke's *Landed Gentry*. But the Garsias were not listed, either under 'G' or '*de la*'. As for Williams, there was hardly a Welshman who wasn't called Williams.

For Birdie's peace of mind it was fortunate that the question, "Who *are* the Garsias, dear boy?" remained unanswered for eighty years. Then, from sources as varied as the telephone book and the Bodleian Library in Oxford, my brother-in-law, Peter, discovered the startling and romantic origin of a galaxy of Garsia/Garcia relatives. Twenty-five years before Peter's revelations, my half sisters and I had wrestled with the old stories until Joy remarked crisply, "The Garsias are weird," and Felicity added mildly, "They are simply incomprehensible." So two lifetimes ago the Garsias, teasingly weird and incomprehensible, also baffled Birdie's anxious search for the facts.

She poured out her concerns to Ted. "The dear boy is infatuated," she cried. "The father was Spanish, a doctor, and dead as well. The mother's father seems respectable, but Welsh. That can mean anything."

My grandfather called Ralph "a damned young fool" but pointed out that his eldest son was a man of twenty-six, and an officer in the army doing his duty for King and country. If he was set on marrying this young woman there was not much to be done about it. But Birdie, not so easily dissuaded, tried a final ploy. Christina was only twenty, and the law required her father's permission to marry. Though Minna had given her consent, legally she was only a woman, and her consent didn't count.

Ted explained to his son that marriage without parental consent was illegal, but Ralph already knew that he could ask the Archbishop of Canterbury to stand in *locus parentis* and give the desired permission. He took the train to London and returned with an impressive sheet of parchment embellished with the pendant Seal of His Grace of Canterbury. It is dated March 25, 1915, and cost ten shillings. Birdie, recognizing she was in no position to take on the Primate of the Church of England, conceded defeat.

On March 26, the London *Times* announced that my parents were married the previous day "very quietly at St. Michael's and All Angels, Copford, Essex." In the announcement my Garsia grandfather is noted as 'the late W.M. Garsia, Esq.' Birdie doubtless preferred 'Esquire'. Doctors were admirable people, and the Rectory doctor always joined the family for a glass of sherry after church on Sunday, but he was never asked to dinner. Medicine, like trade, was not a gentry profession.

Christina and Minna stayed at Copford Rectory before the wedding, and some of Birdie's apprehensions turned out to be groundless. Christina's appealing oval face was not British pink and white, but cautious scrutiny could detect no touch of the tarbrush. She was endearingly shy, and as for Ralph, the dear boy couldn't take his eyes off her. Minna's quiet charm and gentle manner was beyond reproach, her fair hair still abundant, her features delicate, and the eyes a beautiful blue. Altogether Mrs. Garsia was a trim little figure, and Birdie was reassured by her very small feet - a sure sign of gentle birth. There were still obscurities about the Garsia lineage, and the two brothers with their odd names had yet to be encountered. Never mind, her dear boy was so happy and proud of his young wife, and what a pair they made, walking down the aisle together. All might yet, after all, be well.

A month later Birdie, corresponding indefatigably with the family, wrote to her sister Edie's husband, Bertram Kite, then Dean of St. David's Cathedral in Hobart, Tasmania.

> *Ralph is still with his wife at Weston, and I am glad they have this happy time together. The Regt is expecting to go to Salisbury Plain any moment.*

Whatever Birdie's doubts, Christina was now a Ruck Keene and the rather exotic creature so impetuously beloved by Ralph was, for better or worse, one of the family and entitled to her share of warm-hearted affection.

In September Ralph left for the front in time to take part in the advance on Loos, an engagement in which the Germans used gas for the first time. There were huge casualties, little ground was gained, and Ralph was one of the few officers in his battalion to emerge unscathed. Birdie knelt at the *prie-dieu* in her bedroom and thanked God for the safety of her beloved firstborn.

Ralph returned to England for a brief leave, going first to Copford for a hurried visit before spending the rest of the time with Christina.

Much later Birdie told me how, on his last evening at Copford, she went to bid him goodnight. "I said I would pray God to keep him safe, but he put his arms round me and said, with such a bright face, 'Why, Mummy, to die for your country is the very best death a man can die!'"

On January 9, 1916, I was born and a telegram announcing my arrival was sent to my father. His reply came the next day:

> *Awfully pleased, Ruck Keene.*

This seems a little lacking in fervour. He might have been more enthusiastic if I had been a boy; on the other hand army telegrams had to be as brief as possible. Two days later he wrote a letter, headed simply 'France'. Its arrival in England was postmarked January 25:

> *Darling,*
>
> *...I can't tell you how pleased and thankful I am that it is all over and you are all right. How I wish I were with you now to give you a kiss and take you in my arms. I can't tell you the immense relief your telegram was darling. It took ten years off my shoulders. I expect that you are feeling very weak and done up now dear. I will come to you as soon as I can, but at present I'm very busy with my new duties, and must get things running properly before I can get away. Gilbert had no system at all and I must start again. I am afraid you will think this is a very cold letter after all you have been through darling, but I am no good at expressing myself in a sentimental way. But don't think that my love for you is any less for my lack of expression....*
>
> *Goodnight, darling and give my daughter a kiss from me.*
> *Your very loving husband.*

I didn't know about this letter until, after my mother's death, I received a package of newspaper cuttings, bits and pieces about my father and his regiment, two telegrams and the letter. The second telegram was from the War Office, recording briefly that Lieut. R.E. Ruck Keene had died as a result of a bomb accident on January 16.

The letter, postmarked January 25, is folded into a flimsy grey-brown envelope. I see Christina standing with it in her hand, staring at the familiar handwriting, and knowing it was a letter from a ghost.

My father was blown to bits by a made-in-England hand-grenade, then called a Mills bomb. The British soldiers threw them into the German trenches, the bomb fuse timed to explode ten seconds after a pin was pulled out. In a letter of muddled explanation and anguish, my aunt Dorothy wrote to cousin Muriel:

> The darling boy died such a wonderfully brave death, he was instructing the Cheshire regiment (as he was brigade officer) when the accident occurred. He was explaining to the men that if they threw the bombs too early the Germans had time to send them back again (so _many_ deaths have occurred in this way). To further carry out his meaning he let the men throw bombs at him which he picked up and threw on further before they exploded. But evidently one was a short fused bomb and it exploded in his hand. The dear boy did not suffer as he became unconscious in a few seconds and was dead in less than five. I think it was such a beautiful death so extraordinarily brave. His Colonel wrote of him "that he will be such a loss to his regiment he was such a fine officer and absolutely fearless." The darling boy for him it was a glorious death to lay down his life for his country, it's those he has left behind.
>
> My dear whatever do people do these days without religion, its the only thing one has these days to keep one up at all. Poor darling Mum is so absolutely heart broken you know how she adored him, but she is being so splendid and brave. Poor dear Dickie is absolutely heart broken but has been splendid, the baby is such a comfort to her. Poor girl, she adored Ralph. Mum is going to Weston to see the baby as soon as she feels she can bear it.

Early in February the visit to my mother was described in another letter to Muriel:

> But Dickie! It's absolutely too pathetic, I shall never forget her the night we arrived it was just awful. We came in the evening and she was in bed. She just sat up and looked absolutely dazed as though she had no life in her whatever, so

frightfully listless and she didn't cry, I would much rather have seen her absolutely broken down.

...I am so glad she has the baby just imagine if this had happened some months before she was born wouldn't it have been awful.

The christening was too pathetic, it was more like a funeral, but Dickie was wonderful...Daddy came just for one night to christen her and took the service so beautifully. There was only just us and an uncle of Dickie's and a girl friend of hers.

Dorothy took on the task of answering the 200 letters of condolence that poured in to the Rectory. After the first dozen she took time off to spill out her own agony to Muriel:

...I just write and write those awful 'sympathy' letters till my head buzzes. Anyhow it spares Mother, she just makes my heart ache. Muriel isn't this war cruel beyond words? Now we have had this terrible blow, when I look at the casualty list I think of how other people must be feeling like too. The thousands of aching hearts....

"The thousands of aching hearts" rings like a refrain in a Greek tragedy, and at Copford the words masked an unspoken terror - now Ralph was gone, would Ben join up?

After his ordination Ben was accepted at Oxford House in Bethnal Green, the very place my grandfather Ted had longed to work all those years ago. I believe Ted loved Ben above all his children, and the Bethnal Green appointment was not only a source of pride and joy but a kind of blessing on the sacrifice of his own young hopes. Perhaps Ted prayed that this beloved son would not enlist, but as the nightmare of trench warfare claimed more and more lives, Ben was torn between his work in the London slums and the call to fight with his peers.

Ralph's death put an end to indecision. In the summer of 1916, Ben was appointed padre to the Eighth York Battalion and left for France. In September of 1917 he was killed by shrapnel while chatting outside his dugout.

Dorothy, clutching at mantras to reconcile the unbearable with the unthinkable, wrote to Muriel:

...Bens death gets more and more glorious to me as time goes on, nobody knows what it will mean facing life without him he means such a tremendous lot to us, yet the wonder of it all just overwhelms everything else.

A chaplains death is the finest one of all and when you have lived like Ben lived and died like it too, the passing on must be just stupendous. Having served Our Lord so well here, Bens meeting with Him must have been just too glorious for words when he passed on....

Amongst this new batch of sympathy letters were several written by Ben's brother clergy at Oxford House. The following passages are from a writer simply identified as HHL:

> *...Benjy was one of the first people I met in coming here about 6 ½ years ago, I took to him at once and saw a great deal of him after. He always struck me as being one of the greatest certainties for the next world and bliss that I knew he was always so superbly on the spot in a gloriously absent-minded sort of way....*
>
> *One always felt with Benjy that whatever his faults and his priceless way of forgetting unimportant details and his worries over all the dreadful little jobs that were thrust on him to do, that he was really good underneath. He was what I call a 'white man'....*
>
> *And now its all a memory and he has gone over to help poor souls the other side. There is something very glorious when a chaplain dies, the death is so very like our Lord's. It is a sacrifice made for the whole church by one who is living for it, by it, and in it right through. I feel quite certain that it is just what he would have chosen and that his activities have not ceased for one single second. There will be so many for him to help whom he has comforted as they died, there are many to come over who will know him when they arrive. There are some of his bestest friends over there too....*
>
> *I shall pray for him at Mass on Sunday with a certainty that I rarely ever possess and I know that if ever I can become a little like him I shall see him one day very near the Throne.*

In November, a month after Ben's death, Muriel's young brother Ralph died of wounds. He was twenty-one, the only son of Birdie's sister Edie. The wounds were inflicted by British guns whose range was unreliable, so the shells sometimes fell short on British trenches in the forward lines. The curious phrase 'friendly fire' had not then been devised to obfuscate the facts.

After the war my father's old school, Rossall, sent Christina a memorial list of their dead. On the cover is a large blood-red cross, and the words FILIIS MATER (Sons of the mother). The names of the 201 boys killed in the war are listed, and on the back of the folded sheet is a poem. The last verse runs:

> They gave the glory of their coming years;
> The sorrow of an ever-clouded sun
> Of empty homes and desolate we give.
> Oh! ye who here in happier days shall live
> Forget not that your liberty was won
> By bitter sacrifice of blood and tears.

What liberty?

But for all the dis-grace of war, courage remains, a human grace in the unmitigated inhumanity of warfare.

⋘ 5 ⋙

The prayer book is adamant,
so off to the New World.

Christina said of her marriage, "Ralph came like a prince out of the Thousand-and-One Nights, and then was gone. It was like a dream." What remained from this dreamtime was the hitherto undreamed-of world, so beguiling and expansive, of Copford Rectory. It was a little kingdom, a dynasty with family connections spread out across the world, providing a never-ending supply of stories about people whose names Christina strove to remember. Just how much did my mother know about her own relatives, the weird, incomprehensible Garsias? There were Minna's stories about Dr. Garsia in South America and herself in Heidelberg. But did those tales satisfy Birdie? Perhaps this was just one of the unexpected swamps through which Christina needed a native guide to avoid putting a foot wrong.

Mercifully Phil had turned out to be a great help. He was very like Ralph, a little taller but just as handsome, with the same corn-coloured hair and brown eyes, and the same Corrie exuberance and sense of fun. 'They make quite a pair,' Birdie thought, brooding on Christina's oval face and glossy black hair 'such a colourful creature. It was no wonder Phillie was so attracted.'

On a summer visit to Copford Phil offered to take me down inside the windmill. My mother said it wasn't safe but Phil said, "You come too, Christina, then you won't fuss about her." I knew she was afraid of climbing down the little metal ladder, but she pretended she wasn't. Phil carried me on his shoulders and I felt safe, though from the bottom of the well the bit of blue sky overhead was very small, and very far away. My mother kept tight hold of my hand but talked and laughed with Phil, and afterwards, as we walked back to the house, Phil said, "You're a ripping girl, Christina!" Then he put his arm round her waist, and kissed her just as Birdie stepped through the french windows onto the lawn. I ran to my grandmother, crying, "Phillie took Mummy and me down the windmill and the water dripped, plop! plop! but *we* didn't fall in."

Birdie said, "How exciting, my darling!" but she wasn't looking at me and her face said something else.

Later, when I was tucked up in bed and sleepy I saw my mother pick up the prayer book Birdie had given her, and go out on the balcony. I know now that she was looking for the list of people the Church of England said you couldn't marry. It's on the last page of *Articles of Religion*:

A TABLE OF KINDRED AND AFFINITY
wherein whosoever are related are forbidden
in scripture and our laws to marry together.

Underneath this are two columns; on the left it says, *A man may not marry his...* and lists thirty different proscribed female relations; and on the right, *A woman may not marry her...* with a matching thirty forbidden male bodies. The connections make one's head spin: Mother's Sister's Husband, Husband's Father's Brother, Husband's Mother's Brother. But sure enough, seventeenth on the list, was Phil - Husband's Brother. Below the lists the *Articles of Religion* say flatly: *Holy Scripture containeth all things necessary to salvation.*

Christina stood for some while on the balcony, listening to the doves gently cooing as the evening shadows lengthened across the lawn, and the air was sweet with summer. Into her head came one of Marston's favourite Shakespeare quotes: 'This other Eden, demi-paradise.' How did it go? Something about a fortress built by nature...yes...'Against infection and the hand of war./This happy breed of men, this little world,/This precious stone set in a silver sea...'

Marston always spoke the words beautifully. Dear old boy, what fun they'd had putting on plays when they were children, Willoughby building the sets, herself playing the piano, Marston taking the best parts because he could memorize pages and pages without difficulty. She remembered her beloved father choosing books from his library for her to read, encouraging all the children to think for themselves and develop their talents; they'd been a happy breed in their quiet, busy world - and never any ructions, unlike the Ruck Keenes. Yet the Copford ructions were part and parcel of their zestful life in their demi-Eden. Except the hand of war had ravaged it.

Christina leant on the stone balcony, taking care not to break the hanging clusters of wisteria flowers. She thought how lovely it would be truly to belong here; but as she gazed out across the water meadows she knew that her only claim to this enchanted place lay in her being Ralph's widow and the mother of his child.

Not long after our visit Phil got his first posting abroad, and much later he sent a photograph of himself in white tropical uniform. He stands by the rail of a ship and looks keen and naval; on the back is the single word 'PENANG!' The photograph came with a birthday present for me, Hilaire Belloc's *Cautionary Tales for Children*. My

mother read them aloud over and over until I knew most of them by
heart:

> Matilda told such Dreadful Lies
> It made one Gasp and Stretch one's Eyes;
> Her Aunt, who from her Earliest Youth,
> Had kept a Strict Regard for Truth,
> Attempted to Believe Matilda:
> The effort very nearly killed her,
> And would have done so, had not She
> Discovered this Infirmity....

The poems made us laugh, even though terrible things
happened to the children, and I loved the drawings of funny-looking
people in funny old-fashioned clothes. The book and photograph had
taken a long time to reach us. When it arrived I was already five, and we
were with my uncle, Willoughby, in a place called San-Antonio-Texas.

Willoughby once said to me, "When I am in doubt I rest in the
arms of the Universe." One of these reposeful periods most likely pre-
ceded his decision to quit the Slade School of Art and set off to explore
North America - a decision which profoundly shocked my mother.
Willoughby was her favourite brother, and though she was a year his
junior she had styled herself his protector ever since typhoid left him
partially deaf. They grew very close, except Christina never truly appre-
ciated that Willoughby's deafness shielded a treasured inner self. Every
time he suddenly glided away with a disarming, slightly apologetic
smile, she was left nonplussed.

"But why on earth do you want to leave the Slade? Don't you
want to be an artist?"

"I want to travel."

Minna smiled and was silent, but my mother exclaimed,
"*Travel!* whatever for? and why America?"

"They have interesting ideas of healing. I'll never be a great
artist, and there are other ways of healing."

"What's healing got to do with painting pictures?"

"Art can put us in tune with the universe. Being out of tune has
a lot to do with illness."

"I don't know what you're talking about!"

Willoughby said mildly, "Don't you remember, Christina, what
unusual theories our father had about health - didn't he, mother? Like
proper diet and hygiene and exercise instead of filling patients up with
useless pills. And I think he knew something about the ideas of a
German chap called Freud."

"What ideas?"

"I've only read his book on dreams; the others haven't been
translated into English yet. He talks about our unconscious and how it
affects what we do, that we tend to bury things that hurt and the buried

hurt can make us behave quite destructively as well as making us ill. He says dreams have meaning, can help us understand our unconscious."

"Is this what you want to do?"

"No...no, I don't think so. I'm more interested in natural cures, that sort of thing. They go in for it in America. Here doctors won't countenance anything new, just call it quackery."

So off he went.

In a letter to Minna he described visiting a community in Canada. "It's in British Columbia," Minna said as she gave the letter to Christina. "Wasn't that where Ralph was banished? He says the community is at Hundred Mile House, such a romantic name, and the people call themselves Emissaries of Divine Light."

Christina was not impressed. "They sound peculiar to me. I hope Willoughby isn't getting mixed up with weird people. You know how other-worldly he is." But Minna said not to worry.

Several months passed before Christina had a letter from Willoughby which began with enthusiasm about something called chiropractic, and that there was a college in San Antonio where he intended to train as a chiropractor. 'What a queer word,' Christina thought - and then read, unbelieving:

> *Why not come out here and train with me? It'll give*
> *you a career, and we can set up a practice together. Burn your*
> *boats and give it a try! Just sail to New York and get a train to*
> *San Antonio. Nothing to it.*

To this extraordinary suggestion he added that Texas once belonged to Mexico in South America, where Father had been, "so we'll be carrying on the family tradition!"

Willoughby's letter provoked Christina to agonizing sessions with Minna. Christina's world was Weston-super-Mare, with London and Copford the extent of her travels, and marriage her life's ultimate prospect. But a career! At first absurd, then progressively exciting, it was surely better than being a widow with a child, living on a tiny army pension and a very small private income. A career! And Texas! She felt quite breathless.

At last, between terror and excitement, she told Minna she would burn her boats, then wailed, though knowing the answer, "What will the Ruck Keenes think?" And more practically, "However shall we manage alone in huge New York?"

It was Minna's idea to seek help from Harry Ruck Keene, who was my godfather and Ted's favourite brother. Harry was a family maverick who'd flouted the traditional gentry careers and become a ship's surveyor for Lloyd's. "He knows people all over the world," Minna said. "Besides, he's so fond of you and Thelma, and he'll be an ally."

She was right. Harry lost no time in answering Christina's letter. He wrote that she was a plucky girl, and he'd be delighted to arrange for a Lloyd's agent to meet us in New York, and then see that we got on the right train to San Antonio. He added, "If you plan to leave soon after Christmas mind you take warm clothes. New York temperatures can fall below zero in January."

Below zero! Minna advised two pairs of woollen stockings for me, but pointed out that temperatures in Texas would be much warmer, "and desert heat in the summer, darling." Good heavens, imagine freezing cold to boiling hot from one city to the next! Life for Christina suddenly became full of exclamation marks.

When Birdie heard I was to be whisked off to the wilds of America she burst into Ted's study crying "Listen to this!" and read Christina's letter aloud, interrupting herself with "What do you think of that?" without waiting for a reply. At the end she expostulated, "Really, Ted! Dickie seems to forget she is darling Ralph's widow. What does she think she's doing, traipsing off to some godforsaken place thousands of miles away just because that young brother of hers has filled her head with quackery? Yankee bone-setters! Not even proper doctors!"

Ted said nothing. It was always best to let Birdie run out of steam first. She went on, "Why can't Christina train to be a nurse? At least that's a respectable thing for a nice gel to do! Margie has done very well and met plenty of the right people. Goodness knows how our dear child will turn out, running wild with blackamoors and little Yankees with their atrocious accent!"

Ted admitted the news was surprising and he wasn't altogether happy about it. "Not too happy?" Birdie exclaimed. They carried on like this for several days until Ted put an end to the fuss.

"Dickie's a grown woman and has every right to make her own choices. After all, America isn't a pathless jungle, it's a civilized country. You're exaggerating, Lass!"

Birdie thought impatiently that Ted was too susceptible to a pretty face. A brisk exchange with Harry followed. Birdie accused him of "aiding and abetting Christina in her disastrous plans." Harry replied that the girl had lots of spunk, and times were changing.

Ted agreed. "We must get used to the fact that Dickie has a mind of her own; and the war has changed everything. Young people are doing things that would have been unthinkable in our day. You can't turn the clock back, Lass. We must just pray that God takes care of them, and they'll come back safe and sound, with the child none the worse for her adventure."

Early in the New Year Minna came to see us off at Liverpool. My mother held me firmly by one hand; my other hand clutched a bag containing crayons, a colouring book, a pack of cards, a snakes and ladders board (Halma on the other side) and a small box of dice and

Halma counters. Golliwog had been packed in the trunk, but Monkey, my newest, beloved toy, was coming with us. Minna held him for now.

It was very cold. There was a lot of noise, strange hollow bangings, loud creaks and groans from the huge looming wall of ship, and big rough-looking men hurried everywhere, shouting and pushing loaded carts.

"Write often, won't you, dear one," Minna said, not for the first time.

"I do hope I've done the right thing," my mother said, also not for the first time.

"Can we go on the ship now?" I said for the umpteenth time. And then, above the tumult, there was a shout of, "All aboard! All aboard!"

Minna kissed me and said, "Be a good girl, my precious, and don't forget your old Minna," and we left her alone on the dockside. As we climbed up the gangway, my mother kept saying, "Don't let go my hand, Thelma."

Much later, as my mother unpacked our suitcase, I poked around the funny little space of our cabin, where even the soap and towels were very small. It was like playing house, with the added charm that I had to climb a ladder to my bed that was called a bunk.

"Mummy, where's Monkey?" I asked. "I want to show him our house."

But Monkey wasn't anywhere. At this point my world fell apart. I made a great deal of noise, so we didn't hear the knock on our cabin door; but suddenly a steward stood in the doorway, his face one big smile.

"See, see!" he cried, and like a magician, held up the familiar grey shape in its little red jacket with a pocket in front. Then, crying "See, little lady", he pulled from the pocket a slip of paper. "Your Granny stop my friend as he run up gangway, very late, very silly fellow, but your Granny she say, 'Please!' and write your cabin number on the paper. She very kind lady."

The world went back together, we all smiled, and I showed Monkey everything. After supper I climbed up and down the ladder of my bunk until my mother abruptly said, "It's stuffy in here, we must have some air;" and after opening the porthole said in a no-nonsense voice, "Time for both of you to go to bed."

Cosy in my bunk with Monkey I asked sleepily, "The sea won't come in, will it Mummy," and she said of course not. But when I was woken by Christina throwing up and groaning, "Oh God, oh God!" I heard something worse - water! It was splashing through the open porthole, and slish-sloshing around the cabin floor.

I howled, "Mummy, Mummy! The sea's comin' in! Mummy, stop the sea!"

But my mother only groaned, "Oh God, I wish I was dead!" and for a brief moment the cabin filled with a duet of "Stop the sea!" and

"Oh God, oh God!" until my mother rallied to cry, "For God's sake, Thelma, press the steward's button!"

I didn't know about any button so we went on about the sea until, like magic, the door was flung open and the steward was running to the porthole, shouting, "What for it open? You a mad woman?" But the sea stopped coming in. Soon people came to mop up and attend to my mother, while I sat with Monkey and ate a Digestive biscuit with bites of chocolate - my mother's invention she called "a toothsome morsel." It was some time before Digestive biscuits were coated one side with chocolate. "I was ahead of my time," my mother said.

This dramatic start to our voyage was followed by several days of cabin fever. My mother was confined to her bunk and refused to let anyone take me on deck, convinced they might be inattentive and I would plunge overboard. We emerged at last from the depths of the ship, and braced by the tingling cold sea air, began to explore. Our favourite part was the first class, particularly the shops. We gazed at impossible delights displayed behind gleaming plate-glass framed in polished wood.

Christina sighed, "Wouldn't it be lovely to be really rich!" Everywhere thick carpets were underfoot, the air redolent of cigars and perfume. Christina said, "Isn't it opulent!" and for years the word 'opulent' always conjured up a wonderful, desirable world of wealth and plenty, indelibly tinctured with cigars and perfume.

As the ship docked in New York everyone crowded on deck, and my mother kept saying, "Don't leave go of my hand for a minute, Thelma." At last we were on dry land, which felt funny, as if the ground was moving. My mother was fussing about something called 'customs' and having to find our trunk. It was my father's brown leather trunk and we saw it easily as Christina had painted RUCK-KEENE in bold white letters on the lid. But as we waited for the customs man to look at our luggage, she noticed that most people's trunks were being searched and everything rifled through. "However can we get all our things packed in again?" she murmured, for in Weston big Marston had to sit on the lid before it would shut tight.

Our turn came and the customs man said loudly, "Kindly get that trunk opened up, ma'am." My mother struggled with the heavy straps, turned the key in the brass lock, threw back the lid - and then nobody spoke. Golliwog lay spread-eagled, face up, smartly dressed in his red and white striped pants, blue jacket and spotted tie. His fuzz of black rabbit-fur hair was rather flattened but his big red mouth curved in a friendly grin and his white button eyes stared unblinking at the world.

After a silence the customs man said, "Say now, whaddya know about that!"

"That's my golliwog."

"Is that so?" he said. "Well, ma'am, I reckon there's no cause to disturb the coloured gentleman's rest," and slammed down the lid. He marked it with white chalk, said, "Good-day to you ma'am and little lady," and cried, "Next please!"

As we followed our porter outside Christina suddenly laughed. "So this is America!" she said.

&ᐧ 6 ᐧ&

Life, Liberty and Chiropractic
in San Antonio, Texas.

Four days later I sat on the brown leather trunk outside the station in San Antonio. So far there was no sign of Willoughby and my mother was in a fuss, but San Antonio smelt spicy and the sun beamed hot from a bright blue sky. In New York, because it was icy cold outside, I had to wear two pairs of woollen stockings and could hardly move. Inside the flat it was stuffy hot and my mother wanted to open our bedroom window, but couldn't. The best part of New York was being in a flat which scraped the sky, and down, down, down below the streets were full of little ant people driving little ant cars. But I refused to eat anything except Cornflakes and poached eggs, so we were both glad to leave New York.

Just when my mother was saying once again, "Whatever's happened to Willoughby," he turned up, and there he was, the same Willoughby I loved. In the taxi, while my mother told him about New York, I leant against my uncle and knew that all was well. When the taxi stopped he said, "Out you get, Thelma. Now for your surprise!"

"What surprise?"

All I could see was a long stretch of rough grass and funny-looking plants, and a house without any upstairs. The front had a big porch, and a flight of steps on which sat a lady and a little boy. They got up to greet us, and Willoughby said, "This is your surprise, Thelma. His name is Junior. And this is his mother, Mrs. Spangler."

In the old photograph album of that time Christina has inscribed a heading in bold white ink which stands out on the grey paper like a testimonial of triumph:

Christina de la Paz Ruck-Keene, D.C.
Graduate of
The Texas Chiropractic College, San Antonio,

43

Texas, U.S.A.
1921-1923

Here is Christina perched on the edge of the veranda. She wears black stockings, a longish black skirt and a flowered top (home-made, and much like a T-shirt); her ankles are neatly crossed and her black court shoes have rather chunky heels (popular once again in the twenty-first century). Her thick black hair is draped to frame her oval face, and she is laughing. Junior's mother probably took this photo for dispatch to England.

In these first photographs I wear a belted (home-made) cotton dress, white socks and lace-up shoes. Junior is in overalls and a sort of long-sleeved vest which has rumpled up under the overall straps. He looks rather a mess, but Mrs. Spangler has straightened him out for a second picture of us holding the blade of some tropical plant. It's a silly pose and we're both laughing. Junior is the same age as me, but I'm nearly a head taller - a shrimp of a boy, no beauty, but cheerful. In another photograph I wear a sunbonnet.

Here is our bungalow (#309 Garden Street) and I sit in the middle of the veranda steps, barely visible because Christina wanted to get the whole bungalow in, which she did, by a whisker. We live on the right side of the bungalow, the Spanglers on the left.

Mrs. Spangler has agreed to look after me, with Junior, while Christina and Willoughby are at college. In her photograph she looks rather Mexican. There isn't one of Mr. Spangler. He is a travelling salesman and not often at home - luckily. One day shrieks came from the Spangler's kitchen and my mother ran, saying, "Stay there, Thelma!" There were shouts, silence, and then she came back stiffly holding a big carving knife. She looked rather mad and burst into tears just as Willoughby came home. He took the knife away. In bed that night I heard my mother tell Willoughby she found Mrs. Spangler crouching on one side of the kitchen table, Mr. Spangler on the other side, brandishing the knife. "He was roaring, 'I'm gonna carve you up, you bitch!' I don't know how I got him to give me the knife, but I did."

One photograph is of Pedro and his two mules. They look after our lot, mostly rough grass and cacti. Pedro was my friend. Soon after our arrival I saw a snake in the grass and called, "Mummy, come and see the pretty snake!" I bent to pick it up, but Pedro was there first and sliced the snake in two with his machete.

"No good snake. He make you very sick. You see him, you run fast!"

Another time Pedro pulled me away from something that looked like a queer little castle of red earth and was almost as tall as myself. I poked at it, then howled, "Mummy, Mummy!" I was covered with red ants, and had to be hosed down to get the ants out of my hair.

Not surprisingly the English trappings of cotton sunbonnet, belted frock, socks and lace-up shoes didn't last long. The chubby little girl in the first few pages of the album is suddenly replaced by a lanky child wearing a noticeably home-made garment, a sort of T-shirt dress. I've tucked the hem of the dress between my legs, possibly to look as if I'm wearing shorts, like Junior. My hair is no longer neatly bobbed but nearly shoulder-length and thick as a thatch. Junior and I stand together in the bright sunshine, holding hands and laughing, barefoot, scruffy, and merry as grigs.

San Antonio was a paradise, completed by Rover, who turned up one day and settled in. He was a dog of mixed blood, his coat a shiny black and on his chest a large white star (Pedro called him "Lone Star dog") and his ears were pointed, one usually cocked, the other flat. Flying fox ears Willoughby called them and said, "He's a very debonair dog." I loved Rover as much as Junior.

Mrs. Spangler's idea of looking after us was to hope for the best. We were forbidden to play by the San Antonio River which ran, cool and tempting, not far beyond the rough land behind the bungalow: but we often went there, and she said nothing. Sometimes the water was high and fast, sometimes low and sluggish, always just itself, a fine river with wild flowers growing in profusion on the banks. The sunflowers were so tall we had to tip our heads back to get a good look at their brown faces, frilled with yellow sunshine petals. Once two big shapes swept past, their backs covered with great shells that clashed together as they tossed in the tumbling water.

"What are they?"

"Turtles."

"Are they fighting?"

"Sumpin' like it."

"They're awful strong."

"Reckon we keep outa their way."

Were they really turtles? But Junior said they were so we kept a lookout for turtles before stopping to cool our feet in a quiet stretch of water, and laugh at Rover splashing around trying to snap up water sparkles.

We were also forbidden to play on a nearby junk heap, but we did, poking around for treasures among rusty cog-wheels and springs and bits of cars; there was even a whole, springy bench seat to bounce on. After rootling in the junk heap we'd come back extra grubby and Mrs. Spangler would cry, "Land's sakes, jest look at you kids! Better get washed up before your Ma comes home."

One day we took courage to creep inside an old, abandoned truck. A faded, greenish canvas roof covered the back. Inside it was hot and the light an underwater green. Junior found a little bag of multi-coloured jelly babies, toughened by age, which we divided between us. It was warm and secret and we took off our clothes; that was how we chanced on the surprising pleasures of our bodies. We explored these with enthusiasm.

"You first, then it's my turn."

We added this discovery to our list of the many fine things to do - when we were alone, of course, except for the time we got carried away at Junior's birthday party. Three or four small boys were invited, one of whom provoked us to explore another forbidden place, a sort of hut tucked away in a shady corner of our lot. There wasn't much inside - a table and chair and, surprisingly, a bed. One of the boys began jumping about on the bed, and this was when we threw off our clothes.

Somebody chanted "Junior's in his birthday suit!" and we all took it up, "Birthday suit, birthday suit, I'm in my birthday suit."

So there we were, jigging about and laughing, tangling, touching, giggling, not a care in the world, and Junior was crying, "Mine's bigger'n yourn," when I heard a sharp tap on the window, and looking up, saw the faces. One of the boys did the same, stopped jigging, stared and squeaked, "There's my Ma."

Silenced, we stood bare-naked, staring wide-eyed at the faces in the window as my mother's voice said cheerfully, "Whatever are they up to now!" which was followed by a chorus of "Disgusting!... Disgraceful!" before the door flew open and there were angry commands, "Put your clothes on this instant!" and "Your father will have something to say to you, boy!"

The boys did not play with us again. My mother made us tidy up the hut and apologize to Pedro, for it was his place. We really did feel sorry to have made a mess of his bed and promised never to go in there again. Pedro grinned and said, "Don't make no matter" so we felt better.

Hank was another boy we never played with again. Christina knew his mother slightly and invited her to bring her little boy to play with us. The two women sat chatting on the veranda while we initiated Hank into some of our games. He was rather heavy going so we decided to liven things up with our disc game. The disc was a junk heap find, a sturdy metal washer, heavy, but we could handle it. Held with one finger through the hole it could be pitched along a runway of earth, carefully smoothed by the two of us. We took it in turns to see how far we could fling the disc, marking the length of each throw. Whoever wasn't throwing stood well to one side as our first throws had been a bit wild.

Maybe Hank was fed up being bossed about by Junior and me, but whatever the reason he refused to move from the end of the pitch. It was my turn to begin and I cried, "Git out of the way, Hank. Junior'n me'll show you, then you kin have a turn." He didn't move. "Don't be stoopid, I don' wanna hit you." I talked like this in Texas.

Hank made a face and exclaimed rudely, "Youse ain't strong 'nuff to git this fur."

"Aw, c'mon Hank! You stand along of Junior." Hank stayed put. This was not the way Junior and I played games. "Don't you wanna play? Wassa matter with you?" Silence. On the sidelines Junior called, "C'mon over here. She throws good."

"She's jest a gurl. Gurls cain't throw."

"'Course I kin throw! an' I'm gonna throw soon as I count three. So jest you look out!" I began counting - slowly. "One...two..." Hank glared, unmoving, and in a burst of irritation I shouted *"Three!"* and flung the disc - but felt my finger catch in the hole and watched the metal circle fly, not along the pitch, but straight at Hank's head. It hit him just above his nose and with a howl he stumbled away crying, "Momma...Momma...that gurl..."

We saw the blood running through his small fingers, heard: "What's happened?" from Christina, and a wail from Hank's mother, "Oh, my Lord, my baby!" amidst awful cries from Hank. The noise brought Willoughby to the veranda and we heard him say, "Got a handkerchief, Christina?" and to Hank, "Stay still, old chap. In a minute you're going to be a wounded soldier."

We kept our distance but my mother called, "Come here, you two," and then, "How did this happen?"

From Junior, loyally, "He jest *stood* there..."

From me, indignant, "I never *meant*...I *told* him..."

Willoughby interrupted. "Let's go, ma'am. A doctor will put a stitch or two in that cut. He'll be right as rain," and to Hank, "Ready, soldier?" Hank gave a woeful squawk and then the three of them were gone.

The game was sternly forbidden, and for once we obeyed - the blood had been frightening. Later I was taken to apologize to Hank.

"I got stitches in my skin," he said.

"Did it hurt?"

He scowled and said "'course it did!"

As I'd already apologized I couldn't think of anything more to say. On the way home my mother remarked that I should always be polite and thoughtful to guests.

"I *told* him to move, 'n *he* wasn't polite. He made faces."

"That's not the point. It's what *you* do I'm talking about."

Junior and I didn't miss Hank, but suddenly our carefree days were interrupted when my mother decided I should go to school. I heard her tell Willoughby it was high time I learnt to read. "Thelma is six years old. I'm sure we all read long before then: I remember reading *Little Black Sambo* when I was three. Also, she's getting rather wild."

Willoughby said, "She's full of beans and seems happy."

"I think she should go to school, do her good to be with some other children."

I went to the local school, but my mother was upset by some surprising new turns of speech. Willoughby enjoyed my vocabulary. "Did you hear her telling Junior to 'Git up and hump youself!' Pure Huckleberry Finn."

"Birdie would be horrified! She's Ralph's child."

"She's your child too."

"But she should learn to read."

Soon reading lessons were arranged with a governess whose name sounded like Schmid, but my mother said it was spelled Schmidt and pronounced it in a funny way. "But it's not funny," she said, "and you must be nice to her."

Willoughby said, "Maybe Thelma will add a German accent to her collection." My mother said he was impossible, but laughed all the same.

I mostly hid from Miss Schmidt whom I found difficult to understand. When Rover was around Junior had to take him someplace else otherwise he stood outside my hiding place, grinning and wagging his tail. Junior hid with me if Rover was off on his own, and we stifled giggles together in the darkness of the henhouse or whatever hideout we'd chosen.

"Telma, come, come!" Miss Schmid would cry, but rarely found me. She left after a couple of weeks, complaining, "How I teach an empty chair?"

"I give up," my mother said. "At least the children are safe with our Mrs. Spangler," and we returned to our carefree lives.

Something Junior and I looked forward to was the occasional weekend treat of being taken by Willoughby to the college grounds to play on the parallel bars. We'd hang from our knees, twisting and turning like monkeys, inventing new tricks, crying "Can you do this?" Now and again, if Mrs. Spangler had to take a few hours off, we played in the grounds while my mother and Willoughby were in class.

We were always told, "Play quietly, both of you, and stay away from the corpse hut."

My mother told me that the corpses were dead bodies. What for? For students to learn about anatomy. What's a 'natomy? "The bones and everything inside your body," she explained. "I passed this on to Junior the next time we were at the college.

"So that's your 'natomy!" he said, poking me in the ribs.

"And that's yourn!" and we forgot about being quiet.

My mother came out of class and was cross. "You won't come again if you disturb everyone like this. For goodness sake, *play quietly!*"

When she was gone we tiptoed giggling to the corpse hut and pressed our faces against the window, but the glass was dark and we couldn't see anything: so we pretended.

"There's a foot stickin' up!"

"I kin see sumpin'. Cain't you see, stoopid, look, over there!"

Soon we got ourselves really spooked and ran away to the corpse-free parallel bars.

Only twice did the college fail to be a jolly place. The first time was when Mrs. Spangler had to take Junior somewhere and I had to go with my mother and sit in the lecture hall while somebody gave a talk, with pictures. I was dressed in a clean frock and sat at the back of the hall with the younger students. I felt very grown-up, all by myself.

Afterwards my mother said she hoped I could see some of the pictures. "It was all right," I said, but didn't tell her what I'd seen when the student next to me undid the buttons in front of his trousers and out popped a nasty-looking sausage between his legs. I looked away, but he took my hand and tried to make me hold the sausage, which was warm and hard and I didn't like it. I had never seen a man naked, not even Willoughby, and didn't connect the sausage with Junior's small appendage. I snatched my hand away and, cheeks burning, kept my mouth tight shut and breathed through my nose; this was what my mother told me to do if we passed a nasty smell.

Nothing like this had ever happened before, and I was embarrassed by what seemed unmannerly behaviour, but then, grown-ups could often be peculiar.

The second bad happening was a different kind of badness. I went with my mother to the college on what must have been a special party as lots of the students and staff were outside talking and laughing.

I ran around enjoying myself, and seeing a pile of leaves jumped on top crying, "I'm king of the castle, Git down you dirty rascal!" but suddenly hands seized me and I shrieked "AIEEEEH!" My feet were not my feet, they were nothing but shrieking pain from the red-hot center of my castle, hidden under a fresh load of leaves.

In the college my mother held my feet under cold running water - and ah! the pain stopped. But in the air it began again, and I screamed all the way home in a taxi and then lay on my bed choking and crying, "Stop it, Mummy, stop it!"

When telling this story my mother always said she was sure I could have cried myself into a convulsion. Instead, Rover hurtled out of nowhere into my bedroom and jumped straight on my bed. "He knew this was strictly forbidden," said my mother, "but it was as though he knew just what to do."

What he did was flop down very flat beside me, put his cold damp nose against my face and one paw over my chest. I put my arms around his neck as he licked my face and then I stopped crying, and fell asleep.

"Rover saved Thelma's life!" my mother would conclude. "His flying-fox ears must have been psychically tuned in to Thelma's cries. He was quite out of breath, his tongue hanging out, as if he'd run a long way." Well, maybe. But what mattered that day was the blessing of his warm furry body.

The burns were soon healed. I'd run barefoot for more than a year and the soles of my feet were tough as leather, so only the upper parts were burned. They blew up like balloons and for years the skin was almost white and mottled with brown. Back in England Birdie was shocked, and my mother had to explain.

The last batch of San Antonio photographs are about the serious business of chiropractic, including Christina and Willoughby standing together in cap and gown, each holding their rolled diploma. Separate photographs have my mother laughing, and Willoughby soulful under a tree. Then a series of photographs record their patients.

The most important is noted as: *Henry Villanura, 22 months. General Dropsy set in after whooping cough.* Henry was Willoughby's patient. In the first photo Henry stands like a small pumpkin on spindly legs, his stomach blown out and cheeks so swollen his eyes are tight shut. Underneath Christina noted: *Before taking chiropractic adjustments.* Next, Henry is held by his mother. He is still a hefty armful, but his eyes are open. Then comes the last photo of Henry. He is a normal little boy, chubby and smiling on the college steps. Christina notes: *After first chiropractic adjustment he could open his eyes. After 10 adjustments he lost 8 lbs. of water.*

Below this proud record a single line runs across the page like a triumphant shout: *Given up by the San Antonio specialists to die, cured by chiropractic.*

A last photograph of a young boy is headed, *My first patient.* He looks healthy, and Christina gives no explanation. But the point is clear: whatever the Ruck Keenes might think, her venture had succeeded, and no harm had come to me.

The two years of study must have been hard work for both Willoughby and my mother, particularly as she'd never had any formal schooling. Even so, both of them managed to take time off for treats, like a trip to Brackenridge Park which had swings and slides and a Japanese teahouse where we each had a fortune cookie with our own fortunes printed on a slip of paper tucked right in the cookie. But the best treat of all was the Mexican market.

At the market we bought *enchiladas de legumbre* or *tortillas* or *chili con carne.* My mother always rolled *"de legumbre"* round her tongue in a relishing way, and for years I heard the two words as one - *deligumbre,* meaning 'wonderful'. Often we saw cowboys who had just rollicked into town for a bit of relaxation. They wore broad-brimmed hats and high-heeled boots and were big as giants. Sometimes we went to the market at dusk and gradually the sky grew velvet black, the stars blazed, and in the darkness cooking fires glowed and flickered. The flames lit strong-boned Mexican faces, bending intent over their cooking, or raised to cry their wares in words I didn't understand. The air was full of spicy smells and everything, just everything, was beautiful, for we were alive alive-oh! and would live in San Antonio forever.

⊰ 7 ⊱

Paradise 'was'. 'Now' is mostly
one thing after another.

Junior, Rover and I sat by the river in silence early in the new year of 1923. I had just asked Junior if he'd heard of a place with a funny name that sounded like Bwenosiris. He hadn't. I said we might be going there, adding that I'd heard Willoughby say, "If that doesn't work out, we can try Monty...something."

"Are you goin' away?"

I said I didn't know. "Perhaps they'll change their minds."

"Perhaps," but we knew they wouldn't. We didn't talk about it any more.

Did Willoughby and Christina really plan to have a stab at being chiropractors in Argentina or Uruguay? Neither of them spoke Spanish, but perhaps they cried, "We can learn!" and talked of their father's sojourns in South America and their Spanish ancestry; or maybe they just felt young and free and bold.

Three photographs record the next few months, beginning with me in the sea at Corpus Christi where my mother and I had a holiday. Then we embarked on a cargo ship through the Caribbean to Buenos Aires where Willoughby was to join us. No photographs exist of our dreamlike voyage amongst the Caribbean islands. I was spoiled by the captain who brought a goat on board so I could have fresh milk, ordered a swing to be made and hung on the deck, and in his spare time embellished a ship's chart with hand-drawn, coloured hazards - dangerous coral reefs, sea monsters, islands infested with brigands, passages of stormy weather and shipwreck. It was a game with dice and counters like Snakes and Ladders; the chart was mounted on wood and varnished to last a lifetime. He also wrote a poem about me with the refrain, "What will she be at seventeen?" To my chagrin the poem and the game were lost in one of our many moves.

The second photo is of Mr. Brooke-Smith (the Lloyd's agent in Buenos Aires). He sits firmly at the wheel of an open car with his wife and a friend in the back; the two ladies wear hats like flowerpots, and the demeanour of all three implies "We are pillars of Anglo-Argentinean society."

Here we waited for Willoughby. Meanwhile the Brooke-Smiths were probably less than enthusiastic about chiropractic in Buenos Aires, and the next photograph is of me smiling cheerfully under a straw sombrero in Montevideo. We were the guests of another Lloyd's agent, and once again we waited, fruitlessly, for Willoughby. Then Christina must have lost her nerve. A final photograph is headed:

Taken on the S/S Highland Pride.

Left La Plata April 14, 1923.
Arrived London May 10.

A gaggle of children stand lined up on deck, me in the middle, taller than the others and wearing a jersey that's too small for me.

The last photographs of that year begin with my uncle Phil Ruck Keene and his young wife Marguerite (nicknamed Dick). They walk out of a church under an archway of crossed naval swords. The date is December 1923. I am seven years old and a bridesmaid at this wedding.

In the bridal picture I gaze at the camera with a vaguely sweet expression. I am very dressed up, my thick hair flattened by a band of rosebuds, and my ankles are neatly crossed. Drastic measures must have been taken to effect the transformation from long-legged scruffiness to this simpering creature. My rather padded appearance is partly due to being built up on English stodge after whooping cough, and to being forced to pile on woolly under-garments, "or you'll catch your death of cold, Thelma, in that flimsy frock."

Phil is in full dress naval uniform, draped in gold braid; he looks splendid, tall and handsome, his chin up as if he'd just barked out a naval command like "Splice the mainbrace!" or simply "FIRE!" Dick, smiling and slender, is a lovely bride - like my mother she is another exotic, but Irish, with no disturbing touch of foreign blood.

I turn back the album pages to the photograph of Junior and me in San Antonio. There we are, barefoot, laughing, and so full of life it seems to burst out of us, like electricity.

In England I tried hanging on to shreds of life and liberty, such as not wearing shoes. My grandmother Minna let me run around barefoot, but as we prepared for our first visit to Birdie and Ted at Copford Rectory my mother said, "When we are there you will wear shoes and socks all the time."

"But I can't feel the ground!"

"That can't be helped. In England young ladies wear shoes. I don't want Granny and Grandpa thinking you're a hooligan."

"What's a hooligan?"

"You not wearing shoes and socks."

"Was I a hooligan in Texas?"

"No...no, of course not. But Texas isn't England."

"Texas was better."

Maybe it was around this time that my mother began exclaiming, "Oh dear, peaceful Texas, how I loved you."

I wore shoes and socks at Copford, but took them off when Oophats and I were on our own so I could feel the soft green grass underfoot and wiggle my bare toes on his furry belly (sometimes I called him Rover, but he didn't seem to mind). I also forgot where I'd left my shoes and/or socks, so in no time Birdie saw the burn scars on my feet.

"Dear child! whatever happened to your poor feet?"

"Oh, I jest jumped on a bonfire. Mummy says Rover saved my life." I left my mother explaining and went off with Oophats.

In the end Birdie let me run barefoot around the house and garden, but insisted on shoes and socks for church on Sunday.

I didn't give up on the shoe issue, and even went barefoot in London on a visit to Uncle Harry whose agents had been so helpful in New York and Buenos Aires and Montevideo. He said he liked my bare toes, so I was unprepared for what happened in Kensington Gardens where my mother took me for a treat.

We went on a bus and sat on the top which was open to the sky and all of London. "We'll get off at the Broad Walk," my mother said, "and walk up to the Round Pond. That's where children sail their toy boats."

The Broad Walk was uphill as well as broad, with benches on either side where nannies with prams stopped to catch their breath and have a chat with the other nannies. I had no personal experience of nannies, so considered them with interest. They wore spotless uniforms and funny stiff hats and sat up very straight, the gleaming prams safely parked alongside while the older children played nearby - or rather, they played as well as anyone can in clean smart frocks, white socks, and leather shoes with a strap across the instep.

Being used to friendly smiles from passing strangers I was taken aback when all I got from the nannies were unsmiling stares, and the children were as bad. I stared back, then ran ahead to show I didn't care; but for the first time I *knew* my feet were bare, and I was angry. It was rude to stare. I didn't stare at them because they wore shoes.

At the Round Pond I forgot about the stares. All kinds of little boats were bobbing about on the water, and there was a beautiful big one in full sail. The children were standing around in shoes and socks instead of paddling, which seemed silly. At least my bare feet were ready for a paddle. But I'd just put one foot in the water when my mother said sharply, "No, Thelma, see the notice - it says NO PADDLING ALLOWED." She read it in capital letters.

Before we went back to Uncle Harry my mother bought me a pair of brown leather sandals with crêpe rubber soles. She'd pointed out that I'd be going to school soon, and at school everyone wore shoes and socks. The shop assistant said the *crêpe* soles would stand up to hard wear and smiled at me as he fastened the buckles. I clumped out of the store in silence, unable to feel the ground, and San Antonio slipped away out of reach.

We went back to Weston hoping Willoughby would have turned up at last. But he hadn't, and I kept asking, "Will Willoughby be here today?" until my mother said, "We'll see him when we see him," in a voice meaning 'stop asking aggravating questions.' He did come at long last, and soon he and my mother began planning their chiropractic partnership. Then I knew he wasn't going away any more, and everything would be all right.

The two of them were often away in London, searching for somewhere to live and work. Then they had to buy two treatment couches, and yards of white cotton so my mother could make curtains for the cubicles, and gowns for the patients.

It was at this time, when Minna and I were alone together, that she began telling me stories. There was a fine story about my grandfather when he was a young doctor in South America. One night he was whisked away in a coach by masked men. They made him wear a blindfold until they reached a big house, and there he saved the life of a young man with a bullet in his thigh, and he was paid in chunks of gold and precious stones.

The stories about Minna began when she was a child in India with an ayah, which is Indian for a nanny. "I only saw my parents once a day before tea," Minna said, "so I loved my ayah, who told me stories about tigers and wizards, princesses, and princes. But when I was even younger than you, pet, I was sent away to school in Heidelberg, which is in Germany, and I never saw my ayah again."

Of all the Heidelberg stories the best one was about the Military Tattoo. "The tattoo was going to be attended by the German Emperor and his grandson. At that time," Minna explained, "we never dreamt that his grandson would be the Kaiser and be at war with England. No, he was just the young Prince, and we begged permission to buy tickets for the Tattoo and see the Prince. But horrid Frau Mann, the principal of our school, said it was not suitable for young ladies to be in such a crowd. Now it happened that I had a riding lesson on the opening day, and I persuaded my riding master to ride with me to where the horses were getting ready for the parade. It was very exciting," Minna said, "such a hullabaloo of fidgeting horses and jangling harnesses - and then the band in the arena began to play the German anthem and we knew the Emperor had arrived. We kept very still, but when it was over a command was shouted and with a sudden deafening clatter the cavalry, the foot-soldiers and gun-carriages surged forward. I never heard my riding master cry, 'Fräulein, Fräulein, nein nein!' for my horse took fright and plunged ahead of the whole parade. In a moment we were flying quite alone down the parade route - and oh, what a ride that was!"

"Did you fall off?"

"Certainly not! Why would I do that? I could ride almost before I could walk. I gave the horse his head, and though my riding hat fell off and my hair tumbled all down my back, I never gave it a thought until I saw the Royal Box ahead, with the Emperor and his grandson."

"Did they notice you?"

"They could hardly do anything else!"

"What happened?"

"Well, I managed to slow the horse down and, as we drew level with the Royal Box, the young Prince stood up and bowed to me!"

"And you bowed back?"

"Naturally, though I had to twist because I was riding side-saddle. I cantered past the box with my head properly inclined, and all I wanted was to get out of the arena. But there was another surprise: in the crowded tiers of seats people were clapping and cheering, and who do you think they were cheering?"

"*You!*"

"Yes," said Minna, her cheeks pink, her blue eyes sparkling.

She went on, "I was punished by horrid Frau Mann. She shut me in my room for a day on bread and water and I wasn't allowed to ride for a month. But just at that bad time your grandfather came to visit me - I first met dear Willoughby in London when I was fifteen and my parents were on leave there. When they went back to India he promised my mother he would visit me in Heidelberg and send them news of me. The next two years he came quite often. I'd grown to love him very much - I was seventeen, and no longer a child. So when a servant told me he was waiting in the salon, I ran down the stairs, and didn't stop until I'd flung my arms round his neck crying, 'Take me away from here! Please take me away!'"

"And did he?"

"Of course," said Minna.

These stories were repeated, word for word, many times over; I never asked for the gaps to be filled in, so the Garsias moved in the world of myth and fairy tale, where the prince and princess married and lived happily ever after.

Minna introduced me to fairy tales by reading aloud from Andrew Lang's collection, printed in books titled by the colour of their cover - *The Blue Fairy Book*, and the *Brown, Grey, Orange, Violet,* and *Red* fairy books. She explained that Andrew Lang had written down stories from all over the world, and then asked different artists to illustrate them. The drawings ('engravings' Minna called them) were in black and white and as magical as the stories themselves.

I don't know how it happened but soon I was reading the fairy tales for myself - maybe I just decided to try, and it was easy. Curled up in an armchair I read and read, choosing different coloured volumes, until one day Minna gave me *The Tanglewood Tales*. She said these were myths, another kind of fairy tale, from a country called Greece. I read every one, and then read them again, spellbound by something luminous that was different from the fairy tales.

One evening, as the light faded and I couldn't read any more, I sat up straight, shut my eyes and said aloud, "One day I will go to Greece." It felt like a vow, and I spoke out loud so the gods would hear - which they did, in their fashion.

It was late summer when Minna took me, for a treat, to the Waxwork Museum in Weston's Arcade. We started with The Battle of Trafalgar. Minna said the man lying on deck was Admiral Nelson, and he was dying of wounds. The man bending over him was his favourite officer, Hardy, and Nelson's last words were, 'Kiss me, Hardy.' I asked whether Marston would kiss Willoughby if he was dying, but didn't hear her answer for I was distracted by a woman's squeaky voice exclaiming, "Oo, look, the Chamber of 'orrors. Let's 'ave a see." I turned just as a man with a giggling young woman disappeared behind a curtain on the other side of the room.

"Minna, what's the Chamber of 'orrors? Can we go? Is it funny?"

"Horrors, pet: and no, you wouldn't like it, and it's not in the least funny," adding, "You can go when you're older."

"How much older?"

"Oh...perhaps another ten years. Maybe nine at a pinch."

"Ten years...!" Behind her wire-rimmed spectacles Minna's eyes were kind and blue as a summer sky and I knew she was teasing me.

But the seed of curiosity was sown. Some time later I spent an afternoon with another seven-year old whose house was not far from the Arcade. I learnt that she also had never been to the Chamber of Horrors, and we hatched a plan to slip away when we were supposed to be resting after lunch.

We had just enough pocket money for the ticket and made straight for the notice, CHAMBER OF HORRORS UPSTAIRS. Eagerly we pushed the curtain aside - and stopped abruptly at the bottom of a staircase. On both sides of every stair were very lifelike severed human heads. Some had one eye dropping out of its socket, some had open mouths as if caught in a last shriek, all were bloody and frightful. We stared at the heads, and the ones with two good eyes stared fixedly back.

However, fairy tales had accustomed both of us to much chopping off of heads, particularly of no-good characters, so holding hands and keeping carefully in the middle of the stairs, we went on up to see what else we'd find.

We came into a large room dominated by a group of men gathered on a low platform against the far wall. The men wore grey uniforms and spiked helmets and stood around a man on a sort of throne whose uniform was grander, and his leather boots had a spike on each heel. The helmets were vaguely familiar.

There was no attendant in the room, but I whispered, "Let's go over there."

By the platform was a notice which I spelled out, uncertainly. It went something like. *The bloody Bo..Boches at play. The K..K..aiser, attended by Bi..s..marck and his co..horts."*

"What's a co..hort?"

"I don't know."

Not that it mattered. There was nothing mysterious about the bloody little bodies of dead babies: one was being offered on the end of a sword to the man on the throne. It didn't say so, but to me they were eating babies.

I said, "The Boches were bad Germans. They killed my father."

We stared at the Kaiser's hands, red with baby blood. He bent forward, the sharp-nosed face unmistakable under his spiked helmet. The room was very still. Suddenly, without a word, we turned and ran across the room, down the stairs past the severed heads, through the shielding curtain and out, out into the warm arcade where sunshine filtered through the glass roof, and ordinary people with both eyes in place, hands pink and clean, walked up and down buying peppermint rock and Japanese parasols and laughing at what my mother called 'rude postcards'.

Not long after this escapade my companion and I fell ill with whooping cough, and in the new year we moved to London. So we never met again, nor did I tell anyone what we'd done, not even Minna. But I didn't escape scot-free. Whooping cough laid me low with a high fever, and at night, when I heard the wardrobe creak, I knew it was the Kaiser, cramped inside, chomping babies. With beating heart I'd lie very still, willing him passionately not to come out. He never did, but when I was well and the wardrobe only had clothes in it, the Kaiser took to lurking under my bed, and to avoid his outstretched, Boche-bloody hand, I had to leap on the bed from quite a distance.

"Goodness me!" Minna exclaimed, "we should have christened you Kangaroo!"

When we moved to London the Kaiser-under-my-bed stayed put in Weston. But for years the mention of a German prompted a quick, unreasoned dread until, at last, I learned to think for myself.

We spent Christmas with Minna, the tree trimmed with candles and the indispensable decorations my mother had carefully carried to America and back. Then we joined Willoughby in London. In the new year I started school, and on January 9, had eight candles on my birthday cake. In October twenty-nine candles had blazed on my mother's cake, and Willoughby had teased her, "I always have one more candle than you!" They were quite old.

In London we had two floors of a house in a small South Kensington square. On the ground floor were our bedrooms and the big drawing-room where the patients were treated. Downstairs, which wasn't quite a basement, was a roomy kitchen and the dining-room where we mostly lived. Outside, in the middle of the square, was a garden with a lawn, trees, bushes and flowerbeds; it had a strong iron fence, and a locked gate. If you lived in the square you had a key, not otherwise. I asked my mother why everyone couldn't enjoy our garden.

"It wouldn't be very nice if it was crowded with all kinds of people." What kinds? "Oh, Cockneys from the East end, smelly beggars."

"But if we let the beggars into our garden perhaps, like when Beauty kissed the Beast..."

"A fairy-tale Beast," said my mother firmly, "is one thing. Smelly beggars are smelly beggars; besides, the nannies would be put out." I could believe that.

My school, Norland Place, was in a house like ours, facing a square, which had a fenced garden where we played when it was fine. I loved every minute of school, and by the end of the first term I was able to write as well as read, and also to play the piano. Every day I came home in time for tea with my mother and Willoughby, and afterwards I sat at the piano and, rather laboriously, sight-read from my books of nursery rhymes - the two illustrated by Henriette Willebeek le Mair, and *The Baby's Bouquet* which had songs in several languages. My mother's favourite song was, *I had four brothers over the sea*, which had a refrain like a spell:

> Petrum, Partrum, Paradisi Tempore,
> Perrie, Merrie, Dixi, Domine.

After supper I took over the big armchair in front of the gas fire and read *Chums*. This boys' paper came out once a month, bringing revelations about the fascinating world of boys. My mother wanted me to read about girls and bought copies of a girls' paper, but the stories seemed soppy compared with the goings-on in *Chums*.

I still have a battered *Chums* of May 1925. It cost one shilling, for which you got: *Five serials, eighteen long complete stories,* and a colour plate of: *Latest types of motor cycles.* There are 60 pages in all measuring 9½" by 12".

Chums left no doubt about something called - *the right stuff.* Unlike fairy-tale heroes and Greek gods, decent British boys always told the truth. Even the silliest fibs were put to scorn by...*"I say, Smith Minor, that's just not done!"* Decent British boys also shied away from being a muff, a mollycoddle, a sneak or a swot.

"What's a swot?" I asked Willoughby.

"It's what schoolboys call someone who works so hard he's not interested in playing football, or whatever boys like to do."

"Is it bad to work too hard?"

"It's good to enjoy your work."

"Do you enjoy being a chiropractor?"

"Yes. And about work," he added. "People often talk as if work is a burden. But that's because they're not doing the work they really want to do - unless, poor creatures, they have to take whatever work they can get, so they can live." Probably I looked puzzled, for he said, "When you try to get something right on the piano it's hard work, but you enjoy it - don't you?" I nodded. With a smile Willoughby said, "Just keep that in mind."

What was reassuring about the *Chums* world was how everyone seemed to agree on what mattered. A boy worth knowing kept his chin up and wouldn't blub (tears were babyish), he was a good sort and a ripping pal (or chum). I did wonder why none of the boys played the piano or, like Willoughby, painted pictures. But perhaps that sort of thing was acceptable for adults, or even girls, though there were few clues about what girls did in the boys' world - they were mostly some boy's sister.

The boys lived in a rough world. In my 1925 *Chums* is an instalment of *The Red Deluge: a story of World Peril,* which the editor notes...*has Attracted World-wide Interest.* At the top of the page is a summary of earlier instalments:

> The sinister allies, IGNATIEFF, the Russian Red, and HANG LOO SIN intend to destroy civilization...[Russians and Chinese] have captured Harwich and are advancing.

An illustration titled *How the Britons Faced the Red Tide* shows heroic young Hilary Bellamy whacking at the Red Hordes with what looks like a large spade, while his companion thumps them with the butt of his gun - obviously their ammunition is exhausted. The Reds are already surging over the barricades, but their brutish faces mark them as losers, just as the clean-cut British boys (their socks as always pulled tightly up to their knees) will naturally win through. They are plucky (*the right stuff*) and white through and through - like Kipling's *Gunga Din* who was...*white, clear white, inside.* My mother enjoyed reading this poem, giving it much dramatic expression.

Actually *Gunga Din* was an exception. Readers of *Chums* took for granted the rotten streak in outsiders like Jews, Germans (of course), Italians, Russians (unless they were princes) and people confusingly referred to as Frogs. Frogs? Willoughby explained this was an unkind word for a Frenchman.

However, not all the British were decent fellows, particularly war profiteers who were filthy rich and not gentlemen. A rich gentleman was quite all right, but if you weren't a gentleman you had no business to be rich, and to have made money out of the war was despicable (and filthy).

In sum, it was best to be British (preferably a gentleman) and a boy. What luck to be a boy! They lived adventurous lives, were brave and strong and more sensible than girls. Girls in *Chums* were generally good sorts but were rescued rather than being rescuers, and seemed less shrewd than boys. Boys were quick to sniff out treacheries, while girls were trusting and easily taken in. Boys knew that trust was best given to people of the right stuff.

I felt I was the right stuff, even though I wasn't a boy. The next best thing would be to have a friend who was a boy. I didn't, but Jane Boulanger, my friend at Norland Place, was a good substitute.

In the summer holidays I went with Jane and her parents to St. Malo, a little seaside town in France. The old part was encircled by ramparts, and within a few days we discovered that not only could you walk all round the town, but could often see right into people's houses. So we got up early every morning, and "Did you see!" we cried at the sight of a woman in her nightdress or a man shaving. Occasionally we were ourselves seen and then we sank to the ground and, safely out of sight, were prostrated by giggles. One morning a man, covered with shaving soap and waving his cutthroat razor, shouted *"p'tites salaudes!"* and slammed wooden shutters across his windows.

"I say, he was in quite a bate!"

"But why did he call us a salad?"

"I'm not sure it was a salad. Dad says when the French want to be rude they call you things like *un espèce de chameau*, which means 'a sort of camel,'"

"Sounds daft."

"Perhaps a salad is as bad as being a camel." We found this exquisitely funny.

Just before this entrancing holiday came to an end I fell ill with a fever. Jane wasn't allowed into my room, and Mrs. Boulanger kept coming to ask how I felt. But I could only croak at her; my throat hurt, my eyes were swollen, and I felt terrible. But the Boulangers had to get back to England so I was bundled up and propped, more or less senseless, in railway carriages and on the Channel ferry until, breathing hideously, I was handed over to my mother at Victoria station.

Christina's account of this meeting was, as usual, dramatic. "Your mouth hung open, your tongue was sticking out and almost black. I took one look at you and was sure you were at death's door." Being at death's door was one of my mother's expressions, usually far from the truth, but not so this time. Willoughby examined me and said he suspected diphtheria.

In 1924 diphtheria deaths were not uncommon. The only known treatment was to give injections of antitoxins with no guarantee of cure. Willoughby, explaining that it was a notifiable disease, took a swab of my throat for testing at the hospital.

"But they'll take her away," my mother wailed, "and give her those revolting injections!"

"Of course they won't. Don't fuss, Christina, we'll pull her through. She's healthy and hasn't been filled with poisonous drugs all her young life." The test was positive, but already Willoughby had begun daily spinal adjustments, followed by massage with his healing hands. These continued until I was well enough to go back to school in September.

But by then I knew that all was far from well in our house. Whatever was wrong had to do with somebody called Yedra, whom Willoughby liked, and my mother didn't.

When Christina took against a person or something that she disapproved of, the disapproval was fixed. Once, when I was much older, my uncle Marston told me about an early morning visit she made to his flat. "She turned up unexpectedly just as I had finished a breakfast of fried eggs and bacon," he said. "As you know, your mother can't abide the sight or smell of congealed egg and bacon. She walked in, exclaimed, 'Ugh, how revolting!' and before I could stop her she'd seized the plate and flung it clear through the open window."

"Was anyone below?"

"Luckily not, luckily not." Then he smiled and shook his head. "Ah, Christina was a bagsome girl!"

She was a touch bagsome about Yedra, who was one of Marston's ex-girls. He was keen on girls, but when he tired of one, he'd introduce her to Willoughby.

"This is my young brother," Marston would boom. "I am sure you're going to be great friends." Willoughby would politely take the new young woman out dancing and sometimes she had dinner with us - but after a while they all faded away, except Yedra.

She was lively, an excellent dancer, and cultivated her Spanish looks, as well as changing her boring name, Ivy, into Yedra, the Spanish for Ivy. She made Willoughby laugh. My mother liked her at first, but grew irritated as the weeks passed and Yedra appeared to be becoming a fixture.

"She's full of empty gush," my mother remarked crossly one evening, but Willoughby smiled and refused to quarrel.

One night I was woken by my mother's voice, clear and fierce, exclaiming, "You're being a fool, Willoughby. And I mean what I say. If you marry that woman, Thelma and I will leave!" Then a door slammed, hard.

Next morning I noticed my mother's silver fox stole untidily flung on a chair in the entrance hall. The black fur with silvery streaks wasn't exactly soft, just thick and luxurious; the jaws of the little fox face could be opened to clip head and tail together, and when the stole was round my mother's shoulders it set off her glossy black hair. I stretched out my hand to ruffle the fur, but my mother's "Don't touch it!" startled me.

"Why...?"

She snatched the stole, said in a tense, angry voice, "It stinks of Yedra. Willoughby lent it to her last night."

If an open window had been on hand the stole would most likely have gone the way of Marston's breakfast plate. Whatever its fate, I never saw it again, but from then on everything began to go wrong.

❧ 8 ❧

So many changes,
but Copford is forever.

For a time not much changed in our house, and Willoughby showed no signs of getting married. But we weren't as comfortable together as before, and maybe this was why I once or twice found myself slipping down the waste-water hole in the bath, the one just below the hot and cold taps. I liked lying in the warm water and letting my thoughts wander, and when Christina called, "Time to get out now!" I'd lie a little longer until, "For goodness sake, Thelma, stop dawdling!" Then I'd get out.

One day no command to stop dawdling disturbed my lazy contemplation of the waste-water hole and, quite on its own, my body seemed to rearrange itself, and effortlessly began gliding through the hole and down, down a long tunnel. A pinpoint of brightness grew and grew until, light as a bird, I flew out on to golden sand under a clear blue sky. Sunlight sparkled on the sea, and white crested waves fell softly on shore. I ran forward, arms widespread, certain of welcome, calling soundlessly 'I am here!'

I never went down any other hole, only that sad time before my mother took me away from London, leaving Willoughby behind. We moved to a place called St. Alban's, I don't know why, for we weren't happy. Instead of the happy days at Norland Place where I learnt something new every day, I went to a very large school where I was forever trying to be in the right place when bells rang.

"It's so big, Mummy," I complained. My mother said it would be all right soon and hugged me. But 'now', not 'soon', was what mattered, and I missed Willoughby. The piano was still in London, and I missed that too. The only bright spot was a game I invented and played with the girl next door.

The game was only possible on a weekend. We got up very early without waking anyone, and then we ran through the fresh morning air to a brick wall surrounding the kitchen garden of a big house. Unlike many grand English houses this wall had no bits of broken glass cemented on the top to keep thieves from climbing in. So we clambered up and sat for a moment on the top, making sure no-one was about before, silent as wraiths, we dropped into the garden.

This was the best moment - the garden all ours, so quiet it might have been spellbound. We took our time, wandering dreamily along the neat paths bordered by sweet-smelling privet, stopped to admire perfect dewdrops trembling on cobwebs and petals, and breathed in the scent of rambling roses. Then we got down to the taking of spoils.

62

They were token spoils, two flowers each and only humble ones the garden wouldn't miss. We began this stage almost reluctantly, for enchantment was displaced by the need to look out, and the thrill of possible discovery, even capture.

And one day it nearly happened. We were padding quietly towards our bit of scaleable wall when we heard a shout behind us, and turning, saw an old gardener running heavily after us, brandishing a rake. He looked just like Beatrix Potter's Mr. McGregor when he chased Peter Rabbit.

"Thieving young varmints...you'll be sorry..." he bellowed, and the awful word "...police!" followed us as we tumbled over the wall. We lost our spoils in the helter-skelter of escape so I couldn't give them to my mother. This I had done the first and second time we played the game. The first time she cried, "Oh darling, how lovely!" and with her arms round me said, "So you do love your old Mummy!" But neither this time nor the next did she ask where the flowers came from.

When school ended we went to stay at Copford. On a sunny hot day my mother and I spread a rug under the elms and played a game of checkers. I won and wanted to play one more game, but my mother said, "I want to talk to you about a new school."

"Can I go back to Norland Place?"

"No," she said, "no, that's not possible," and went on quickly, "Birdie and your grandpa feel you would enjoy being at a boarding school, like the boys in *Chums*." From where we sat I could see the windmill, and overhead the rooks cawed. "Grandpa has chosen a school and I'm going to see it while you stay here with Birdie and Abbie and Emma and Oophats."

I listened to the rooks, then said, "When are you coming back?"

"I won't be back. Birdie will put you on the train in charge of the guard."

After a moment I asked, "Will I sleep at the school?"

"Yes - like the boys in *Chums*. I'll rent a house in the town so I can take you out during term." Then I asked if Willoughby would be there and she said briskly, "Now Willoughby and Yedra are married, they have a house of their own in London." I sat very still, feeling as if Willoughby had, with a little deprecating smile, gently closed the door of his house in London.

Birdie and I saw my mother off at Marks Tey station, and Abbie made a chocolate cake for tea. That night, as a great treat ("just this once, Thelma") Oophats was allowed to sleep in my room. When Birdie came to say goodnight she sat on the side of my bed and told me that, when the boys were young, they would smuggle the dogs upstairs, and if Abbie came back to see what they might be up to, the dogs would dive under the eiderdowns. Birdie said, laughing, "The dogs would lie still as mice and flat as pancakes while the boys tried to keep straight faces. I'm afraid they were often very naughty."

From then on the telling of family stories was a nightly ritual, and gradually my father, in spite of being always quite dead, became someone who had been very much alive - after all, the great fight with my grandfather had happened on the landing right outside my bedroom.

The stories were told in instalments like the serials in *Chums*. The great fight and what happened afterwards took a couple of nights, ending triumphantly with my father walking down the gangway at Tilbury "looking every inch the gentleman, darling!"

One morning at breakfast Birdie remarked to Grandpa that someone I didn't know "wasn't quite out of the handkerchief drawer." I asked if being every inch the gentleman meant you were out of the handkerchief drawer, and was that the same as being out of the top drawer? She chuckled, exclaimed that I was sharp as a needle, and said, "When you've finished your breakfast we'll go upstairs, and I'll show you something."

What she showed me was a miniature chest of drawers in her bedroom. It stood on top of a larger chest with bigger drawers. "Isn't it a pretty little chest!" Birdie said. "It was made of walnut veneer when good Queen Victoria was a girl." Then, pulling out one of the little drawers, she added, "and this is where I keep my handkerchiefs."

"There's not much room in them," I said. "There's more room in the top drawer of the big chest."

"So there is," Birdie said. "But there's plenty of room for people like us in the handkerchief drawers, darling."

Those days at Copford were happy, and every night I looked forward to the stories about the boys and their cousins who often came to stay in the summer holidays. Birdie said, "Sometimes there were enough young people in the rectory to make up a family cricket team to play against the village." I imagined the house full of laughter and jokes, and Birdie said, with a sigh, "They were such happy times, darling, wonderful summers...and all the gallant boys with us."

One night she told how my father died. It was a rather complicated story, which ended when he was blown to smithereens in a dreadful place full of mud and danger. But before that shocking moment I saw him laughing as he caught each bomb, and then turn to throw them into the German trenches, easy and careless as if the bomb was a cricket ball.

Birdie said, "But one bomb had a short fuse and blew up in his hand." I couldn't see that at all, but Birdie went on quietly, "Such a brave boy, darling, and such a glorious death. Never fear, he loves you and will watch over you in heaven and keep you safe from harm."

As the days passed and the stories were told, the Ruck Keenes entered the marrow of my bones.

From time to time Birdie talked about the first school my father went to when he was even younger than me, and she brought out a leather-bound book with a crest stamped in gold on the cover. Inside was my father's name:

> R.E.Ruck Keene.
> iv.B. Mod. Class Prize.
> Summer Term, 1902.

I couldn't read the squiggle at the bottom but Birdie said it was the headmaster's signature. The book was a prize because my father had worked hard that summer of 1902. It was about someone called Caesar. There weren't any pictures and the book didn't open very easily as if, perhaps, he forgot to read it.

Birdie said that when he was thirteen he went to a public school called Rossall. "He made many friends there - just as you will, darling, at the school your grandfather chose specially for you. It has very good music, so those clever little fingers will get good teaching, and every day in the beautiful chapel you will say your prayers and sing hymns, and give thanks to God for his mercies." When I asked why they had their own chapel she said, "Because St. Agnes' is a convent school, run by very nice sisters."

"Sisters? Are they a big family? and what's a convent?"

Birdie laughed and said, "They are God's sisters, darling, and work together in God's service. Their house is called a convent." It didn't sound much like the boys' schools in *Chums*. "Are girls' schools the same as boys' schools?"

"Oh, girls' schools are much nicer. Boys have quite a rough time of it and are beaten if they get into trouble. You wouldn't like that, would you!"

I'd never been beaten so let that go, and thinking that St. Agnes' might be all right, I began to feel quite important.

"I'm going to boarding school," I told Abbie and Emma.

"Let's hope you behave yourself," said Abbie, and Emma chimed in, "Well, I never!"

During the last days at Copford, Oophats and I made goodbye rounds together. Every morning Abbie gave us two chewy ginger biscuits from the big crock in the larder, and we'd usually stop to watch her poking through the reeds around the pond, trying to find some moorhen eggs and muttering, "Drat they silly birds!" After that we went into the kitchen garden where I snapped open the pea pods, for we both liked the juicy young peas. Then we wandered into the orchard and I shared the first ginger biscuit with Oophats under apple trees that already promised a good autumn harvest.

We took our time to say goodbye to the water meadows, and when we reached the windmill I told Oophats about going down the well with Phil, and how I was so young I had to be carried. "Isn't that funny!" I said, and Oophats grinned and wagged his tail. There was no chum like Oophats.

We kept the dell for the last day. Oophats scrambled ahead as I clambered down the tree roots to the carpet of brown, sun-dappled beech leaves. We scuffed through the leaves and after a while I sat with my back against a tree. Oophats flopped down beside me and I scratched absently behind his silky ears, feeling teased by a sort of expectation. It was beautiful and quiet, but nothing happened. That was all right: it was good to sit, feeling neither sad nor happy, just there.

The next morning everyone was outside to see me off. I hugged Abbie and Emma saying, "I'll see you soon!" and kneeling beside Oophats, laid my cheek against his coat that smelt so beautifully of dog, and pulling back one silky ear whispered, "I'll see you soon, my beautiful boy!"

At the station, Grandpa gave me a shiny silver half-crown and shook my hand. He was too tall to hug so I thanked him and said I would see him soon. Birdie called me her darling gel and when I said, "I'll see everybody soon" she cried, "Of course you will, my precious." In the train I called from the window "Goodbye, goodbye, I'll see you all soon!" Then the whistle blew and the train chugged away under the open sky. I stared out at the lovely flat fenland, sniffed the friendly scent of dog and pipe tobacco on my fingers and thought about going to school, and that I'd be ten when I came back to Copford for the summer holidays. But it was twenty years before I came back again.

At St. Alban's I found my mother busy making some of my school clothes. She was stitching Cash's labels onto handkerchiefs and wasn't pleased when I exclaimed, "The name's wrong! It shouldn't have a hyphen, Birdie told me." I gave her the benefit of Birdie's history of why Ruck was forever coupled with Keene, concluding with Birdie's insistence that, "Nowadays too many people of no consequence put a hyphen between names."

My mother exclaimed, "Oh, hoity-toity! Anyway it's too late to change them," and picking up another handkerchief said, "I can't imagine why you have to have *twenty-four* of these. At least I shan't ever have to buy any more." She was wrong there. I never explained that when school food was extra revolting I'd flick gobbets on to a handkerchief spread ready on my lap. This I'd fold and stuff up the leg of my horrible navy bloomers; later the whole package went down the lavatory.

I wandered around looking at what my mother had made, and seeing a blue wool frock with smocked top exclaimed, "Do I have to wear this?"

"It's for Sundays in winter," said my mother. "In summer there's another like it but in tussore silk. Kind Minna is smocking it for you."

"But only babies wear smocking!"

Ignoring this my mother held up a Vyella blouse, white with blue stripes. "Look, these are pretty! In summer you have cotton ones with pink stripes."

As some clothes couldn't be made at home we went to Schoolbred's in London and bought a navy serge gym tunic, hideous black woollen stockings, something called a Liberty bodice, and the navy bloomers. At home my mother had made what looked like white cotton knickers and said they were called 'linings'. "You wear the linings underneath the bloomers," she explained.

"That's awful," I cried, "I'll die of heat." But my mother said there was nothing she could do about the rules, and she didn't want to hear anything about the Liberty bodice. This garment was made of ribbed cotton, strapped with broad white tape from top to bottom, the ends looped to take suspenders which held up the beastly black stockings. As my breasts developed the Liberty bodice flattened them mercilessly.

The last straw came when my mother said, "At least I don't have to provide the pinafores."

"Pinafores?"

"Blue cotton ones. You wear them over everything." Pinafores! like those old-fashioned children in my nursery books. How lucky boys were! I wished I was a boy.

One comfort was that all this paraphernalia was packed into my father's old leather trunk, the one which went with us to Texas and back. Unfortunately Christina had painted a hyphenated *T.RUCK-KEENE* in large white capitals on the lid. I thought about my father keeping an eye on me from heaven and hoped he'd overlook the hyphen. The wooden tuck box also had my name, with hyphen, painted in black to match the metal strapping on the box (my mother felt strongly about things matching). The box was packed with jam, sweets and a cake. Apparently we were allowed to eat ten sweets every Sunday.

"What if I only want six sweets or maybe twelve?"

"You'll soon find out."

The night before I left home my mother came upstairs and putting her arms round me said, "I'll miss you terribly, darling." I hugged her, but couldn't say anything.

The next afternoon my mother delivered me to the sisters of St. Agnes'. I was nine years old and felt sick. It was September, and wrapped in layers of frightful winter clothes I felt more like a parcel than a person. We were met by a lady in a white bonnet thing and long black dress with wide sleeves like wings. She handed me over to an older girl who took me upstairs to an empty dormitory. In the passage outside I noticed my trunk and tuck box and cried, "There's my trunk!" but the girl just nodded, said, "Sister says you're to wait here," and left. So at least I knew now that the lady in the bonnet and black robe was a sister.

I sat on one of the beds which were lined up on either side of the large room, each with a white sheet turned down over a red blanket, both tightly tucked in all round. They looked like beds for soldiers to lie on at attention, arms clamped to their sides, toes together, legs straight. I waited. Nobody came. I wondered why the sister wore the bonnet thing, and why her hair and ears and neck were completely covered with white cloth. I'd hate to be all wrapped up like that.

I wished someone would come. It was very quiet. Sun streamed through the tall leaded glass windows. Was I forgotten? When I heard footsteps I jumped up but sat down again quickly as a sharp child's voice exclaimed, "Look at this! TRUCKEENE! What a name!" followed by giggles and a chant of "Truckeene is a silly bean." They seemed to be thumping my trunk to mark time. I hoped they'd go away. What sort of children had my mother sent me to live with?

I was at last found by a sister who cried, "Dear me, Thelma! Whatever are you doing here? You should be in the nursery."

"*Nursery!* Why do I have to be with the babies?" I asked.

"They aren't babies, dear, simply the youngest children. When you are ten years old - in January you say? - well then, next term you'll be in a big dormitory."

In the nursery I was presented to a half-dozen children and a nurse. At least she looked normal in a nanny uniform and big white apron, and in front of the fireplace was a tall fender with a brass rim, just like the one at Copford where towels warmed when, long ago, I had a bath in front of the nursery fire. By bedtime I felt more like myself - until the shocking discovery that I was supposed to sleep in a cot, a real baby's cot. It had high rails all round and one side let down so you could get in. When I was in, nurse pulled it up and locked it in place.

"I don't like being shut in," I said.

"Now Thelma, that's enough. Sleep tight."

I slept, but woke suddenly with my head gripped fast by thin cold fingers. I tried to pull away but the fingers held me tight and hurt my ears and "Let me go! Let me GO!" I croaked, and went on until a voice said, "Hush, Thelma, you'll wake the children. Goodness me, whatever are you doing!"

What I had done was ram my head through the cot rails, and was stuck. Nurse had to put Vaseline around my ears so she could slide me out, meantime shushing the other children who'd woken and were crying for their mothers.

The next night I came out of sleep to find myself bending over the top of the fender. I had a poker in my hand and was scrabbling in the fireplace muttering, "I can't find it!" Luckily only a couple of children were disturbed this time.

Not so the third night when I woke with a start and felt someone messing about with one of my feet. I saw a witchlike shape, lumpy-headed, crouched at the end of my cot, and I sat up like a Jack-in-the-box shouting "Go away! Go away!" trying to pull free - and then the nightmare figure resolved into nurse, wearing a grey dressing-gown, her hair in curlers. By this time all the children were awake and crying so she went off to settle them down. Left alone I discovered that my foot had been tied with tape to the bars of the cot.

"Why am I tied up?" I asked.

"You were sleep-walking last night, dear. I can't keep having the other children wakened."

"I'm not a dog!"

"Don't be impertinent, Thelma. Go to sleep now."

I slept, but in my sleep must have tried to get out of the cot, and as my foot was still tethered I toppled over, crashing against the metal rails and causing another hullabaloo. So I was untied. I drifted into sleep feeling I'd prevailed against odds, unmindful that dealing with an apparition and a strip of cotton tape was child's play compared to coping with more puzzling phenomena.

⤙ 9 ⤚

Encountering phenomena from the very good to the truly awful.

Until I went to St. Agnes' God was, in a manner of speaking, a Ruck Keene who played a major part in all the daily ritual gatherings of the family. We gathered for breakfast, followed by family prayers, then at lunch, tea and supper, and at each gathering God was praised and thanked (though not mentioned at elevenses). His big day was Sunday when we all gathered with the village in my grandfather's church. There God had organ music and songs, plenty of praise and thanks as well as frequent requests for forgiveness. It was a lot of words, like my grandfather's sermon, but the gatherings were friendly and came round daily, like clockwork.

In the nursery world of St. Agnes', the God of Copford gatherings reappeared at mealtimes, morning school assembly and chapel-on-Sunday. I knew my grandfather Ted had chosen this school for me, so God was to be expected, though there were rather too many new words, especially in chapel. I stuck with what I could remember from Birdie teaching me "Our Father which art...." However, morning assembly regularly included something called the 'collect for the day' which everyone (except me) seemed to know by heart. So I set about making approximate sounds, speaking firmly, but quietly, not wishing to be conspicuous, particularly when the sounds became words which didn't make much sense. What, for instance, could be the meaning of "O God, Thee or Thor, piss and conquer"? Piss wasn't in my vocabulary, but Thor was the god of Thursday and in my reading gods were quarrelsome. Perhaps pissing was a bold military move leading to conquest. I carried on with "O God, Thee or Thor...." until one remarkable day my words slithered into "O God, the author of peace and concord." It was a triumphant moment.

On balance the school, chapel and convent was a not uninteresting foreign land where I was a traveller learning the language. 'Sin' and 'guilt' were new words which I was soon repeating cheerfully, not connecting them with the everyday business of being naughty, until a puzzling incident left a suspicion of something sneaky, but a little exciting. Nurse had left us briefly alone in the nursery, and an older girl suddenly appeared and told us urgently about something she called a 'period' and how we would bleed from 'there', making a swift, unmistakable gesture. We stood transfixed as she produced from under her pinafore a pad with loops at either end, but at this moment nurse returned and briskly hustled her away. What was it all about? No explanation was offered.

Next term in the big school I recognized the girl and learnt she had nearly been expelled the previous term. Expelled! That meant you'd done something really bad. I asked what she had done. Nobody knew. But I guessed, sensing a new meaning of the word 'sin', pregnant with question marks, anxiety - and a smidgen of excitement.

On the whole I rather enjoyed the first term at St. Agnes' and when my mother came in a taxi to take me home for the Christmas holidays I was full of information, starting with the names of everyone in the nursery and about nurse and the teachers and prayers and jumping over the horse in gym, and how I'd written a play about a princess which we performed in front of the whole school and I was the princess and also played my one piano piece in the intervals. "There were two intervals," I explained, "but I only had one piece ready, so I played it twice."

As I paused for breath my mother said, "You don't seem to have missed your Mummy one little bit!"

I hear her voice, see the expression on her face, and recall feeling as if I'd been swinging merrily down an open road and bang! I'd fallen over a ruddy great rock. Surprised and at a loss I stopped talking. Didn't she want to know what I'd been doing? She always had before. Did she want me to miss her? But she'd sent me away to school. I looked out of the taxi window and didn't understand.

In the summer of 1926 a school photograph was taken. I am ten years old and stare glumly from beneath a fringed mop of fair hair, wearing the summer uniform of long-sleeved shirt (pink stripes) and dark tie; the navy skirt and black stockings are hidden by the row of children in front. I am near the end of the third row; my best friend,

Josie, is at the opposite end. We are both taller than our contemporaries who sit in the front row, cross-legged on the ground. Josie looks as if she is about to burst into a fit of giggles, which is probably why we are separated. The teachers all wear unbecoming mob-caps of white cotton, the frilly edge encircled by a black ribbon. The caps are required because the school is part of the convent, which is hallowed ground. We, being little innocents, can remain uncovered.

In the photograph Miss Tovey, our secular principal, wears a mortarboard. She is the sister of Donald Tovey, a renowned musicologist, and thus the source of our music. She also teaches English with infectious enthusiasm, striding into the room crying "Listen to this!" which could be anything - Shakespeare, Alfred Noyes, Milton, Shelley, Rupert Brooke, Tennyson - and she makes us learn poems by heart. We laugh at her but like her.

I also like my music teacher, Miss Griffin: she has a long, delicate nose, a gentle expression and is altogether long and thin with long thin feet which turn inward. She walks rapidly, her long body bent forward, seeming in imminent danger of tripping over her own feet.

The fat French teacher appears likely to murmur her frequent complaint, *"Ah, comme j'ai mal à la gorge aujourdhui!"* This gives hilarious point to a perennial schoolboy joke relayed from someone's older brother. Translate: *"L'Anglais avec son sang-froid habituel."* Answer: "The Englishman with his usual bloody cold" (except we would never dare say 'bloody' as we are fined sixpence for every overheard 'damn').

Jolly Miss Keeble grins at a private joke; she teaches gym and drama and is unquenchably cheerful. The junior teachers look depressed; several are old girls, returned to earn a pittance as teachers in training.

Flanked by the teachers are three sisters. Sister Catherine, in charge of the sanatorium, is young and slight with a pixie face; we like her and don't take her seriously when she discovers us being naughty and cries, "You are all Possessed!" (by the Devil, of course).

Mother Superior is in the centre, presumably imported for the occasion for we have no contact with her; she is dumpy and resembles a cottage loaf in a wimple.

Next to her is Sister Hilary, our other principal. She runs the school and is clearly not someone to overlook. In the photograph her head is slightly turned as if, having just looked back to make sure no gigglers are about to ruin the picture, she now concentrates on the camera-man, to verify he is not fooling about wasting time, or even daring to ogle the prettier older girls in the back row. As his head is mostly under a black cloth he has little chance of ogling, and for all intents and purposes he is simply a pair of legs in grey flannel trousers. Sister Hilary is handsome, her face full of intelligence, a striking person, accustomed to being in command. So there we are, all sixty of us, lined up for posterity, backed by the gothic windows of the yellow sandstone convent buildings.

1926 was a year of crisis in England when the trade unions voted to support the coal miners in a general strike. Perhaps the sixth form of St. Agnes' discussed the threat of Bolshevism and the revolt of the working classes, but such subjects were not mentioned in the lower forms. Anyway, by that summer I was deep in a crisis of my own, and probably wouldn't have cared a jot for the plight of the miners.

One day Josie and I were playing Hangman in the junior sitting-room. You started by drawing an outline of the gibbet and then drew different bits of the hanging body, adding imaginative details until there was no justification for more. This ghoulish game was unfinished when I was told Sister Hilary wanted to see me.

"I wonder what's up?"

Josie said helpfully, "We haven't done anything lately," and promised not to add anything to the body while I was away.

I knocked on Sister's door with no more than the usual faint undercurrent of apprehension, the price of living in close proximity to Sister Hilary and God. So it was a nice surprise to find my mother in the study, though I wondered why a man who'd been around in the summer holidays was sitting beside her. Also why was Sister Hilary grinning as though it was Christmas?

I hugged my mother and asked, "Have you come to take me out?" but before she could answer Sister Hilary said something about good news and "This is a happy day for us all, Thelma."

My mother still had her arms round me and said, "Darling, you remember Edward?" I said I did. Beyond the closed door the buzz of school sounded normal.

My mother started again. "Edward and I, darling...we're here today...you see, pet, we wanted you to be the first..." and then in a rush, "Edward has asked me to be his wife and...my dearest, he will be your new father and...and I know you will love him as he loves you already, and we will all be a happy family together."

If you look up the verb 'shock' in Roget's Thesaurus you'll find "daze, numb, stupefy...flabbergast...stun...outrage, displease, horrify." Well, take the lot, roll them into one and that just about describes what I felt, plus one more - immoveable. Christina de la Paz Ruck Keene was Ralph Ruck Keene's wife and apparently intended to marry this man Edward who obviously wasn't my father and never could be.

I was allowed to go out to tea with the two of them - very likely it was a difficult outing. Back with Josie I said, "My mother's going to be married. I have to go to the wedding. They took me out to tea. His name's Edward."

"That'll be queer, seeing your mother married."

"I don't see how she can. She's married to my father."

"People do when the father's dead, like mine."

"Your mother hasn't."

"I don't think she's interested. We get along all right on our own."

"We got along all right too."

Maybe, after all, the three of us might have got along all right. Edward wasn't a patch on Willoughby, but he was kindly in his rather unimaginative way and liked a quiet life. But Edward's mother, Hanna, interfered.

Edward Willis-Fleming had been in a cavalry regiment during the war, and Christina framed a photograph of him wearing gleaming cavalry boots and well-cut uniform. This photograph displaced the one of my father sitting cross-legged and laughing (wearing puttees, not boots). Edward also had a vaguely romantic Swiss connection through his mother; he spoke fluent French and had worked in Paris after the war. Now he was a solicitor, which wasn't all that romantic, but my mother, undaunted, opted to call him 'Tony' which she felt was less pedestrian than 'Edward'. However the change didn't last long, for his mother, Hanna (daughter of Baroness de Bondeli) disapproved.

I also earned her disapproval during a dismal visit doomed to failure from the start. It was to be made on the first Christmas day the three of us had spent together.

"But we *always* have Christmas at home!" I cried.

"I do understand, darling, but it's only for lunch and just this once. I tell you what, I'll put a sticky pudding to boil and we'll have it for a supper treat. So be a good girl. The visit will make your new grandparents happy, and I'm sure you will like them."

Edward's father came from respectable landed gentry, had plenty of charm and was a likeable, easygoing man. Hanna was not easygoing and, like a dog sensing danger, I knew Hanna was no friend of mine. She sat very upright, was gracious in a discomfiting way, and everything in the house was just so. There wasn't even a Christmas tree. My step-grandfather was quite jolly, but when I got a bit jolly too and addressed my stepfather as Edward, I noticed Hanna purse her lips and her head gave a little jerk. By the end of the visit I was quite jerky myself and thankful to be off.

At least the sticky pudding was waiting for us. This was one of my mother's curious cooking inventions, made by piercing the top of a can of Nestlé's sweetened evaporated milk and boiling it for hours until, reduced to a caramelly mass, it was turned out in a glass dish, stuck with peeled almonds and eaten with *petits fours*. When we got home my mother said, "I'll take the pudding out now so it'll be cool for supper." Then she opened the kitchen door and cried, "Oh, my God!"

The can of Nestlé's milk had exploded and most of the sticky pudding hung like caramel icicles from the ceiling - my mother had failed to punch a hole in the can. Memory blots out the immediate sequel, leaving only a bleak sense of misery. But the visit had another sequel, less easy to clear up than sticky pudding on the ceiling.

Directly after the visit I became aware that my mother was trying to steer me into calling my stepfather 'Daddy'. I continued to call him Edward, but in self-defence started getting his attention with "I say!..." or "By the way..." which seemed a brilliant ploy; unfortunately it didn't serve when writing letters from school.

Not without distaste I began my first letter, 'Darling Mummy and Edward.' He wasn't my darling, but I couldn't think of a way to call my mother 'darling' and Edward something else. However, my mother's first letter asked me point-blank to write, 'Darling Mummy and Daddy.' I replied, with what seemed to me seamless logic, that Edward wasn't my father. But this did not settle the matter, for in due course Sister Hilary sent for me and made it plain that my mother had written to her about this Daddy business.

She dismissed me with "You will feel happy, dear, if you do as your mother wishes." I made no comment and with a frown she added, "I don't expect to hear any more about this."

When I told Josie about this encounter she exclaimed, "But it's none of Sister's business." That helped, but nothing could ease writing the unspeakable 'Darling Mummy and Daddy.' But I had to do it every Sunday afternoon for the next five years. I would heroically have written 'Daddy' in my own blood, but gloomily accepted it might miss its dramatic impact by looking like red ink.

It was a pity my mother didn't explain why 'Edward' was so suddenly a forbidden word and 'Daddy' imperative. Years later she told me that, after the Christmas visit, Hanna lost no time in making my mother understand that it was unacceptable for a child of ten to call an adult by his first name. My mother mimicked Hanna saying, "Telma is a charrming child, but *ma chère* Chrristina, she would profit if she were - how shall I say? - a leetle more *convenable.*"

My mother made a face and said, "I had to ask Edward what '*convenable*' meant and we quarrelled when he said that children could be pretty poisonous if they got their own way all the time, and his mother was right. What was I to do? I wanted Edward's parents to like me, and I even wondered if I was spoiling you, you were changing so fast. Besides, I didn't know you felt so strongly about your father. You never mentioned him."

No, I never mentioned him. Nor did I think about him all that much; but he was my father, however dead.

In the Easter holidays I held out over 'Daddy', but my mother persisted in her campaign, which became a miserable nightly ritual following her goodnight kiss. She would look at me sadly and say something like, "Is Daddy such a difficult word, darling?" and when I remained silent she'd add the refrain: "It's such a little thing, Thelma? Don't you love your Mummy?"

Before long the nightmares began. They weren't real nightmares, for I wasn't asleep. I would simply become aware of a gradual gathering of figures right at the foot of my bed. They were grotesque, like different-sized toadstools, and in nightmare fashion they vaguely resembled how I had seen the Boches when I was very young and knew they had killed my father. As they materialized they groaned and globbed and made blubbery, shifting movements which threatened to engulf me.

The first time they appeared I ran sobbing down the passage to my mother. They came again, and yet a third time which was when Edward took me back to my room, told me to stop being a baby and upsetting my mother. I got into bed, he pointed out there was nobody else in the room and left, shutting the door.

They came back later, crowding at the end of my bed while I lay stiff as a post, heart beating, willing them not to come and glob all over me. But suddenly, as if I'd received an electric shock, I sat up in bed filled by an almighty rage, and heard my voice shouting, "Get out of here! Go on, GET OUT!" and when nothing happened I got up on my knees and bawled, "Are you deaf? I'm sick of you, this is MY room. Get out!" I was so furious I could hardly see clearly, but I could still shout, "You're not allowed in here...not any of you...don't you dare...!"

Then, unbelieving, I stopped shouting and stared as the Boches wobbled, undulated and began to lose shape. Hardly above a whisper I cried, "Be off! and never, ever come back again!" Faintly globbing, they grew indistinct and, rather pathetically, oozed away. I lay down, trembling and amazed that I'd exploded the Boches. Why, I could stand up to anything or anyone if I tried.

They never came back. But something had happened to what I can only call the territory or landscape of my mind. Until this time my mother had been right there in the centre, the place that was home. Now she was off to one side in a new, somewhat devastated territory where I was the lone centre. The territory was not uninhabited, but an unfamiliar tension existed because I wasn't sure, for the first time in my life, whether anyone, including my mother, loved me. 'Don't you love your Mummy?' she had asked, and to that I asked, 'Don't you love me?'

I returned to school asking the same question, 'Will the girls like me?' At least Josie was the same as ever, staunch and matter-of-fact, and letters from Birdie helped. I'd not been back to Copford since going away to St. Agnes' and her intermittent letters spoke of my grandfather being very ill with bronchitis. Now she wrote that they were looking for a house in the south of England where he could get well, "and then, my darling, you will come to stay and brighten our lives once again."

This was something to look forward to, and I thought more about my father, who had known I was born, and loved me. I thought of him walking down the gangway at Tilbury looking every inch the gentleman, and this mingled with Chaucer's "verray perfit gentil knight" who "loved chivalrye, Trouthe and honour, freedom and courteisye." Miss Tovey read these words aloud to us at the beginning of the Easter term. She wrote them on the blackboard so we could see how Chaucer spelled them 500 years ago and I thought, 'My father was a parfit knight,' and then, 'My goodness - those words are music!'

⤛ 10 ⤜

About music, words, and being 'possessed'.

Although the God of St. Agnes' was boringly preoccupied with sin and guilt, he had a taste for fine words and was a glutton for music. Every weekday, morning and evening, we tramped through the cloisters to chapel for matins and compline. For these two services we sang only one hymn to ease the chatter of praise and thanks and regrets for being sinful. But Sundays and saints' days were command performances. The plump, elderly priest was clothed in vestments embroidered by the sisters in glowing colours, threaded with gold or silver. His movements were slow, grave and decorous, little bells rang and the sisters in the minstrels' gallery filled the chapel with antiphons, alleluias and Gregorian plainsong. Sometimes we sang Gregorian arrangements of the psalms, reading from a curious score of square notes instead of round. The wonderful, bare music soared serenely as clouds of aromatic incense drifted up to the great rose window above the altar. On bright days shafts of sunlight poured through the glass mosaic, infusing dust motes and incense with rose and blue, green and gold. On those days the chapel was joyous and it seemed mean-spirited to keep saying we were miserable sinners.

It was a while before I understood that the lovely music, the incense and bells and embroidered vestments were practices adopted by Anglo-Catholics, which the Church of England said made them no better than Roman Catholics. I was glad we weren't Church of England because their *Hymns Ancient and Modern* weren't nearly as singable and satisfying as those in our Anglo-Catholic hymnal. Occasionally we sang from the A & M book. Our favourite was a rousing Salvation Army hymn beginning "Hold the fort for I am coming!" We roared the words so exuberantly that it was finally banned.

The ramifications of religious differences were beyond us younger children, but we tended to feel rather superior about being Anglo-Catholics. We had our special prayer book, paid homage to the Virgin Mary and all those masses of saints, and there were esoteric beliefs like transubstantiation which hinted at strange Mysteries. The Sunday drama of lavish vestments and clouds of incense testified to a sort of holy *cachet* appropriate to us, the daughters of gentry. Admittedly we were disadvantaged gentlefolk, the majority of parents being either poor clergy, or dead like my father, or absent on service abroad. As gentry we were unlike the children of St. Michael's, a day school also run by the convent.

St. Michael's was attended by the children of local tradesmen. It was in another part of the convent grounds, and we were segregated from them without explanation. We secretly envied their greater freedom of movement, but argued that we were kept apart because the children were 'common'. One idle day I told Nancy McBride, a particularly snobbish Scots girl, about Birdie's 'Not out of the handkerchief drawer, darling.' Nancy approved of this fine distinction and proposed listing which St. Agnes' girls were handkerchief drawer quality. We whittled it down to a dozen (out of sixty), including of course, ourselves.

As well as St. Michael's the sisters cared for orphaned children and what were called 'remedials'. The orphans, remedials, the sisters, and ourselves all ate in the same refectory, a huge room with a beamed ceiling like the chapel, each group shut off from the other by tall oak partitions. At breakfast the sisters listened to readings from holy books so we all ate in silence, broken only by whispered requests like "Pass the butch!" This request dumbfounded me on my first morning, until followed impatiently by, "Pass the bread-and-butter, you idiot!" We were allowed to talk at other meals, but we never heard a murmur from either remedials or orphans.

The orphans were described by the sisters as poor little innocents, implying the death, or possibly abandonment by one or both parents. The school underground had the more interesting explanation that they were illegitimate, born out of wedlock, and now saved from further sin by being trained as servants.

"But they didn't choose to be illegitimate," I said, "so why are they saved from *further* sin?" I was told not to be silly. We saw the orphans, subdued and drably dressed, clustered at the back of the chapel for Sunday mass, and it was a mystery where they slept or what they did all day. The remedials were slightly less mysterious since most days we saw them scurrying about the school, cleaning or polishing.

I asked Sister Catherine why they had such a queer name, but her answer was vague. "They are poor girls, dear, who are being trained to go into service." Why didn't she call them *servants?* I didn't ask. An older girl was more explicit. It seemed that the remedials had 'fallen' (meaning into the frightful pit of sin), a condition somehow connected with men and shame, thus needing remedy. The explanation had a touch of melodrama, but the poor remedials, whatever their torrid past, retained no hint of drama. In the school they usually worked in pairs, looking pinched and cold and rarely speaking, though once I did hear one of them ask the other to name her two favourite colours.

After a pause she said shyly in a Cockney whine, "Pile pink and pile white."

I told the story in the junior sitting room, emphasizing the Cockney, and made everyone laugh. "Pale white! whoever heard of such a thing!" I laughed too, and immediately hated myself. That night I thought about the remedials in their unchanging winter/summer uniform of cotton dress and apron, to which, in winter, was added a mousy grey woollen shawl that they clutched round their shoulders with work-reddened hands. I hoped they wore woollen vests and knickers, otherwise they'd likely die of cold. I was cold enough myself despite the ungainly bundle of uniform, cotton underwear, woollen stockings and pinafore of strong, blue cotton. Like all English dwellings the school passages were unheated, but we could huddle over radiators (though girls with bad circulation developed agonizing chilblains) and in break we jumped around in the assembly hall. The remedials never huddled or jumped around, just skittered through the icy corridors like nervous little mice. I wished I hadn't laughed at them. It was a cheap way to be liked. Later I searched through the sin lists at the back of our Anglo-Catholic prayer book, wondering if laughter at someone's expense was a sin, but couldn't find anything to cover 'I've been cheap.'

The sin lists were intended to help us when we made our first confession after being confirmed, but we pored over them, fascinated by all the sins you might commit. The effect was similar to reading a medical dictionary - had one perhaps committed them all? Some, like murder, could be ruled out, leaving mainly boring sins, like being vain or lazy or rude, but a few were phrased in rather muffled language, hinting at the unmentionables of what men and women did, or shouldn't do, together.

We heard a lot about the pit of sin which I imagined as a frightful place, broiling with hissing serpents, a trap devised by the Devil who undoubtedly made sure the pit was craftily concealed so if you failed to keep your eyes skinned, in you'd fall. Every day we chanted *Kyrie eleison*, Lord have mercy, three times, to make sure God heard. He was all-powerful, all-seeing and a God of mercy, yet inattentive. Inscrutable also; he never gave a helping hand to the martyrs who refused to commit the sin of denying their faith, and allowed them to die horribly.

One of the sisters had written and illustrated stories of selected saints, "A gift for God," she said, and told us how many years she had spent striving to make the book as beautiful as a medieval manuscript -

and so she had. The first elaborate letter on each page was coloured and illuminated with gold leaf, and the margins decorated with delicate paintings of trees and vines, flowers, birds and all manner of creatures. The details of each saint's martyrdom were minutely presented in full-page colour.

It was meant to be a treat for us younger children to sit round her and hear the stories and look at the pictures. There was always a clamour to see little St. Agnes, not all that much older than me, whose breasts were torn off because she refused to deny her belief in God. Some children gloated over the story of St. Agnes and her bloody bosom and murmured devoutly when sister concluded, "and never did she utter a single cry, only praised God for his love."

I found this peculiar. St. Agnes and her awful fate seemed at odds with the illuminated letters and enchanting tapestry of nature's lively goings-on around the margins, all patiently created by the sister to delight God. Did God also delight in St. Agnes' poor mangled body? I didn't ask. Questions about God were not well received.

For the same reason I kept quiet about Jesus and his humility - there was no sense in his agreement to die on a cross to make sure God forgave our sins. Jesus might have done better to take a leaf out of Abbie's book and give God whatfor, tell him to make up his own mind about forgiveness instead of letting his son have such a terrible, bloody death. The 'holy' cards we collected and swapped between us portrayed Jesus with beams of yellow light radiating from his bright red heart, squarely set in the middle of his bosom. It wasn't surprising his heart bled with sorrow - he'd agreed to being nailed to a cross (with a ghastly crown of spiky thorns jammed on his head) to make sure everyone was forgiven their sins, and would presumably make an effort not to sin any more - but they just went on sinning. Jesus must have felt badly let down by God.

These conundrums buzzed around in my head but weren't discussed with anyone, not even with my two so different friends, Josie and Olive. Josie, a lanky girl with a sardonic sense of humour, said God could look after himself and she couldn't be bothered with him. Olive, a romantic girl with a gypsy mop of black curls, was more interested in the sin lists than God. So I kept my puzzlements to myself, spending much spare time in the practice rooms playing the piano, or getting lost in a book.

The school's library was small but well-stocked with all kinds of books, and I gobbled up the easy classics - *Pride and Prejudice, The Tale of Two Cities, David Copperfield, Wuthering Heights, Jane Eyre* - as well as rollicking stories like *The Scarlet Pimpernel,* and funny books by P.G. Wodehouse and Jerome K. Jerome. I read Jerome's *Three Men in a Boat* during a French lesson, the book open on my lap, a handkerchief on my mouth to stifle giggles, until Madame asked, *"Tu es enrhumé, ma chère?"* and with tear-filled eyes I mumbled, *"Pas beaucoup, madame."*

We were lucky to be taught English by funny old Miss Tovey excitedly bursting into the classroom crying, "Listen to this!"

She also brought musicians to perform in the assembly hall to enthuse us about music, and once (just once) a man came to enthuse us about Shakespeare. Unfortunately he was doomed the moment he appeared on the platform wearing black velvet knee breeches and carrying a large cushion covered in matching black velvet. He cast the cushion on the platform with a careless gesture, knelt with hand on heart, and began to intone famous, familiar lines. But already we were convulsed in an ecstasy of giggles. At the end we gave him a rather too rousing ovation, quelled by Sister Hilary with "That will do, girls."

We took Miss Tovey for granted, laughing at her protruding teeth and disordered grey hair, but she made sure we read books, learnt pages of poetry, and acted in plays for the joy of it.

In the autumn and spring terms Miss Keeble put on a play, all kinds of plays for all ages. In *'Robella and the Robbers'* I was the fairy queen, with sparkles on my dress, a wand, and white socks pulled over gym shoes to avoid splinters in my feet. The older girls did *'The Prisoner of Zenda,'* and when I was thirteen I was Jessica in *'The Merchant of Venice.'* Joan, on whom I had a 'pash', was Lorenzo.

All this was pure enjoyment, and even grammar was a sort of game - spelling and punctuation and parsing. I didn't realize how important these skills were until, when I was a bit older, I read Thackeray's *Vanity Fair*, and chanced upon a paragraph which took my breath away. It was the passage following a description of the ball in Brussels when whispered orders were passed round the ballroom, and the young officers slipped quietly away to the battlefield of Waterloo:

> *No more firing was heard at Brussels - the pursuit rolled miles away. The darkness came down on the field and city, and Amelia was praying for George, who was lying on his face, dead, with a bullet through his heart.*

That single word, *dead*, felt like being shot myself, and all because of a series of well-placed commas. It was amazing.

My twelve-year old excitement at discovering the classics gave me intellectual pretensions and I scorned the schoolgirl stories that filled a few shelves in the library. Angela Brazil's books were the most popular, with titles like *The Leader of the Lower School* and *The Youngest Girl in the Fifth*. But during the Easter term (the year I was twelve), I cut my knee badly and had to stay in bed for a week. Sister Catherine brought me three or four Brazil books and said I'd enjoy them. Disdainfully I read one, and then read the others.

I have an ancient copy of *The Girls of St. Cyprian's*. The opening paragraph is typical of how the girls talked:

"If there's one slack, slow business in this wide world,"
said Bess Harrison, stretching her arms in the exigencies of a
combined sigh and prodigious yawn, "it's coming back to
school after the Easter holidays."

The St. Cyprian girls had awful names and in this book most of the first names begin with M - Maggie, Mildred, Mona, Myrtle, Maudie. Perhaps Brazil worked steadily through the alphabet, book by book (she wrote a great many). The girls, like us, exclaimed "Oh goody!" but unlike us often spoke to one another in a rather literary way: "True, O Queen!" and "Mona mine!" This was not at all like the boys in *Chums,* though the girls were ripping and good sorts, and like the boys despised slackers and upheld loyalty to the old school. The head mistresses were invariably wise, kind and firm and even had a quiet sense of humour, and were often imaginative with the girls who didn't fit in and behaved badly.

I had a fellow-feeling for the misfits. When the fuss about calling Edward 'Daddy' was at full blast my end-of-term report noted, "Thelma's behaviour has been disappointing this term. We hope she will do better in the future." My mother was upset, not least because my school fees were paid by the Freemasons. She explained that my father had been a Freemason, which was a sort of secret society with plenty of money to help the widows of members. But the Freemasons expected good reports, otherwise no money. I promised to behave better and the next term's report was all right. It was hard to remember my good intentions and my reports were variable, but the funds weren't cut.

So I did understand about not fitting in, and didn't need Angela Brazil to point out that to be ripping, hearty and good chums with everyone made school life pleasanter. Grudgingly I even found the hearty Brazil girls rather enviable; they were so assured and successful while the misfits were unhappy and failures. Spurred by their example I decided to have a go at being hearty, and once my knee was healed I joined the school troop of girl guides.

I tried to get Josie and Olive to join with me but Olive said it was a bore and the uniform was hideous, and Josie just laughed and enjoyed mocking the badges I sewed on my shirt sleeve. "I say, how ripping to have a badge for tying knots. Have you done your good knot-tying turn today?"

"The knots are jolly useful," I said crossly, and obstinately spent a week at guide camp during the summer holidays. Back at school Josie asked what camp had been like. "It wasn't half bad!" I said speciously.

Josie grinned. "Well, well! How was the rain - not half bad? I bet you had lots of scrumptious food."

I made a face, exclaimed, "O bother you!" and couldn't help laughing. "All right," I said, "If you want to know it was cold and wet and boring, and the food was repulsive - dead earwigs in the stewed plums." That was the end of my guiding and the end of being hearty.

It was my idea, as a sort of final salute to Angela Brazil, to have a midnight feast in our dormitory. Brazil girls, even the good ones, did this sort of thing, though I don't remember any of their picnics ending quite like ours.

Josie and Olive agreed it would be fun, and we persuaded the others in our dormitory to join in. This was useful, for those who were taken out by visiting parents picked up extra good things, and on the night of the picnic we shared a fine feast of cold sausages, hard-boiled eggs, cake, cookies, apples, raisins and even candy saved from our Sunday allowance. We washed it all down with rationed sips of sweet cherry pop, and when everything was eaten and we felt rather sick I said, "Let's go down to the cloisters!"

Exclamations of "We can't!" and "You're mad!" and "We'll be expelled if we're caught!" eliminated everyone except Josie, Olive and me.

It was a warm night in early July, and wearing just our night-gowns we crept barefoot down the creaking polished wood stairs, ran along the cold tiles of the passage to the big iron-studded oak door between the school and the convent.

The door was locked, but Josie said, "At least the key's on our side." It was a very big, old-fashioned iron key with a decorated head. We tried to turn it quietly, but the clang of the lock seemed enough to wake everyone - children, teachers, sisters, remedials, orphans. We held our breath until Olive whispered, "Come on! They won't look for us the other side."

We shut the door carefully and stood still. Nothing happened. The stone-flagged cloisters, through which we clattered daily to chapel or the refectory, were empty and silent; shafts of silver moonlight fell between the arches, interspersed by dark pools of shadow. Slowly we stepped out of the cloisters on to the moonlit grass, dew-damp under our bare feet, and walked deliberately to the centre of the lawn. For a moment we stood unmoving as if enchanted, and then, without a word, we began to dance. Even Josie was caught in the magic. We didn't leap about, but silent and rather stately we met and separated, turned to bend and pirouette, than met and separated again, and again. No Sister Catherine was there to cry that we were possessed. On the contrary, for once we were in possession - gloriously in possession - of our own selves.

Family, and belonging.

Three years had passed since I cried to everyone gathered outside Copford Rectory, "I'll see you all soon!" Then I had no doubt that Copford was forever; but now I was going to visit my grandparents in another place altogether.

"Why did they have to leave Copford?" I asked my mother. "I loved the big house and the windmill..."

"Whatever would two old people do with thirteen bedrooms!" said my mother. "Besides, Ted is far from well and had to retire - Lymington is by the sea and will help his bronchitis. Of course they've called their new house Copford. It's nothing like the rectory, but it's a cosy house, and close to the sea with lovely walks for you and Oophats along the dikes."

"Will Oophats remember me?"

"Of course he will! And they're all looking forward to seeing you again. Poor old dears, they had a hard time looking for the right house - you know what Ted is like." I didn't, and even Birdie was a bit foggy. "But they haven't changed, and gave Edward and me such a warm welcome. I really love them, in spite of everything." I was going to ask what 'everything' was, but she went on, "Don't be surprised that they've aged a great deal. I don't think they ever got over the dreadful year the three boys were killed, one after the other."

"Three?"

"Your father and Ben, and young Ralph, Edie's only son."

"Who's Edie?"

"She was Birdie's favourite sister. The other child was Muriel. She married Bernard, a rather peculiar young man, very clever and in the navy. They had six children and the second child, Elizabeth, is the same age as you. The family takes their summer holiday every year on the Isle of Wight, just a short ferry trip from Lymington, and Birdie's keen for you to meet your cousins."

Cousins! On the train to Lymington I thought about having cousins, and that they'd be the first I'd met. Cousins were family. The Garsias were family, but there weren't any cousins, only my two uncles, and nobody my age. I wondered what my cousins looked like and then, as the train slowed down and drew in to Lymington, wondered whether I'd recognize Birdie, and what would I do if she didn't know *me?* I was only nine when she saw me last, and now I was twelve, and bigger.

I needn't have worried. As I jumped down on to the platform I heard, "There's my darling gel!" and in a moment Birdie's arms were round me and I was kissing her cheek, the skin soft as silk but deeply lined. Her body felt soft as a cushion, and was oddly familiar, but she was quite small! Did old people shrink? Then she exclaimed, "Look Jackie, how tall she's grown!" and the bearded man beside her stared at me intently, the eyes very blue and the stare also familiar. "Just look at her," Birdie said, "isn't she the spitten image of Ralphie?"

Jackie, who must be my uncle, grinned and said, "Welcome, brat! Come along, Mother, let's not keep Polly waiting, it's time for tea." Polly? Was Jack married, or was Polly a horse with a pony trap? In fact she was a car, grey, round-nosed, rather like a bath on wheels.

"She may not be much to look at," Jack said as he chucked my suitcase on the back seat, "but she's one of the best. In you get, Thelma, room for three in front."

I squeezed in between him and Birdie and thought, 'This is family,' and felt very snug. As we drove through Lymington Birdie gave me a running report of family news. I didn't know half the names and couldn't hear everything she said, but it didn't seem to matter, she just carried on. We stopped on the way so she could pick up something for Abbie, and I stayed in the car with Jack. He sat in silence until I plucked up courage and asked why the car was called Polly.

"Short for *hoi polloi*."

"Hoi...?"

"Greek for the proles. Don't they teach you Greek at school?"

"No. The proles...?

"The proletariat, the workers. Polly is sound peasant stock, reliable, and knows her place. Some people make rude remarks about her shape - don't they, old girl? But she's not had a breakdown yet, which is more than can be said for some of the fancier cars around." Later I discovered that Jack loved having to salvage a visitor's car, and would set off crying, "Polly to the rescue again!"

I said shyly that Polly was very handsome and Jack told me she was a Morris Oxford, and showed me how you put windows in when you needed them. They had metal frames with pins on the bottom which slipped into holes on the top of the doors, and the window part was made of mica which Jack said scarred easily and spoilt the view. "So I just put them in when it's cold or rainy," he explained. Then he showed me the windshield wiper which had to be worked by hand. "If you're with me on a rainy day," he said, "you can work the wiper for me. That'll be a help. Otherwise I have to drive with one hand and work the wiper with the other." I said I would like that very much and hoped we would have plenty of rainy days.

We drove out of the town and it seemed almost like country when Jack stopped the car and said, "Here we are! Out you get." I walked round the car and stopped to look up at a comfortable-looking house with dormer windows. Trees surrounded a lawn and Jack said, "Big enough for croquet and badminton," but I was remembering the big rectory and exclaimed, "However does everyone fit in?"

Birdie gave a little chuckle and said, "See the dormer window right at the top? It was put in the attic to make an extra bedroom, and when our neighbour saw it he said the Ruck Keenes had burst out of the roof!" Her wrinkled old face creased more than ever with laughter, and behind me Jack said, "Proof positive that nothing can keep the family down!"

I started up the front path and suddenly Oophats came grinning and wagging his tail, and I cried, "There's my beautiful boy!" and then saw Abbie by the front door.

"Well now," she said, "here's quite the young lady!" and straight away I knew that if I was in a crowd and heard the slight burr of her voice with a sort of smile in it, I'd know at once it was Abbie. I ran and hugged her, and she smelt of soap and new-baked bread.

In the kitchen I helped pile bread-and-butter, jam and cake on a tray, and asked where Emma was. "Her mother's ailing," Abbie said, "so she couldn't rightly come away. Besides, there's no call for the two of us. I manage nicely, with a daily help three times a week." Not that there would have been much room for Emma in this kitchen. The old Copford kitchen had room enough for the whole family, but at least Abbie's rocking chair and the rag mat were, as ever, in front of a gleaming range.

"Do you rest every afternoon like you used to?"

"Indeed I do, and I'll thank you for not rampaging in until I've had my forty winks."

"Or you'll give me whatfor!"

I felt greatly daring to be teasing Abbie, but she said, "That I will!" with a little smile, so the teasing was all right.

We had tea in the dining-room. The familiar Chippendale chairs (broad seats, tapestry-covered, plenty of room for ample bottoms) were ranged round the dining table which was big enough for all the family and room to spare - except here the chairs and table seemed to fill the room. Then, as I put down the tray, I saw that space was taken up by a sort of makeshift study, and there was Grandpa in his old leather armchair, his books filling shelves on either side of the fireplace. I'd heard his rasping cough as I crossed the hall and it sounded bad, but when I saw him sunk in his chair with a plaid rug across his knees, I knew it was very bad. Birdie looked old, but poor Grandpa, who once had seemed seven feet tall at least, and full of fire, now appeared - well, just ancient. But as I bent to kiss his cheek, dry as parchment, I caught a gleam of the old fire from under his white but still fierce eyebrows.

"You must tell me what you've been up to, Thelma. Lots of changes, eh? School, and all that?"

I said, "Yes," tongue-tied.

"Yes. Yes indeed. But tomorrow, tomorrow. You'll be wanting your tea now." To Birdie, "No, Lass, I'm not hungry. Just a cup of tea," and to me, with another glance from those formidable eyes, "Sit down,

child, sit down. Got a good appetite after your journey, I'll be bound."
Then he coughed again, his old veined hand against his chest.

After tea I mooned around discovering old friends. The dining-room, drawing-room and kitchen opened on to a central hall with bookshelves under a bay window. One shelf was full of children's books, and I pulled out *Carrots, or Just a Little Boy* by Mrs. Molesworth. Printed right on the pale green cloth cover was Carrots, a very Victorian little boy with a mop of carroty curls and wearing red-and-white striped socks.

I sat on the floor with the book in my hand. On the wall opposite hung a familiar print of an old man with an ugly, warty nose. On his lap a pretty little girl sat gazing lovingly into his face, warts and all. From the past I heard Birdie saying, "You see, darling, if you love someone it doesn't matter what they look like." Further along was a big old oak chest. 'J H' was roughly carved on the front, and above it hung a framed, hand-written letter, brown ink on brownish paper. I was trying to read it when Birdie came in.

"That was written by Oliver Cromwell," she said, "one of your ancestors on the Berners side."

"Berners...who were they?"

"They came into the family through your grandfather's father, your great-grandfather, darling, who was the Rector at Copford Green. He married Mary Berners, and way back in the 1700s one of her ancestors married another Mary, and she was the great-great-granddaughter of Oliver Cromwell."

"I say! that makes history real. What else?"

"Let me see...well, about names. Your great-grandfather was Benjamin Ruck Keene, and the father of his wife Mary was Ralph Berners, so that's why we called our two first boys Ralph and Ben." She pronounced Ralph as if it was spelt 'Rafe' and I asked why. "It's the old pronunciation," she said, "dating back to the Norman times when your grandfather's ancestors came over with William the Conqueror."

"Is the big chest anything to do with them?"

"Oh no, that's from my family," Birdie said. "It belonged to my mother's ancestor, Sir John Hawkins - see, those are his initials on the front. It's solid oak, and he took it on all his voyages. He lived in style on his ships, and his cabin was always sumptuously furnished with brocades and tapestries, and he dined off gold and silver plate. Imagine that! He was famous for his good manners, and he looked after his crews very well. Of course, the poor blackamoors..." She didn't explain, and I was busy tracing the J and H with my finger, so she went on cheerfully, "We put him and Cromwell together for family company, though you'd be hard pressed to find two more different people." I asked who Hawkins was and Birdie said, "He was a great Elizabethan navigator, darling, though I'm afraid he was one of the first to ship the poor Africans as slaves to America. Those were different times, cruel times - but Queen Elizabeth loved him. In those days the Spaniards wouldn't allow their settlers in the New World to trade with the British, and Hawkins kept intercepting their ships and plundering them. The Spaniards called him a pirate."

A pirate! I laughed and was going to ask Birdie if Hawkins made his captives walk the plank, but she said, "Wait there, darling, I have something to show you."

She came back with a leather case out of which she pulled a leather-bound bible and prayer book, the pages gilt-edged. "Your grandfather and I want you to have this," she said, "when you are confirmed next year." She opened the prayer book so I could see the elegant hand-written script on the flyleaf:

> *Robert Archibald Hawkins, 20th Oct. 1860*
> *The gift of his godfather Adm. Hawkins*

"Now look on the next page," she said, and I read:

> *Ralph Edgar Ruck Keene.*
> *This book is given in memory of*
> *Robert Archibald Hawkins*
> *who died the 1st of Sept. 1864,*
> *by his godmother Eliza Hawkins*
> *Nov. 24th, 1896.*

"My father!"

"He was seven years old, the dear thing, and proud as punch to have such a handsome bible and prayer book all his own." The pages opened stiffly, as if rarely used, but perhaps it was only for special occasions.

As Birdie put the books back in their case I went over to a big glass-fronted cabinet that was squeezed against the wall by the stairs. Something familiar had caught my eye and I exclaimed with delight, "Here's my favourite china, the white ones with blue fruit and flowers!" Two shelves held the collection of little round dishes and small tea bowls without handles, queer narrow mugs, a big fruit bowl with a scalloped edge and, best of all, little dishes shaped like vine leaves, the veins standing out as if they were real leaves.

"Crescent Worcester, darling," Birdie said and picked out one of the dishes, turning it over so I could see the small blue crescent underneath. "That shows when it was made, I forget now, maybe late eighteenth century. Such pretty pieces."

But I was distracted by a rather ugly little blue glass dog sitting amongst the Worcester china.

"I don't remember that dog. It looks sort of funny here."

Birdie picked it up and laid it in the palm of her hand. "I wouldn't part with this, darling, not for all the gold in China. Your father won it at a fair when he was just a little boy. He came running into the house crying, 'Mummy, Mummy, where are you? I won you a dog!'"

"May I hold him?" The little dog sat in the palm of my hand and suddenly I saw my father like Carrots, wearing striped red-and-white socks, Ralphie, or Just a Little Boy. I put the dog back in the cabinet, and said, "I think I'll go and unpack my suitcase now."

On my way upstairs I heard my father's "I won you a dog!" and thought if he'd won me a dog I'd never part with it either, not for all the gold - but *gold?* Wasn't it for all the *tea* in China?' But it didn't matter. That was just the way my grandmother talked, funny, and familiar.

I went for long walks with Oophats on the dikes which, Jack said, had been built to keep out the sea. The dikes stretched for miles, flat as the fens in Essex, the paths raised above water-filled ditches edged with tall, rustling reeds. Sometimes Jack walked with me. I was a little shy of his abruptness but suspected that he was quite soft underneath. Like my other uncle, Phil, he was in the navy. He had a funny little room of his own halfway up the stairs, where he had his drawing and painting things. He'd drawn a beautiful Ruck Keene coat-of-arms, and pointing to a sort of leafy shape said, "That's the *fleur-de-lys* from our French connection, who came over with William the Conqueror." Jack also loved playing the player piano. You put in a fat roll of thick paper pierced with little holes and set it going. By manipulating keys for slow and fast, loud and soft, the music sounded almost like a piano, and Jack produced impassioned performances of Chopin and Lizst and Tchaikovsky. He showed me how to use it too, but said he liked to hear me play the real piano, and wished he'd learnt to play it. "But," he said, "boys didn't do that sort of thing when I was young." I nodded, remembering the boys in *Chums*.

During the next few weeks I gleaned all kinds of stories about the family. Breakfast was a particularly good source. As Birdie sipped her gruel she read the personal columns of *The Times*, her reading punctured by exclamations - "Poor old Duncan!" or "Such a lot of trouble with that young scapegrace," and "Listen to this, Ted" until my grandfather said, "That's enough, Lass. Let Abbie clear the table."

Many of these stories were nothing to do with the family, but one morning Birdie came across a reference to Assam, and putting the paper down, murmured, "I wonder where poor Bob is now." I asked who he was and why he was 'poor', and after a little hesitation, she told me.

"His father was my brother," she began, "and a tea planter in Assam (that's in India); so when Bob was seven or eight he was sent to prep school in England. Dear Bob, such a bright lad, full of pranks and jokes and chatter, sharp as a needle. He loved his holidays at the Rectory, but hated school. Of course I said all our boys went to school and he wouldn't want to be different from his cousins." She shook her head. "I never guessed what he would do."

"What did he do?"

She repeated, "What did he do?" and with a sigh went on, "A few days before the holidays ended he went down to the local railway line and put his hand on the rails. The driver never saw him. It was a wonder he wasn't killed, but the arm had to be amputated, just below the elbow."

"How awful!"

"Yes," Birdie said, "it was indeed, and I'll never forget that when he understood what had happened he whispered, 'I won't have to go back to school now, will I?' Poor lad! That was why he did it." She sighed and shook her head "But he was brave as a little lion, wasn't he, Ted?"

"Damned young fool!" Ted growled.

"But a proper little fighter," said Birdie. After a moment I asked what became of him. She said vaguely that he learnt to fly airplanes, and was doing well.

Out on the dikes with Oophats I thought how desperate poor Bob must have been, knowing he couldn't make anyone understand why he hated school so much. The awfulness of what he did to command attention was terrible, crazy perhaps; but he had learnt to fly, and that was amazing. I heard Birdie's "Brave as a little lion," and to my pantheon of family heroes, Hawkins the pirate, and my father, the parfit knight, Bob Corrie was added, flying high, one-armed, mythical.

On the evening before our expedition to meet my cousins on the Isle of Wight I asked Birdie to tell me who they were and what to expect. I was nervous about meeting them, though I kept that to myself.

Birdie was always happy to talk about the family. "Their mother, Muriel, is my sister Edie's daughter," she began. "You'll meet her, but not their father. Bernard is a very busy man. Such a brilliant boy, and doing very well in the city now, though it was a sad blow when he was axed after the war."

"*Axed!*"

"By the government, darling. They cut down the navy after the war - such folly! - and Bernard was one of many officers who had to leave." Birdie then ran through the names of my cousins. "Mary is the eldest, and Elizabeth is just six months younger than you, then the twins, Ralph and David, followed by Hilary and Martin, twins also and much younger than the others, quite an afterthought."

"An afterthought?"

"Oh well, darling" said Birdie, "babies don't always come when you expect them," and changed the subject. I wished adults weren't so delicate about explaining. Though at another time, perhaps the following year, she wasn't at all delicate. Somehow, surprisingly, we got onto the subject of making babies, and though I had no idea what men and women did, I airily passed on what Olive had confided at school, that men enjoyed it more than women did. To this Birdie, smiling up at me like a mischievous old elf, said, "Don't you believe it, darling. We enjoy it just as much as they do," and I, speechless, thought, 'Her and Grandpa...' but got no further.

Our expedition to the Isle of Wight included Birdie and me, Jack, Abbie and Oophats. Without Abbie there were muddles, and if Oophats was left behind he disturbed the neighbours with howls of misery. The crossing was a bit rough and Oophats embarrassed us by vomiting onto the deck below. Abbie led him away muttering, "Drat the dog, nothing but a nuisance."

We meant to picnic on the beach, but by the time we met with my cousins it was raining, so we picnicked under the roof of an empty bandstand. I was shy with all these children who knew one another so well and had private jokes. Also I had been rather put off Elizabeth when Birdie told that "she's as good as gold, darling." Later Elizabeth admitted she'd also been put off me after hearing I was "so brainy." Mary just ignored me and it was years before she admitted, "I hated you. You were such a beautiful child, and I wasn't." So we ate our sandwiches in silence, ignoring the grown-ups' hopeful, "You children must get to know one another."

The rain let up at last and we wandered off together to look for treasures on the beach. I found an empty bottle and Ralph pounced on it. "I say," he cried, "let's write a message and put it in the bottle like shipwrecked sailors," adding quickly, "I'm the tallest and throw best so I'll throw it out to sea."

"...and someone will send out a search boat," Hilary began, followed by Martin, "but they won't find us..." and Hilary interrupted, dancing about, "they won't find us 'cause we'll be drownded."

"Drowned, you fathead," David said and then we argued about what message to write and forgot to dislike each other.

I told Grandpa about Oophats being sick and the bottle and message and he said, with a chuckle, "When Harry and I were boys we put a message in a bottle: 'Food nearly gone. Must eat cabin boy. Help!'" Another chuckle. "Rum lot, boys. Savages under the skin."

We laughed together, and I decided I mustn't be shy of my grandfather. Maybe next summer...and thought how nice it was to have next summer to look forward to, especially because Elizabeth would be at Copford with me. Having things to look forward to made school more bearable. Even the prospect of being confirmed next Easter wasn't too bad, for Birdie and Ted were so pleased about what they called 'this important step.' I fell asleep in a glow, close to feeling good as gold, like Elizabeth.

✎ 12 ✐

Confirmation, Copford,
sex, and sin lists.

For a while I carried the glow of goodness through the rather heady time of being prepared for confirmation at St. Agnes'. Six of us met every week for a session in Sister Hilary's study which endowed us with a sense of being chosen for higher things. Sister discoursed on the nature of God and the Devil, and particularly on Jesus, who suffered little children to come unto him, and whose bride we would become on the day of confirmation. Fired by mystical concepts, our multiple marriage posed no problem, and in our prenuptial state we received and exchanged showers of 'holy' cards.

Josie and Olive were not being confirmed, presumably on instruction from their parents, and Josie pricked my high-flown condition with occasional astringent gibes. "How's the halo holding up? Nice and bright?" and "A polish a day keeps the devil away!"

"Oh, very witty!" I'd retort, pretending I didn't care. Anyway, for once I was in Sister Hilary's good books, even when my zeal came a cropper over Denise.

Denise must have been about eleven, a scrap of a child with very black hair and an alabaster-pale face. She looked like an orphan, and we weren't surprised to learn that her handsome father (a wonderful sight for us) had brought her to St. Agnes' after term began, because her mother had died. I was reading *Dombey and Son*, and Denise looked much as I imagined little Paul Dombey who, so obviously, was destined for an early grave.

We were sorry for this waif and her sadly widowed father, and I went out of my way to talk to Denise, earning praise from Sister Hilary. Time passed, Denise chatted away and I felt a do-good glow. Then one day she began talking about her father's interest in me.

"But Denise, he doesn't know me."

"Of course he does, I've told him about you," and added, "He thinks you're beautiful."

"How on earth...?"

She broke in, "He sees you on our walks. He drives past us so he can see how I'm getting on. That's when!"

I told Josie, casually, about this unexpected turn of events but she said, "Oh, what bosh! She's just got a pash on you." Stung, I told Olive, whose liquid brown eyes sparkled as she exclaimed, "How exciting! Older men are so passionate." Conversation with Olive was fun, though sometimes too much like eating lots of sticky buns. On the whole I preferred Josie's peppery broadsides.

I let Denise keep reporting on her father and his interest in me. It did seem a bit outlandish, but added a touch of gilt to the gingerbread of being the object of a pash. After all, the previous winter term I'd had a pash myself on Joan (a cheerful girl who was captain of games) so what was the harm? Not until the outcome of Denise's pash did I admit that my pash on Joan had been very different.

It began when I was Jessica to Joan's Lorenzo in *The Merchant of Venice*. I longed for rehearsals, especially the moment when, reclining together on a fake grassy bank, Joan spoke of love, murmuring, "On such a night as this..." Wonderful Shakespeare, wonderful Joan, filling my heart with honey.

The first night went splendidly until, having run up the ladder to the mock balcony, I whispered ardently, "Here, catch this casket..." then, dumbstruck, stared down at Lorenzo/Joan who stood, with arms outstretched, ready for a flawless catch. I muttered, "'tis worth the pains" - but it wasn't, for I had forgotten the casket.

Giggles broke out in the audience, and though smartly shushed, they set me off. I clapped my hand over my mouth and thundered down the ladder, the casket was thrust into my hands and I was pushed on to the stage, where Joan (Lorenzo) seized my arm and dragged me, by now senseless with laughter, into the wings.

Our exit met with huge applause. Happily Joan had no vanities and laughed me out of apologies. After that the pash faded in the light of day.

It never crossed my mind that a pash had anything to do with sex, and this was not surprising as we had no words to furnish our curiosity. At St. Agnes' we regularly prayed, with fervour or absent-mindedly, that God would keep us pure in heart and mind. The body was not mentioned, and the Sisters kept us physically busy, hitting balls with bats, sticks and racquets, leaping around in the gym or taking long walks in crocodile. But the body's fund of pleasures did not go away, though without words its existence lurked undefined, unpronounceable, vaguely sinful.

Yet, naturally, nothing stopped our lively fascination in anything that touched on what we couldn't name. Titillating rumours tended to flourish, one of which surfaced after a cricket match with Roedean - an exclusive, very 'advanced' girls' boarding school. The rumour hinted that the boy who cleaned the shoes would, for a fee of sixpence, do unspeakable things with the girls in the boot room. But the unmentionable question was what did he *do?* Olive didn't know, but wished she did; predictably Josie simply said the story was poppycock.

The rumour was provoked when the Roedean girls arrived for the cricket match wearing cotton shorts. Moreover, instead of joining us for tea after the match, they and their shocking garments were bundled off in their school bus. We envied them the freedom of their shorts, and mocked the nuns for being stuffy. But what were they being stuffy about? It was perplexing, though someone pointed out that, when we were on the playing field, we weren't allowed even to roll up the sleeves of our pink striped cotton blouses, and someone mimicked Sister saying, "We don't want rude boys from the town staring at us over the fence, do we?"

So men were the clue, though the outcome of stares over the fence was unclear. Indeed, our ideas on relationships between men and women were limited to three unsatisfactory categories: the optimistic (living happily ever after); the tragic (lovers cruelly separated, the flavour vaguely spiritual); or the unmentionable (steeped in a fog of sin, guilt and general gloom). The rude boys seemed incidental, and, come to think of it, where did the boot boy fit in? There were no answers and, besieged by ignorance, we made do by having a pash on God, Jesus, poets (Rupert Brooke), dead but romantic composers (Chopin), horses, dogs - and other girls. Having a pash was often referred to much as if you had measles or a headache.

So I blundered along with Denise, pretending that my intentions were blameless - until the day Josie passed us, and her one raised eyebrow spoke volumes. Suddenly I was ashamed. Denise was expatiating on her father's interest in me and I, roughly abrupt, exclaimed, "Honestly, Denise, I think you must be mistaken."

At once her face puckered and she cried, "Why don't you believe me! I've told you and told you, he really likes you and...and he wants to marry you so you can be my mother."

I could only think, 'This is my fault,' and muttered, "I'm sorry, Denise, it's all right." She calmed down, but it wasn't all right. I spent an hour not liking myself at all, not knowing what to do, and then in desperation went to Sister Hilary and blurted out the whole sorry story.

I don't know what I expected, but all she said was, "I'm glad you've told me, Thelma. Don't worry, I will deal with the matter." And that was that. No questions, no explanations, just not to worry. But I did worry.

Not many days later Denise's father took her away. By mischance I met them as they were leaving and stood aside, hoping to be invisible. Denise, paler than ever, looked diminished, and her father's glance passed over me without recognition.

I went upstairs to a practice room and played Chopin's Twentieth Prelude loudly and with passion, making the repeat poignantly soft. But the worry remained: I was ashamed of myself and I understood nothing - not myself, not Denise, not anything.

At Christmas I received a book inscribed in rounded, childish writing, *With love from Denise*. The words lay on the page like a reproach. In the new year I was given a small pocket diary with a gilt cover. I wrote only one entry: 'I want to love and be loved more than anything in the world.'

The sorrows of that winter had faded by the spring morning of our confirmation, and the glow of goodness had returned. I wore a small gold cross given by Birdie and Ted, and was ready to be exalted, picturing myself like the Infant Samuel, whose Victorian portrait had him kneeling with the light of heaven beaming down on his innocent, upturned face. As the six of us walked gravely into chapel wearing our new white frocks and veils, it seemed appropriate that the sun was pouring through the many-coloured mosaics of the great rose window.

As a Bride of Christ I repeated, "I do" with fervour, and when the priest laid his hand lightly on my veiled head, saying "Defend, O Lord, this thy child with thy heavenly grace..." I was moved by the words and waited for joy. The hand was removed, the vestments rustled away, and in the minstrels' gallery the sisters sang my favourite hymn, 'Immortal, Invisible, God only wise...'

Back in our places the sisters raised their clear voices in beautiful, rejoicing music. But I was still just me. Where was God? Obviously Immortal, Invisible - and Absent. It was rather a disappointment.

Confession proved more rewarding. From the sin list I copied the ones I'd definitely committed and confessed them to our old priest in what seemed to be his book-lined study. After being absolved I was told to kneel in the chapel and as a penance repeat three times 'Hail Mary full of grace...' I did this solemnly and emerged from the chapel feeling clean as a new pin, and rather nerve-wracked to be so good. I walked carefully through the cloisters as though wearing a floaty dress of purest white: but however was I to avoid getting it dirty? Or, much, much worse, staining it indelibly with the sin against the Holy Ghost? This sin was never clearly spelled out but it was undoubtedly rock bottom bad. All in all, what Birdie called 'this important step' seemed to have landed me with more questions than answers.

At the end of the summer term I went straight to Lymington with only one day at home. 'Home' was a new house my mother had designed, "on the American plan, Thelma, lots of space not broken up with chilly passages." But now everything was at sixes and sevens and I was glad to be off to the solid life of my grandparents and Abbie and Oophats - and my cousin Elizabeth. She came a few days after my arrival, and I was full of seeing my uncle Phil for the first time since I was his and Dick's bridesmaid, years and years ago.

"He came here after seeing Dick," I told Elizabeth, "for the awful thing is she has TB and is in a sanatorium in the New Forest. 'Such a sad place, darling,' Birdie says, 'so chilly with all the windows open' - you know how she talks - and Phil is out of his mind with worry, but the doctors say she'll be all right. Luckily Phil's got a submarine command and is at Gosport which isn't far away. So you may meet him because he visits Dick as often as he can - as Birdie says, 'riding his motorbike like a maniac, darling.'"

It wasn't difficult to mimic Birdie. Elizabeth laughed and said I shouldn't, and we both agreed that Birdie was a dear and how worried they must be about Dick. "Poor Phil!" Elizabeth said. "My mother always talks about the Ruck Keenes. Copford Rectory was a second home for her, and her brother, Ralph, who spent his school holidays there. My grandfather was Bishop of Hobart, so Ralph was sent to prep school in England when he was only seven - poor little boy! My mother lived at Copford for several years, and I think she fell in love with all the older boys, one after the other. Are they wonderful?"

"Yes!" I said emphatically, "I haven't seen Hugh since I was very young, but I do like Jack - he's a bit different, quieter than Phil who's full of life, and so handsome!" I didn't tell her that when he came roaring up the road on his motorbike I was in my bedroom, and ran to greet him. Halfway down the stairs I saw him hugging Abbie and hoped he'd hug me. He didn't, though he exclaimed, "Why, there's my beautiful niece!" which made me blush and was nice, but a hug would have been better.

Elizabeth and I took long walks over the dikes and talked endlessly about the family, and ourselves. I loved the dike paths which meandered for miles alongside reed-lined ditches, the wide bird kingdom of sky arched overhead, and away in the distance, on sunny days, the sea was a glint of silver. We rarely met anyone else, and on hot days we lay on our backs, watching the birds flying free as we mulled over happenings at Copford.

Elizabeth wanted to know about Frank, the husband of my aunt Dorothy. They had been at Copford with their small daughter Stephanie when I arrived, but left the day after seeing Phil.

"It's a pity you missed Frank," I said. "He's Phil's best friend. They're both in submarines and met ages ago. Phil took Frank to Copford Rectory and he fell in love with Dorothy, and everyone was delighted."

"What's Frank like?"

"He has very blue eyes," I said, "and a way of looking at you intently, which gives me a funny feeling, and so does his voice - it's husky and slow, sort of mocking as though he might be sharing a joke with you. He talks to me as if I'm grown-up. I like him a lot."

"What about Dorothy?"

"She's awfully gushy, but she sings beautifully. She's going to have another baby. Maybe that's why she's a bit queer." This led to talk of marriage and divorce, and that there'd never been a Ruck Keene divorce. I told her that Birdie said marriages are made in heaven and divorce is a sin, and asked Elizabeth if she agreed.

"Yes...but sometimes...I don't know...my parents..." Her voice trailed off and Oophats, returned from a private foray, slumped down beside us. Elizabeth said no more about her parents and we drifted into talking about what sort of life we wanted. Elizabeth knew, quite clearly.

"I want to get married and have children and a home with a garden and a dog and cat."

"What sort of person?"

She sighed, thought for a moment, then said, "Someone I can trust, who's wise and kind and - oh, brilliant, of course! Maybe a poet or musician."

"Do you remember the musician in *The Constant Nymph* who marries the wrong woman and loves the girl he's known all his life; and when he realizes what an awful mistake he's made they come together, and she dies."

"Yes. It was dreadfully sad, I could hardly bear it." Then she asked, "What about you?"

I sat up and stared at the distant strip of silver sea. "I want to explore, and have adventures and see other countries. And I want to love and be loved, passionately. And play the piano beautifully. And leave school."

"Do you hate school?"

"Oh, it's hard to say. I just don't fit in. I'm supposed to want to be a prefect later on, but I don't. I'd be a rotten prefect; I don't believe school's the happiest time of my life, and I'm not absolutely sure about God, so I'd hardly go down well as a prefect in a convent school. You're lucky to be at day school."

"I went to a boarding school for a term when we were rich," Elizabeth said, "but I was sick with misery and came home. Now only the boys are away at public school. We aren't as rich as we were." I asked why. She shrugged and said vaguely her father was having difficulties, and then we talked about Dorothy and Margery and their different husbands.

"Margery's Billy is nice, but a bit boring," I said. Billy was a clergyman and housemaster at Lancing, a public school in Sussex. Elizabeth and I had separately stayed a few days at Lancing and I said, "Birdie told me the boys buzzed round you like flies round a honey pot."

Elizabeth laughed. "I don't remember that at all. I was miserable there. I had to share a room with the matron who was a horrid old thing."

"The boys didn't come near me."

"Perhaps you scared them away."

"How would I do that?"

"Well," Elizabeth said, "you're so attractive and you can't help looking sort of eager and ready for anything. You go rushing up to people as though you know they'll be pleased to see you."

Disconcerted I said, "Do I really? How peculiar. I suppose I don't know much about boys or what's going on in their heads. You're lucky having brothers and their friends coming and going. We've moved twice since my mother married again, and in the new place we won't know anyone." I rolled over and tickled Oophats behind his ears. "It will be wonderful to be in love. Do you ever wonder if you'll manage all right?"

"Manage what?"

"Oh, life" I said, veering away from unmentionables. "Like what would I do if a house was on fire. Would I be brave enough to plunge into the flames and save people?"

"I'd call the fire brigade."

We laughed, and on the way home I said, "The trouble with you, Elizabeth, is you're so worthy."

"Oh well, we can't all be wonderful like you!"

It was jolly having someone like a sister. We even had a family likeness, except her hair curled and mine was just thick. She was pretty, and although a bit shy, she had an enviable way of gently defusing uncomfortable situations with a little joke. Altogether she was nicer than me, but not so adventurous.

When I got home the new house was more or less in order, and my mother said she wanted a rest and had booked rooms at a farm for the three of us. "We'll have a holiday together before you go back to school" she said. She liked expeditions and change, and also believed that if we did things as a family we'd be one, and I would call my stepfather Daddy.

The farm was in Sussex and the only other guest was a young Cambridge undergraduate. He was shy and seemed very old (at least twenty), and I was equally shy, but he knew about plants and I began asking him the names of wild flowers I picked. This led to our wandering together through the fields and woods, collecting and naming flowers. It was like having a big brother until, turning to show him a new discovery, he clasped me, and awkwardly planted a kiss under my right ear.

I was startled and stiffened, untouched by rapture. He let go of me and, confused, we regarded one another with burning cheeks.

"I say, I'm awfully sorry," he said. I studied the ground. "You must think me a bounder. I...really...you're...I don't know..." and then suddenly, "I say...d'you mind...how old are you?"

I told him, then thinking he might feel better if I was older, added, "I'll be fourteen in January."

He said, "I didn't know..." I said it was all right, and in silence we walked back to farmhouse tea. He left the next morning.

As imagined kisses went, mine was a let-down. In pictures and stories lips met and often the woman swooned because it was utterly glorious. Not so my kiss. Was the promise of ecstasy a lie? Or maybe he just wasn't good at kissing? But what I had to decide was whether a kiss - not just any kiss but a kiss *by a man* - was, or wasn't, a sin.

The decision was important because, at the beginning of each term, Sister Hilary arranged the dates for our confessions. So I'd have to prepare my list of sins. The problem was that anything connected with men bristled with implications. Yet men and women kissed. Perhaps only some kisses were a sin? Say I'd shrieked and fled, then surely I would be sinless? On the other hand, if I'd swooned, limp and willing, I would, very likely, be sinful.

In the end I decided that, however unsatisfactory the experience, it was best to be on the safe side, and settled for sin. But what should I say? 'I was kissed by a man' sounded idiotic, as though I'd simply been available, sort of sinning by default. I combed the sin lists in the *Anglo-Catholic Prayer Book,* but nothing obviously fitted. Finally I chose one sin, mainly because it included two genders: "I have had illicit relations with a member of the other sex."

❧ 13 ☙

Confession. Saved by books and music, but beware the Jubjub bird!

The priest greeted me kindly and I knelt on the hassock beside him. The room was cosy, sun shone on bookshelves and the carving of his high-backed chair. After the preliminaries I read steadily through my list of unremarkable sins, concluding firmly, and without a pause, "I have had illicit relations with a member of the other sex."

Silence followed; my confessor seemed deep in thought. I bowed my head and waited, possibly for the wrath of God. As the silence continued I wondered what would happen if absolution was withheld. Would I be excommunicated? I shifted nervously on the hassock, and my confessor gave a slight start.

'Now for it,' I thought. But I wasn't 'for' anything, other than absolution, a penance of one Our Father, three Hail Marys, a blessing and kindly dismissal.

Later that day I sought out an older girl and asked what 'illicit relations' meant. She told me, and though short on explicit details, concluded, "and that's how babies are made."

"So illicit relations could make a baby?"

"Yes, but that's just bad luck. If you're married and do it with someone you're not married to, that's the sin of adultery. It's fornication if you do it with someone when neither of you are married."

"So just a kiss isn't a sin?"

"No, not unless it leads to fornication."

I said, "I thought fornication had something to do with forsaking God and worshipping idols."

"Well...if you sin, you're forsaking God, aren't you?"

I brooded on these absolutes and finally reached some of my own. First, if I'd fornicated properly I might have been going to have a baby, which would be illegitimate and perhaps all set for being a poor little innocent orphan in the convent. Second, if the old priest didn't listen or never bothered to find out what I was talking about, what was the use of telling him a sin which could lead to this predicament? Third, if I was God and had been forsaken I'd not be so easily mollified by a meagre penance of one Our Father and three Hail Marys.

It was clear that the priest never listened to our confessions. I couldn't blame him, they must be very boring. Therefore from now on I'd tell my sins personally to God - and if he was absent elsewhere I'd manage without him. Telling Sister Hilary my decision was another matter. She would not be pleased, and when she wasn't pleased her nostrils flared and she became - well, intimidating. Then I told myself not to be feeble. She couldn't force me to go to confession; after all, Josie and Olive didn't go, so why should I? In January I would be fourteen and, braced by this prospect, felt bold and invincible.

In January, when Sister Hilary summoned me to her study, Josie grinned and said, "Keep your chin up!" and I made a face, feeling neither bold nor invincible. Sister greeted me with a pleasant smile and said, "Father will be hearing confessions next week, Thelma, so I have put you down..." She checked a list and identified the day. I said nothing, so she asked, "Is anything the matter, dear?"

I managed, "It's just...well, I don't...that is, I don't wish to go to confession any more."

Sister Hilary considered me in silence, her nostrils expanding slightly as she drew in a breath.

"I beg your pardon, Thelma. You don't *wish*...?"

"I *decided*." That was better.

She gazed at me, frowning. "May I ask what has prompted this...this extraordinary," she pursed her lips, "decision?"

"I...I just decided."

Another breath, nostrils fully stretched. I stared at the simple wood cross which hung against her black habit. She said, "My dear child, one does not make decisions which can affect your whole life, indeed your immortal soul, without good reasons. Come, Thelma, I thought better of you."

I kept my mouth shut. After a pause she said, "I suggest you pray God to help you. I will pray for you and we will talk again in a day or two." More silence, then, "I am sure you will come to see your...your *decision*...differently." She picked a paper from her desk, and added shortly, "You may go now."

I did not see my decision differently, even though there were three more sessions in Sister Hilary's study that term. The sessions had a routine, beginning with an invitation to sit on the hearthrug, "So we can both be comfortable." Instead I felt cut down in size and, in defence of being talked down to, occupied my mind with the fire irons - their design, blackness and size. But they did not exclude her warnings about the sin of self-will with parallels to the fate of the Arch Rebel, Satan, and the pit of sin prepared for those who rejected God.

During the third session, men and sin were somehow connected with the way I looked. I didn't know what she was talking about, and sat mute until, with a burst of exasperation, Sister Hilary exclaimed, "I do not understand you, Thelma. You have not shed a tear of repentance for the pain and worry you are causing. Do you not long to be reconciled to God?" All I longed for was to get out of her room, so I said nothing.

These sessions left me with unanswered questions boiling angrily in my head. Why was it a sin to think for myself? And what did my appearance and men have to do with not going to confession? Without answers, and no outlet for protest, I began breaking rules. I didn't break them all the time, and just little ones that seemed pointless. One was the ban on our talking as we walked through the cloisters to the refectory. We were told this would disturb the sisters in chapel. But once in the chapel you couldn't hear anything as the walls were thick stone and the door was solid oak. So I talked, quietly, and at the same time thought, 'They can't kill me!'

The sessions continued throughout the autumn term. After each one I'd shut her door behind me, wishing I could shut her inside until she decided to stop badgering me. At least, if a practice room was free, I could play the piano to my heart's content; failing that, books were waiting, each one a passport to a different world.

Some books were an invitation to a dreamy banquet of love and marriage and adventure, ending with the good triumphing over the bad. Other books led into a different world where good did not always triumph, sorrow really broke hearts and, surprisingly, the villains were not always thoroughly bad - like Shylock in *The Merchant of Venice* crying, "Hath not a Jew eyes? Hath not a Jew hands, organs, dimensions, senses, affections, passions?...and if you wrong us, shall we not revenge?" Why yes, of course!

But Shakespeare's Shylock was a Jew, and other writers implied that Jews were definitely not the right stuff, especially the rattling good storytellers like Buchan, Sapper and Dornford Yates. All three, in different ways, wrote about *Chums* heroes grown up and still saving England from the routine list of *Chums* enemies - Jews, Yellow Devils (Arabs, Chinese, Japanese), Russians and, of course, the Germans. In the British Empire there was a fine distinction between the native who was disaffected and thoroughly bad, and those who were loyal, grateful, and splendid fellows - "You're a better man than I am, Gunga Din!" wrote Kipling with genuine feeling.

I never cared much for Sapper's meaty hero, Bulldog Drummond; he was too like a *Chums'* bully and his bullying often included rather beastly torture. But whether torture or simply a spot of murder was at issue, the heroes had nothing to worry about; they were gentry, and as everyone who mattered knew each other, the death of a foreigner or two was readily overlooked.

More to my liking was Sapper's Jim Maitland. In one story, dressed as a 'fanatical Moslem', he was about to set off for Khartoum on a counter-espionage job:

> ...to find out just how widespread the influence [of the German agents] was and feel the pulse of the natives. There were ten of us on it, and between us we got in eight reports. Not bad going, especially as the two who were murdered were not really up to the standards required - poor devils.

Poor devils - not everybody could be white through and through. At least Maitland was sorry for them.

I mooned over Jim Maitland - lean, hard-bitten, wearing a monocle nobody dared joke about, speaking in a pleasant drawl, an absolutely fearless man with a grip like a steel vice. I tried to imagine him loving only me, but it didn't work - he loved somebody else.

John Buchan's stories were exciting, but the women weren't interesting. He was either tiresomely sentimental about them, or they were thoroughly bad. But the Dornford Yates women were beautiful, brave and witty.

Berry & Co. was the first book about Berry Pleydell, his wife Daphne, his brother Boy (and his American wife Adèle), Berry's young cousin Jill, and her brother Jonah. When they weren't chasing villains at breakneck speeds (up to eighty-five miles an hour!) in a Rolls Royce Phantom, they lived together in an ancient family estate of unparalleled beauty called *White Ladies*. Their retinue of servants remained loyal and adoring, despite being constantly tied up by the villains and threatened within an inch of their lives.

One attribute of the Pleydell women was puzzling - they had shining ankles. At last I decided it was because they could afford an unlimited supply of silk stockings. In the holidays I wore silk stockings on special occasions, but caught every run and darned holes, hoping shoes or skirt would cover the mending. The Pleydells had no such anxieties: they never thought about money, or talked about it (that was bad form), so were free to pursue their life of elegance and leisure, spiced with danger, secure in their loyalties and good fellowship, ready to exchange witty abuse and take no offence.

I thoroughly enjoyed being Daphne (or Jill who never said an unkind word to anyone), and matched *White Ladies* with old Copford Rectory, pairing the Pleydell servants with Abbie, Emma, and Benty. Admittedly Jack's Polly didn't measure up to a Rolls Royce, but ancestors presented no difficulty - Oliver Cromwell and Sir John Hawkins were a presentable line-up.

A sharp antidote to the Pleydells' fascinating lives was the world portrayed by Dickens and Thackeray. In *Vanity Fair* I met cynical, depraved aristocrats, women without grace or honesty, and a stupid, cowardly middle class, besotted with wealth and status. But Thackeray never moved me as Dickens could. I wept over the death of little Nell, and even more over poor Jo, the crossing-sweeper in *Bleak House*, whispering:

"It's turned wery dark, sir. Is there any light a-comin'?"

As I mopped my eyes, I told myself that Dickens and Thackeray wrote about lives in another age. Surely now the world wasn't quite so bad?

Books and music - it was a toss-up which I cared for most. What was exciting about books were the revelations, like reading the passage in *Vanity Fair* about George lying dead on the battlefield, and realizing what well-placed commas could do. Then there were the subtle revelations, more like a shaft of light opening up a dark place.

That happened one day when I was searching for a poem by Blake and chanced on an unfamiliar one about a struggle between Urizen and Los (a footnote explained that Urizen represented Reason and Los was Love). Alone in the library I read how the struggle came to a crisis when Los, captured by Urizen, was imprisoned underground. At last, after a long, bitter confinement, Los broke out: but something horrible had happened. Imprisonment had gradually transformed Los into Red Orc, a creature consumed with rage who stampeded over the land, spreading waste and desolation.

I put the book down and sat very still, letting the poem settle in my mind. It was truth. But for the life of me I couldn't exactly have explained its meaning.

Music was another language, as full of meaning as words. When someone played beautifully, or when I played something just right, the sense of it flowed through my whole body. That sort of experience happened out of the blue, as it did one day in the summer term when I cut through the gym on my way to a cricket practice.

The gym had a cranky old piano on which Miss Griffin thumped out hymns for morning assembly, and marches when needed, and I noticed some sheet music propped above the keys. I stopped to have a look, saw it was unfamiliar, and sat down - just for a moment - to try it out. The first part was too difficult, and I turned to the slow movement. It had a wonderful grave opening, and then began to sing. I played all the singing part and then began to play it again, and was thinking, 'I could die right now, and not mind at all,' when a voice behind me said testily, "Whatever d'you think you're doing, Thelma? Everyone's waiting for you."

I said I was sorry, but before getting up I checked the title page and saw I'd been playing part of Chopin's No.2 Sonata in B flat minor.

I floated away to the playing field, the music humming in the tips of my fingers, and in this exalted state imagined that, after all, I might one day be chosen to have lessons with George Woodhouse in London. When less exalted I knew this was a forlorn hope; though the Freemasons paid my school fees, they didn't pay for 'extras', and George Woodhouse was an 'Extra'.

But towards the end of the summer term something amazing happened. Miss Griffin, my music teacher, told me I was to begin lessons with Woodhouse in September. Her thin, sallow features were quite rosy with pleasure as she said, "His lessons will make demands that you need, Thelma. But I know you'll work hard, and repay your mother for making the lessons possible."

I said I would indeed work hard, and when my mother fetched me from school for the holidays, I hugged her, and thanked her from my heart, feeling we were close once again.

For the next little while everything felt better than it had for a long time. Sister Hilary gave up on her confession campaign, and I was specially looking forward to my annual summer visit to Lymington because Elizabeth would be there. I had a lot to tell her, not only about lessons with George Woodhouse, but also that I'd made friends with three boys - three in one go was a change from having no boys at all.

The first two, Peter and Mark, I met at a Christmas dance. They were a year or two older than me, but the third boy, Geoffrey, was my age. He lived miles away in Rhodesia, but his mother and mine were old friends, and they spent a day with us when they were in England during the Easter holidays. While our mothers talked about old times, Geoffrey and I went off to explore a little wood nearby and dammed a stream to make a paddling pool. It was fun to have a boy to play with, and a pity he was going back to Africa. But before he left we agreed to write to each other.

"That's a deal," Geoffrey said, and we shook hands, grinning, a little self-conscious. It was a light-hearted compact, with not a hint of future trouble.

Out on the dikes at Lymington I told Elizabeth first about George Woodhouse.

"But that's wonderful!" she exclaimed.

"Yes, it is wonderful!" I said, then to my surprise added "But..."

Elizabeth waited, then asked, "But what?"

I picked up a stick for Oophats, threw it for him, and said, "Well...what I want is to go on to the Royal Academy of Music and study all the things Miss Griffin hasn't taught me. I've learnt lots of pieces - Chopin, Schumann, Schubert, Brahms, Beethoven, Mendelssohn and even modern composers like Scriabin and Moeran - but I don't know any theory, I don't play scales, and my sight reading isn't brilliant. I just hope Woodhouse..."

It was a lovely day, sunny with a light breeze, the maze of footpaths outspread to meet the sea, and above us the sky arched away to the other side of the world. Elizabeth said suddenly, "Next summer we'll be fifteen, and the one after that we'll be sixteen and have left school. D'you still want to travel?"

"Oh yes," I said, "*and* go to the Royal Academy. But how to do anything without money? My mother hasn't much, I'll have to work after school, but at what? We're not trained for work at St. Agnes'. Only one girl is going to university. She's very clever and rather plain, and everyone thinks she's odd. We've been taught the ladylike accomplishments, and yes...I play the piano quite well and won the school music prize last year. But with only sixty children in the school there's not much competition."

Elizabeth said, "But you are the best."

Frowning I countered, "I won the best holiday essay prize two years ago. It was on Scott's poem about Lochinvar, remember?"

"O, young Lochinvar came out of the west,/Through all the wild Border his steed was the best." Elizabeth laughed, and chanted the famous couplet: "So faithful in love, and so dauntless in war,/There never was knight like young Lochinvar."

"How could you not write a good essay on that!" I exclaimed. "It makes me go all tingly saying it aloud. And writing isn't difficult. Perhaps, like my mother says about the Ruck Keenes, I've just got the gift of the gab. Playing the piano is much harder. And I don't know if I'm really good. And if I'm only just 'accomplished' the future comes down to getting married and having children." Oophats brought the stick back and I threw it, hard, saying, "Probably that's why we have to darn our hellish black stockings in a perfect lattice. 'A thing worth doing is worth doing well, dear' says Sister. Anyway, what about you?"

"Oh, I'll stay at home for a while and help Mum with the twins. We have a German girl, and mother likes her because they play piano duets together, but she's rather moody - I mean the girl, not Mum. I just want to get married and have a family of my own."

This got us on to boys and falling in love and I told Elizabeth about Geoffrey and Peter and Mark. "The dance I met Peter at was my first, and I didn't know anyone. Then he asked me to dance, and this summer I've played tennis at his house; that's where I met Mark. Peter's sixteen. His name is Harmsworth and his uncle is Lord Rothermere. He owns the *Daily Mail*. My mother calls it 'that awful rag.'"

"Aren't they very rich?"

"Presumably. Lord Rothermere is also Peter's godfather and he's going to give Peter a car for his eighteenth birthday."

"What's Peter like?"

"Sort of ugly-attractive. He's going to join the Guards. Peter flies hawks. They wear beautiful little leather hoods with a feather, but I'm not sure I really like the idea."

"What about Mark?"

"He's different, serious about being a doctor. The family is mad about flying, have their own airfield and play a treasure hunt game, flying low to look for clues. Mark has crashed twice but always steps out without a scratch. He's awfully nice. He makes me feel...oh, that I can just be myself. Peter's other friends are nice too, but they do things I don't do, things like coming-out balls, shooting in Scotland, holidays in the South of France. I just listen."

One day we talked about the fuss over my confession and after we'd giggled about 'illegal relations' I exclaimed, "What I don't understand is why Sister Hilary is so angry with *me*. It's as though...oh, I don't know. I wonder if she sometimes wishes she hadn't become a nun. Somebody told me they have to wear a cotton shift when they have a bath so they don't look at their naked bodies. In the dormitory we're even on our honour to report if we catch a glimpse of someone in the next cubicle without their clothes on. It's dotty."

Elizabeth said, "If someone really has a vocation, they must have to struggle against..." and ended vaguely, "well, all the temptations." We didn't discuss the temptations.

But by coincidence our interchange about vocation had a kind of sequel at school. Not long after the autumn term began I was hurrying past Sister Hilary's study and through the open door saw that she was bending over a book with a young priest. This was so out of the ordinary that I slowed down to have a good look. They were very absorbed, and made quite a pair, for Sister Hilary was handsome and so was the priest. Then he glanced up at her with a smile, and must have made a quiet joke, for suddenly they both burst out laughing.

In the senior sitting-room I told Josie and Olive what I'd seen, and said, "She looked quite different, really young and...and happy."

Josie said, "Mum likes her, says she's very intelligent and wonders why she ever became a nun. She's very county gentry - hunted, came out, went to balls, all the gentry things." Olive said maybe her lover was killed in the war and she fled to the nunnery with a broken heart. Josie said she had more sense.

For a while we mulled over the mystery of having a vocation, until I said slowly, "I really could like Sister, but can't be sure where I am with her. When she flies into a bate she's...she's kind of dangerous, like a big black bird, about to swoop."

Josie gave a snort of laughter and cried, "Beware the Jubjub bird," and we took it up together, "and shun the frumious bandersnatch!" We stumbled, laughing, through the enchanted word-games of the *Jabberwocky* verses from Lewis Carroll's *Alice Through the Looking-Glass*, and Olive sketched Sister Hilary swooping through the tulgy wood, the big sleeves of her black habit outspread like wings.

A couple of weeks later I had my first piano lesson with George Woodhouse in London.

❦ 14 ❧

More music, more sex,
and that's it for school.

Almost everything about the lessons with George Woodhouse was wonderful - that is, once I got over the first sight of him. The small plaster busts of composers in Miss Griffin's room had fed my imagination, shifting between Wagner, his flowing locks topped with a funny flat hat; or Beethoven, growly under an unruly shock of hair; or Chopin, sensitive and doomed. Instead Woodhouse was a little, rather untidy, sandy-haired man, and I soon discovered that he liked to nestle up against me on the long piano bench and surreptitiously pat my bottom. Behind us, and a little to one side, Miss Griffin fidgeted, her kind horse face peering anxiously as she tried to monitor what was going on.

The other St. Agnes' pupil, Margaret, didn't have her bottom patted. She was a rather stuffy girl, a year older than me, a prefect, and rival for the school music prize. We didn't like each other much, so I shared the joke about the bottom patting with Josie and Olive.

Woodhouse taught in a big room like a crowded Victorian drawing room, full of sofas and easy chairs, plants on stands and two grand pianos. That first lesson he insisted on my playing chords and single notes with curved, springy fingers, so when they struck the keys they sank down and back, as if landing from a height. "This will make the notes sing," he said. And it did. He gave me new music to learn, and I forgot to wonder about learning theory or getting help in sight-reading. I had new work to explore, and a new way to touch the keys - that was enough.

The studio was on Wigmore Street, and after the lesson we went to a teashop where Miss Griffin ordered tea for three and iced cakes ("One each, Thelma," she said gently as I stretched for a second). This became our routine, and the lesson, followed by the small ritual of tea and cake, was like coming up for air from the confines of school. Wigmore Street was *the* music street of London, and the first day we walked the hallowed ground I set my hideous school hat at an angle (ignoring Margaret's frown), feeling quite dashing and enjoying smiles from passers-by. 'This is the life!' I thought, and commanded London, 'Wait for me, I won't be long!'

During that term Miss Griffin took us to hear Arthur Rubinstein play Chopin. Everything, the delicacy and spirit of his playing and his happiness in sharing it with us, left me wanting to leap about and shout for joy, and at the same time keep silent, as if the joy was tender and might be shattered by unruly noise.

I didn't know my mother was pregnant, until I came home for the Christmas holidays, so was taken aback when she told me I would have a little brother or sister in May.

Shocked, I exclaimed, "But aren't you too old?"

She laughed and said, "I'm only thirty-seven, darling."

I was away at school when Felicity was born. I couldn't feel any connection with her, and the prospect of a baby in the house was disconcerting. My mother delayed Felicity's christening until my summer holidays, and after the ceremony she put the baby in my arms saying, "Your little sister, darling." I held her gingerly and didn't blame her for breaking into a wail. I'd never held a baby before and felt like Alice when the Red Queen lands her with the howling baby who turns into a little pig. Not that Felicity was piggish, she was just a baby and I was afraid of dropping her.

After a couple of weeks at home with a baby in the house it was a relief to be off to Lymington. I'd come bouncing in after tennis or a picnic with the Harmsworths, and my mother would appear, finger to lips whispering, "Hush, Thelma! you'll wake the baby." I'd say I was sorry, but thought crossly that at Copford babies and young children were often underfoot (Phil's wife Dick called them "the tiny tots brigade") but life went on without all this shushing.

Naturally at Copford everyone was glad about Felicity, including Elizabeth, who loved babies. "Aren't you pleased?" she asked. "Hilary and Martin were adorable when they were babies; I felt they were my own property." I was non-committal, and muttered that I was away from home most of the year. Elizabeth didn't press the subject and talked of other things. I liked her for not going on about it.

Copford was full of family, including Frank and Dorothy with their two little girls. I felt shy with the children, but one afternoon I came into the drawing-room just as Frank was about to read to them. I asked what book he was reading, and he said, "A book by a man called A.A. Milne."

"What's it about?"

"A little boy called Christopher Robin and his friend, a bear called Winnie-the-Pooh, a donkey called Eeyore, and others."

"It sounds rather silly," I said.

"Now you are being silly. This is classic stuff. Sit down and listen."

So I sat down, and as I told Elizabeth afterwards, I was captivated. "It's funny and charming and the characters are so real and have such wonderful names." Elizabeth said she often read the book to the twins, and they adored it. After a moment I said, "It was cosy listening to Frank, feeling like a child with the other two, part of a family."

"Don't you feel a family at home?"

"No...not like that. I did when I was little and we lived with my grandmother Minna, and there was Freda, and my uncles came sometimes. It was best of all in Texas with Willoughby, and in London. But my mother quarrelled with Willoughby and we left London and went off to dreary St. Alban's. Then I was sent to St. Agnes'. I haven't seen Willoughby since. Marston takes me to a pantomime at Christmas, but the Garsias are kind of thin on the ground. I know all about the Ruck Keenes, but nothing about the Garsias; they sort of spring out of nowhere. But I'm going to visit Willoughby when I've left school. I loved Willoughby."

"What about your stepfather?"

"Oh, that went all wrong after my mother tried to make me call him Daddy, and I couldn't. She's given up now. But I don't call him anything. I just mutter, 'I say!' or 'by the way' to get his attention."

Elizabeth giggled. "Like the Bellman in *The Hunting of the Snark* who answered to 'Hi! or any loud cry.'"

I laughed, and said, "Maybe I could try 'Fry me!' or 'Thing-um-a-jig!' But he wouldn't be amused. He isn't too bad, just rather boring."

"A pity we can't choose our parents," Elizabeth said soberly.

"I'd choose Frank any day," I said. "Have you noticed his voice, it's...well, it sort of strokes you."

She said, teasing, "Maybe you've got a pash on him."

"That's nonsense," I retorted quickly, and after calling Oophats, said we better start back, it was nearly time for tea.

In September I moved into the Sixth form and our lessons were galvanized by the Cambridge School Certificate examinations which we were to take next summer. The previous year Sister Hilary had discovered that the Fifth form was lamentably ignorant of geography, and began teaching us herself. In the lower forms we had suffered from the dismal lessons given by the Old Girls who returned as pupil teachers. I never recovered from my confusion over anything to do with mathematics. Those questions about men picking apples, and how long would it take them to fill their baskets, left me with a clear picture of their cheerful faces and the apples hanging, plentiful and rosy red on trees - but how many and how long was a closed book.

So we had to work hard. We were told that the Cambridge Certificate was a respected examination that would be invaluable when we went out into the world.

Josie said acidly, "How else will they know we're educated?"

But the hard work was exhilarating, and I snatched times to study the new pieces George Woodhouse had given me - Schumann's Papillons, a Chopin Impromptu and a promise to start, after Christmas, on a piano transcription of Bach's organ Toccata and Fugue in B minor. With so much of interest to be done the months passed quickly, and I wasn't tempted to be a nuisance to anyone. So when, halfway through the Easter term, I was summoned to Sister Hilary's study, I knocked on her door with only a tinge of automatic apprehension.

I'd no sooner shut the door when she began, smiling very pleasantly, "I have some good news for you, Thelma. George Woodhouse has offered you a music scholarship."

For one giddy moment I thought this meant a scholarship to the Royal Academy of Music. But it wasn't. Sister Hilary reminded me that Woodhouse had an arrangement with a finishing school for foreign students in Wimbledon. Every year the school gave board, lodging and time for piano study to one of his pupils, provided she helped the foreigners with their English.

"As you know," Sister Hilary concluded, still smiling, "Margaret took up a similar scholarship last year and is very happy there."

I stared at the floor, knowing I should be beaming with pleasure, but all I could see was a school where Margaret was happy. It could be all right, especially if I could study the things I'd never learnt from Miss Griffin. But what if I just went on learning pieces? On the other hand, it was music.

At this point I distinctly heard my mother murmuring, "Never look a gift horse in the mouth, Thelma," and "Beggars can't be choosers." So I pulled myself together and said I was very grateful and Sister said, somewhat briskly, "I would hope so, Thelma, it is a great compliment for you."

Afterwards I buoyed up my spirits with the thought that there was only one more predictable term at St. Agnes' to get through - and then I could begin living my own life.

As it turned out, the last term was anything but predictable. The trouble began when two girls, Molly and Betty, complained about the 'unsavoury atmosphere' and loud playing of gramophone records in our sitting-room, which was shared by the dozen seniors who were not prefects. Sister Hilary reported the complaints to us, saying she wished to hear the records, and we were to tidy up the sitting-room and be ready when she came the following afternoon.

Nobody took this very seriously. Molly and Betty couldn't help being the daughters of a clergyman, but they were priggish and extra holy. "What a pair of toads," someone muttered as we made the sitting-room presentable. I piled the records neatly, not putting them in any particular order, and wondered why anyone would disapprove of our current favourites - Mendelssohn's *"O for the wings of a dove"* sung by an angelic choirboy, and sad, romantic *"I'll see you again"* from Noel Coward's *Bittersweet*. Unsavoury? Some people were daft - and then remembered Kate telling me about what happened when her so-called 'uncle' took her out in his car. That would undeniably rate as unsavoury. And oh dear! there were the letters.

The letters were mine and those of two sisters who spent their holidays in Paris. Barbara and Jane kept their letters in a bundle tied up with pink ribbon, safely tucked away in their lockers. Barbara said they were love letters - and in *French,* which made them especially romantic. Mine were not romantic or tied up with anything. They were from Geoffrey in Rhodesia who wrote sporadic, hearty letters about treks in the bush and football matches, ending invariably, "So long, old girl."

The snag was that we were not allowed to receive letters from anyone other than parents or relatives. I don't know how the letters reached Barbara and Jane, but Geoffrey's mother included his letters with those she wrote to my mother, who forwarded them in her letters to me. My replies followed the reverse route. It seemed the simplest process, requiring only one stamp. As for the rule, it was silly. But might our lockers be inspected? Surely not - they were the one private place we had at school.

So much for the letters. The other sudden anxiety was very different - something, I believed, known only to me. Kate was the best actress in the school and beautiful - slender, with fine features, a wide mouth which smiled easily, and enormous brown eyes fringed with long, dark lashes. We weren't close friends but I liked her. Then, by chance, the two of us spent time together preparing for some event and, for once, talked about ourselves. This was when she told me she wasn't a virgin.

"Really?" Astounded, rape and fornication rattled in my head, jostling with my mother's recently frequent admonishment, 'Never make yourself cheap, Thelma.' What did she *mean*? She also sometimes referred to 'that sort of woman.' I stared at Kate and mumbled, "Did you...I mean...was it...well, all right?"

"Of course. It's wonderful."

"How...I mean, when?"

"Last summer. I went into the garden one night with a cousin I like and he took off my clothes."

"What about babies?"

"Oh, men do something about that," she said airily, and smiled; she had an enchanting smile, and was naturally an enchanting person, not at all 'that sort of woman,' whatever that might be. Then Kate laughed. "You know the uncle I go out with sometimes? He isn't really my uncle, just one of my father's assistants. He's quite old, about thirty. But nice. We do it in the back of the car."

"Do you...do you love him?"

"Oh, I don't know. I like him, he makes me laugh. Don't tell anyone."

Of course I didn't, but from that time on, whenever Kate returned from an uncle outing and lay on the floor looking limp and contented, I knew why. It was amazing that she was doing this unspeakable, dangerous, wonderful thing. I tossed between envy and anxiety - how would it be when this happened to me? Even more, how I wished I knew who did what, and what went where.

Though burdened with this private knowledge I stood looking polite and innocent when Sister Hilary strode into our sitting-room for her inspection. She sat down in the only comfortable chair, and we sat on the others and stared at her.

"We will begin with one of the records," she said. Nobody moved. We were all aged sixteen, but suddenly most of us were in that peculiar, almost delirious condition of being very near ungovernable laughter. "Come along now," Sister said impatiently, "a record, please."

Josie whispered, "Go on, you tidied them." So I got up, took the first record on the pile, managed to put the needle in the right groove and sat down just as a howl came from the gramophone, "Ee-eee-eeee! ain't it graa-aand to be bloomin' well de-e - ead..."

There was hardly time to register astonishment before Sister Hilary was on her feet. "Take off that crude rubbish!" she exclaimed, and breathing deeply, nostrils flaring, said, "I will return," and left so vigorously that her habit flew out and overturned a couple of empty chairs.

Josie murmured, "Beware the Jubjub bird," and the laughter exploded as we asked each other where that frightful record came from - we'd never heard it before. Then someone cried, "For goodness sake, shut up. She said she was coming back."

When she came back she made no mention of records but asked us to open our lockers. She discovered the letters and after glancing at them remarked crisply, "You will be hearing more of this," and took the bundles away. I thought how sensible Kate was: though ravished, her locker held no shred of evidence.

I was the first to hear more - far more than remotely expected. I barely had time to shut Sister's door before she began vehemently, "I would like you to understand, Thelma, that you have brought me to the end of my patience. If it isn't one thing with you, it's another. Now I find you have been receiving letters I knew nothing about. If the summer term did not have less than four weeks to run, I would expel you forthwith."

Expelled? For Geoffrey's, 'So long old girl'? I stared at her, nonplussed. She didn't ask me about Geoffrey, or how the letters were exchanged, but continued headlong, "I have instead decided to write to the finishing school in Wimbledon about your behaviour. Anything less would be a dereliction of duty. It must be their decision whether or not to accept you."

I left the room half wanting to be rid of the scholarship. I was fed up with school, and adults who didn't ask the right questions, and weren't interested in what I thought and felt. I'd broken a rule, but so had my mother, and couldn't she be trusted to let me write letters to a friend? And even if Barbara and Jane really were receiving love letters, they were just letters. Kate was another matter, but letters? I was even more perplexed when nothing happened to Barbara or Jane, no punishment - so why *me?* The question stirred a fleeting remembrance of the day I saw Sister Hilary laughing with the young priest. Was she jealous of us all, or more particularly of me?

There were no answers, and no speculation prepared me for the next summons to Sister's study.

I was at once surprised when she quietly asked me to close the door and sat silent, looking at me intently until she picked up a letter and said, "I am afraid, Thelma, I acted hastily and in anger. I should not have written as I did to the Wimbledon school. On reflection I sent a following letter to assure the principals I believed you would do your best. I have now heard they are willing to accept you." As I said nothing she added, "I am glad your future has not been jeopardized."

I said "Thank you" and may have said I was sorry. Possibly not. Two weeks later I left St. Agnes' for good.

There was, however, an unexpected, curious sequel to the muddle that ended my seven years at St. Agnes'. About a year after leaving school I spent an afternoon with Josie and her mother, and from them learnt that Sister Hilary was no longer principal of the school. "And they *punished* her," Josie said.

"What on earth for?"

"A lot of bugaboo," said Josie's mother, "about having to humble herself and renew her spiritual discipline. Too many women cooped up together. The whole thing is unnatural."

"How was she punished?"

"Oh, everything short of burning her at the stake" said Josie's mother. "She was put in solitary confinement, and allowed a brief spell in the garden once a day, alone, weather permitting - and you know what last winter was like. When I got wind of it I went straight off to see Mother Superior."

Josie broke in, "Mum was grand. She went to Mother's room and said, 'Do you want a death on your hands?' and then sat down and said she was staying put until it was agreed she could take Sister out every weekend."

"You wouldn't have recognized her, Thelma. She had been confined and silent for far too long. She stared at me as if I was a ghost. But she never complained, not once. A few months ago she was sent to another convent. She seems content."

I couldn't imagine the Sister Hilary I'd known just being 'content' and though she'd made me miserable, I could have liked her. But there was no resolving that now. This was my time, and I had my life in my own hands - that is, more or less, since freedom, so longed for, was turning out to be rather a rum go.

❧ 15 ❧

Freedom!
And what is love?

The two weeks before I left for Lymington were full of tennis parties at the Harmsworth's and spur-of-the-moment outings in Peter's new car. I was always glad when Mark joined us. He would amble in, easy and good tempered, a bit untidy, dark hair flopping, rather too long, across a broad forehead, his brown eyes taking in everything. He didn't come the day we went to all-in wrestling at Brighton, but I understood why after watching great hunks of hairy men (one was called Rough-house King Carts) thump and twist, and even jump murderously up and down on each other. Peter said it was a performance and a joke, and joined in the cheers and roars of laugher. I told Mark I thought it was disgusting and not at all funny.

"No, it's not funny," he said. "But some wrestlers are really skilled, and wrestling isn't as harmful as boxing."

Then we talked about Peter's passion for falconry, and I said, "I'm in two minds about it, but it does have a kind of medieval magic." Mark had never been out with the falcons, so I told him how Peter made me put on one of his heavy leather gloves so I could carry one of his peregrines on my wrist. "With the other hand I held the jesses, those strips of leather attached to the falcon's legs. Mine sat so still, carrying his little head high as if he was pleased to wear a beautiful leather hood with a tiny feather on top."

Mark asked why I was in two minds about hawking, and I said, "It seems cruel to confine their heads in a hood, but Peter says that the hood and jesses stop the falcons from bating off after unimportant prey. Of course, it's exciting when the right quarry is sighted. I was quite deft at slipping off the hood and jesses, and then I bawled "Hi-loo-loo-loo! and flung my peregrine into the air."

"So what then?"

"Well," I said, "it was wonderful, but also sort of hateful," and with a frown admitted, "Secretly I'm thankful that Peter's birds often don't catch anything." Mark grinned, and said I better keep that under my hat.

I enjoyed being with Peter and his friends. They were young and fun and glamorous, but (except for Mark) they never talked seriously about anything. Mark made jokes and was never solemn, but he didn't mind if I asked questions - he even seemed to like it, and he had a way of looking at me as though he really saw me.

A few days before I left for Lymington we all, including Mark, went to a big fun fair. Everyone wanted to go on the huge roller-coaster and, pretending the idea was great fun, I stood frozen with terror, waiting our turn. Just before we boarded this monster I felt an arm slip through mine and heard Mark say, "Sit with me, you'll be all right." It seemed a miracle that he knew what I was feeling, and even more of a miracle that with him I really was all right, and even enjoyed being terrified.

When I first met the Harmsworths I told Birdie that Peter's godfather was Lord Rothermere, whose brother, Lord Northcliffe, owned *The Times*. I thought this would impress her, as she always read *The Times* at breakfast. She wasn't impressed.

"Harmsworth? Oh yes, newspapers," she murmured, implying that they were not out of the handkerchief drawer, so not people who *mattered*. I sometimes wondered how the quality of *mattering* was measured. Peter was my friend: did that not matter?

Unfortunately it was Peter's fault that what was to be my last visit to my grandparents had such a disastrous start. The day began cheerfully. Peter offered to drive me to London, and as we set off he said, "Let's lunch at the Ritz, and afterwards we'll feed the ducks in St. James' Park." I'd never been inside the Ritz and thought, 'This is the life!'

It was exciting to walk into that famous place and be ushered into the restaurant by courteous flunkies. When people's heads turned as we walked to our table, I bit my lip so I wouldn't smile too much. At lunch Peter made me slip a couple of rolls into my handbag for the ducks, saying "We'll have plenty of time before your train goes." I had a glass of wine at lunch, feeling very grown-up, and we took our time with the ducks. That was why I only just caught the train.

Not until it stopped at every station did I ruefully admit that it was a slow train and wouldn't reach Lymington until long after I was expected. For what seemed interminable hours I sat in a fidget of anxiety wondering if Birdie would be worried, and if I'd be met, and would they be cross?

It was such a relief to see Frank on the platform standing right opposite my compartment that when the train stopped I jumped out, dropped my suitcase and threw my arms round his neck crying, "I'm so glad to see you!" But there was no responsive hug, and I drew back, abashed: of course, hugging Birdie and Abbie was all right, but not my uncles, it wasn't their style. So I began babbling about why I was late, while Frank picked up my case, smiled, and said nothing.

In the car he asked, in his slightly mocking, husky voice, "So what have you been up to?"

That was better. I slithered comfortably down until my head rested on the back of the bench seat and talked about having lunch with Peter at the Ritz, and the ducks, and the awful slow train, until Frank stopped the car and said, "You better calm down or Birdie will think you've been drinking."

"I only had one glass of wine at lunch," I protested, and after a silence Frank asked what Peter was like.

I said he flew hawks and was in the Guards and was fun to be with, and was kind to me. Then, in a burst of confidence, added, "He wants to marry me when we're old enough."

"Would you like that?"

I sighed, not because the question was troublesome but from pleasure. I loved my uncles but I hardly ever saw Phil or Jack, and they never asked questions as if they might really want to know the answers. It was a treat to have Frank to myself, asking questions in his beguiling voice, and waiting for an answer. I said slowly, "I don't know. I've only just left school. I do like him, he takes trouble with me, but..." I turned my head, smiled up at Frank, and said, "it's just...there's something kind of missing." The next moment he'd slipped an arm round my shoulders, bent his head and gently kissed me, full on my lips.

It was a long kiss, and I never wanted it to end. But it did, and without a word Frank pulled his arm away and started the car. We didn't speak until, on reaching Copford, he said, "Go and make your peace with your grandmother, I'll bring your case."

I went in and found Birdie and Jack standing unsmiling together, and Elizabeth half way down the stairs; it was as if we were part of a scene in a play, complete with the family props of Hawkins' sea chest, the Cromwell letter, and the big cabinet with the Worcester china alongside my father's blue glass dog. There was no, "Here's my darling gel!" Instead everyone stared at me in silence, Birdie's old face crumpled and frowning - she didn't even look like herself. Then Abbie appeared from the kitchen and I stumbled into an explanation about having lunch with Peter Harmsworth and catching the wrong train, but Birdie cut me short.

"What have you and Frank been doing?"

"Doing? But I've told you..." and then the blood rushed to my cheeks. She couldn't know...how could she? But what was all this about?

Birdie said, "I find it hard to believe you," and I heard Frank come in and stand still behind me.

I couldn't think of anything to say and for a moment we all stood like waxworks in a show until Elizabeth broke the spell by coming down to greet me, and Abbie said briskly, "Time you was in bed, Mrs. Ruck Keene. I'll bring your hot drink upstairs," and turning to me added in a very whatfor voice, "I've kept some supper warm. You best eat it in the kitchen."

Uncertainly I kissed Birdie on her soft, wrinkled cheek and she patted my arm, saying something about everyone feeling better after a good night's sleep. In the kitchen Abbie said, "Another time you best mind what you're doing, Thelma. Your Granny was worriting her head off and for all anyone knew you might of been taken by the White Slavers."

Later Elizabeth came into my bedroom and said, "Everything seems to be going on as usual but Birdie's very strung up, Grandpa coughs and coughs, and Jack and Frank behave as if they hardly know each other. Dorothy's really queer and Frank goes around looking hangdog. Something's badly wrong."

"Has he been unfaithful?"

"Who knows? Obviously Birdie doesn't think he's safe with any woman, and certainly not you - you came rushing in looking as if..."

"As if what?"

"Don't be so fierce! Did anything happen?"

I sat down on my bed and said, "He kissed me."

We stared solemnly at each other. "What sort of a kiss? An uncle kiss?"

I shook my head. "It was wonderful," and after a pause, "Do you think he's in love with me?"

"If he is he oughtn't to be. Don't be silly. It was just you looked so nice and he wanted to kiss you."

"It felt more than that."

I lay awake, feeling the kiss. Surely no-one kissed like that unless they were in love? And if you were in love, didn't you want to marry? Before I went to sleep I knew what I must do next day.

I waited until after lunch when Frank was reading alone on the sofa in the drawing-room. By then I felt sick, and would have liked to change my mind, go for a walk, anything but what I did, which was to march in and sit at the other end of the sofa. "Hallo!" he said.

But I was in no mood for 'hallo' or chit-chat, not with a question bursting in my head, so I said bluntly, "Are you going to tell Dorothy?"

After a silence Frank asked, "Tell her what?"

"About us." He said nothing. I now wanted to vanish, never to be seen again. But I had to know. I felt a jab of anger. Couldn't he help me? After all, he did kiss me. So I said in a rush, "Don't you want to marry me?"

Frank closed his book, marking the place with a strip of leather. Then he said, "No."

"But..."

"Thelma, I am married to your aunt, I am thirty-two years old with two daughters. You are sixteen and below the age of consent."

It was too much. I leapt away from the sofa and cried, "Then you shouldn't have kissed me like that!" But Frank wasn't even looking at me, his blue eyes were fixed on something behind me - it was Jack, standing in the doorway. I exclaimed, "I'm going for a walk," and pushed past Jack, but he came after me.

"Just a minute, Thelma." I stopped, hating everyone as he asked, "Has Frank been bothering you?" Through the open door of the drawing-room I saw Frank listening, intent, staring straight at me. I shook my head but Jack insisted, "Are you sure...?"

Hadn't I wished Jack would ask me questions he really wanted me to answer? Now I'd got my wish. I heard myself say, "He just kissed me. It didn't bother me," and then wished I was dead.

"If Frank does bother you," Jack said, very deliberately, and not really to me, "don't be afraid to tell me, Thelma. Promise?" Cravenly I muttered something, and fled.

Out on the dikes with Elizabeth I told her what had happened and was put out when she laughed. "Oh dear, you are an ass! I wish I'd been a fly on the wall and seen you waltz in and demand to know Frank's intentions."

"All right, I suppose it is funny. But I wish I hadn't told on him! It was mean. He'll hate me."

"I don't know about that. But you could have said nothing."

"I know. It's awful. But...but the kiss - I don't understand."

"The trouble with you," Elizabeth said, "is you don't seem to realize the effect you have on people. You'll have to stop being so come-hitherish, or else not mind when they do come hither."

"Come-hitherish? But I was just sitting in the car." And so we went on until I said gloomily, "I suppose if I was...well, sophisticated, I'd just have said something light-hearted and witty like the women in Dornford Yates' books. But, Elizabeth, I never knew a kiss could sort of hit you all over. You hardly know if you're coming or going, or even where you are."

We sat in silence, listening to the birds crying and the reeds rustling in the light sea breeze. It was very peaceful, and after a while I asked, "Is growing up always hard?"

"Probably most of the time," Elizabeth said.

Frank left Copford the next day. I longed to say I was sorry, but didn't have a chance. A few days later Jack's leave was up and he drove away with Dorothy and the children. It was a relief to see her go. Once I'd chanced on her sitting alone, twisting her hands and muttering "My God! My Frank!" She looked terrible, her hair all over the place. Adults weren't supposed to behave like this.

"D'you think it's my fault?" I asked Elizabeth.

"No, you just made everything more difficult."

"I wish we knew what was going on," I said. "It's awful feeling everyone is so unhappy."

I never did know what had been going on until, after more than sixty years of ignorance, I started writing about my life. Soon I came up against missing dates and gaps in family stories, so I sent off a list of questions to Phil's wife, Dick, and in no time received a reply headed UNSATISFACTORY ANSWERS TO YOUR QUESTIONS. Dick was rising ninety by this time, but nothing had dimmed her irrepressible Irish sense of life's absurdities. Many of the first questions I sent her

117

needed only brief, factual answers, but to the one about what Aunt Jessie had done with the silver teapot, I was treated to the following reply:

> *It was a COFFEE pot and roused great dissension in the family as for generations it was always bequeathed to the "WRONG PERSON." I have an idea Jackie got it in the end.*
>
> *Aunt Jessie was a charming person married to Grandpa Edmund's deadly dull brother George and lived in Colchester. She was always spoken of with hauteur by Birdie and on my very first visit to Copford I was told that Aunt Jessie had been 'a flower girl' which surprised me, having just come from China where this is what girls in brothels are called. It had a cheering effect on me (I was very young and the Ruck Keenes were rather daunting), and was disappointed when Phil told me that Aunt Jessie did not have a torrid past but had worked for a short time in a VERY up-market sort of Constance Spry flower shop in Mayfair.*

This was far from an unsatisfactory answer and for two more years, questions and answers passed frequently between us. In one letter Dick unexpectedly wrote an account of what indeed had been going on when Frank kissed me, that evening in the summer, more than sixty years ago:

> *...It occurs to me you never heard the full story of poor Frank's fall from grace as it would have been kept from your tender ears. What happened was this. Doshy and the two little girls were at Copford while Frank was cruising around in his submarine. An Engineer-Commander's wife, a good deal older than Frank, invited him to dinner, alone, as her husband was away. After dinner she seduced him on the sofa. Frank, knowing Doshy's strong views on marriage vows and fidelity, etc. was immediately consumed with guilt and the silly old Ninny went straight to Lymington and Confessed All to Doshy. He must have been bonkers. Doshy went nearly out of her mind. Phil and I were at Lymington a short while after and she was like a mad woman. Jackie was there and suggested I should take Doshy for a walk round the dikes and give her some worldly advice, which I reluctantly did. I told her that once only on a sofa didn't count and was merely a one-off bit of nonsense, but it didn't do any good. She was just given over to Shattered Dreams of Lasting Fidelity and Betrayal and so on and it was impossible to cheer her up. Poor old Frank. It was only what the Austrians so deliciously call a Sidespring (seitensprung). And it didn't help that while I was delivering my homily, ribald memories of Mrs. Patrick Campbell's historic remark were humming round my head -*

"Oh, the bliss of a double bed after the hurly-burly of the chaise longue!"

A second letter followed on the heels of the first; it was prefaced apologetically:

...I wouldn't like my jokey way of writing to be misconstrued, it could seem very heartless when it was a woman's whole life in tatters...Frank didn't confess ALL at once as I vaguely remembered. It was much, much worse. After the sofa romp he was engulfed in an evangelistic group called the Oxford Movement, started by a Dr. Buchman in Oxford. It spread through England like some nasty virus affecting the most normal and reasonable people. The main tenet was that one should confess all one's sins to all one's friends and get them (the sins not the friends) out of one's system. There were dreadful scenes when people got up and confessed their sins and misdeeds to audiences of perfect strangers. Well, Frank got sucked into this madness and went to Copford where he waited till Birdie, Grandpa and Doshy were all assembled and THEN and THERE confessed to the Sofa Sidespring. It must have been mayhem let loose. I remember now that Frank tried to confess his sins to Phil and me and was greeted with ribald laughter and unsuitable comments. But no wonder Frank was under a cloud when he had his charmed moment with you, so fresh, beautiful and desirable. The poor toad. Little did he guess the traumas he was causing, for you also, so vulnerable as one is at that age.

A third letter carried the story a step further:

...In the end Frank met his Scarlet Woman in America during the war - a prim little spinster handing out tea and buns at the Union Jack Club for visiting English sailors. Before this Frank had an awful time with Doshy trailing round with him but refusing to go out or meet any of his friends and spending a lot of time being miserable in a dressing-gown. Robbie was born during this unhappy time...I don't really know what happened after that, except Doshy was plonked into a Home and Frank moved in with his 'femme fatale'.

What brought Dorothy's plight to a dismal conclusion was Ted's death two months after my last visit. About a year later Birdie had a stroke and lay paralysed and speechless, until she died in 1934. However, before her stroke she begged Abbie, "Look after poor dear Doshy when I'm gone."

When she'd gone and Copford was sold, Abbie, now in her seventies, kept her promise and for several years helped Frank care for the children - and Dorothy. But as war approached there was a new problem, for Frank was in submarines, and could be ordered anywhere; so the family intervened. Abbie was installed in a little cottage at Copford Green, and for a while Dorothy and the children lived with my aunt, Margery, and her family. But at last Dorothy became unmanageable, and a suitable 'home' was found for her (she wasn't exactly 'plonked') and there she lived until she died of cancer, aged sixty-eight. Dick wrote:

> *...poor old Frank went to her funeral and, according*
> *to Margie's ribald report, wept copiously throughout...*

'Ribald?' The word shocked me, it seemed heartless. But it was Dick's way, a buffer against the tragic absurdity of foolish Frank and 'poor dear Doshy,' mired in a swamp of sentiment and relentless religious imperatives. No wonder Frank was fair game for Dr. Buchman, an American cult figure which, for the English in the 1930s, was a phenomenon.

Buchman was a one-time church minister, a clever man who realized the potential value of British reserve. For several years he made a handsome living in England persuading people that public confession of their wrongdoings could relieve them of guilt and, as he remarked adroitly, "change their lives from selfishness and lust to purity and service." Buchman preferred changing lives of the well-to-do and found good pickings amongst wealthy young Oxford graduates. The whole group travelled around England, staying in expensive hotels or as guests in grand country houses. When Buchman was asked by a sceptic why he and his Oxford 'groupers' always stayed in such posh places he replied, "Why shouldn't we...? Isn't God a millionaire?"

Poor Frank, the poor toad, and poor Dorothy. In 1916, after my father, Ben and young cousin Ralph were killed, Dorothy wrote in one of her many letters to Ralph's sister, Muriel:

> *...My dear, whatever do people do these days without*
> *religion, its the only thing these days to keep one up at all.*

Alas, religion didn't keep Dorothy up, not at all, not even when her life was in tatters. Nor did their God do much for Birdie - or Ted, so intelligent and thoughtful yet in thrall to an implacable godhead who was supposed to be forgiving. Dick wrote to me about Ted's death, and described him, with unexpected passion, in another light:

> <u>What</u> *a dull, boring life he had and with all that*
> *potential to be stuck in a small country rectory all his life...*
> *I think he was bored to SOBS by all those Tiny Tots always*
> *underfoot. He really unbent to me and was so kind and easy to*
> *talk to, not at all the OGRE he was made out to be...*
> *He seemed fascinated by my accounts of La Dolce Vita in*
> *Shanghai and Hong Kong. I don't think he had ever met*
> *anyone frivolous before and I was a feather-brained minx*

who was quite different from anyone he'd ever met. I loved
him deeply and was desolated when he died....

I never returned to Lymington, nor did I see Birdie or Frank or Dorothy again. In a way that last visit, and what happened immediately afterwards, seems now to have been the end of my childhood.

When I got back home Peter was away in Scotland, but Mark came the next morning to suggest driving to the Downs for a walk and lunch at a pub. "We'll have some days on our own for a change," he said, and thus began a week of being together, on our own.

The weather was fine and sometimes I made up a picnic lunch, other times we aimed for a pub where Mark knew the beer was good and they made a hearty ploughman's sandwich (bread, cheese and pickles). We talked with ease of many things, and in one of our conversations he spoke about the exhilaration of flying, and how his family was mad about it.

"Isn't it dangerous?"

"No more than driving a car, though the chap my sister's engaged to has made her promise not to fly after they're married. Having our own airfield meant we could fly as soon as we were old enough to handle a light airplane. The only accidents I've had were when I got careless."

One day we talked about the future. Mark said he hoped to work as a doctor in countries where there was much sickness and poverty, and I told him about Willoughby and chiropractic, which he didn't call quackery but was interested, and said he would like to meet him. I told Mark about my scholarship and the finishing school at Wimbledon, and he asked if music was very important to me; I said music mattered a lot, but I wanted to do about six things at once. He laughed and asked, "Like what?" and I said, "Oh, travel, and...and enjoy being *alive!*" I could have added, "and most of all to love and be loved," but didn't, for every day I was happy, and kept thinking, astonished, 'Is this love? Can loving be so simple?'

On our last day we had dinner together. He drove me home and we stood for a while talking idly until, after a little silence, Mark said, "I've got two more years of medical school before I'm an intern. That's when I'll have a salary. I've always had plenty of money, but a salary will be earned - and much better." Then he put his hands on my shoulders and said, "Will you wait for me?"

I felt such a burst of joy that I couldn't speak and just looked at him - it didn't matter, silence was all right with Mark. He kissed my lips, gently, very sweet, different from Frank's kiss, and said, "I won't come in, if you don't mind. I'll see you at Christmas."

A few days later my mother and I were waiting for Edward at a restaurant in London before going to a matinée. The lunch and theatre were my mother's idea, a send-off for me. Edward was late and we waited, consulting the menu, chatting, and at ease together. With the thought of Mark glowing in my mind, I was in a new landscape where my mother, and even Edward, were welcome.

At last Edward arrived, apologized for being late, and as he sat down my mother gave him the menu. But he ignored it, and held up a folded newspaper.

"Have you seen the news about that young fellow - you know, the one you said liked playing around in airplanes? Courting trouble, if you ask me."

I felt my mother stiffen, and into a hole of silence I carefully dropped, "Is he...um...is he all right?"

Edward, suddenly uncomfortable, said, "Well no, 'fraid not. Playing some sort of game, looking for clues, flew too low. Killed outright. Seemed a good lad. Very sorry." There was a silence, then perhaps hoping to save the day, he asked, "So what have you both chosen for lunch? Got any suggestions?"

The rest of the day was a polite blank. I couldn't think about Mark, or feel much except a bleak, fierce desire never to speak to Edward again.

The next few days I kept my mother at arm's length, got ready to leave for Wimbledon, and didn't speak to Edward. I suppose something had to blow up and when it did it wasn't over anything serious. Probably I got in Edward's way for he gave me a slight, impatient push - and I whipped round and bit his finger to the bone.

"Good God, Christina, she's drawn blood!"

I didn't wait to hear more. Upstairs in my bedroom, the door slammed shut, I was face down on a pillow so no-one would hear me as I wept for my Mark, no longer a solid, glowing thought with the promise of Christmas shining bright ahead: instead Mark was simply not there, forever. My mother knocked on my door, but I said I was all right and later slipped out of the house to walk for a long time trying to come to terms with how happiness could fly so close, and then fly away, without ceremony.

❧ 16 ❧

Freedom sounds good,
but it's hard work.

The Wimbledon finishing school was in a typical, turn-of-the-century suburban house, built for the *nouveaux riches,* but with primitive central heating. I was told I could practice on the grand piano in a big room upstairs, sparsely furnished and very sparsely heated. As the weather grew wintry I had to keep padding off to the bathroom to unfreeze my fingers in hot water. Unfortunately more than hot water was needed to unfreeze either the foreign students, or the French principal. The English principal was all right, quite friendly, but Madame was a dragon. Sister Hilary's first letter to the school, though followed by a kind of retraction, seemed to have left Madame ready to pounce and exclaim to her colleague, "Did I not warn you about this girl?"

The foreign students posed a different kind of problem. I was supposed to talk English to them at meals, on expeditions, during morning and afternoon break, and routine social evenings. But I might have been a leper - they just wouldn't engage in conversation. It was ridiculous, and inevitably Madame pounced and called me to account. It was too idiotic to say, "The girls won't talk to me," so I mumbled an excuse and was dismissed with, "You are not here to amuse yourself on the piano all day."

I left Madame, seething with injustice, and ran into my one friend, Gerda. She was an Austrian baroness who stood out amongst the other students for her charm and forthright character. "You mope," she said. "Is that a good word? What is wrong?" I told her. "The silly sheep!" she exclaimed. "Leave them to me." "What d'you mean by 'sheep'?"

"Stupid - *dummkopf.* I will tell you. Margaret, that girl from your school, she said you made trouble, should be given a cold shoulder to put out your nose," and with a shrug added, "Your English language...*sonderbar* - how you say...peculiar?"

Whatever Gerda said to the students I stopped being cold-shouldered and was able to be seen by Madame paying for my keep. This was better, but I kept wondering what I was doing in this stable. No memory stirs of even one lesson with George Woodhouse, or any programme of study. He can't only have wanted to pat my bottom without Miss Griffin fidgeting in the background. But I badly wanted to know whether there was any likelihood of my qualifying for the Royal Academy. If there was, then I'd go to work with a will and take the finishing school in my stride. Conversely, if Woodhouse said I wasn't Academy calibre, but a year's study would lay a sound basis for years of pleasure, that would be worthwhile. But that would still beg the question of how I was to earn a living.

It was depressing to be encumbered with these uncertainties and I looked forward to the weekends when we were free, provided we got permission, to go out with friends. One Saturday I'd been allowed to get up late after a bout of influenza, and as I lay in bed, wishing I was somewhere else, the telephone shrilled on the landing outside my room. It went on ringing so I answered it, and heard Peter saying, "Hullo, that's you isn't it?" and when I said it was he cried, "What a bit of luck! I was afraid it might be the French dragon. It's a ripping day, come and have lunch. I'll pick you up." I told him I was supposed to be convalescing in bed, but he retorted, "Then you need cheering up." I explained I had to ask permission, but he said, "What is this place - a prison? I'll be there within an hour. That'll give you time to have a word with the dragon ladies."

Feeling better already, I dressed and went off to get the requisite permission - preferably from the English principal. But they were both out. I hesitated, then thinking, 'May as well be hung for a sheep as a lamb,' I left a message saying I'd gone to lunch with a friend, and went off with Peter.

The next morning Madame called me into her study and accused me of "planning your sickness very well." I said hotly that this wasn't true, but she cut me short with, "I am not interested in your protests," and curtailed my weekend freedom for a month.

The following Saturday Phil Ruck Keene telephoned; he and Dick were in London for a few days and hoped I was free to lunch with them. I explained why I wasn't free, then was inspired to add, "But you can help. Could you come here before you leave London and put in a good word for me with the principals? I need it."

Two days later I told the English principal that my uncle and aunt were coming to see me and would like to meet with her and Madame. She murmured something courteous and I felt hopeful that this might make things more comfortable all round. Phil and Dick arrived punctually and I took them into the drawing-room after sending word of their arrival. Dick said, "I rootled out my naval officer's wife's hat, isn't it hideous? And *flat-heeled* shoes. Will we do?" I said they were obviously pillars of the navy, and we settled down to exchange news.

After we had waited for more than half an hour, Phil offered to rap authoritatively on the principals' study door, but Dick and I discouraged him. "What a pair of old toads!" Dick said. Phil looked at his watch and said they could wait another half hour. We waited, no word came, and they left.

I caught both principals in their study after supper and asked why my relatives hadn't been received. Madame told me to sit down, so I sat and listened to her elaborate on my sly schemes to wriggle out of the consequences of my behaviour. I sat very stiffly while she carried on, and as my anger grew, so did the vivid impression that my spine was a ramrod of steel, and I would take no more from this odious woman.

When she left off I didn't wait for second thoughts but said firmly, "I don't think we'll ever get on together, Madame. There isn't any point in my staying here. I wish to leave at once."

The English principal murmured something emollient, but Madame said, "Let it be as she wishes."

That night I packed my case, bid Gerda goodbye, and left the next morning.

At home my mother had her hands full with two-year old Felicity scampering around, and I was impatient to get on with my own life. I decided to stick to music a bit longer, and try for a job as an assistant piano teacher at a school. I didn't like schools and knew nothing about teaching, but I could learn to teach, and keep my sights on music. So I made an appointment with Gabbetas and Thring, the best known scholastic agents in London, and set off full of hope.

A few months later I happened to read Evelyn Waugh's *Decline and Fall* and was hugely amused to find Gabbetas and Thring wickedly lampooned as Church and Gargoyle. The glum fellow who interviewed me at Gabbetas and Thring might have been the twin of Waugh's Mr. Levy. I knew just how the luckless Paul Pennyfeather felt when Mr. Levy cut him down to size and after offering him an 'unexpected vacancy,' a frightful school, explained:

> "...Between ourselves Llanabba hasn't a good name in the profession. We class schools into four grades: Leading school, First-rate School, Good School and School. Frankly...school is pretty bad. I think you'll find it a very suitable post."

My interviewer was less expansive than Mr. Levy, but after grinding down my expectations to his satisfaction, he said, "However, I think we have the very thing, Miss Ruck Keene. An unexpected vacancy, you understand...a nice little private school on the east coast, very bracing." He added that the school's owner, Mrs. Ramsbotham, was in London, and he arranged for me to meet with her the next day. When I left he said, as if scripted by Evelyn Waugh, "I think you will find it a very suitable post."

Mrs. Ramsbotham interviewed me on a bench in Victoria Station. She seemed eager to get the interview over and I felt sure that I was her last hope for the unexpected vacancy. She was an implausible bundle exuding respectability in black bombazine. Her eyes were sharp, and her fat little face was crowned by a sort of helmet, black felt, with feathers.

"We have only the best sort of children, you understand," she said.

I murmured, "Of course," and asked how many students I'd have, adding that I wished to work under an experienced teacher.

"Yes, yes," she replied vaguely and went off into something about the 'tone' of the school and how, as junior staff, I must pay proper respect to the senior teachers. I might have been a prospective kitchen-maid, and the wages were comparable. But it was music, and a live-in job. I accepted, and she bustled away, urging the porter to hurry.

The east coast of England in November was bitter rather than bracing, and the school was in a grim row of Victorian houses which opened straight on to a street without a blade of grass or a tree. Inside a kind of cold, grey atmosphere pervaded everything - rooms, staff and children. The latter were drawn from local tradesmen's families and I guessed their parents hoped they would get a 'superior', rather than Board School education. But at least board schools had government grants. Private schools did not, so Mrs. Ramsbotham saved expenses all round, on heat, food, and salaries.

The one decrepit piano was, like the rest of the house, in a minimally heated room and – replaying Wimbledon – I had to keep unfreezing my fingers under the hot tap in the bathroom during my brief practice hours. As for working with a senior music teacher, there wasn't one - hardly surprising, for I had only one pupil.

She was a small child who played the piano with gritted teeth, as if the notes were multiplication digits and getting them in the right order was all that mattered. At our first lesson I praised her accuracy and asked if she liked music.

"Not much, miss."

"Are your parents fond of music?"

"Not much, miss, but me mam says as I should." She seemed resigned. I suggested she should tackle the next piece in her book and she said, with something approaching animation, "Mam will be that pleased," and we parted amicably. I sat alone afterwards wondering what I was doing in this improbable place. But here I was, and it was my choice.

With only one weekly piano lesson to give I was handed plenty of playground stints, supervision of study times, a spelling lesson with the youngest children, and a class in what was called Divinity. Maybe Mrs. Ramsbotham had noted my school certificate credit in Religious Knowledge, but she hedged her bet by presenting me with a pile of small paperbacks, saying "These will help your Divinity lessons, dear. I have always found the little stories most uplifting."

The little stories were sickening, mawkish stuff about pious little girls drawing drunken fathers and cowed mothers together, and at least one deathbed for more uplift. I put the paperbacks away and stuck to the Bible stories.

On a diet of thin stew and watery vegetables, junket and over-stewed plums I was soon possessed by hunger, and a longing for

126

cheerful company. So I cut practice times in the icy room and escaped to buy a cheap cup of hot tea and a sticky bun in one of the warm cafes near the fishermen's wharf. The teachers murmured nervously about Mrs. Ramsbotham and the tone of the school, but I took no notice. The wharf smelt of fish and tar and brine, smells belonging to a real world, rough and lively, and the fishermen were always ready for a joke and a friendly chat.

Inevitably Mrs. Ramsbotham got wind of my harbour expeditions. I was called to her study, a stuffy room crowded with menacing aspidistras, and prim little crocheted mats lay on the backs and arms of all the overstuffed chairs. Without asking me to sit down she said acidly, "I understand you are hobnobbing with rude men in the harbour. That is no place for a self-respecting girl to be, and your behaviour lowers the tone of the school." I pointed out that the fishermen were not at all rude, but she interjected with a sniff and a curt, "You are impertinent, Miss Ruck Keene. These visits must cease at once."

A few days later Mrs. Ramsbotham slipped into my divinity lesson, but after about ten minutes she left, saying, "I will see you in my study after the lesson."

In her study she began brusquely, "Why are you not reading the inspiring little stories I gave you?" I replied that the Bible stories were also inspiring, but this did not go down well. She launched with vigour into giving me a dressing-down until, all of a sudden, I was out of patience with the whole performance. When she'd finished I gave her notice that I would leave immediately, and as I packed my case that night I thought without mercy that Gibbets and Thring would have yet another 'unexpected vacancy' on their books.

As it was clear that schools and I did not agree, and as I had no training in anything, I decided to work in a shop, and not just any old shop, but a really posh one in London.

I started from Piccadilly Circus and walked up Regent Street with an eye to luxury, and after studying the furs in the window of *Reveillon Frères*, I walked in. Rather to my surprise I was taken on straight away to work in the fur salon; the salary was ten shillings a week for a ten-hour day, six days a week, except Wednesday, which was a half-day when shops closed early. I was told to fit myself out with a white collared black dress, black court shoes and black silk stockings. As my mother had passed on her rather slapdash sewing skills, I went to John Lewis and bought some black material and a ready-made white collar. At home I cut and tacked, and sewed up this funereal outfit on the old Singer sewing machine, and reported for work the following Monday.

I caught a train at seven so I could be at the shop by eight-thirty. There were two other women in the salon and at eleven we took turns for a ten-minute break in a small windowless room where we also spent the half-hour allowed for lunch, and a tea-break at four. For the rest of the day I stood in the showroom wearing my new court shoes, and though there were several elegant chairs and a sofa in the salon, they were only for clients.

At the end of that first day I hobbled from the station and fell into a hot bath. My mother said, "Are you sure you want to do this?" and I said grimly that I'd find out.

It took only a month to find out. One afternoon I modelled a sumptuous white mink jacket for a client. She had a friend with her, and after I'd done my bit the friend drawled, "That's a pretty thing," meaning the jacket, not me, "Would you mind, dear, if I order one like it? We live in such different parts of the country."

Dear didn't mind at all: but I did. Something was amiss in a world where a mink jacket, costing far more than I would earn in several years, could be purchased as casually as a loaf of bread. I had no solution to this anomaly, but felt disenchanted with *Reveillon Frères*, and decided to work somewhere else.

A few days later I scrapped my lunch half-hour and belted along to a store I'd recently discovered - Liberty's. It also was a place of luxuries, but they were luxuries on a different level of value, for the shop was full of wondrous things made by craftsmen, not only from England but from all over the world.

I made an appointment with the staff manager and was interviewed the next day. By good luck he'd been an officer in my father's regiment and was moved by my fatherless state. "Gad sir, bad show!" he muttered, called me a plucky little filly, and hired me to work in the costume department.

Before I left he confided, "Between you and me we're always glad to hire a lady - decent accent, y'know, pleases our clientèle. Queen Mary likes to drop in, and of course the little princesses have summer frocks made in our workrooms - Tana Lawn, finest cotton from the Sudan, I expect you know it." When we shook hands he beamed kindly at me and said, "Delighted to have you, you'll feel at home here." Full of glee I sped back to *Reveillon Frères* thinking there was much to be said for being out of Birdie's handkerchief drawer and one of the people who *mattered*.

Liberty's still stands on Marlborough Street, a block behind Regent Street, and when I went to work there in 1933 the building itself had been a London phenomenon for nearly ten years. It was built of brick and Portland stone, timbered in the Elizabethan style with teak and oak salvaged from two great double-decker sailing ships, and the span of one of them - *HMS Impregnable* - exactly matched the length and breadth of Arthur Liberty's store.

The store was a maze of innumerable interconnecting showrooms linked by three open spaces rising up three storeys, giving the impression of inner courtyards in an ancient hostelry. On each floor the open spaces were surrounded by carved oak balustrades; from one floor hung fine carpets and, from another, cascades of Liberty's famous oriental silks, printed in their own workshops at Merton Abbey. To my eyes it wasn't a store, it was the journey's end of an Elizabethan adventurer who'd called on the craft guilds to line his walls with linenfold panelling, lay floors and staircases with gleaming deck timbers, and then enrich it all with carpets and silks and an intoxicating array of printed yardage, weaving and embroidery, ceramics, jade, enamels, and jewellery.

Gradually I learnt the story of Arthur Liberty. He was fifteen when he came to London in 1858 as an apprentice to the wine trade. But all he cared about was the theatre and art. At the Second International Exhibition of 1862, he saw the first public display of work produced by William Morris & Co., and also a ravishing collection of porcelain, silks, fans and other exotica from Japan - the latter had hitherto been virtually unknown in England because of Japan's trade isolation.

That year Liberty left the wine trade and went to work at the elegant Shawl Emporium on Regent Street: two years later, aged twenty-one, he was appointed the manager of a new department featuring work from Japanese craftsmen. Ten years later Liberty opened his own small store on Regent Street.

In 1924 the extraordinary Elizabethan structure called Liberty's was ready for business. Sadly, by then, Arthur Liberty was dead, but his vision remained and prospered. The vision was simple: public taste could be enriched and transformed if people were offered the chance to browse amongst (and buy) beautiful things made by skilled hands.

In 1933 Liberty's still housed around eighty skilled needle-women on the upper floor where they made clothes for adults and children (including the little princesses). There was a special room for embroidery, another for pleating and a third for Paul Perrot, designer and head of the costume department. His clothes were very different from the famous 'Liberty gowns', originally designed for the Victorian Aesthetes - the movement of 'Art for art's sake', championed by Arthur Liberty's friend, Oscar Wilde. In 1933 Liberty gowns were still in stock and advertised as 'Never out of fashion.' This was patently untrue in the cocktail age of little sports cars, jazz and nightclubs. The high-waisted, floor length Liberty gowns had a medieval air, the prints inspired by William Morris, the silk draping gracefully, softened by Liberty's innovative dyes. I wished I'd been employed a few years earlier when each of the senior lady shopwalkers floated around the store in a Liberty gown, their hair bound with one of the famous Liberty silk bandannas.

The interior of Liberty's was eccentric. The interconnecting rooms were divided by massive oak pillars behind which shoplifters concealed themselves. The whole layout was also a source of confusion to customers who were forever asking how to get out. The English, accustomed to eccentricity, were at home with this peculiarity, but it surprised the American visitors who flocked to buy Liberty's cashmere twin sets.

Altogether the clients were much nicer than the fur-coat people, though a few were a little batty, like the lady who would collect a heap of frocks and then get stuck in one, and start to choke, requiring attention and glasses of water. I got stuck with her once and thought she was going to die.

The most delightful person I served was an elderly gentleman who put me in mind of Tenniel's White Knight in *Alice-in-Wonderland*. He had the same disarming air of being game but bewildered. He wanted an evening jacket for his wife, so I asked if he knew her size.

"About your height," he said gravely, "but - well, she's a...um, what you would call a fine figure of a woman." He smiled hopefully. I asked if he'd measured anything of hers and he cried, "Yes, yes, how foolish, I forgot. Here it is!" and from his overcoat pocket drew a large white handkerchief. He held it out between two opposite corners saying, "The bottom of her old jacket is four times this length."

Unless she was a very large lady this measurement was implausible, so I suggested we discreetly consider other customers in the hope of finding a look-alike. He entered the game with a will, and before long cried "That one!" rather too loudly. The lady started, but seeing only a faceless salesgirl and the guileless features of my customer, went on her way.

"Whew!" he murmured, "I feared we were in for a spot of trouble," and blew his nose on the handkerchief. We found a jacket that pleased him, and as I gave him the package I said he could return it if it wasn't right. He didn't, and that pleased me.

I wasn't, however, at all pleased by two customers, a man and woman whom I'd met a few times at the Harmsworth's. I stepped forward smiling cheerfully, but met no answering smile. So I did my job, and as I handed over their purchase gave them a friendly grin. Surely by *now...!* But their expressions only stiffened slightly, eyes like pebbles. I said, "Thank you sir, goodbye madam," and as I watched them depart, made a vow: I would always remember that shop assistants were human beings, not faceless riffraff.

I learnt a lot working the wrong side of the counter, but never dreamt that Arthur Liberty's vision would, forty years on, redirect my life in Canada.

Much as I enjoyed Liberty's the daily train journey and the long store hours took a toll and I was given sick leave. During this time my grandmother Minna came on a rare visit. For the last ten years she had been looking after my aunt Freda, and her daughter, Jacqueline. There was a bit of a mystery about Freda, who married unsuitably and reappeared, with baby and no explanation. From then on Minna cared for them both.

She was obviously tired, and happy to sit and talk with me, and I began to remember how she'd always been there when I was young. "You told such wonderful stories," I said, "and do you still have a bag of sugared almonds ready when things go wrong?" She laughed, and I added, "I've missed you."

"I've missed you too, pet, and you've grown up so fast." Then she asked what I planned to do when I was well. I had no idea, but from this and other conversations my future was, unknown to me, put on a new course. Minna decided I must have a profession, and told my mother she would pay for my training as a shorthand-typist at a college in London, and also pay my board and lodging in a London hostel until I could support myself.

When all was agreed, Minna presented me with her plan, concluding, "I know shorthand and typing doesn't sound very romantic, but you can go anywhere with it, and live your own life."

"My own life!" I exclaimed, and flinging my arms round her neck I thanked her and promised to work hard. That afternoon I sat on the floor beside her while she talked about her years in Heidelberg. I asked, "Weren't you very lonely at that school? You were so little."

She smiled, "Not for too long, pet. The older girls were very kind to me. I remember a country walk when I insisted on jumping over a water-filled ditch. I was told to cross by a little bridge, but I was sure I could jump just as well as the others, so I jumped - and in I fell. Oh dear! Fräulein was very angry but the girls said I was a dear thing and shouldn't be punished."

I said that I seemed to be forever falling in ditches and Minna observed gently, "If you jump across water, you may get wet."

Dear Minna. She was wise and kind, with a gentle sense of humour, and knew when to give and when to withhold. This was our last meeting: she died three years later.

∽ 17 ≈

London!
and new aspects of freedom.

The hostel had white curtained cubicles in the dormitories, depressingly like school. Altogether it was rather a sad place, with lots of girls who drifted through their evenings polishing their nails and washing their hair, fretting about their boring jobs, and longing to escape through love (hopefully) and marriage (definitely). There were two girls I liked, and one remained a long-time friend - but I went out a lot. Peter was in London and I had a giddy time with him and his friends - dinners, theatre, dancing. In contrast the hostel seemed a kind of interim penitentiary that would end as soon as I had a job. That would be the day, when I could rent a room and be independent. I tossed off the disadvantage of never having learnt to cook, but I could make tea and toast and boil an egg, which was a beginning.

As money was tight I walked everywhere, taking a bus or underground only when time or weather insisted. The secretarial college was in the Strand, and most days I'd walk there along the Embankment and enjoy the multifarious river traffic on the Thames and, in fine weather, stop to watch the little boys called mudlarks, ferreting for treasures at low tide. They were cheeky little Cockneys, irrepressible and full of life, straight out of Dickens - or so I thought, forgetting poor Jo, the crossing-sweeper, and the terrible place called Tom All-Alone where the street boys starved and died. No, I couldn't imagine anything like that, not in my wonderful London of 1934.

I started at the secretarial college in early September and the trees in the parks were still green. By October they were carpeting the grass with gold and copper, and in November the blue skies gave way to clouds and rain until fog crept over the city. Then the parks became ghostly places, bare trees emerging out of the fog like black skeletons in a formless world which invented itself with every step. One day the fog was so thick I couldn't see beyond my outstretched hand, and padded three times round Trafalgar Square before I found the exit to the Strand, and was late at the college.

The acrid smell of fog blanked out the other London smells which grew so familiar - I was sure that if I walked blindfolded through London, my nose would signal where I was. At the entrance of underground stations a warm blast of greeting came from below, a smell all its own, combining dust and oil and bodies. Tidy residential districts were fresh and clean, while Soho was redolent of spices and exotic unfamiliar gourmet delights. But in spring came something special - the flower ladies with their baskets of violets and daffodils. They sprouted like gardens along the sidewalks, and settled on the steps surrounding Eros in Piccadilly Circus (just like Eliza in Bernard Shaw's *Pygmalion*). Pearly drops of water lay on the petals, and the ladies chanted, "Buy me pretty vi'lits, la'idy, only sixpence a bunch!" Was it sixpence? or less? "Buy me pretty vi'lits!" The lilt of their Cockney voices was an echo of old street songs.

The flower ladies were just one of the sounds in London's street symphony. At street corners the Cockney newsboys cried out the headlines, the more dramatic and horrid the better; through residential streets the rag-and-bone men often pushed their carts crying, "Any old iron! Any old iron!" and around tea-time the muffin man would appear, ringing his little bell, on his head a tray of fresh-baked crumpets and muffins wrapped in a white cloth. For entertainment on Sundays the costermongers in Petticoat Lane competed in selling their wares with such an indefatigable brilliance of Cockney patter that it took your breath away. There were also other kinds of patter - the percussive pitter-patter of children running, the tip-tap of high heels, and the measured drum thumps of a Bobby making his rounds. All these were clearly defined in a London that was not overwhelmed by crowds and traffic. Later I had a bicycle, and even in Piccadilly Circus could prop it against the sidewalk and leave it there while I shopped, knowing it would be unmolested until I returned.

It seemed a long time ago that I'd walked along Wigmore Street with Miss Griffin and Margaret, had cocked my hideous school hat and smiling at passing strangers thought, "Wait for me, London, I won't be long!" Now, here I was - and still smiling at strangers. One day in an underground train, a gentle old man leant forward and said, "Permit me, young lady, to thank you for your beautiful smile!" Of course I smiled even more - I was seventeen, alone in London, with my life in my hands.

The Secretarial College was no more than a few rooms in an office building where a lady of eccentric character put a dozen girls through the stages of learning to be competent secretaries. We typed to music to overcome hitting the keys in jerky bursts, we plodded through ever-increasing shorthand dictation speeds, learnt to contract common phrases into single shapes, and occasionally received homilies on office behaviour.

The only advice I remember (because it made us laugh) was, "You may place a vase of flowers on the desk of your employer, but do not place yourself on his knees." The implication was plain: one should be ladylike and keep out of trouble, and if you did get in trouble it was very likely your fault. We were not given instruction on self-defence, other than not sitting on your boss's knees, which sounded daft anyway.

As soon as I was settled in London I got in touch with my Garsia uncles. Willoughby and Yedra lived in a pretty little house in Kensington where he was quietly building a solid chiropractic reputation. I had not seen Willoughby since my mother had stormed away from London because of Yedra, but he was still my dear Willoughby, quite unchanged. Yedra was all right, though a bit weird. She was caught up in the current fascination with the psychic phenomena of séances, automatic writing, table turning, and poltergeists. She and Willoughby had both experienced a poltergeist in Spain where they spent several weeks searching, fruitlessly, for the Garsia family castle. Yedra gave a lively description of the poltergeist making objects fly around the room in a most interesting fashion. Willoughby listened quietly, saying in conclusion, "Anything is possible, isn't it, Thelma?" Later he talked about the pleasure of sometimes leaving his body and floating around London. "It's delightful," he said ruminatively, "to be free of my body for a while," and added with that suddenly familiar, deprecating smile, "Luckily it is always there when I come back." I thought how good it would have been to grow up in the same house with Willoughby; I could have talked to him. Too late now. At least I had the benefit of his healing hands, for he gave me occasional adjustments, "to keep you fit," he said.

Marston was quite a different kettle of fish. He was well on the way to being a reasonably successful barrister. His resonant voice and phenomenal memory had served him well in the courts, and when he was young he'd made quite a name for himself by writing an excellent textbook. For years the book had a steady sale to law students; but Marston wrote it when he was struggling to survive between briefs, and when his publisher offered to buy the copyright for twenty pounds he accepted eagerly. "Twenty pounds was a fortune to me just then," Marston said sadly, "but the book was a goldmine for the publisher."

Marston enjoyed being a man-about-town and an inveterate theatre-goer. He'd long abandoned the dream of being an actor, but one never-forgotten season in 1920, he played Fellows (the butler) in John Galsworthy's *The Skin Game* at St. Martin's Theatre in London. When I married he gave me a copy of the play with a handwritten 'Gratefully yours, John Galsworthy' on the flyleaf, and all the performers' signatures. A sheet from the programme is glued inside the cover, showing 'Marston Garsia' third in the list of characters in their order of appearance. He must have been very fond of me to part with that little volume.

The dinners I ate with Marston developed a pattern. He felt I needed instruction on some of the unwritten imperatives of high society, particularly how to behave at dinner parties. So I would be taken out to expensive restaurants by Marston and his great friend, Guy Fossick. Guy was dapper and rich, a dilettante in law, and very much a man-about-town - he said "Doncherknow" just like P.G. Wodehouse's Bertie Wooster.

As soon as we were handed the menu Marston or Guy would pontificate on which wines to drink with what food and throughout the meal one or the other would clarify important matters, such as the proper use of knives and forks, making sure I remembered when a dessert should be eaten with a spoon, or with a spoon and fork, "But never, Thelma, with a fork alone." I must also always *break* (in bite-size pieces) the bread or roll on my sideplate, and never, never *cut* it. When Guy asked, "Which is the right word, 'napkin' or 'serviette'?" they both waited gravely for my reply.

"Napkin," I said firmly, and they nodded, approving.

All this was rather fun, a game, but Marston had an obsession which did make me jittery. He insisted that at dinner parties I must be amusing and never allow the conversation to flag. As I was often shy with older people, this command was burdensome and for a while, if conversation languished, I'd be struck dumb and sit, longing to faint and be carried away beyond social reproach. Mercifully chance released me from this nonsense.

At one dinner party I sat next to an older man (at least thirty) whom I didn't know, and inevitably our conversation lapsed. I was wondering if we would ever speak again when he said idly, "You know, I used to be most awfully shy, stammered, couldn't think of what to say, felt a peasant. I'm sure you've never been so afflicted, but I'll tell you a funny thing. I was sitting next to a young woman I didn't know and we were making heavy weather of our conversation until, quite suddenly, I realized she was as shy as I was. D'you know, I was so surprised and sorry for her I decided to help her out. But the funny thing was, that when she left with the ladies she turned and gave me a radiant smile - and I realized *I'd* quite forgotten to be shy!"

"And she hadn't been shy either," I exclaimed. "Whatever had you done?"

"Well, people love to talk about themselves, so the easiest thing is to ask them anything - if they live in London, are they fond of dogs, that sort of thing, nothing complicated." He added, "You can think of it as a sort of game. Let's try it and you'll see what I mean."

So we tried it and I did see what he meant. Gradually it became second nature to avoid the unforgivable solecism of letting conversation peter out. But it was a long time before I realized that if I made somebody feel they were interesting, they very often were: and anyway, it was just common courtesy.

Clothes were a much harder proposition to handle. A long dress was mandatory for a dinner party, theatre or dancing; country house weekends demanded tweeds, and for my one appearance at the Eton and Harrow cricket match I needed another kind of long dress and a picture hat. There was no escape from the fact that clothes were an etiquette all their own - to wear the wrong clothes was as bad as farting in public. So I walked everywhere and saved money to buy silk stockings, waited for sales at the shops on Shaftsbury Avenue before buying a new dress, and relied on inexpensive hats at *Bourne & Hollingsworth* on Oxford Street (Regent Street or Bond Street were not for me).

Luckily clothes didn't matter when I joined college friends for a cheap meal in Soho - and I mean cheap. A huge dish of pasta cost as little as sixpence, and for no more than a shilling each we shared a Chinese banquet of delicious little dishes and mounds of rice. Nor did clothes matter when we went to hear Shakespeare, high up in the gods at the Old Vic, or stood throughout the promenade concerts in the Queen's Hall.

In a way the easygoing, inexpensive outings with the college students were almost more enjoyable than having to cope with the subtle codes of speech and behaviour amongst my wealthier friends. Yet many of them were interesting and very amusing, and kind, and wealth made their lives somehow spacious. On the whole it was a challenge to be with people whose lives were so different from mine, and sometimes it was a joke - planning, for instance, a way to arrive at the Cecil Harmsworths' London house in suitable style?

Cecil was another of Peter's uncles, a charming courteous man with a kind, hospitable wife. I stayed with them when Peter planned to spin out an evening until the early hours at a nightclub. I liked the Cecil Harmsworths, enjoyed their kindness and, no less, the comforts of their house. It was one of those stately 19th century houses with a butler and an impressive double front door, brass handles and bell-pull gleaming like gold, the sort of house visitors arrived at by car or taxi. I could easily walk from the underground station at Hyde Park, but I couldn't bring myself to trail up to that double front door carrying my overnight suitcase. The butler was a friendly man and would not have made me feel small - but I couldn't do it. Equally, I couldn't afford a long taxi journey. So I took the underground, walked to within a block or two of the house, hailed a taxi, and paid an affordable fare of sixpence. This way I was sure the butler would hear the taxi grinding away when he opened the door with a welcoming, "Good afternoon, Miss. Her ladyship is expecting you." My case would be handed to another minion and I would glide off to greet Lady Harmsworth as if to the manner born.

But I wasn't born into opulence. The old Copford Rectory, for all its beautiful things, had never been opulent, nor was Minna's 'Woodford' in Clarence Park, Weston-super-Mare. But opulence was beguiling. At the Cecil Harmsworths' it was a treat to wake as the fire was lit in my bedroom, and then drink early morning tea in bed, cosy under a silk eiderdown, propped against a pile of soft pillows.

Opulence. Suddenly I see my mother and I exploring the shops on the first class deck of the ship taking us to New York. We are walking on soft carpets in an aroma of cigars and perfume, and my mother cries, "How opulent!" and "Wouldn't it be lovely to be rich!" Well yes – and beyond cigars and perfume is ease and the world wide open for being alive-alive-oh! On the other hand the Old Vic and Soho are no less beguiling.

So I wasn't envious of opulence, and lay in bed, looking forward to a delicious breakfast of porridge and cream and the choice of eggs and bacon, or scrambled eggs, or sausages, or whatever was on offer, each in a separate silver dish kept hot by little spirit lamps. 'This is the life!' I thought, and saw no reason to jettison any experience, or miss out on whatever came my way.

An altogether new experience came about through another Harmsworth, Peter's cousin Eric, who took me to a literary party in the city one foggy December night. Eric was older than Peter, and unlike him was interested in music and literature and art. It amused him to introduce me to his world which included a very grand party where I was taken in to dinner by the exiled King of Greece (I was mightily pleased to dine with a king). On another evening we went to a musical soirée at Mrs. Washington Singer's, an American lady who really was the hostess with the mostest. We sat on little gilt chairs subduing a dreadful desire to giggle while a majestic Personage sang rather badly. At a more serious musical party I met Walter Legge. He was the first Jew I'd met, and I liked his un-English warmth, as well as being awed by his knowledge and passion for music. He talked a lot about working with someone called John Christie on a new kind of opera house at a place called Glyndebourne in Sussex, unaware that it would become a world-wide mecca for opera-goers, not only for its beautiful setting but for a new approach to the presentation of opera. When he discovered I'd never been to an opera, he took me to hear Wagner's *Tristan*. During the great love duets he breathed heavily at me and I, unsure how to respond, was overwhelmed, not by rapture, but embarrassment. We met occasionally, my last contact a brief letter of bitterness and horror about what was happening to the Jews in Germany. Later he married Elizabeth Schwarzkopf, and through EMI did great things for the recording of fine music.

Eric's literary party promised to be a new kind of experience. After we arrived he went off, saying "Stay there, I'll get us some wine." and with a grin added, "See if you can pick out the celebrities." Feeling conspicuously uncelebrated, I was trying to decide whether the slender lady with a long cigarette holder was Virginia Woolf or Rosamund Lehmann, when a young man introduced himself (John Grey Murray - didn't mean anything to me) and told me who the slender lady was. He seemed to know everyone, so I asked if he also was a writer. He chuckled as if such a thing was a great joke and said, "Nothing so grand. I just print the books they write!" He followed this with a sort of 'Ho, ho!' as if he was gently mocking himself, and life. He was tallish, loose-limbed, blonde hair slightly longer than common fashion, a broad brow and mobile face, part clown, part poet, not routinely handsome.

Eric returned with wine and seemed to know my companion, whom he called Jock. When John/Jock left us, saying he had to talk to some people and would be back, I asked Eric, "Who is he? and why did you call him Jock? He told me he was John."

"Most people call him Jock," Eric said, "but he's going to be the next John Murray." When I looked blank, he explained that John Murray's was the oldest private publishing house in England. At this point we were joined by a couple of Eric's friends and for a while I was absorbed in trying not to be shy in the company of people who seemed either to be writers or know writers personally. In time John did come back, and asked if he might take me home; Eric was agreeable, so John and I left the party together.

We came out into a very foggy night and John at once exclaimed, "We'll go by way of the Temple. You have to see the Temple in a fog."

Marston had introduced me to these Inns of Court - Lincoln's Inn, Gray's Inn, the Middle and Inner Temple - founded for the study and practice of law some 800 years ago. That night in 1933 the courtyards were temples of quietness. Pools of light glowed round the base of gas lamps, and the treetops were lost in fog. John tucked my hand in the crook of his arm and we wandered around, stopping here and there to trace the names of great men, long dead, the names written in gold on wooden boards at the bottom of stairwells. From time to time we stood still, fogbound, not a sound to be heard: we might have been the only people in the world.

Alas, one cannot stand forever in a gaslit fog. But that night I knew what it was to be delicately poised at the centre of the universe.

Not long after our first meeting I received a note written in a small, distinctive and unfamiliar script, firm, legible, and delightful to look at. It was an invitation to dine at the Berkeley, and signed 'John.'

I liked the Berkeley, which was a favourite with Peter and his friends. I felt at ease there, and after we'd settled our menu I asked, "Which name shall I call you - John or Jock?"

"Well," he said, "I could answer to Hi! or any loud cry."

I was up on Lewis Carroll and *The Hunting of the Snark,* so the quote rolled easy off my tongue, "Such as 'Fry me!' or 'Fritter my wig!'" and we went on together:

"Or 'What-you-may-call-um' or 'What-was-his name!'

But especially 'Thing-um-a-jig!'"

Carried away by these word flights I suggested, "Or why not Jonah?"

"Ah yes," said John, "the great deep of the whale. Warm, and rather smelly."

He sounded oddly sad, and I said, "But I will call you John."

He smiled and said, "Shall we dance?"

After that evening with John I continued to dine and dance with Peter and Eric and their friends, but what I was waiting for was another note in John's neat, unmistakable hand, inviting me to dine.

We invariably went to small restaurants where a few musicians played you-are-my-heart's-delight music, not too loudly, just enough so you could talk quietly while dancing. We would choose our meal, drink an aperitif, perhaps eat an *hors d'oeuvre*, then "Shall we dance?" from John, and I'd try to steady the thumping of my heart as he put his hand on my waist, try not to melt away altogether when his cheek rested lightly against mine.

The evening usually ended at 50 Albemarle Street where, John told me, Murray's had been publishing books for 150 years. He lived somewhere in an upstairs attic, but there would be a good fire blazing in the beautiful main room, curtains drawn across tall windows, the firelight flickering on portraits of famous dead authors, and glinting on a glass case filled with a jumble of precious literary memorabilia. John sat on a leather chair by the fire, told stories and made me laugh. I sat on the floor and was utterly happy. We never kissed, never hugged, just were there, together.

This happiness was very different from the brief joy of being with Mark and thinking, 'Can loving be so simple?' With John happiness verged on a kind of anguish. He had a way of whisking off into some otherwhere place where words played games which sometimes I followed, but sometimes couldn't. I seemed to be heading somewhere I longed to fall headlong into, yet at the same time wanting to cry 'Please wait! Please wait!' though what for I couldn't say.

'What about John?' I sometimes asked myself, and one day the question was compounded when he sent me a copy of Andrew Marvell's poem, *The Definition of Love*. It began:

> My Love is of a birth as rare
> As 'tis its object strange and high:
> It was begotten by despair
> Upon Impossibility....

The last verse ran:

> Therefore the Love which us doth bind,
> But Fate so enviously debars,
> Is the conjunction of the Mind,
> And Opposition of the Stars.

I read the poem many times, uncertain what to make of its hopelessness, and pondered a verse about Love's oblique lines meeting at every angle, which ended:

> But ours so truly *Parallel*,
> Though infinite can never meet.

I lay in bed perplexed that love seemed to be as much pain as pleasure. It was a conundrum. Finally, not getting anywhere, I decided it was futile to feel forlorn. The future must take care of itself, while I took care of that part of my future which was not dependent on anyone but me. The college course had a couple of months to run, but already I'd reached proficiency speeds. It was time to look for a job.

✑ 18 ✒

The Foreign Office, a room of my own, and soul muddle.

Somebody in the secretarial college casually said that a job at the Foreign Office was the best ever. The Foreign Office! There was a promising ring to the words. I asked what the Foreign Office did.

"Foreign affairs, of course - embassies, that sort of thing."

"Sounds interesting."

"Well, don't think you can just march in and ask for an interview. You have to write an application with references from top people like bishops or members of parliament, and that's only the beginning. There's a long waiting list of debutantes with the right connections, and even if you do get interviewed you might wait a year before there's a job opening."

This seemed a tedious procedure which needed speeding up. A day or two later I set off down the long street from Trafalgar Square to the Cenotaph, checking every brass plate on every splendid building, but not one said FOREIGN OFFICE. Then halfway down the street I caught up with a man carrying under his arm a neat, official-looking red box, and when I asked for directions he replied cheerfully, "You come along o' me, Miss. I'll take you right there. No, not out o' me way, I'm going next door."

'Next door' turned out to be Number 10 Downing Street and my companion was a King's Messenger taking papers to the Prime Minister. But he carried on past Number 10 saying "Just a step more to the F.O." and a moment later we stopped outside a daunting building fronted by a marble pillared portico and a broad flight of marble steps. "There you go, Miss," he said, "and the best o' British luck." I faltered, but the King's Messenger grinned confidently, so I kept going.

The doorman treated my request for work with a barely detectable raising of the eyebrows, and said kindly, "Fill in this application form, Miss, and maybe the lady who employs the secretarial staff will spare a few minutes to see you."

I waited in the huge stone-flagged entrance hall feeling small and willing the lady to spare me a minute - and she did. We went together to a small room where, after a few questions, she asked why I wanted to work in the Foreign Office. This took me by surprise and having no impressive answer ready, said truthfully, "I don't know anything about foreign affairs, so I thought it would be a good place to learn." The corners of her mouth gave a little twitch and I thought, 'How absolutely awful, she's going to laugh!' But instead she proposed giving me a test straight away.

Two weeks later I was at work in the shorthand-typing pool at the Foreign Office. From this experience I learnt not to bother with formalities, unless unavoidable.

The Foreign Office required a minimum shorthand speed of 120 words a minute, and that was my maximum. It was all very fine saying I wanted to learn about foreign affairs, but this off-the-cuff answer hid my profound ignorance of countries and people beyond my own life. In the first months at the Foreign Office I often had no idea what the dictation was about. The girls in the shorthand-typing pool were sent to whatever department needed us, so one day I'd struggle with Egyptian politics and the spelling of Egyptian names, the next day it could be Africa or Japan, France or Germany or some outlandish place I had to look up on a map. But somehow I got by and began to enjoy myself, and sometimes, as I checked the finished typescripts, a turn of phrase would jump off the page for its wit or humour. Most memorable was the concluding sentence of a report on discussions with a visiting dignitary who was generally mistrusted:

...I accompanied the minister to the lift, and as it sank to the depths below I seemed to detect a faint whiff of sulphur.

Occasionally the routine days were enlivened by staying late to take dictation from a youthful under-secretary who wanted to practise dictating a report after his half-dozen colleagues had left.

Evelyn Shuckburgh was such a one (Mr. Shuckburgh then, Sir Evelyn in later years). It was a lovely evening in early April, and the big windows gave a view of St. James' Park bathed in gentle sunshine. Young Mr. Shuckburgh was not much older than me and was what my aunt Dick would call 'a dish'. He was nervous, so I sat quietly while he unravelled his thoughts; after a while a very small mouse tippetted across the parquet floor to nibble a few biscuit crumbs close to us. I was amused that young Mr. Shuckburgh was oblivious to the mouse.

After a month or two I was assigned to work in the morning for the Foreign Office librarian, Sir Stephen Gaselee. He was reputedly one of the most brilliant scholars in Europe, and was rumoured to have been the lover of Queen Marie of Romania. But however inflamed his past I soon learnt he was a happy family man, whose wife knitted the scarlet socks he regularly wore with his formal dark trousers, frock coat and stiff collar. He also daily came to work carrying a large canvas shopping bag - for sandwiches? I never asked.

He was a tall man with a great presence and a grave courtesy. Every morning he rose to his feet when I came in, stood as I walked with pen and notebook across the expanse of carpet, and remained standing until I was seated by his desk. One morning I wore a rather odd dress which I'd made myself of dark brown velveteen with a small ruff of green tartan silk. As usual Sir Stephen waited until I sat down and then, with a slight inclination of his head, remarked, "Permit me, Miss Ruck Keene, to say that your dress becomes you very well."

I probably sparkled a bit after this well-turned compliment, for when our session ended and I was preparing to leave, he went over to a cupboard, took out a bottle of wine and said, "This was presented to me yesterday by that Balkan gentleman. Let's give it a try. You look festive today."

We sat on either side of the open fire as he poured the wine into two coffee mugs. We raised them in a toast, I sipped cautiously - and as I gasped to catch my breath saw Sir Stephen spit his mouthful slap into the open fire, followed by the rest of his wine, which exploded with a roar up the chimney.

"Good God," he exclaimed, chuckling, delighted, "Could this be a plot!"

I greatly enjoyed these interesting lessons on foreign affairs.

With my first salary cheque in hand I gave notice to the hostel and rented a room in a faded Victorian row-house in Chelsea. It was charming, though decrepit, minimally furnished and lit by one bare gas jet. But it was mine, my certificate of independence, and by walking to work most days I could just afford the rent.

Chelsea was the next-best thing to living in romantic Parisian Montmartre. In 1934 it was the haunt of artists and writers who had very little money, cared not a jot for clothes, and talked their heads off about whatever interested them. It was fun to go for a drink at the pub called *The Six Bells* and see people with familiar names. One evening I met Dylan Thomas because a friend of his, James, lived in the room above mine. Dylan was drunk and I felt shy and never saw him again. Not long after this meeting James had an attack of delirium tremens and when he was recovering I took him some food, and sat on the side of his bed while he described how Dylan had saved him from going crazy because of the mice.

"Really! I don't have any mice."

"Probably they all come here, marching to and fro, to and fro. In platoons. Tramp, tramp. It was terrible."

"What did Dylan do?"

"Great man, Dylan, no-one like him. Inspired. You see, he had similar trouble, but not mice, it was General Booth."

"Good heavens, the Salvation Army man?"

"Good Heavens - that was the trouble. Saving souls for God, all that. The General didn't say a word, mind you, just peered through the window and wouldn't go away. Very obstinate man, the General."

"How frightful. And Dylan...?"

"Scotched him good and proper. I'll tell you how, but keep it a secret. He got one of those little clockwork tanks with guns, you know the kind of thing? So, whenever that damned General began peering, Dylan set the tank on the floor, guns firing, and - poof! poof! - General gone!"

"Did it work with mice?"

"Like clockwork! No trouble, poor little buggers couldn't run fast enough, tumbling over themselves."

Poor James. A year or two later I heard that he died in hospital of cirrhosis of the liver.

I was happy in Chelsea, occasionally rather hungry but could rely on two or three good dinners a week with my agreeable wealthy young friends. These helped to spin out my spare homemade meals, mostly a boiled egg and bread-and-butter or baked beans heated on a shared gas ring on the landing. For lunch on warm days I'd buy a bag of fruit from a street vendor and eat the lot, sitting on a bench in St. James' Park, watching the ducks.

There was piquancy in the contrasts of this time in London. In Chelsea I felt carefree, poor and bohemian. Then I'd dress up for an evening of high life - a delicious (free) dinner, or an early supper before floating into the stalls or dress circle at the theatre. Often the dinners were at the Berkeley Hotel where I first dined with John. It was at the Berkeley that Peter Harmsworth threw a birthday party for me, memorable because he paid the bill from a wad of pound notes. I looked away, embarrassed - I could live for weeks on that largesse. That party seemed a long time ago. I still dined out with Peter and other agreeable young men, pleasant, inconsequential evenings in between hoping for a note from John.

Then one day I received a different kind of note - a formal card, inviting me to a party at the 'printing house' in Albemarle Street. On the back was hand-written, 'Come early!' This was a wonderful note, for it was the first time John had asked me to meet people in his own world.

The party was in the room so familiar from our evenings together. I felt a little shy to be just one of many guests, none of whom I was likely to know. I hesitated in the doorway, saw John standing by the fire chatting to a stranger, and was about to join him when the stranger looked up and stared - and as if propelled by an invisible hand, I turned smartly and walked to the other end of the room. Here I attached myself like a limpet to a group of people I'd never met before.

A few minutes later a voice behind me asked, "Can I persuade you to have one of these?" It was the stranger. He held out a plate of canapés and said, "These are especially good. And may I introduce myself? Arthur Lyons."

His expression was approving and his smile cheerful, but I stared at him tongue-tied while a voice in my head said very clearly, half mocking, half resigned, 'Oh well, too late now!' That's all. Not another word. I pulled myself together and took a canapé.

The rest of that evening is a blank, except for meeting George Bernard Shaw. This was very exciting but, being young and shy, the pleasure was mixed with the horror of what to say. I was eighteen, overawed in this roomful of intellectuals who had so much to talk about. But Bernard Shaw was not like those unbearable people who, having been introduced to you, look around for someone more socially rewarding. G.B.S. behaved as though I was the most interesting person in the room. If he uttered a Shavian quip or unique epigram, they did not register. Instead I remember the kindliness of his blue eyes, the ease of our exchange and how afterwards I marvelled that someone so famous, and so very tall, would take the trouble to make me feel important.

In the months following the party Arthur Lyons asked me to dine and, in a gentlemanly, unobtrusive way, began to court me. The dictionary definitions of 'to court' include 'to pay courteous attention,' and 'to woo (with a view to marriage)...' There is no crude implication of getting someone between the sheets in short order. John, flitting in and out of my life, wasn't exactly wooing with a view to marriage, and as other young men were paying courteous attention to me, Arthur was just one of them. He was merry and well-read, had travelled in Europe and America and knew lots of interesting people. I enjoyed his company, and meanwhile continued to be in love with being in love with John.

Arthur and John had been friends since they were at Eton, and the three of us occasionally spent a weekend together. In the spring of 1935 we drove across the country for a weekend at Port Meirion in Wales. In later years Port Meirion became famous and lost some of its early flavour, but at this time, though it hadn't long been opened, knowledge of it was passed around the world of artists and writers and travellers as a place worth going to.

The hotel, originally a charming Edwardian country house, stood at the head of a peninsula overlooking an estuary. Port Meirion was an estate which had been bought by a Welsh architect, Clough Williams-Ellis. To the hotel he added some whitewashed, red-roofed cottages for private rent, and in a flight of Italianate fancy added a campanile with an antique statue of St. Peter holding his Keys and Book. The Book was soon dubbed 'Jim's Black Book' for Jim Murphy, the Irish hotel manager, was known to keep a record of guests he found boring, and unless business was slow these unfortunates rarely found it possible to book a room.

In the spring the peninsula was covered with wild rhododendrons in full flower, and the hotel felt like a well-appointed country house in which everyone was a privileged guest. Before dinner Jim routinely gathered all the guests for cocktails and conversation, and on the first evening John and Arthur kept pointing out and introducing me to notable people. At bedtime, overwhelmed by all this excitement, I was thankful to go to my room and be alone.

I put on a pink satin nightdress I'd recently made, got into the comfortable bed, and was drifting off to sleep when there was a quiet knock on my door. Before I had time to answer, John came in. He wore a dressing-gown and pyjamas and, after closing the door, walked in silence to my bed.

Once, at the Cecil Harmsworths', I was fast asleep when the light snapped on and I woke to see a strange young man who exclaimed, "Good God! I'm s-so sorry!" and vanished. At Port Meirion John did not vanish; nor did either of us speak.

I watched his approach, thinking illogically, 'Arthur is in the next room,' followed by the wish that this silent, unfamiliar John would go away. Instead, and without a word, he tried to remove my nightdress.

As it happened this nightdress was one of my least expert creations, and being a little tight round the bosom, it resisted John's efforts. Under less startling circumstances I might well have given John every assistance. But I was frightened. Once stripped naked, what would come next? And if I co-operated would I be making myself cheap? Would John then think I was 'that sort of woman?' Miserable and inarticulate, I lay inert as a corpse. The unequal tussle with my pink satin nightdress was brief and John, defeated, left me. Neither of us had spoken one word.

I spent a desolate night.

But resolution returned in the morning. I got up early and found John alone in the small, sunlit breakfast room. He tried a greeting, but I was too nervous to think of anything except the question I had to ask. Alas, my purpose received no warning from that not-so-distant summer when Frank had kissed me.

Point blank I asked John, "Do you want to marry me?"

I had only to see the look on his face to know full well that this was not a good question to ask anyone, especially John. We stared unhappily at each other - and then Arthur blew in and demanded cheerfully, "A lovely morning. What shall we do today?"

When we left Port Meirion, Jim Murphy said kindly to me, "Thank you for looking the way you do." I was touched but could have wept; what did my looks matter when I had lost John forever?

A month or two after our visit to Port Meirion, Arthur took me to Paris, where he confined his courting to a chaste goodnight kiss. I was excited to see Paris and, grateful to Arthur for such a treat, and could have enjoyed everything had it not been that I was in this wonderful place with the wrong person. In the middle of the Champs Elysées I burst into tears.

"What's wrong, my darling?" Arthur asked, and offered me his spotless handkerchief.

Incoherently I mumbled through the handkerchief, "Paris is so beautiful," and blew my nose.

British reserve forbade my saying honestly, "I wish you were John," or trying to unravel the difference between loving someone as a friend and being 'in' love; but British reserve was not the only barricade. My wits had been addled on the subject of love by the bewildering but insidious convent implications that men and sin were closely connected, and by my mother's inexplicit "Don't make yourself cheap, Thelma." The key word (though unspoken) was virginity. Yet men were apparently eager to break down this valuable asset, rendering the non-virgin cheap, with ruined chances of eternal love and permanent wedlock. In addition, Elizabeth saying "The Ruck Keenes have never had a divorce" had left no doubt that marriage was a permanence. Anyway, a divorced woman was held to be 'fast', significantly referred to as a 'divorcée' - and often was not invited to dinner. Added to this was what giggling girls called 'petting' and 'necking' and the importance of not going 'too far'. The first two made you cheap, the second could end in an illegitimate baby.

It wasn't surprising that John's silent visit put my knickers in a twist. We could have laughed about it, but didn't, not even through our long years of friendship. The absence of a good laugh can cause a pack of trouble.

Not long after our trip to Paris, Arthur asked me to be his wife. At the same time he gave me a pair of exquisite diamond and sapphire earrings. I stared at them, rather wildly suspecting a taint of purchase, and wanting to refuse both marriage and earrings; but this seemed churlish when Arthur said, "I just wanted to see you wearing the earrings, whether you marry me or not."

Rather desperately I asked Arthur for time to reflect. I knew John would never marry me, not because of what happened at Port Meirion, but because I wasn't the right person for him. This was not brilliant self-knowledge, I just knew.

I also knew that I enjoyed Arthur's company - he was kind, amusing and interesting. But how did I feel about him? For a start he was quite old - thirty-two, and though John was thirty, Arthur seemed much older. He gave me a studio photograph of himself, and I put it on the mantelpiece of my Chelsea room. He gazed from the photograph with a lively expression on his pleasant face, a good-looking young man, poised and well-groomed. In truth he seemed rather out of place in raffish Chelsea, though I soon discovered that many of his friends were oddballs, and he was a bit of an oddball himself. Instead of going to university or choosing a gentry profession (army, navy, or church), he joined up with a maverick member of the Lyons Corner House dynasty (no relative) who'd started his own business making meat pies. The firm was called Ticky Snacks because the pies sold for threepence each, and 'ticky' is Cockney for threepence; also 'ticky-nap' was a game with a stake of threepence. Ticky snack, ticky nap - Arthur found it a great joke and was amused by his oddball choice of profession.

It did not occur to me that I might be an oddball choice for a wife. I was twelve years younger, gentry but not a true-blue product of the 'finishing' school, the presentation at court, and the débutante balls - the stuff of 'people who mattered'.

There was nothing oddball about his parents, who were true Victorians and lived in one of the lovely houses overlooking Regents Park. His father, Sir Henry, was rubicund and dignified, and enjoyed his little jokes and gentlemanly courtesies. Arthur said his father was knighted for service with Kitchener in Khartoum (ages ago, around 1900), and that he was a member of the Athenaeum.

"What's that?"

Patiently he explained that there were Athenaeum Clubs in other countries but the London one was the most famous in the world. I was impressed, but liked Sir Henry best for his little jokes and the contented life he passed amongst his books.

Arthur's mother was from an old gentry family, a petite person, charming and solicitous. Arthur was the apple of her eye, and though she made me welcome, I suspected she found me wanting as a possible daughter-in-law.

Arthur and I were married in Chelsea Old Church a few days before Christmas of 1935. My mother, who at forty-one had recently given birth to a third daughter, Joy, took little part in the arrangements. The weeks before the wedding passed in a rather mindless whirl of preparations, including being photographed for *The Tatler*. I looked very stiff in the small picture that appeared in print, but the photographer sent me another which he'd taken without my knowledge. I'm wearing the dress that prompted Sir Stephen Gaselee's charming compliment, and sit relaxed in a high-backed chair. My head is half-turned against the chair-back, giving no clue to what I might be thinking.

Lovely Chelsea Old Church was decorated with holly and poinsettias. My sister Felicity, aged four, was the one bridesmaid, Arthur's sister Marjorie, and my cousin Elizabeth were maids of honour, all of them dressed in red velvet to match the holly berries and poinsettias. My white veil was held in place by a diamond tiara, given by my mother-in-law; Phil Ruck Keene, resplendent in gold braid, gave me away; and John was best man.

Musicians played at our reception, and all the guests enjoyed themselves greatly. So, in a manner of speaking, did I, except for not feeling quite myself. In fact a few hours earlier I'd come very close to not being at the wedding at all.

I stayed with Arthur's parents for two nights before the wedding, and they had already left for the church when Phil arrived. He came bounding up to my room, exclaimed, "There's my beautiful niece!" and after formally giving me his arm, we set off down the curving staircase together. But halfway down I stopped short.

"Phil, wait a moment!"

"Forgotten something?"

"No. Not exactly. It's just...oh Phil! I don't want to marry Arthur."

Years later Phil confessed he simply didn't think I was serious. "I'd have taken you away at once," he said, and so he would, adding one more story to the family saga. Instead he smiled broadly, said not to worry, just nerves, happens to everyone, and concluded, "Everything'll be all right. Arthur's a decent chap, and good stock."

I loved my uncle, who was the next best thing to a father. So we went on down the stairs together. I was nineteen, and amongst a morass of other mixed emotions was in a panic. Not for a moment did it occur to me that Arthur, in some unacknowledged recess of his psyche, might also be subduing panic.

⤜ 19 ⤛

Marriage.

Our honeymoon began sumptuously with a night at the Ritz, then to Obergürgl, a little-known village high in the Austrian Alps which could only be reached by sleigh. Everything was set for romance - except us.

Except us - but, as the voice in my head had remarked crisply, 'Oh well, too late now.' So we carried on according to the accepted script, I ignorant as a babe in arms about what to expect in the marriage bed, never having seen a naked man, especially one ready for action. I blindly trusted that Arthur, aged thirty-two, knew what to do. This presumption, I discovered, was at fault. On the first night Arthur lay on top of me, without preliminaries, moved a little and then, with a sigh, rolled away. He said nothing and I, shy and confused, lay hoping for a clue. None came. The same bewildering, non-event was silently repeated at Obergürgl. Then one night, side-by-side and silent, I was moved to put out my hand to touch Arthur's hip - but hesitated. Might so bold an initiative be cheap or embarrassing and make whatever was wrong, worse? For a moment it was touch and go - or no touch, and no go. Arthur lay unmoving and, with a sort of hopelessness, I withdrew my hand.

Only once, after yet another no-go night, Arthur muttered, more to himself than me, "I always thought you might be difficult." I should have banged him on the chest and cried, "What do you mean?" But I was shrivelled by the implication that whatever was wrong was my fault, and rather desperately I felt that the least I could do was not ruin the honeymoon entirely by being miserable. So, as Arthur was always an amusing companion, and by now I was quite good at keeping

148

the ball of conversation rolling, we chattered away and ate excellent meals after hard days of skiing. Arthur was expert and I'd never skied before, but I strapped the sealskin strips on my skis, plodded up to the tops of mountains and (mostly) traversed cautiously down. The mountains were beautiful and quiet, and at the end of the day I fell swiftly asleep.

While I was writing this part of my story, my aunt Dick sent me a postcard she had found amongst my uncle's papers. It was written to Phil from Obergürgl and began, "We are so glad you enjoyed the wedding - so did we!..." and it goes on about everything being wonderful. I read it, amazed at the flow of my duplicity; on the other hand a postcard was not the place to shriek, "I am married, but still a virgin, and understand nothing!"

Back in England Arthur took me to a doctor who pronounced blandly that I needed 'expansion'. To this end I was installed in a clinic where glass tubes were pushed into my vagina. It was degrading and painful, and as the tubes grew larger I begged, without avail, "Please not again! please!" Once, after asking if such a punishing procedure was necessary, I was told, "It will make all the difference, dear."

The promised difference enabled us, technically, to live as man and wife, except I failed to become pregnant and was occasionally not very well. We did not talk about having a family, but Arthur sent me to a surgeon who said my womb needed turning. In 1937, wombs facing the wrong way tended to be righted by a surgeon's knife, and after the operation our doctor told Arthur I should convalesce for a few weeks in the South of France. Doctors of the well-to-do often gave this advice, which made them popular with their patients. So Arthur saw me off at Victoria Station, and away I went with a ticket for Nice and a room booked at the *Hôtel Negresco*.

After waving goodbye I sank onto my seat, suddenly relieved to be alone, and not humping around a load of blame. By now I was sure Arthur deemed me 'frigid' - a vague term for a sexually unresponsive women. But if she was keen on sex she tended to be dubbed a nymphomaniac. The categories seemed waspish, and missed the point of 'Why?'

The *Negresco*, a famous old Edwardian hotel fronting the *Boulevard des Anglais,* was gracious and comfortable, but the wealthy, sophisticated guests living their expensive, pleasure-filled lives didn't interest me. What I wanted was everyday France. So I moved to a room above a pastry-cook where I at once fell ill. For twenty-four hours I lay feverishly oppressed by monster scarlet roses, big as cabbages, which bore down on me from the wallpaper. Starvation scotched the fever and, needing food and sunshine, I bought something from the pastry cook and ate it voraciously, sitting on a park bench and chatting to a friendly American couple. They were sympathetic and advised cheerily,

"What you need is mountain air. Take the bus to St. Paul, you'll just love it."

That afternoon the bus set me down in the little walled village of St. Paul-de-Vence, and I took a room in the hotel on the square. The view from my bedroom window stretched away to the Mediterranean, and below my window was an orchard of peach trees, each russet brown tree trunk encircled by a painted band of turquoise. Next morning I woke late, and sensing sunshine got up, threw back the shutters - and cried aloud, "Oh, thank you!" Sunshine poured from a clear blue sky and the orchard had blossomed, peach pink above russet and turquoise.

As the easy days passed I became familiar with the village. It dated from the middle ages and was surrounded by ramparts. Some of the cobbled streets were so narrow that if you stood in the middle with outstretched arms you could almost touch the walls on either side. In the square outside my hotel there was a little fountain where, on weekdays, women gathered to wash their clothes and gossip. On Sundays the men took over the square, and played *boule* with their hats on. Just off the square was the other, more expensive hotel, the *Colombe d'Or*. It was a beautiful old building, but the dining-room was astounding, the walls being covered by paintings signed with names like Dérain, Bracque, and Léger, many with a message of thanks and friendship. I asked a waiter about them, and with a smile he explained that when the artists were young and unknown they came to paint at St. Paul. "But they had no money, so our *patron* gave them board and lodging. A good man," he concluded, "and still our *patron*."

Apart from the *Colombe d'Or*, lodgings were cheap and St. Paul attracted all kinds of people. There were two Russian refugees (husband and wife) who earned a few francs doing what they called '*hautes giguettes sur les ramparts*' - lots of galloping to and fro on horseback, picking up a handkerchief with their teeth, that sort of thing. I can't vouch for *giguettes* (from *gigue*?): their French was phonetic and verb tenses were ignored in favour of the infinitive - *je dormir, vous dormir, ils dormir*. It was a restful system. The husband had fought with the White Russians under General Wrangel against the Bolsheviks, and had slipped away to join his wife as the hopeless resistance crumbled. Together they reached the South of France and holed up in an abandoned shed outside Nice. They were found by a woman who owned several houses in St. Paul, and in one of them the two refugees were installed. From that time on they camped happily on the ground floor amongst their few belongings, not bothering to use the bedroom upstairs.

In another house lived an Englishwoman, a dancer, whose Spanish lover (a *woman!*) was reputed to keep a dagger tucked in her garter. The Englishwoman had rigged up a tiny theatre in her house. On certain evenings she danced to music from a gramophone, which she wound up in the wings before leaping, or gliding, on to the stage. Amongst the artists was a handsome Frenchman, Paul, with a beautiful wife from Indo-China. One day he chased me over a stretch of prickly vegetation on the mountainside above the village. I tripped, but when he grounded me I cried, *"Non!"* very firmly - he had no business to be philandering. With good grace he desisted and called me his *"princesse lointaine."* I wasn't sure what to make of this, but it was France, and I loved it.

Fritz was the most fun. He was a young, coltish American and quite unpredatory. One day we collected a good haul of donations for the Russians as they galloped up and down on the ramparts. In exchange for this sudden bounty the wife made a pile of *bleny*, measuring in depth from elbow to wrist (the measurement seemed to have significance). We ate them with caviar and sour cream; Fritz had to go outside and throw up, but came back for more.

I spent a month at St. Paul. It was wonderful to eat breakfast on the terrace among pots of orange trees, and on Sundays to sip a Dubonnet as chickens were turned on a spit above a log fire in the dining-room. It was bliss just to be alive, feel light-hearted, laugh and do silly things. I was grateful to Arthur for this holiday, yet found it hard to think about him. Did he hope I'd have a torrid affair in France and come back to England, rampant for sex? I don't know. But I did return rampant, though not for sex - for travel. Even so, I didn't plan to run away when I was in Paris that summer. One thing simply led to another.

My cousin Elizabeth had never been to Paris, and in June I persuaded her to spend a couple of weeks with me there. Arthur saw us off on the train and told us cheerfully to enjoy ourselves. He'd recommended the *Hôtel Saint-Pères,* "It's cheap and in the Latin Quarter, the best part of Paris," he said. Here we shared a room, and I began whirling Elizabeth around the city. But I was too exuberant and tired her out. She caught a cold and said she'd better go home. I saw her off at the station, and rather put out by her lack of stamina, set off to walk through the city. It was somewhere on that walk that I decided to stay in Paris, and get a job. Just that.

Arthur had given me a travel allowance but I had no bank account of my own so work was a priority. As my French was poor I scoured the telephone book for organizations whose names included *'Anglais'*. One dreadful old man offered me a job, but he leered so meaningfully that I fled. He chased me down a long corridor, but I ran faster and left him panting far behind.

To conserve dwindling funds I ate meagrely, and took an inexpensive attic room in the hotel. It overlooked a landscape of grey mansard roofs, and chimney pots with unique personalities - unknown territory, potentially romantic. But Elizabeth had left me her cold. One afternoon, after another fruitless search for work, I took to my bed and slept, but woke sharply when Arthur burst into the room and, before I could gather my wits, demanded furiously, "Where is your lover?"

Astonished, half awake, I asked, "What lover?" Then I noticed he was carrying a horsewhip - and suddenly was so sorry that he should have been goaded into such melodrama for nothing. When the lover problem was cleared up I was further touched when he produced a Fuller's walnut cake, my favourite. I ate it gratefully, feeling ill and foolish. Did we talk about what I'd done? The only memory is that we returned to England and carried on as before.

On the surface Arthur and I led an enviable life. We moved into a charming Victorian house in Fulham, and with two lively Irish girls as cook and housemaid, my time had no domestic demands other than ordering meals. Friends came and went, including John, but infrequently. He was deep in the work he loved, a future cast when the Murray family chose their relative, young John Grey, to be the sixth head of John Murray's publishing house. That was no mean future: Murray's had been founded at 50 Albemarle Street in 1768, and their authors included Byron, Walter Scott and Thomas Moore. John added his own inimitable discoveries – John Betjeman and Osbert Lancaster, Freya Stark and many more.

So although we saw less of John, Arthur had interesting friends, and we gave dinner parties, were entertained by friends, dined out, danced, went to the theatre, spent weekends in the country, and took holidays in Europe. After the outbreak of the Spanish Civil War we housed two refugees, an elderly couple of especial interest. The husband was a pianist and colleague of the cellist, Casals; in exchange for our hospitality he offered to give me piano lessons, provided I would study only Bach. This was a wonderful few months, during which my fingers began, for the first time, to feel the structure of music.

That was a time when I felt most like myself. I had nothing to complain of, except for the recurrent unease of not being quite myself. I didn't put this into words, but one evening an odd thing happened, and words came. We were at a gala opera night in Covent Garden. During an intermission I was walking down a wide staircase and was struck by a young woman coming towards me. She wore a long, slim-fitting black velvet dress, and a diamond tiara sparkled in her hair. For a second I wondered who she was: but it was only a second before I knew she was myself, reflected in a floor-to-ceiling mirror. I felt a stab of pleasure to be cutting such a dash, but with it came a small cold query, 'What am I doing in this *Tatler* world of mirrors? Who am I?'

It wasn't an easy question to answer, since I was in Arthur's world, into which I was trying to fit. And why not? It offered so much. I was, for instance, rampant for travel, and we not only travelled regularly in Europe, but Arthur taught me how to travel. He insisted on my reading about the countries we visited so I'd be prepared not to offend the people, and get the flavour of each place. For the same reason he preferred travelling third class. This meant sitting up overnight on hard wooden seats, but Arthur said, "This way we meet the real people," and we shared rough wine with friendly peasants and ate bread, onions and olives as they did. Though often fiendishly uncomfortable, we definitely got plenty of flavour. Often I wished Arthur and I were just friends and travelling companions, and could forget about being married, and be easy.

However, a major change came into our lives when, in 1937 I learnt that my grandmother, Birdie Ruck Keene, had left me a legacy of £1,000. This was a windfall that needed brilliant spending, and with Arthur's agreement, I decided to buy a cottage in the country.

My cousin Elizabeth joined in the search, and for several weeks we scoured Hertfordshire. Then one evening we arrived at the village of Albury. It was nearly dusk when we walked up a stone-flagged path to the thatched cottage which stood on half an acre of rough garden and orchard, with a view across a valley. The property was a little forlorn, but we both cried, "This is it!" The price was £450.

"Lovely plums, ma'am, Victorias," the caretaker from the village told us, "and the apples are a treat - yes, ma'am, Cox's Orange Pippins."

The cottage had once been two small ones, side by side. The thatch needed repair, but the structure was a sturdy oak framework supporting walls of wattle and daub (a plaster of mud and straw adhering to strips of wood). The fireplaces, framed by broad oak beams, were almost big enough to sit in, and upstairs the bedroom ceilings were the underside of straw bundles tied to the exposed beams. I used to like lying in bed, listening to little creatures rustling companionably overhead.

Before buying furniture Elizabeth and I spent a couple of bitterly cold nights on camp beds. We lit a fire in one of the fireplaces and tried to trace the draughts with a lighted candle, but the flames blew out all the time. We found that there was no damp course (a layer of slates inserted between walls and earth) and plants pushed through from outside and sprouted palely inside at floor level. The damp was pervasive.

Over the next couple of years our weekend guests did all kinds of useful jobs, like building a more comfortable outside lavatory. When a part of the garden became very wet we called in a water-diviner and watched his willow wand turn down to point at a spot where he dug, and revealed a broken section of old terra-cotta drain. A local thatcher repaired the roof cap which, according to tradition, he edged with the signature of his own pattern.

Gradually the cottage became habitable, the garden was tamed, and the pruned fruit trees bore generously. Apples were stored on racks in what we called the studio, a frame building with a large room downstairs and storage space above. From harvest-time to the new year the studio was full of the clean, sweet smell of Cox's Orange Pippins. Downstairs two pairs of double glass doors opened onto the orchard

153

and valley beyond. For two summers the piano was moved from London to the studio and often, after a day of hard work, everyone gathered round the piano to sing a fine mix of songs - *Sumer is icumen in, - Frankie and Johnie were lovers; Green Grow the rashes-oh; She was poor, but she was honest.* They were good times, except for the flaw at the centre of our marriage.

I loved this cottage deeply. It was my one true possession, and a link with the rooted country life of Copford Rectory. Albury was a typical English village. There was a pub called *The Labour in Vain* (the sign depicted a woman scrubbing a little black boy), a post office and village store, a school, a church, a blacksmith (a handsome old man and wonderful craftsman), and a farmer with a glorious baritone voice. Some of the old people even remembered a witch being dunked in the pond just outside the cottage.

Arthur sometimes stayed nights in London and for companionship I acquired Mr. Potter, a brindle border collie of sterling character. His only weakness was a sensitivity to music in a minor key. There was no way of knowing whether his doleful howls reflected pain or pleasure, or were simply his contribution to a duet. We spent many peaceful days together. It was a rather dreamy existence, in which it was possible to push aside personal problems, and the black clouds of war boiling up in the world around us.

⊷ 20 ⊷

The chemistry of impending war.
War, and Budapest.

1935 was the year I worked at the Foreign Office with the object of learning about world affairs. But my own life was more real. School curriculum had not included either contemporary history or the art of reading a newspaper. War belonged to a past in which my father had died heroically, and England was victorious. Of course. Also, in 1919 the United Nations was formed "to save future generations from the scourge of war."

More than sixty years later it seems that ever since 1919 the world was moving steadily towards war. In that year the Treaty of Versailles imposed war reparations on Germany, which included huge cash payments, and the confiscation of their rich industrial and coal-mining areas in the Saar and Rhineland. I remind myself about what happened next with a list of dates and events.

1922: Fascist Mussolini becomes premier of Italy. Germany defaults on reparation payments.

1931: Japan invades Manchuria.

1932: Hitler appointed Chancellor in Germany and establishes the State of National Socialism.

1934: the Nazis assassinate Dollfüss, the Austrian Chancellor.

1935: Mussolini occupies Abyssinia. A plebiscite in the Saar results in its return to Germany. Later both Germany and Japan withdraw from the League of Nations.

1936: German troops occupy the Rhineland and militarize the Saar. In Spain, General Franco's Fascists precipitate civil war; Germany and Italy support the Fascists, Russia the Republicans.

1937: Japan occupies Manchuria. Italy, Germany and Japan form the Anti-Communist Pact against Russia. In Palestine an abortive plan is initiated to partition the country between Jews and Arabs.

1938: *Kristallnacht* - November 9, Nazis smash windows of Jewish-owned stores in Berlin.

During these foreboding years the League of Nations was riven with rivalries and dissensions, and failing to act effectively, gradually disintegrated. This brief summary suggests that the nature of victory is dubious: and the nature of war? Viewed dispassionately it appears to be a prime incubator for yet more wars.

In 1935 I had no clear opinions on world affairs. I was always rather overawed by Arthur's grasp of such matters, and felt ignorant as a post when I listened to him and our friends discussing Germany's invasion of the Rhineland, and prophesying war.

Arthur did his best to help me understand what was going on. But when information began circulating about the outrageous treatment of Jews in Germany, I looked at him in astonishment, and cried that it was medieval, and was he sure it was true? Then Sir Oswald Moseley and his Fascist Blackshirts provoked anti-Jewish riots in London. Arthur remarked drily that Peter Harmsworth's godfather, Lord Rothermere, was openly calling Moseley 'the one hope England had against socialist and communist hordes.' But I said I'd heartily disliked Rothermere when I met him with Peter.

"Good for you," Arthur said, and I felt I'd gained a point.

At various times Arthur tried educating me in a hands-on fashion. During a trip in Wales he made a diversion through the Rhondda Valley. We stopped at an abandoned village whose coal mine had been closed. It was a ghost place, the only sound a repeated dull clank as the wind stirred a loose sheet of metal against the rusting pithead.

"This is where the miners who sing on the streets come from," Arthur said. "Unemployed, poor devils. The socialists and communists think they have a better system to offer."

In London we went to a rally of the Hunger Marchers - two hundred out-of-work men who walked from the north of England to protest unemployment. I was impressed by the young woman with a shock of red hair who'd marched with the men and spoke passionately about hunger and the disgrace of having no work. She was about my age. I envied her passion and purpose and felt useless as well as ignorant. Her name was Barbara Castle, and Arthur said admiringly she would make a name for herself in politics. He was right - the one-time rebel became the respected Baroness Castle.

In 1938 we visited friends in Austria where house-party conversation was dominated by denunciations of Hitler as a bandit and barbarian. *Kristallnacht* had not occurred, but the word *anschlüss* kept cropping up, and Arthur explained that it meant annexation. "Hitler now means to annex Austria," he said. "That's why he got rid of Dollfüss in 1934."

"But what if they don't want to be annexed? How can the Germans allow it? After all, they elected Hitler." I cannot have been a stimulating companion on these subjects.

"They allow it because Hitler tells them that Germany will rise glorious from the defeat of 1918; that German Aryans are the super-race born to create a new world order; and that non-Aryan Jews are the incarnation of evil, and must be eradicated."

"Eradicated? Wiped out?"

"The Jews are Hitler's trump card," Arthur said. "They give Germans a license to hate."

"What d'you mean?"

"Wait till we're in Germany. You'll see."

On our way through the lovely German countryside we stopped for a lager at a village which greeted us with a notice, handwritten in capital letters: *"JUDEN HERAUS!"* I read it aloud, and then, unbelieving, cried, "Does that really mean 'Jews get out'?"

"Just so, plain and simple. This will be interesting."

At the village inn we drank lager with a couple of young boys - friendly, fresh-faced, typical tow-headed German boys - and I was emboldened to ask in halting German *"Warum 'Juden heraus'? Das ist nicht...gemütlich."* I meant 'polite' and should have said *höflich* - not that any word was right. Eerily the boys' open expressions glazed and, as if reading from a prompt card, they intoned mantras about the Fatherland's need for *lebensraum* (living space), the purity of the Aryan race, and finally, rising to their feet, raised an arm in the theatrical Nazi salute, barked *"Heil Hitler!"* and left.

Arthur said, "We can just make a Hitler rally tomorrow. That'll give you a taste of what's going on here."

It was dark when we arrived and the rally was in full swing. Flaming torches illuminated the blood-red banners (crooked cross black on a white circle), and lit the posturing little figure above us. Hitler's high, obsessive voice spat out words I didn't understand, prompting yells of *"Heil Hitler!"* and *"Sieg heil!"* No reason here, just the heart pounding, the crowd exulting together, anger and hate let loose in jungle roars – *"Sieg heil! Sieg heil! Heil Hitler!"* In a horrible way it was exciting.

"Demonic, isn't it?" Arthur said.

The following year, 1938, we took a late, tetchy holiday in France and came back while Neville Chamberlain and Daladier were meeting Hitler and Mussolini in München. When Chamberlain returned he stepped from the aircraft waving a bit of paper and announced, "I believe it is peace in our time!"

Arthur was furious. "Peace in our time? What a donkey the man is!"

"But why is peace so bad?"

"Because that ass Chamberlain has betrayed Czechoslovakia into ceding the Sudetenland to Germany. Sudetenland? That's the part of Czechoslovakia bordering France, Hungary and Poland. You watch - Hitler wants all that borderline territory. The München treaty won't stop him. War's inevitable."

A year later German forces invaded Poland. On September 3, 1939, Britain and France declared war on Germany and that morning the air raid sirens wailed for the first time in London. By then I was back at work in the Foreign Office.

It's easy to say the war changed our lives, but that wouldn't be quite true. In the uneasy years before war was declared the chemistry of change was everywhere, transmuting familiar elements, hinting at chaos. This chemistry worked on the fragile balance of our marriage, and early in 1939 chance, in the person of James Robertson Justice, gave it an added push.

James entered our life unexpectedly not long after we were married. Arthur and I were standing on the sidewalk waiting to cross Shaftsbury Avenue when he exclaimed, "Good God, there's James!" and added, half joking, "Come on, I don't want you to meet him, he always spells trouble." But it was too late; James, six feet and more, bearded and exuberant, was already crossing the road, shouting greetings.

Arthur had known James for years and pulled him out of numerous fixes long before he made quite a name for himself in films - *Doctor in the House; Scott of the Antarctic; Whiskey Galore.* He'd fought for the republicans in Spain where he was wounded and decorated, but in England his communist connections made jobs hard to get. He'd been educated in Heidelberg, spoke French and German perfectly, was a riveting storyteller, and could draw on a huge repertoire of songs in several languages. He was also nice about my piano playing.

After our chance meeting James came often to our house in London and to the cottage. In the spring of 1939 I was in bed with some mild malady and feeling unusually depressed. Arthur had brought a big bunch of flowers, later admitting with slight impatience that he'd assumed I was pregnant. I wasn't pregnant and, lying in bed assailed by failure, was glad when James came upstairs to see me.

He cheered me up with stories of his student days in Heidelberg, and dwelt lovingly on his mistress. "She was a beautiful red-head, with that marvellous creamy-white skin red-heads sometimes have." He stared out of the window, chuckled and added, "I ordered black satin sheets to be made for our bed. *Wünderschön!*"

"Oh James," I exclaimed, "how romantic!" - and all of a sudden I blurted out, "Our marriage hasn't been like that." I didn't mean to blame Arthur, and in a confused way said I wished he was just a friend, and that we shouldn't have married. But once started, I couldn't stop.

When I did stop James said gently in his beautiful, warm voice, "You know, Thelma, you don't have to live a lie."

It was a common catch-phrase, but I shied away from it - after all, James was Arthur's friend. "What d'you mean?" I exclaimed, "Arthur's not a monster, it's just that we're..." But what were we? Suddenly impatient with pretence I said flatly, "Do you mean... divorce?"

"People do it and live."

"The Ruck Keenes have never had a divorce," I retorted. But 'People do it and live' lodged in my mind like grit in an oyster shell. The fact was that physical love with Arthur had been an unresolved non-event. Moreover, Arthur's muttered, "I knew you would be difficult" had settled like another piece of grit, posing the question "Is it my fault?" No answer came.

Throughout June and July of 1939 'People do it and live' was part of the war chemistry, the feeling of being on the brink of a huge unknown, demanding decision and change. Then in August a letter came from the Foreign Office saying there was urgent need for secretarial help in the suddenly-expanded Communications Department. Was I free?

With Arthur's agreement I closed the cottage, returned to London, and was back to work at the Foreign Office by the end of August. On September 1, Germany invaded Poland. On September 3, Britain declared war on Germany, and that was when the air raid sirens sounded over London.

The Communications Department overlooked the Horse Guards Parade, and at the first spooky howl of the sirens I went over to the big window to see what was happening outside. Usually the Parade was busy with people strolling around or hurrying to work; now they were standing still, looking up at the sky. But there was nothing to be seen, and one person started walking away. The others seemed to hesitate, then someone began to run, and suddenly everyone was running. At this moment we were taken down to the vaults and walked a long way to the air raid shelter, heavy doors clanging behind us. After a while we went back upstairs, and found that nothing had happened.

Two weeks later Russia invaded Poland and then followed the strange lull called the 'phoney' war. There were no air raids, just a pervading bustle of preparation for the real war ahead. Blackout was mandatory, everyone (except a few rebels) carried gas masks round their necks, and there were plans to evacuate children from London to the country. For several months my cousin Elizabeth had been living with us in London so she could complete a secretarial course. When war was declared she applied to the Foreign Office, was accepted and assigned to the Communications Department. We were soon joined by a most unlikely person, Terence Rattigan. Terence was a humourist as well as an upcoming dramatist, and I still laugh at an exchange in his very first play, *French without Tears*, produced when he was twenty. Someone asks, "How would you say, 'She has ideas above her station?'" The reply is, *"Elle a des idées audessus de sa gare."* The use of *gare* (railway station) instead of *position sociale* is not deathless wit, but having Terence around made our Department a jolly place. Then, without warning or explanation, I was sacked.

Outraged, I wrote for an appointment with someone who would explain and, impatient for a reply, gave the letter to Terence very early one damp, grey morning. We met at the Cenotaph and I said, wanting him to be serious, "You *must* deliver this yourself."

"Yes ma'am," he said, saluting smartly, which made me laugh.

My letter produced an appointment with Gladwyn Jebb (inevitably he was later *Sir* Gladwyn) but it wasn't much use. He was a very tall man encased in diplomatic courtesy, and told me nothing, very politely. Much later it was Terence who told me what had happened. It might even be true.

"Somebody," he said, "discovered a serious information leak, and to narrow the field of suspects everyone employed in our department before the outbreak of war was dismissed. That's why you had to go and Elizabeth and I stayed on. Well, like the Mounties, the F.O. got their man - he was a cipher clerk!"

"But how...?"

"You know how light-heartedly the deciphered telegrams are bundled up, tied with pink tape and chucked into a cupboard. It must have been easy." Terence grinned and said, "But listen to this. The clerk had not only been selling information to Germany since the end of World War I, he'd sent his son to Eton on the proceeds. A nice touch. Long live the dear old *Alma Mater!*"

I laughed and said he ought to make a play out of it, then asked, "D'you think spying really makes any difference - I mean, to winning or losing? It's like a silly game."

Terence shrugged, said, "Whatever would writers do without M.I.5 and their little capers! Perhaps I will write a spy play." I keep forgetting to check whether he did.

Barely a week after being sacked, I received a curt telegram from Phil Ruck Keene, now in command of the submarine base at Harwich. The telegram read:

Fool of a secretary is Oxford graduate
only types one finger come immediately.

I went immediately, assuming I was a stopgap and would soon be back in London. But I stayed for six months, working with Phil on the base ship. It was an odd period. Submarines left on regular patrols in the North Sea, but there was little action and no losses. The sailors were tensed up for action and restless from the lack of it, so I organized a mammoth variety show in one of the dockside warehouses. A few London professionals agreed to take part and I filled in the programme with some rather bizarre local talent. To my surprise it was a riotous success and Phil was delighted. Not for a long time had I felt so alive and useful - and happy. Amazing! I was happy.

By March of 1940 I decided to provide Arthur with grounds for divorce. Sounds simple, but it wasn't. As the decision was mine it was proper that I should satisfy the divorce law by providing evidence of adultery. For this I needed a lover and didn't have one. Finally one of Phil's submariners agreed to stand in as co-respondent, but said, "I'll have to have a false name or be nameless. Ruckers would kick up a frightful fuss if he found out. Anyway, I'm engaged to be married."

He slept on the sofa in the hotel room. I heard all about his fiancée, we gossiped about the base, and talked about life, and war and whether we'd die before it was over. When the waitress brought our breakfast in the morning we were sitting decorously together in bed. I asked her name and tipped her generously to make sure she'd remember us in the divorce.

After she'd gone I said, "D'you remember Bumble, the beadle in *Oliver Twist?*"

"Of course! '...the law is an ass - an idiot.'"

We laughed, but I said, "It isn't easy, deciding."

Nor was it easy to determine what to do next. Phil could at any time sail off to another command, and I was, presumably, on a Foreign Office blacklist. But, as if my decision had acquired a life of its own, a letter arrived from the Foreign Office.

I had to read it twice to be sure I understood that I really was being asked, once again, if I was free, and this time not for a job in London, but at the British Legation in Budapest. My dismissal from the Communications Department was vaguely referred to as "an unfortunate emergency," and no mention was made of my married state. But I wasn't going to ask questions. I replied that I was free. Then I returned to London and told Arthur what I intended to do.

I have no recollection of how my announcement was received, only that he finally said, "Maybe we can talk better in the country." I would have been no better than a block of wood not to hear the anguish in his voice, and agreed.

For some reason he drove to Blenheim Palace (Winston Churchill's overblown family pile near Oxford). The grounds were open to the public and we walked around in the chilly April sunshine. Then we sat on a bench and Arthur tried to change my mind. When I refused he said, "How do you propose to live? You haven't any money."

"I'll have a salary. I don't expect anything from you; it's my decision." Lamely I added, "I'm truly sorry to grieve you, you've been a good friend. But we aren't...we don't...it doesn't work, Arthur. It's not your fault we...well, we started badly, and it never did get right. Anyway, I've decided."

I knew this was an inadequate excuse for hurting him, but even though he was such an agreeable person, and loved me, I had to get away from him.

Forty-two years later I met Arthur and his second wife. I had just completed a six-month journey from Canada through Asia and Europe, and was staying with John and Diana Murray in Hampstead. The meeting was Diana's idea. "Time to heal old wounds," she said.

They arrived, and after the first greetings and pouring out of tea, Arthur sat down by me. I said something about him looking just the same, which was reasonably true. To this he replied, with a bright smile, "Well, I wouldn't have recognized you if we passed in the street."

I looked at him in surprise, thought, 'That's rather a crass thing to say.' I had been twenty-four when we parted in 1940 and was now sixty-five - but I knew I'd aged well. Yet there was something familiar about his remark. However, I let it go. I liked his wife, who was American, a few years younger than me - and also a pianist. She said, "Now I've raised four daughters I'm taking piano lessons. You know how it is; you have to play all the time or you just get frustrated." We smiled at each other, briefly connected.

Ten years later I was writing about our honeymoon, and once again I heard Arthur utter, "I always knew you would be difficult." Then, quite suddenly, his unmannerly remark about being unrecognizable made sense. Both of them were put-downs - of course they were, each one a way to ease a wound. But on our honeymoon I did not understand this, nor did I in April 1940. But by then it would not have made any difference.

I stayed with John and Diana while my travel papers were fixed, and on a fine April day I boarded the train to Budapest. I would not be back in England until April 1944.

∽∾

My father, 2nd Lieutenant, 1914.

Me, 1918.

163

My mother, Christina de la Paz Garsia.

My grandmother, Minna Garsia.

Birdie and Ted Ruck Keene with my father, Ralph, age 3;
Margery, 6 months; and Ben, nearly 2. April 15, 1891.

Copford Rectory, Eight Ash Green, Essex.

Abbie and Emma.

Junior and me, San Antonio, Texas, 1922.

Willoughby and my mother with Diplomas in Chiropractic, 1923.

Wedding photograph of Phil and Dick Ruck Keene with me as
bridesmaid.   December, 1923.

Me with Oophats, Lymington, 1928.

Hogs Hill, my cottage in Albury, Hertfordshire.

Arthur Lyons and me, 1938.

Engagement photograph for the *Tatler*, 1936.

"Positively the Popsiest Picture I ever Produced."
Taken by James Robertson Justice, 1939.

Kalanthe survivors. The hospital party on Kimolos, April, 1941.
Peter Fleming at left, me in the middle holding child.

Me with Kassab, 1941.

Me on the balcony of the Spears Mission, 1942.

Dinner in Beirut, 1942. From left: unknown couple, me,
Sandy Mitchell-Innes, Tony Lambert, Dick Usborne.

Leo, 1954.

Leo and me on our first visit to Canada, 1965.

Leo and me in Vancouver, 1997.

PART TWO

If you dare cross water,
you may get wet.

African proverb

⤞⤝

1940 – 1944

Hungary, Greece, Egypt, Lebanon, Sicily

21

Beautiful Budapest,
bedbugs and other problems.

I had the compartment to myself and read the familiar notices - *NE PENCHEZ PAS AU DEHORS - NICHT HINAUSLESEN* - DO NOT LEAN OUT OF THE WINDOW. Did some unfortunate once *hinauslesen* and have their head knocked off? The question slid away as I read the notices aloud in impeccable pronunciation, feeling travel capable, in spite of a slight twittery sensation overall. The train rumbled through peaceful countryside, past children romping home from school, hungry for tea with bread and jam and slices of cake. Did I envy those strangers their settled, routine days? 'No,' came the answer, without hesitation, 'I am twenty-four and on my way to the Balkans, alone. That's enough for now.'

I went in to the first service of dinner and a waiter showed me, with a flourish and a smile, to an empty table. A small shaded lamp cast a pool of light on the white tablecloth and folded napkins, and there were fresh flowers in a slender silvery vase. Quite Orient Express! The tables filled up quickly, and a stocky youngish man asked, with an amiable grin, if he could join me. As I smiled agreement he added, "It's crowded tonight. Must be a last dash before the doors slam."

He spoke with a slight northern accent ('middle-class' I registered automatically) and wore a nondescript raincoat, the sort worn by spies in the movies. He folded this garment neatly and laid it on the seat beside him just as if he had secret papers sewn in the lining. We introduced ourselves in the formal English way, but we must have got quickly on to first names for I only remember him as Fred, who was on his way to Belgrade.

After we'd chosen our meal I asked, hoping he wouldn't think me stupid, "Why did you say 'before the doors slam'?"

"Sorry, it was a bit cryptic; you must have missed the news about Scandinavia. The Germans have invaded Norway and Denmark. Looks like dirty work from inside one of the countries. If Europe's next..." I missed the rest, I was thinking of Harwich and that the submarines would no longer patrol the North Sea without loss. Should I have stayed? But Phil had said it was going to be a long war and I could serve anywhere.

I told Fred about Phil and Harwich and he told me about his family. By the end of dinner we might have known one another for years, and for the rest of the journey we ate our meals together. It was the first of many here-today-and-gone-tomorrow meetings in the limbo war, the transience adding an intensity which, not infrequently, produced revelations.

Fred didn't go in for revelations, but talked about his fascination with hypnotism. "It began as a hobby," he said. "You know how it is, you play around with something until one day there's a challenge to be serious. This happened after Pete, my son, had his tonsils out. He was scared stiff by the anaesthetist and his nosebag of chloroform, and the poor little tyke kept throwing up after the operation. So when my daughter Penny had to have her tonsils out I knew what I had to do - skip the anaesthetic and keep her in a trance right through. I couldn't have done it if the surgeon hadn't been a friend, though he nearly had a fit when I told him. But he agreed in the end."

"Weren't you scared it mightn't work?"

"You know, when something needs doing the only way is to fix your mind on doing it and keep it steady while you stay quiet inside. Then it's easy. Penny knew I'd send her to sleep, that I'd be there when she woke up, that her throat would be sore but she could have lots of ice cream (she's a tiger for ice cream) and that's just how it went. Best of all she was at home." With a grin he added, "The operation was done on the kitchen table. I had to promise my doctor never to tell anyone, but I think it's safe to tell you!"

Fred had another story about hypnotism. "I was at a party," he began, "and one of the guests, a middle-aged chap I'd never met before, was carrying on about how he'd lived in Russia until he was six, had a Russian nanny and spoke the language fluently. But now - nothing, not even one Russian word. He got quite worked up about the waste."

With the twitch of an eyebrow Fred went on, "As it happens I speak Russian, and here was a chance in a thousand. I asked if he'd mind being hypnotized, explained I might be able to dig up his Russian, and once he understood what I was after he was keen as mustard."

"What happened?"

"It was funny. Once he was well under I spoke to him in Russian. He stumbled a bit at first, but in no time was chattering away, no problem - except (it was comical) his vocabulary was roughly that of a child of six."

"So we don't forget anything! All the lines of poetry and what you did when you were three..."

"That's it. You just have to ease it out, kindly-like."

Funny how a casual phrase can stick. "Focus your mind, and keep it steady while you stay quiet inside" is really useful in moments of panic. Fred's cheerful companionship was a blessing, easing my way into an uncertain future.

In Budapest I waved goodbye to Fred as his part of the train rumbled off to Belgrade, then went to the luggage van, hoping my suitcase would be one of the first to be unloaded. I watched as trunks and cases and untidy boxes tied up with string were slung out of the van, watched as they were claimed, watched until there wasn't any more luggage. I stared at the few bits of unclaimed luggage, peered into the empty van, and willed my case to materialize. But it didn't, nor did the person from the legation who was supposed to meet me.

What next? All I possessed was a small dressing-case with a nightdress and toilet stuff. I only had enough money to live on until my first pay cheque and couldn't possibly buy another supply of clothes. Help was imperative. So I accosted a passer-by and explained my predicament in English. He replied in Hungarian. This was hopeless, so I tried pantomime. All that did was draw a crowd and in no time everyone was yammering away in Hungarian to one other as if I wasn't there. In sudden exasperation I shouted, *"Sprechen kein man Deutsch?"* and mercifully an answer came from someone in the crowd, *"Ja, ja, ein moment bitte."*

He listened patiently to me, and after more crowd discussion I understood that my luggage was, in all probability, on its way to Belgrade. "Belgrade!" I exclaimed, *"Wie?"* meaning 'How do I get it back?'

It was a bad moment, but an English voice behind me said, "You must be Thelma Lyons. I'm sorry I'm late." I turned and was faced with the obviously English person from the legation.

The station-master was found, promised that my luggage would be returned immediately, and some of the crowd, who had stayed to see what would happen next, now beamed goodwill and offered congratulations. The suitcase did come back after several days, but by this time I was stuck with a worse problem.

We drove from the station through Pest, which I was told was the new part of Budapest, and that the legation was in the old city of Buda. My companion said that a room in Buda had been taken for me, and it was in the house of a baroness. I longed to ask if this meant luxury and sophistication, but didn't, for just then we left Pest by a bridge across the Danube. I looked down eagerly at this famous river, saw it wasn't at all blue, and then the car began climbing the hill to Buda. Above the trees I saw a slender spire rising from a pointed golden roof which shone in the sunshine. I asked if it was a castle.

"No, that's the thirteenth century church of St. Matthias. Hungarian kings were crowned there. You can see it best from the Fisherman's Wharf." We drove on up the hill, past graceful old houses with delicate wrought-iron balconies and I caught an occasional glimpse of inner courtyards. Once there was a burst of gypsy music as we passed a restaurant.

"That's a czardas! Do the musicians often play?"

"All the time," said the person from the legation sourly. I didn't care. He could be as sour as he liked. I was here in this wonderful place, and I was going to live with a baroness. For the moment I forgot I was here because of a war.

The taxi stopped at one of the gracious old houses, just the kind of house I'd hoped for. A maid opened the door - but after that the imagined life of luxury and sophistication took a knock. We stepped into a gloomy passage smelling faintly of cooked cabbage and crowded with very large pieces of furniture. A moment later we were greeted by the baroness.

She was a rather witchlike figure who came at me with a clatter of bracelets crying, "I am sure we will be grreat frriends."

We followed her down the passage until she stopped and flung open a door, saying, "This is your rrroom!"

It was a very large room indeed and held traces of former glittering receptions. Tall windows were draped with faded red velvet curtains looped up by rather tatty tasselled silk ropes, and a sort of truckle bed had been set up in one corner. Small gilt chairs lined the walls, occasional tables were scattered here and there minus the usual bric-a-brac, and there was a constellation of paintings in gilt frames crammed on every wall - except one. On this wall hung a huge painting, in an elaborate gilded frame of a hideous (surely more than life-size?) pug dog, squarely placed in lush landscape.

"You like?" asked the baroness. "You see the eyes, they follow you always! Dear Puggy, he was our frriend so long!"

At least Puggy stayed put on the wall, unlike the creatures which made themselves known later that night. I was nearly asleep when a persistent itch brought me sharp awake. I wriggled. It made no difference. Then I lay thinking, 'This can't be true, not in the house of a baroness.' But the itch was unmistakable: there were bedbugs in my bed.

I was well acquainted with bedbugs. In our travels Arthur liked to seek out country inns whose restaurants were recommended in *La Guide de Sans Guides* (the best travel book ever). The food was always marvellous, but sometimes there were disadvantages. A French friend once remarked, "In France the excellence of the cuisine is frequently in proportion to the squalor of the lavatories," to which we added, "and the resident bedbugs." The only way to deal with them was to turn on the light quickly and catch, one by one, as many bugs as possible. This wasn't easy as, bloated with blood, most of them scurried away out of sight. The trick was to trap each one between finger and thumb, then position the thumbnail so you could quickly chop the bug in two. I became a skilful bug slayer.

But the odd night at a village inn was one thing. Bugs on a regular basis, however baronial, were not acceptable. But I couldn't complain to my landlady, it was too embarrassing. I spent a troubled night and decided to ask someone at the legation to help me find another room.

I arrived for work, ready to please and be pleased, and eager to describe the bedbug problem. But it didn't take long to find the chancery staff markedly unfriendly, almost hostile. The chancery is the administrative centre of any diplomatic mission abroad. It was the place where I would type the letters and reports dictated by the minister or members of the legation hierarchy, such as the first and second secretaries who were Foreign Office employees, and the naval, military and other attachés who are loaned from their career base. Budapest was not the capital city of a major league country so it rated a legation headed by a minister, instead of an embassy and an ambassador.

The head of chancery in Budapest was a thin, disgruntled man, and I thought perhaps the rest of the staff took their cue from him. Whatever the cause, the atmosphere was glacial, and when the minister sent for me I went off with my pen and notebook as if reprieved.

The minister's pale blue eyes stared rather coldly at me through steel-rimmed spectacles, but he was pleasant enough, and when I went back to the chancery I remarked, in a general way, that he had been very kind. This was greeted by silence. Nonplussed, I wondered if it was something about me? Did I irritate people, bouncing in expecting everyone to like me? Clearly I'd have to sort this out; but first I had to get help in finding another place to live.

By the end of the day I'd decided there was only one friendly person around and that was the young Hungarian doorman. He'd been helpful when I arrived in the morning, had shown me where to go, said his name was Michael and he hoped I'd like being in Budapest. So I appealed to Michael.

"I'll ask my dad," he said cheerily, sounding not at all Hungarian. "He's the golf pro at the club and knows everyone. I'll let you know tomorrow."

I endured another night of bug slaughter and was overjoyed in the morning to be met by Michael with a beaming smile. "I've got an address," he said. "My dad says she's a nice lady...and...that is, if you like...I mean, I can take you there after work. If you like."

I said that would be perfect, and maybe on the way he could point out restaurants where I could get good Hungarian food, but not expensive. He went rather pink. He was very fair, more English-looking than Hungarian, rather a handsome boy, and said, "Do you like music? Would you like...I can take you to one with a good gypsy band. I'll show you how to dance the czardas...that is if..." I said I'd love it, subduing a slight discomfiture about him being just a doorman. Anyway, he was friendly and young and Hungarian and class divisions were stupid.

The house overlooked a cobbled side-street. It was small and old, but elegant - like its owner, who was a handsome lady with a touch of distinction and much more my idea of a baroness. She greeted me courteously and no nonsense about being great friends, just a firm, "My maid will show you the room."

The room had French windows which opened on a miniature balcony overlooking the quiet, cobbled street. The furniture was very European, formal but pleasing and comfortable, even if there seemed just a little too much of it. But that was because of the bed.

When I saw the bed, I laughed. I couldn't help it, and then felt badly because Michael asked anxiously, "Don't you like?"

"Of course I do. I love it." How could I not love that absurd and joyous bed, generous and downy, with satin cushions tumbled against a padded, buttoned-silk headboard which rose up and up, ending in a sort of crown from which flew a chubby baroque cherub. He was the real thing, no cheap reproduction, and in one fat little hand he held a filmy cascade of white muslin which floated to the floor on either side of the bed.

Michael said something to the maid in Hungarian and they both smiled at me. The maid was no beauty, but friendly, and we agreed I would move in as soon as I'd given notice to the baroness. Then Michael took me off to his restaurant.

It was just the sort of place I'd hoped for, nothing grand but full of cheerful townspeople tucking in to delicious food. As for the music, it was wonderful, though I wasn't sure how to deal with the violinist who came to play at our table. Every note was a caress, a sob, and his melting brown eyes gazed into mine.

"What am I supposed to *do*?" I whispered to Michael.

He grinned and said, "I'll ask him to play a czardas so we can dance." And so we did, slowly at first, hands on each other's hips, until suddenly the rhythm quickened and Michael put his arm round my waist and we flew around until the rhythm slowed once more, then fast again and slow again, on and on until the music stopped and so did we, breathless and glowing.

Between dances our conversation laboured a little, so I relied on asking Michael about himself, and how he came to speak such good English. He said his dad was English, his mother Hungarian.

"Which d'you feel - English or Hungarian?

"I don't know. Hungarian, I suppose. I don't bother much." He seemed a happy-go-lucky young man, but it was easier to dance than talk.

I gave notice next day to the baroness. I was afraid she would be offended and I made the excuse of wanting the privacy of an apartment to myself. She was nice about my leaving, but I felt badly. Maybe she needed the rent. Maybe I should tell her about the bugs. But I scarpered, thankful to get away.

Michael carried my suitcase to the new apartment and once again we supped and danced. After supper he made diversions through the old streets, pointing out shops where I could buy food and restaurants where meals were good and cheap. I was longing for the weekend when there'd be time to explore, to get lost, try to talk to people, follow my nose - and be alone.

When we reached my front door I began thanking Michael for his help and the dancing and everything, hoping to forestall another invitation. But he cut me short and, very confidently, put his arms round me and tried to kiss me. I was astonished. What did he think...?

"Please Michael, no!"

He drew away abruptly, frowning. We stared at one another and he said suddenly, "I thought you were hot!"

"*Hot?*"

He didn't answer - and suddenly it was my cheeks that were hot. He meant hot like a bitch in heat. I couldn't think what to say. But Michael nodded rather curtly, said, "That's all right. I'll be off."

Later I lay at ease in my great bed, the cherub in flight above my head and my thoughts every which-way. I remembered Elizabeth telling me I was too come-hitherish. Was there a fine line between being friendly and implying 'come-hither?' I had forgotten what it was like to be single and, as it were, available. *Hot.* I didn't like that. Certainly not from a doorman, however personable.

Into my head came the French word '*allumeuse*', meaning a woman who enjoys 'firing up' men and then opting out. A bitch, in other words. Was I a bitch? Was it bitchy to like being attractive to men, to enjoy the sparkly exchanges, fizzy as champagne?

The answers were hard to come by. I was used to heads turning when I entered a room or walked down a street, and out of nowhere came a memory of my young self jumping over the cracks of paving stones on a sidewalk. Behind me my mother walked with a friend and I caught snippets of conversation, chatter chatter, not interesting, until I heard my name. My mother had murmured something to which the friend exclaimed, "My dear Dickie, your Thelma's a beautiful child. She'll go far."

How funny to remember that. It was quite clear, the sunny street and me skipping along, cutting the leaps fine so there was danger of landing on a line, and registering that I was beautiful. Fairy-tale princesses were always beautiful, and married the handsome prince and lived happily ever after. Except things hadn't worked out quite that way. Moreover beauty could be a bore, prompting unwelcome expectations, like Michael thinking I was hot.

I tried dispassionately to think what I looked like: 5' 6", thick light-brown hair ("Jeannie with the light-brown hair, tra-la"), broad forehead, green/brown eyes, a straight nose, white teeth, a mouth like everyone else, a longish neck on well-set shoulders (not Birdie's ladylike sloping ones), and the rest of me fairly slender and limber. Someone saw a likeness to Ingrid Bergman, which was very nice, but I bet her cheeks were never disgraced by occasional hateful spots, and her hair was always cut just right. At least passing strangers smiled at me as if what they saw cheered them up.

None of this answered the question, 'Do I chase men?' All I knew was that men certainly chased me (remembering Paul galloping after me on the hillside above St. Paul-de-Vence). Sometimes the chase was exhilarating, a light-hearted game; sometimes it was tiresome, like Michael. If a handsome Hungarian prince had seized me by the waist and kissed me, would I have been so affronted?

For a while I wrestled with the problem of class distinctions and how it was easy to step over the class line, and bang! you were in foreign territory with a different language, including words like 'hot.' Crossly I blamed the unfriendly chancery staff. I wouldn't have gone out with Michael if even one person had made me welcome, or at least not been so disagreeable. I lay listening to footsteps passing in the street below, to a snatch of conversation and a burst of laughter. From my landlady's room came the faint murmur of a man's voice. I wondered who she was or might have been. Maybe the flying cherub was a clue; or maybe it was just her taste.

Next day at the legation Michael wasn't at the door, and didn't come back. I asked if he was ill. Someone said that his father had fixed him up with a better job, concluding with a laugh, "Michael's a bit of a lad, I expect his father wants him to sober down."

A bit of a lad. Oh well, good luck to him. There were lots of lovely Hungarian girls he could be a lad with. I needn't pretend I wasn't glad he'd gone, except for one regret, that he might have thrown some light on my new landlady.

What made me curious were the firm, unhurried footsteps which, on many evenings, passed by my room. There'd be a quiet knock on my landlady's door, her reply answered by a deep voice, followed by the door opening, and quietly closing. The deep voice was not always the same, but the sober tread and measured tones spoke of respectable pillars of society. I imagined the visitor raise and kiss my landlady's hand, take his usual seat, and after courteous preliminary enquiries about each other's health, settle down to happy hours of gossip and scandal, and maybe talk of the war and the Germans and how to keep out of trouble. Surely she was much too old to engage in anything more lively? No good asking the maid an offhand question - she knew her place, and anyway, it was none of my business.

What was my business was the snooty chancery staff, and tomorrow I'd challenge their unfriendliness.

22

'Belinda'.
A new name, and much else new.

The next morning I was ready for action, but what action was unclear. Maybe I should demand attention, ask "Why are you being so odious to me? I'm not a leper, I don't smell, what's wrong?" As things turned out I didn't have to bother.

The first secretary called me in to take dictation and this being the first time we'd met he asked how long I'd been in the Foreign Office. This was obviously routine courtesy and not a burning concern of his, so I answered briefly, and for good measure said, "I spent a few months early in the war on the submarine base ship in Harwich. My uncle, Phil Ruck Keene, is the base commander."

"Ruck Keene? Are you one of the Oxfordshire Ruck Keenes of Swyncombe?"

Cheered to find he was aware I was a person, not just a handy factotum, I said, "They're my cousins. D'you know them?"

"My parents' place adjoins Swyncombe. A beautiful estate. You must know it well?"

"Actually I've never been there, but I know Rowley and Bill quite well. Phil and my aunt Dick are much closer to them..." I trailed off, aware that interest had cooled.

He rearranged a few papers, already neatly piled, and said, "We must have you round some time." I murmured something polite and wondered what 'round some time' would prove to be, and when. It was a nice surprise when the first secretary's wife invited me to "drop in for a cup of tea" the following weekend.

I found her alone. She apologized that her husband had "an unexpected call, he's so sorry to miss you." I said I was sorry, and we had a pleasant chat. I wondered if I would be asked again.

Shortly afterwards I was invited to dine with the minister and his family. His wife Anne had published several books, and I'd read *Peking Picnic* and could say truthfully that I'd enjoyed it. Jane, their eldest daughter, had spectacles and mousy hair and was only interested in her plans to get back to England and university. Her younger sister, Grania, was quite different. She was slight, with fair curly hair, full of life, and friendly. I was happy to like them all, and Grania invited me to go swimming with her the following day. As for the minister I was prepared to find him charming, though puzzled by his comments on Hungary and Hungarians.

"A good-for-nothing lot," he said. "The sooner the Germans take over the country the better."

His wife exclaimed, "Really, Owen, you exaggerate. They're not all time-servers," and she mentioned Hungarian names I didn't know. Grania smiled and said not to take any notice of her father. I smiled back, listened to Jane talking about her travel plans, and paid attention when her mother spoke of English writers, beginning, "I, as a writer..."

I enjoyed the evening, but the next morning the chancery staff were, if possible, more icy than ever. I was puzzling over whom to tackle when I was told to take dictation from the naval attaché. During the next half hour, everything changed.

He finished dictating and I was about to leave when he asked, "I hear your maiden name was Ruck Keene. Are you related to Ruckers?"

"Why yes! Phil is my uncle. Do you know him?"

He also knew Jack, now in a destroyer somewhere, and two young Ruck Keene cousins on *HMS Hood*. We talked about Harwich and my heart gave a lurch when he said, "The submarine base is going to be pretty busy with Germans swarming all over the North Sea. That damned traitor Quisling - I hope the Norwegians give him his come-uppance."

"Quisling?"

"A nasty piece of work. Army officer, sneaked plans to the Germans before they attacked Norway. Denmark and Holland could be next, then Belgium and, unless the French can stand firm at Liège and the Maginot line..." He paused, then added, "Jane will have to get going if she wants to reach England before the doors slam on France."

"France! So getting back to England through Europe will be..."

"Awkward," said the naval attaché.

At this moment Eleni, the chancery administrative assistant, came in with some papers. The naval attaché smiled at us both. "Oh well, that's war, that is. By the way, Eleni, my wife's presented me with a daughter." Eleni said the right things and asked what name they'd chosen. "We've settled for Belinda. Rather old-fashioned, but we like it." I said it was a lovely name and wished someone had suggested it to my mother.

"What's the matter with Thelma?"

"Oh, it sounds like one of those frightfully expensive Bond Street shops, the ones with a hat and necklace in the window and no prices. My mother got the name from a Marie Corelli book. I've never read any, they sound trashy. Thelma was a heroine in one of them. My mother described her standing by the sea with her hair blowing about, the waves dashing against rocks. She sounded like Elfine in *Cold Comfort Farm*, dancing soulfully on the moors in an arty cloak."

The naval attaché laughed. "All right - let's call you Belinda. Then every time I see you I'll think of my daughter. Will that do?"

Amazed, I exclaimed, "Oh yes, it will do wonderfully," and repeated, "Belinda. Yes, I like that. And thank you, I'm honoured," and smiling at Eleni and the naval attaché said I better get to work, and left them, feeling that the world was, after all, a friendly place,

I was halfway down the stairs when Eleni caught me up. She was slight, rather elegant, and her Greek name fitted her - her profile reminded me of Athene on old Greek coins, the nose coming straight down from the forehead. She stood out amongst the rather lacklustre chancery staff, and I felt she had some fire in her. So far she'd been singularly offhand with me so I was surprised when she said, "Perhaps we'll like you better as Belinda."

"Well thanks! But what did I do?"

She hesitated, then said, "Come and have a cup of tea after work and I'll tell you about this place."

Eleni's apartment was my first taste of Greece - white walls, bright cushions, rugs that looked hand-woven, blue-and-white pottery cups for tea. While she put out tea things I asked, "Why is the minister so sarcastic about Hungary and the Hungarians? He's been very nice to me."

"The old Irish blarney," Eleni remarked crisply. "Let me tell you about our respected minister."

She began with an old story, back when the minister was young, with a promising career opening up in the Foreign Office. But the promise was dashed over what the London newspapers called 'The Bradley-Dine Affair.' Mrs. Bradley-Dine had a suspiciously lucrative flurry on the stock exchange which it was suspected had been made possible through access to classified information. There was an enquiry which finally led to the lady's young friend in the Foreign Office. There were blurred edges, but he was demoted and his advancement set back beyond redress.

"As a result," Eleni concluded, "our minister is ending his career in the minor posting of a legation."

"But did they prove he'd been responsible?"

"Maybe careless rather than deliberate. But discretion is the better part of a diplomat."

I said, "He's an odd man. I like Grania. They're all worried about whether Jane will get through to England safely."

Eleni shrugged, dismissive. "The chancery can't stand him. He makes a point of boasting that he's never travelled outside the city, he's rude to his wife, everyone knows he has a mistress, and he deliberately partitioned off the big reception room so he had an excuse for cutting down on entertainment. Suits him. He still gets an entertainment allowance and the gossip is he's salting it away to renovate his house in Ireland for when he retires. He can't wait to get out of here. All he wants to do now is see that nobody in the legation rocks the boat while he waits for the Germans to arrive." Eleni drew breath and wound up, "And he's such a snob! Do you know what he calls the chancery? The Kitchen Quarters."

I did know, and that he dubbed the chancery staff "a bunch of Bolshies." So I nodded.

"You wait till the great Christmas party," Eleni said. "Once a year we go through a pantomime of goodwill and then everyone heaves a sigh of relief until the next year."

"Are all legations and embassies like this?"

"I've only worked here. I suppose it depends a lot on who's at the top, but the Foreign Service is a bastion of the British class system. Your la-di-da accent didn't endear you to us!"

"That's unfair: I don't talk like that on purpose, it's just the way I talk. After all..."

But Eleni wasn't listening. "Here's a story everyone knows. It's about Lady Waterlow who was the minister's wife at the legation in Athens before the war. There are stories about Sydney Waterlow too, he was a real stuffed shirt. Anyway, she had the legation store of wine divided into three levels: good wine for Very Important People, not-so-good for the less important, and table wine for the diplomatic riff-raff, like consuls. One night all the consular officers came to dinner. The butler poured claret into her ladyship's wine glass, she took a sip and then exclaimed loudly, 'My dear Sydney, surely not the *best* claret tonight?'"

I laughed and admitted that gentry manners could be insufferable. "It's as though they don't know what they're doing. They don't mean it, it's just that if you're not one of them you aren't..." I hesitated.

"Aren't what?"

"Oh well...just not one of them!" Then I told Eleni about my invitation from the first secretary's wife.

"Typical! You're the kitchen staff and don't quite fit in, whatever your ancestry, so a cup of tea will be good enough for you. My father was English. He was all right, but a lot of them are bastards and the British class system is medieval. It's got to change. You wait. The war's going to blow it inside out."

From this time on my relations with the chancery staff became quite normal. As for the minister, I questioned Eleni's view of him until I had an uncomfortable lunch with the family after Jane had set off for England.

We took our places at table and I was about to ask if there was news of Jane when the minister's wife picked up an envelope lying on her side-plate, and crying, "Thank heavens!" took a knife to slit the envelope open. Finding that it was already open she pulled out the letter, but after reading only a few lines, looked up and asked, "When did you get this, Owen?"

"This morning," he said, his voice non-committal. "Nothing to worry about."

But Anne pushed back her chair, stood up and shaking the letter at him cried, "My God! You filthy twerp! You never told me she was all right...all these hours...!"

I blanked out on what was said next. From then on I did not care much for the minister.

That was the last meal I shared with the family. But Grania and I continued to meet, and it was through her I met Ted Howes. He, and a colleague of his, Bob, were correspondents for two London newspapers, and during May and June the four of us often dined together.

In May and June 1940 it was no wonder that our dinners were lively with hot discussions about the crescendo of disasters in Europe. I was hard-pressed to keep abreast of the other three, and mostly listened as their opinions clashed and forecasts differed.

At least I was roughly informed about what was happening elsewhere, for every day at the legation we listened to the BBC morning broadcast. In mid-May Belgium was overrun by the Germans, and as their troops advanced towards Paris the BBC vividly described the thousands of British, French and Allied troops pouring in from devastated Europe to the beaches of Dunkirk. Between May 26, and June 3, we heard how men scrambled aboard whatever floating vessel had made its way across the channel - an armada of everything from destroyers to private yachts and row-boats. Following this evacuation the fortress of Liège and the Maginot Line were breached, Italy joined up with Germany on June 10, and on June 14, the Germans entered Paris. Four days later General de Gaulle began rallying his compatriots to join the Free French Forces in London.

This was the stuff of history, magnificent and terrible - and we weren't there. It felt odd, not being there, and odd to know that now France had surrendered, the doors of Europe were truly slammed shut. It was also odd that we didn't know what would happen next. I wondered about Phil at Harwich. But that was miles away, and I was here - and, to be truthful, I was happy.

After my first meeting with Ted I asked Grania about his wife. "She's a ball of fire," Grania said. "Ted adores her, though she does rather push him around. But you know how good-humoured and gentle he is. He just smiles and lets her walk all over him. He was very down after she went back to England with Emily, that's his daughter. She's a little pet. Ted really misses her. You've cheered him up no end."

That pleased me, for I liked him very much. Before long we began dining out and exploring the countryside on our own, and so got to know one another better than is possible in a foursome. I enjoyed being with him, liked his dry humour, his firm opinions contrasting with a hint of shyness, and was touched by his love for Emily.

"I keep wondering how big Emmy will be when I see her again," he said. "I hope she'll like me. They change all the time."

"What's she like?"

"She's a red-head like her mother, and just as bossy! We had a sort of cook-nanny and Emmy ordered her about like a little Turk, often in very funny German." He laughed, *"Wo bist mein sockel?'* she'd cry, meaning sock - *'sockel'* is the word for foot." He grinned and added, "It was marvellous having a nanny. She looked after my clothes as well as Emmy's. I must confess I find it hard to cope with looking after myself. I'm not much good at ironing."

Despite the war and Ted's anxieties, the summer was infused with a kind of innocent happiness in the pleasure of each other's company. At first I'd been a little awed by the fact that Ted was a journalist and knew so much about the ramifications of the war, its background, and what was going on behind the scenes in Budapest. But he never made me feel an ignoramus, so I gradually became a little less ignorant.

Meantime life in Budapest continued merrily on, and the food was wonderful. Hungarians are cook artists. One restaurant where we made an occasional splurge was a visual delight the minute you entered. On a long buffet were always displayed mouth-watering fruit flans, the succulent glistening fruit arranged in perfect circular designs, like mandalas, and the pastry was light as a feather. Even the most unpretentious restaurants had their special delights - the simplest was a humble place that served a whole cauliflower, covered in buttered breadcrumbs: just that, delectable to look at, and to eat. As for goulash, that was Hungary, full of flavour, spicy and colourful as red paprika.

There was, as yet, no wartime food rationing (except for coffee, which was prohibitively expensive), and sometimes we felt a bit guilty to be eating so well. Ted said we were wallowing in fleshpots, and to prove his point he took me to the hot spring baths on Margit Island in the Danube, just below Buda.

"Have a look at this," he said, "fleshpots in person."

'This' was a series of shallow pools fed with water from the hot springs. In the pools huge, overfed Hungarian men lolled at ease like great seals. "They pretend they're losing weight," said Ted.

"They look rather sub-human," I said. Ted remarked sombrely that he could think of less kind ways to describe some of them, but I expostulated, "Be fair, Ted. Not all Hungarians are like this lot. Think of the marvellous music and...oh! you know what I mean, the nice ordinary people in shops and everywhere..."

"Music's the icing on the cake," Ted said. "You must meet Josef. He's the yeast in the cake. He'll be back soon." I asked from where, but Ted said to wait until I met him, adding that he was a Jew.

So I met Josef. He was well over six feet tall, a powerful man with a mop of black curls, a rugged face and steady, dark brown eyes that missed nothing. What he was doing was getting as many Jews as possible out of Hungary before the Germans took over. "After that," he said, "it will be too late."

His escape routes, which were presumably over borders to adjacent Balkan countries, sometimes succeeded, sometimes failed: always it was touch and go. One story was unforgettable. He was lying in a ditch, timing the border guard's routine with a stop-watch, making sure how far he went each stretch, how long before he turned, how much time there would be to climb out of the ditch, lie low, make a dash, another wait, another dash, repeated until he was safely out of the guard's hearing.

Josef said, "One night in rough country, with the nearest village some way off, I didn't expect a visitor to my ditch." He paused, grimaced, went on, "I didn't hear him until he snuffled in the undergrowth just above my head - of all things, a dog! I'm no believer but I prayed he wouldn't pick up my scent. Poor old dog. He did, and scrambled down into the ditch with me, just a big, friendly dog, tail wagging, pushing at my hand, you know how they are." He paused. "But I couldn't take a chance." Another pause.

"A chance...?"

"It was the most horrible thing I've ever done," Josef said.

"And...?"

"And I strangled him."

Before we parted I asked if he knew how many Jews he had saved so far. He shook his head and said sadly, "It is never enough."

One evening Ted and I joined some friends at one of the grander restaurants. Across the room was a very classy party of young Hungarians, one of whom Ted identified as a prince with great estates. He had an arm round a pretty, laughing girl, and in his other hand he waved a wine glass and called for more wine, and more music. It was pure musical comedy; at any moment the young prince might well burst into song, and the waiters join in a rousing chorus.

"It's a bit overdone," I said.

Ted grinned, then added, "This country is due for a shake-up. Not long ago a friend of mine went to spend a weekend with a princeling at one of his great houses. As they drove through the village the prince threw coins to the bobbing peasants. My friend was shocked, and to make matters worse he had bugs in his bed. Just like you did."

"I can't understand it. Surely bugs come from dirt?"

"Great houses in the Middle Ages were magnificent and very dirty," said Ted. "Parts of Hungary are still medieval. It won't last long. But it's a pretty picture while it lasts."

It was indeed very pretty. One Saturday, driving unhurriedly through the country roads, we came to a typical village, the unpaved road lined with small, brightly painted cottages, and flowers everywhere. Ted said, "It's a feast day, look!" and I saw three girls ahead, wearing their traditional dress, colourful as the flowers.

Ted parked the car and we walked down the street behind the girls. Their hair was braided with ribbons, around their necks were kerchiefs printed with a riot of luscious red roses, and as they walked their full skirts swung from side to side over a froth of petticoats.

Dan said, "They wear as many as ten underskirts, the more the better. Hungarian one-upmanship."

The girls walked with a spring, their arms round each other's waists, chattering and giggling. We heard music, and found it was from a fair, a real, home-grown fair. Even the merry-go-round was on a very human scale, turned by two small, sturdy boys walking round and round on the flat top, pushing something which kept the painted horses spinning below, not very fast, but the riders were very young. Inevitably someone was playing a fiddle. We wandered round the booths and Ted bought a large gingerbread man.

"This is the saintly King Matthias," Ted said. "He was crowned in the cathedral here six centuries ago." The king was decked out in coloured icing with added sparkles and I said he was very kingly.

"But now just gingerbread," said Ted.

One summer weekend Ted took me to visit friends who lived on a small estate in the country. Joan was English, her husband, Otto, a Jew from Czechoslovakia. Ted said, "Joan is a lovely person," and added with a grin, "and very county, just up your street." I laughed, and gave him a dig about putting on his barefoot boy act, and asked for more information. "Well, Joan's family didn't have much money and she came out here before the war as a governess to one of the princelings. This was where Otto met her and fell hopelessly in love. He's quite a bit older than her, tubby, no Prince Charming but a very nice man. Joan said 'no' to his first proposal, and kept saying 'no' until he followed her to England and went on proposing. She said she hadn't the heart to keep turning him away. They seem very happy. Their daughter Margit is the same age as Emily, just three, a pretty little thing. She's living proof that children can learn to speak several languages at once without trying. She talks Hungarian to the nurse, English to Joan and sometimes German to her father. She turns from one to the other without a pause. Otto says 'Why not?'" Ted concluded, smiling, "You'll love them, especially the house."

I loved them all, and the old stone house was beautiful. It was built in the shape of an E without the middle bit which was a spacious raised terrace with terra-cotta urns full of flowers. At Ted's insistence Joan showed me her storerooms where preserves were lined up in orderly rows, the glass bottles full of glowing peaches and apricots, fat red tomatoes, green beans and paprikas.

"It's everything the heart could desire!" I exclaimed.

"Yes," Joan said, "the shelves are very reassuring," and as she locked the door added, "especially in times like these."

I wanted to ask her what might happen to them if the Germans occupied the country, but we'd only just met so instead I said, "You look like a medieval chatelaine with your bunch of keys hanging from a belt round your waist. Do you wear them all the time?"

She laughed, said, "No, only during the morning routine when I give out whatever the cook needs for the day. It's the custom." She looked at me with a very sweet smile and added, "Otto likes to follow the old customs."

As Ted and I drove back to the city I asked him whether Otto worried about what might happen to all of them if the Germans took over Hungary.

Ted broke in and said firmly, "Not *if*, Belinda, but *when* they take over. Otto won't leave, though Joan wants him to. The estate's his lifeblood and he feels responsible for every tenant farmer and every peasant worker on the place. He's feudal in the best possible way. Joan won't leave him. So we all hope the Germans will be too busy in the cities to bother with one Czechoslovakian Jew living quietly in the country." After a pause he went on, "I think he refuses to realize that the Germans have gone crazy, simply can't accept what they're up to in their own country, let alone what they may very well do here."

"What are the Germans up to? Do you really know?" And that was when I learnt about the concentration camps. But even then the whole, obscene reality was not fully known.

In August Arthur wrote that everyone in England was in a fever about rumours of invasion by the Germans, and that he was working in one of the government ministries, but also took shifts as a volunteer fireman in the City of London. He said they sat around drinking tea and the nights were long. It sounded boring. That was August. In September the blitz on London began. In a second letter Arthur wrote that he'd been on duty when the city around St. Paul's went up in flames. 'Pretty terrifying,' he wrote. 'I'm all right, but the warehouse with all the furniture from Fulham, including the Blüthner, was blown to bits.'

I put the letter down, truly glad that Arthur was unhurt, felt a pang for that beautiful piano, and then tried to imagine London in flames, and Arthur in a blazing inferno of crackling wood, buildings crashing, and all the hurt people, and the dead. This, like Dunkirk, was history - and, like Dunkirk, was miles and miles away. It might be on another planet.

But for Ted, England was not another planet. Though his wife and Emily were somewhere in the country, he was worried. "I think the German invasion panic is over," he said, "but the bombing raids will almost certainly spread beyond London."

"Surely they'll be all right, tucked away in a little village?"

"I know. They should be all right."

"Bloody war!" I said. But I knew that, whatever the war might bring, I was happy, sitting with Ted after a picnic on one of the wooded Gellert hills south of Buda. Sometimes a bird sang, and the early autumn sunshine was mellow.

"That was a good lunch," Ted said lazily, leaning back against a tree. He shut his eyes and we sat in silence until he said, "How nice it would be just to be happy, not haunted by the war and the feeling I shouldn't be here, and not..."

"And not what?"

"Well...doing something worthwhile."

"Don't you feel your job's important?"

He shrugged. "Here it's a matter of waiting until the Germans flood in. It's pretty futile. There's not a lot we can do. Except..."

"Except what?"

"Well...I suppose you've guessed that being a newspaper correspondent isn't really the most important thing I do." I didn't know, so said nothing. "Basil's in the same outfit."

I'd met Basil Davidson at parties. He was a tall, good-looking young Scot, with curly fair hair, rather intense, but had a nice wry humour. At a recent party he'd asked me if I'd do a bit of volunteer work at his news agency, and when I asked what sort of work he said, "I'll call you next week. I'm away for a few days." So Basil wasn't just running a news agency. I wondered whether I'd be involved in 'the same outfit,' whatever that was.

We lingered on the hill and had a leisurely supper together in Buda. Afterwards Ted came upstairs to my apartment and stayed all night. It was quite unplanned - and for the first time in my adult life I discovered the tenderness of sex.

∞ 23 ∞

Three full months,
then farewell, Budapest.

Ted and I moved into an apartment together at the beginning of October. It was my idea, though I wasn't planning a love-nest. Not at all. The idea was born the morning after our night together. Ted left before breakfast and returned before lunch, wearing a badly ironed summer jacket and pants, looking unexpectedly diffident. I looked at him and my first thought was a great rush of gratitude for that night, but we couldn't continue as lovers: he had a wife in England. It wasn't a thought, it was an instinct, and was followed by a second thought: that it was absurd he should be holed up in a miserable poky room when we could share the expenses of an apartment - and a servant, who could iron his clothes.

194

In 2001 a roommate may, and may well not, be a lover: in 1940, amongst the conservative diplomatic circle, we were a scandal, of which I remained, for some time, ignorant. Ted did hesitate, but I was carried away by my idea, which opened the prospect of being able to hire a piano. So I blithely set out to find somewhere to suit us both.

I found an apartment in Pest, the 'modern' city on the left bank of the Danube, where rents were less than in beautiful old Buda. The apartment was on the top floor of a turn-of-the-century building, and was gorgeous. The enormous living-room must have been designed as an up-market studio, for half of one wall and part of the ceiling was glass. At night the lights of Pest twinkled below - it was rather like living in a tree house, Peter Pan style. There was a kitchen, a couple of bedrooms plus a very small one for a maid, all the floors were wood and a monument of a tiled stove radiated heat (and gobbled quantities of fuel).

When Ted came to see the apartment I made him shut his eyes, led him into the big room and said, "You can look now!"

"Good Lord!" he cried, "it's a palace!"

"Isn't it better than your gloomy old room? Between us we can afford a maid to do the cooking and cleaning, and your ironing. And there's masses of room for a piano."

So we took the apartment.

After we moved in I didn't hire a piano straight away because I began doing a daily stint of work with Basil Davidson. I had to get up very early and walk across the city to his office, and then do a day's work at the legation. This was enough to get on with.

It was some time before I learnt that Ted and Basil were members of the SOE, or Special Operations Executive, a war-emergency section of Intelligence designed to stir up resistance in countries overrun, or likely to be overrun, by the enemy. Ted and Basil both worked as newspapermen, a blind behind which unspecified activities were carried out.

Meanwhile, all I knew was that Basil's news agency was openly providing British news to Hungarian radio and newspapers. Hungary was putting on a performance of being neutral, so the Hungarian newspapers were happy to make a show of reporting news from both sides. News releases were regularly cabled from the Ministry of Inform-ation in London, but these became intermittent as the *Luftwaffe* stepped up their nightly bombing raids leaving the agency dependent on the BBC.

My task was to monitor the BBC news, record as much as I could in shorthand, and type it out. It was fascinating to be part of a kind of *Chums* adventure, even though I was a bit vague about its purpose. Unfortunately the reception was very rough and croaky, and I was further handicapped on two more counts: my shorthand speed of 120 words a minute wasn't up to taking the broadcasts verbatim, and with a superficial understanding of what was happening in Europe it was beyond me to do more than make a stab at what the broadcasts were all about. I soon suspected this didn't matter too much to Basil. As Allied disasters mounted and the Germans gradually encroached on Hungary, Basil's free-flying news reports became remarkably upbeat.

I thoroughly enjoyed this freelance interlude, rising early to be at the agency to catch the first broadcast at six a.m. I had to be at the legation by nine, but work there was grinding to a dull routine and I looked forward to my daily uplift of helping Basil persuade the Hungarians that the Allies were a good bet.

What I liked best during this interlude was walking through quiet streets in the clear morning air. This was the time of day when the city was very human; voices were individually distinct, a quick laugh rang like an exclamation mark, a broom swished softly as débris was swept from the sidewalk, shutters clattered open, and from a bakery every morning came the delicious fragrance of fresh bread.

On my first day Basil told me not to say a word about what I was doing. "That Anglo-Irish gentleman you work for will kick up a hell of a rumpus if he knows you're mixed up with us."

"Why? Doesn't he support all you're doing?"

"My dear Belinda, the minister is convinced the war is lost so the diplomatic thing to do is maintain a bland front and make sure no-one in the legation does anything irregular."

I thought Basil must be exaggerating, but he wasn't. After I had been working at the agency for a few weeks, the minister called me to his room and abruptly asked me what I thought I was doing "playing games with those SOE types."

In spite of Basil's warning, I was shocked. "I'm not playing games. It's hard for Basil to gather reliable news now for the local press. Isn't the truth important?"

The minister made the sort of noise usually written "Tcha!" and said, "You are a member of the diplomatic service. Your behaviour must be above reproach. You are to stop this tomfool work at once."

Hotly I exclaimed, "I don't even have enough work to do here, I spend half the day teaching myself German. It's ridiculous, with a war on."

The minister, radiating displeasure, curtly dismissed me.

I told Eleni about this exchange afterwards. "Above reproach!" she exclaimed. "I like that. What about his mistress? Everyone knows about her. Or the staff member whose acrobatics with a prostitute were recorded by hidden camera? That cost the legation a pretty penny. Above reproach! Really, Belinda, stop being so naïve. Our minister is not one for toil, sweat and tears, and in the diplomatic world truth is rationed."

I could not disobey the minister, but he could not disapprove of my taking music lessons and I hired a grand piano - nothing less would do for that splendid studio - and after a chance meeting with a violinist called Sandor Vegh, I arranged to have lessons with his friend, Sandor Veres.

Veres was a colleague of Bela Bartok, and Vegh was the first violin in the orchestra which gave daily open-air concerts of classical music in the park. You could sit close to the orchestra, or in a restaurant a little apart from the serious listeners. The chatter and the click of cutlery on china plates was a bit distracting, but it was a jolly, *al fresco* ambience with everyone enjoying themselves in their own way.

The first time I went to a park concert Sandor Vegh made rather a point of noticing me. I felt sure that if he had been a gypsy violinist in a restaurant he would have played his fiddle soulfully in my ear. Instead he came down in the first interval and invited me to join him for coffee later. He was a rosy young man with a consciously histrionic mane of black hair, but for all the show he was a really talented violinist, and had a good heart. I never imagined that the Vegh String Quartet would, after the war, earn a sound international reputation.

The two Sandors were long-time friends. Sandor Veres was gentle and modest, a pianist and a fine musician. For several years he and Bartok had scoured the countryside, laden with primitive little wax discs, intent on recording the unspoiled music of Hungarian gypsies. They went to rural cafés, weddings and festivals where they would find musicians who hadn't succumbed to the exaggerated pathos popular in city restaurants.

When Sandor played one of the recordings for me at his house, he said, "This violinist was an old man, probably in his late seventies, perhaps eighty. I didn't ask. He made his own violin and never had a lesson in his life."

The sound from the wax disc was far from sophisticated, but the beat of the czardas was passionate, the rhythm compelling, and the playing so explosive I felt that at any moment the little disc might shatter into smithereens.

Sandor Veres insisted on my playing Bach. One day after a lesson we sat idly discussing Bach's music, and this led to a story about a country wedding he and Bartok had gone to. There'd been no opportunity to ask if they might record the wedding music, but they were made very welcome. In return they offered to give a concert before the guests dispersed.

"We decided to play nothing but Bach," said Sandor. "We had no idea what they'd make of it, so we were prepared to play something else if they seemed bored." He laughed, and went on, "They weren't at all bored. They kept calling for more, and we went on and on, all the time playing Bach. It was an amazing evening, proof that music is its own language. You can talk Bach or folk and everything in between to people who are unlettered, but true musicians."

"What do you mean, 'unlettered'?"

"Real folk music that's been played and sung over centuries isn't cluttered up with musical fads and pretty-prettiness. Folk music is very free, full of personal elaborations and style, but never out of touch with where it comes from. It's very pure."

One evening Sandor took me to meet Bela Bartok after a concert of his music. As we went backstage Sandor said, "He's a very sick man, but you must meet him, if only to shake his hand." It was a very small hand, limp, white, feeling rather like a cold chamois leather glove filled with fragile bird bones. I held it gently for a moment as he looked past me rather helplessly, white haired, white-faced. That was all, simple, but important. Five years later he was dead.

When Ted finally told me about the SOE I was secretly rather excited as old spy movies ran through my head. During the months we shared the apartment some unexpected things did happen, but they weren't very dramatic. There were the frequent telephone calls when all we heard was heavy breathing, a click, and silence. This became rather a joke. Then one day Ted beckoned me over to a window from which I could see a corner by the entrance to our building.

"See the little fellow in a long black overcoat, standing against the wall, looking cold?"

"Yes...why?"

"There are two of them, turn and turn about. Nothing to worry you; it's just the other side keeping an eye on my comings and goings. You're all right, diplomatically immune and all that."

"How do they know you're not just a journalist?"

"Contacts aren't always reliable. Some poor sod gets persuaded to co-operate."

Part of me enjoyed this view into an unknown world, but at the same time it seemed rather silly and hard to take seriously, even when it was obvious that someone was searching the apartment at fairly regular intervals. I kept my music on the piano in a particular order and would find it disordered, and the same would happen to papers on Ted's desk. Our maid never touched them - but I did wonder how they got in.

I asked Ted if he thought our maid was being bribed, but this was a disagreeable thought, for we were fond of her. She was a real peasant. When she came to live with us I prepared the little bedroom for her, but she insisted on sleeping under the kitchen table on a straw-filled mattress which she unrolled each night.

"It is the custom," she said firmly.

Ted remarked, "Let her be. She's happier that way." As for her being bribed by snoopers he said, "They won't find anything. Don't let's upset her, she's a marvellous cook!" She was indeed. Her steamed rice pudding in a zabaglione sauce was a masterpiece, but very expensive, so we had to ration it.

Only once was there a hint of drama, and I didn't care for it. Ted came and went at all hours of the day and night and one evening he was unusually silent and restless, wandering over to the window, mooning back to pick up a book and not reading it. Finally I asked what was wrong.

After a pause he said, "I've got to get rid of someone."

"Get rid? How? Sack them?"

"That would be easy."

"What d'you mean?" He shrugged and stared out of the window. So I asked, hoping to sound matter-of-fact, "D'you mean...kill?"

"That's about it."

"But Ted, just like that, not even a fight? How?"

"I don't know. Shove him in the Danube, perhaps." He looked miserable. I couldn't probe, but I believed him; he wasn't given to play-acting.

A couple of days later he suggested that if I came back from work and there was anything unusual happening I was to take the bright cotton coverlet from the spare bed and hang it out of the window. Then he would keep away until it was removed.

"What sort of happening?"

"Hard to say, Belinda. It's probably unnecessary. I leave it to you to judge."

I never had to judge, and never knew whether Ted did rub someone out in cold blood. But the more I thought about what he'd said it seemed squalid, a sickening game in which ordinary human beings had their kindly feelings twisted in the name of...what? Patriotism, Freedom, Justice? Even the unspeakable Nazis and Fascists drew on the same vocabulary. It didn't make sense.

At the end of October the first snow fell. The old city was lovely as a Victorian Christmas card and city noises were muffled. Walking up the hill to the legation in Buda the only sounds were the crunch of my footsteps and the soft shus-sh..sh as a clump of snow fell from the branch of a fir tree. By December the Danube was frozen over. Earlier Ted had taken me to a fur warehouse where I bought, very inexpensively, a fur coat, fur hat and fur muff. The fur was treated sheepskin, dyed and transformed to look like something more costly.

I'd never had a fur coat before, and every time I wore this outfit, especially the muff, I felt Balkan and romantic. But that was only when I was pretending everything was all right, which it wasn't. I blamed the worsening situation in Hungary, or the bad relationships at the legation, or the short winter days, and ignored what was under my nose.

The first warning blast came about a month after Ted and I moved into our apartment. The blast was from the minister.

"You're a very headstrong young woman," he said, which could have been friendly but wasn't. "I've told you before that your behaviour should be irreproachable. Now you're living with a married man, and one of the British community for good measure. Have you thought that Ted's wife was popular here, and some people won't like what you're doing and will make sure word of it gets back to England?"

I was angry with him for interfering with my personal life, and said as much, without telling him that Ted and I were simply roommates. But the truth of what the minister said stung, and it was no surprise when Ted, looking wretched said, "Belinda, I've had a letter from my wife."

"What did she say?"

"That if we continue to live together she'll divorce me. I'll write..."

But I interjected, "Don't be an idiot, Ted. I'll move out."

"Don't be so quick, Belinda. Where will you go? I'll explain..."

"What can you explain that she'll believe? Do you want to be divorced and lose Emily and marry me? You know you don't. I'm not staying. I think Janet will take me in." Janet was the wife of an American newspaperman who was away on an assignment.

"Belinda..."

"Please Ted. I've decided."

I lost no time in asking Janet to take me in. She was delighted, saying "It's lonely without Bud." I took my stuff to her place a couple of days later, and then went out and bought an outrageous hat. It was shaped like a sombrero, made of brushed felt, very hairy, honey-coloured, encircled by a brown ribbon. It helped a bit, but not all that much.

Inevitably I longed to get away from Budapest, but how and where to? Then I remembered something the day I read the Foreign Office letter asking if I was free to go to Hungary; my first thought had been, "From there I can get to Greece." So why not now? I couldn't just up sticks and go there. I sat glumly at the legation pretending to learn German as December rolled on towards Christmas. Ted and I had earlier been invited to spend Christmas with Joan and Otto. Now I assumed he wouldn't go. Perhaps I shouldn't. I felt hollow with sadness and indecision. Then out of the blue Eleni told me that the naval attaché in Athens needed a secretary.

"The attaché is an admiral," Eleni explained. "A young naval lieutenant is acting as his secretary and is mad to get away into action. You always said you wanted to go to Greece. Here's your chance."

"How did you know, about the job?"

"I hear things. Just get a move on and write an application. We're only hanging on here by the skin of our teeth, and you may as well get out before the Balkans are swarming with Nazis. If you write today I'll slip it in the diplomatic bag to Athens tomorrow."

"You're a friend!"

"Oh! get away with you! Go and write that letter."

So I did, noting the six months spent with Phil at Harwich, said I could leave Budapest at short notice (a wild promise, but nobody could stop me) and gave Eleni the letter. Then came the wait, fidgeting for an answer, willing things to turn out right, saying nothing to anyone except Eleni. In fact the answer came quickly in a personal cable from the naval attaché: 'Application accepted. Come soonest.'

I decided to wait until after the legation Christmas party before confronting the minister. The party turned out to be as frightful as Eleni predicted. Nobody was at ease, the minister exuded an embarrassing bonhomie, and more than once I saw Anne, a cigarette in a long holder held rather stagily aloft, her head thrown back as she announced in her penetrating voice, "Of course, I as a writer..."

The last time she said this someone caught my eye and raised an eyebrow, and suddenly I felt a stab of pity. It couldn't be easy being the wife of a diplomat, and worse still when he was so unpopular. I hoped there were compensations, but had my doubts. These were strengthened the following morning after my meeting with the minister.

I presented what I thought were irrefutable reasons for my leaving, explaining how the job in Athens would release a naval officer for active service, and pointed out that there simply wasn't enough work for me to do. "I'm lucky to have anything to type from one day to the next," I concluded.

He heard me in silence. When the silence continued unbroken I guessed I was in for trouble. Finally he said, "You sound confident, Belinda, that I will agree to this...this irresponsible suggestion. Your place is here. I do not agree to your leaving. It is important to maintain our position in Hungary until we are forced to go."

So I said, "Then please accept my resignation."

After an icy silence the minister retorted, "I shall do nothing of the kind. If you go, I shall withhold your pay."

I remembered Anne calling him a 'filthy twerp' and sympathized, but shut my mouth and left the room. If he supposed he could deter me from leaving he was in for a surprise.

I wrote a cable to the naval attaché in Athens confirming I'd report at the legation by January 1, and Eleni put it in the diplomatic bag to Athens. After that I bought a ticket for the train journey through Yugoslavia to Greece, leaving on December 29.

I worked at the legation until a few days before Christmas, feeling this was the proper thing to do. I decided not to go back after spending Christmas with Joan and Otto, so on the last day I tidied my desk, and then went to say goodbye to everyone, starting with the first secretary. I made sure he was in his room as I had a bone to pick with him.

He was obviously not quite sure how to treat me, but he wished me well. I thanked him and then said, smiling pleasantly, "There's one thing I'd love to know. Why was I never asked more than once to your house? You know my family, and I don't eat my peas with a knife."

He cleared his throat, shuffled a few papers, moved a paper-weight, muttered, "You must realize..." then cleared his throat and began again, "You must understand...difficult to mix...things can get awkward..."

"Awkward?"

He mumbled something and gave up, so I let it go. I'd broken all the rules of what was and wasn't 'done', but I didn't care - I felt absurdly pleased to have struck a blow for the liberty and equality of chancery staff, wherever they might be.

Joan had told me Ted wasn't coming for Christmas but I searched the platform for him all the same. He wasn't there. Of course.

I had been told that a sleigh would be waiting outside the station, and there it was, straight out of a Russian romance. The graceful lines of the sleigh were of painted wood, the padded seat piled with furs, the horse and driver steaming gently as they breathed into the cold night air. It was a beautiful clear night. The stars crackled in the blue-black sky and all around the snow lay, as it should, deep and even. The only sounds were the jingle of bells, the driver's occasional little grunts and encouraging cries, the soft thud of the horse's hooves, and the whisper of sleigh runners over snow. I was warm as toast in a fur wrap, the crisp air made my cheeks tingle, it was all delicious, a delight - and damn! oh damn! I wished Ted was with me. But I knew one thing: I would not allow myself to get too fond, ever again, of a married man.

Everyone gave me a great welcome, but after supper I just had to ask Joan if Ted was expected. She took my hand and patted it. "He won't come, Belinda. You were quite right to leave, Ted's family means a lot to him. Now come and help me with the Christmas tree."

It was an enormous tree, almost touching the ceiling of the big drawing room. We clambered about on a couple of ladders hanging brightly-coloured glass baubles and making sure the candle-holders were safely fixed.

Joan said, "I'm always nervous of fire. It would be so awful..."

"I'm being careful," I said, and promised with absolute confidence that nothing awful would happen.

The next evening the tenant farmers and farm hands came with their wives, children, and grandparents - the whole gamut of village connections. Joan and Otto greeted them one by one and the room soon filled with adults exchanging greetings while the children gazed at the great, glittering tree. Time passed. I knew Otto planned to hold a small service of thanksgiving and wondered why we were waiting. Perhaps someone else was expected? Finally he moved off to stand by the tree, heads were bent devoutly, and the service began.

The candle flames flickered on silver tinsel and glass, the whole glimmering mass spreading a soft glow over us all. The tenants were resplendent in their beautiful festive clothes and just in front of me was a very little girl, her braids of black hair threaded with ribbons and, in her full skirts and bright kerchief, she was an enchanting miniature adult. She stood between her mother and father, absolutely still, her head tilted to encompass that miracle of a tree, ten times taller than her little self.

When Otto said, "Let us pray," everyone knelt - except the little girl. Her mother pulled her hand, her father hissed in her ear, she did not move. Finally, with a brisk movement her father lifted her up and her mother bent her knees, just as if she was a jointed doll, and then she was set on the floor, kneeling at last. More than once her legs were straightened or bent as the need arose. She submitted, oblivious.

This performance was so delightful that I barely registered the telephone ringing, or Joan leaving the room. But when she came back it was clear something was very wrong. She whispered to Otto and I saw his face stiffen. He nodded, concluded the service and slipped out. Joan presided over the gift giving, and Otto returned to share cake and wine. Only when all the guests were gone did I learn what had happened. Some dear neighbours, driving to join us, had been hit at the unguarded rail crossing. The young son, who was driving, had been decapitated.

Joan kept saying, "I taught him to drive."

I don't remember what happened to the other people in the car, only that the boy was decapitated, and Joan repeating, "I taught him to drive, I taught him to drive."

I stayed over Boxing Day, helping to make a good show of Christmas cheer for Margit's sake, but left the next day. "We must meet after the war," we said, but as the sleigh whispered over the snow to the station I felt a fear of grievous times ahead for the kindly, honourable Jew, his gentle English wife and Margit, who was the same age as Ted's Emily.

Journey with incidents.
Athens, Alexis, and war at closer quarters.

I hung out of the window looking anxiously for Basil Davidson as the train pulled in to Belgrade, unsure how long it would wait and hoping he would be on time. Our meeting mattered a lot for he had promised to lend me some money, having been outraged when I told him that the Minister had withheld my pay.

"I can't lend it now," he'd said, "I'm just off to Belgrade. But I'll meet your train there. Look out for me!"

It was dark when the train stopped but I picked out Basil's tall figure under the station lights, rather dramatically wreathed in steam from engines snorting into the bitter night air. I waved exuberantly from the open carriage window and he loped over, waving an envelope.

"I put in enough to keep you alive for a month," he cried above the station din.

I showered him with thanks, and as the train drew away for the long haul to Salonika he called out, "Good luck, Belinda!" and I shouted, "Keep out of trouble!" knowing he wouldn't. Nor did he. Basil's next assignment was to liase with Marshall Tito's partisan guerrillas in Yugoslavia. Now, sixty years later, when the Balkans are yet again a powder-keg, Basil's post-war book, *Special Operations Europe,* is worth reading.

The train to Salonika had no sleeping berths, also no restaurant, and before leaving Budapest friends had earnestly advised me, "For goodness' sake, Belinda, don't get shut into a compartment with Yugoslav soldiers," and proffered forebodings of thievery and rape.

The absence of a restaurant was tiresome, but I dismissed the warnings of rape etc. as silly - happily for my peace of mind, for just before leaving Belgrade my compartment filled with cheerful, rumbustious Yugoslav conscripts. Soon I was being urged to share their bottles of wine, and at the first train stop, having discovered I had no food, they bought a quantity of sweet, very substantial bun-like things and cried. "Eat! eat!" delighted with themselves. I ate, we smiled and nodded at one another until I fell asleep, exhausted by wine, buns and camaraderie.

The journey seemed timeless. I slept sporadically as the train grumbled steadily along in darkness, waking when the rhythm altered for yet another stop, brakes complaining, followed by rattles, bumps, lights, voices and doors banging. The soldiers got out at one of these stops, and rough hands gripped mine in farewell with what seemed to be blessings on my journey.

Around midnight we reached Salonika and stepped out into total darkness, absolutely no light anywhere. Was this a dire emergency? Then I remembered. It was a blackout, for Italy had invaded Albania in October and pressed on into the mountains north-west of Salonika where the Greeks were holding out against invasion.

For a while the platform was bedlam, compounded by conflicting information about the connection to Athens. People milled around, banging into each other, demanding directions until the connection at last steamed in, and confusion became a mad scramble to find a place. This was when I collided with a well-padded body who apologized in French, shone a flashlight into my face, ascertained I was on my way to Athens, and, grasping my elbow, propelled me to his compartment.

I say 'his' because he seemed to have taken over sole possession of it. When other people peered hopefully in he said grandly, *"Reservé, corps diplomatique."* I disapproved of his dog-in-the-manger attitude, but better feelings were overcome when he brought out a hamper of delicious crisp baguettes, Brie, excellent wine, fruit, and mouth-watering pastries. I was famished and we shared a congenial meal.

After a polite post-prandial interval we made ready for sleep, and only then, as I arranged the basic railway blanket and pillow, did I have a twinge of misgiving. When my companion was absent in the washroom I lay down in the armour of my clothing and pulled the blanket up to my nose. On his return I wished him a sound sleep and shut my eyes. After a pause he murmured, "You are comfortable, madame?"

I yawned, delicately but with emphasis. "Yes, indeed. Very comfortable."

"Permit me to tuck you in!"

As he bent to this task I quickly interposed, "There is no need. You are most kind," and with a flourish added, *"Dormez bien jusqu'à demain."* I turned my back and thought, 'bother men and their tedious assumptions.'

He lay down and all was quiet. But I wasn't comfortable for long, and the reason was damnable and unmistakable - bedbugs. I tried not to wriggle, but failed, and in a flash my companion was on his feet.

"Il y à quelque chose...?"

I sighed as if in deep sleep, and lay motionless, confronting choice - either suffer the bugs stoically, or fend off the wearisome expectations of my host. Crossly, I settled for bugs.

Early in the morning the train stopped and someone entered the compartment. I fell asleep again and on waking found that the newcomer sitting opposite me was a young German. This was unexceptionable, for Germany was not at war with Greece. However, my Frenchman sat in his corner emanating a ponderous, disapproving silence. It was a curious situation. Should I hate this poor fellow, who was young and embarrassed? The answer was 'No' so I offered him an orange. He took it with confused expressions of gratitude. The Frenchman exuded disapproval, and we all looked out of our respective windows in silence until the train pulled in to Athens.

On the platform the Frenchman had a gratifying *corps diplomatique* reception. The German slipped away, and I stood alone under a cloudless blue sky. The air was mild as a blessing, and right in front of me was a wild bush of mimosa in full golden bloom. 'I made it,' I said silently to the gods to whom my young self, long ago in Weston, had vowed, "One day I will go to Greece." So on New Year's Day, 1941, I gave them thanks. For two pins I'd have hugged the mimosa. Instead I picked up my suitcase, and the cold, darkness and heartache of Budapest fell away.

Two days later I was happily sitting in Omonia Square smiling at everything and everyone, including a young man with a feisty wire-haired terrier who made his way through the haphazard scatter of tables and chairs and asked if he could join me. He introduced his dog, Felix, and himself, "Cy Sulzberger, Balkan newspaper correspondent of the *New York Times*." I told him who I was, and before long confided that I was staying in a hotel but hoped to find an apartment in Athens. Cy at once said there was one in the house where he was living which belonged to Greek friends of his, the Ladas family, and it was only a few blocks from the British Legation on Kifissia Street. He offered to arrange for the young son of the family, Alexis Ladas, to collect me that evening from my hotel and show me the apartment.

Alexis was alone in the lobby and looked up as I walked down the stairs. I smiled a greeting and was disconcerted when he simply continued to stare. I was accustomed to stares, but nothing quite so fixed. Perhaps I reminded him of someone? When I'd seen and agreed to take the apartment, I asked if he always stared at strangers as if they were ghosts.

"I'm sorry," he said. "I didn't mean to embarrass you. It was - well, you weren't what I expected."

"What's that got to do with glaring at me?"

"Well...you see...to be honest I didn't want to come, I mean, to show you the apartment. I thought you'd be some old English trout and a bore. And you weren't." We both laughed. It was one way to start a friendship.

The apartment was perfect and included two servants - young sisters from the island of Ikaria whose family had for years served Alexis' family. The two girls looked after both apartments, Cy's upstairs, mine below. Early on an aged relative (mother? grandmother? no matter) took up residence, presumably with the two girls. Their room wasn't very big but it managed to accommodate them, and the kitchen was big enough for the steady coming and going of other family members. Later an ancient uncle spent hours contentedly cracking nuts by the kitchen fire while the room filled with chatter and laughter. It was a happy household. Also, from the flat roof, was an incomparable view encompassing the Acropolis and Mount Lycabettus: away in the distance was Piraeus, the port of Athens.

To add to these delights the legation was also a happy place. Eleni had been right. The atmosphere depended on the person at the top. The Minister, Sir Michael Palairet and his wife, were gentle people in every sense of the word, and everyone in the legation was easy and friendly. The naval attaché's office was in the legation building but separate, a little kingdom of its own, with far wider responsibilities than his counterpart in landlocked Hungary.

The naval attaché was an ebullient admiral who reminded me of Phil. Like my uncle he was a big man with a tendency to roar under stress, so I felt quite at home with him. There was plenty of work, particularly at first for the filing system was a muddle, but soon the office was running smoothly. Gradually I realized the seriousness of the war happening far off in the mountains where the Greeks were ill-equipped and outnumbered in their desperate resistance. But over and beyond all else, Greece had me hooked. Everything, including the Ladas family, conspired to suffuse Athens with delight.

Alexis' mother Dora (known as Dodo) had been widowed seventeen years earlier. His sister, Marina, was nursing wounded front line soldiers in an Athens hospital; and his aunt, Roxane, was married to Shan Sedgwick, the *New York Times* correspondent for Greece. Cy was an honorary family member and I suspected Marina was in love with him, though what Cy felt was unclear. He referred to himself as a news jackal sniffing out how men kill each other in war, and I reckoned it wasn't easy to combine courtship with jackalling all over the Balkans. Cy was a Jew, had black boot-button eyes and a bullet head, was an incomparable storyteller, quick-tempered and fizzing with electric energy. Felix, his terrier, was very like him.

I fell in love with all of them. There were evenings with the family when Cy told gripping, hilarious stories of roving the Balkans before the war, when Dora talked about pre-war Greece, and Shan would make sly jests about young men seeking my attention (accompanied by galloping sounds) which made me blush and giggle. Marina (eighteen, slight, large brown eyes, gentle) was often tired out by long days of nursing, but she told us how the wounded soldiers raged against being made captive by their wounds. She spoke with passion and pity and I sensed that Shan wasn't exaggerating when he said, "My niece Marina is a walking beatitude." Shan's wife, forthright Roxane, was fiery, opinionated and had an acerbic wit. I liked her, even though she was a bit hard on Alexis, upbraiding him for being childish or flippant. I guessed he minded, but he took it with deprecating humour and unfailing good manners.

Dora, quiet, wise and loving, was the lynch-pin of the family, and one unforgettable day she told me about a summer on the island of Ikaria where she took the two children when they were very young. Alexis often referred to this summer, and Dora's description stayed with me ever after as a summer of happiness out of time, like a dream of paradise.

"On Ikaria," Dora said, "there was no doctor or chemist, no shops, and the ship arrived once a week, as long as the weather was fine. The three of us lived in one huge room with camp beds and blankets and a first aid kit, without a kitchen, lavatory or running water, and we cooked outside on a fire laid between two stones."

Dora laughed. "As for a lavatory, the islanders told us to go where we liked, nobody would look at us, and offered us, with a sweeping gesture, the Mediterranean to wash in!"

For Alexis it was a carefree time, before his father died and he was suddenly the man of the family - that's hard when you're only twelve and a bit of a dreamer. On Ikaria he and Marina lived naked as little pagans and swam like minnows in the warm sea. They gathered wood for the cooking fire, scraped salt from hollows amongst the rocks, and picked greens on the mountain-sides. Fish were caught, octopus speared, and when one of the roving half-wild goats was shot it was divided up in the village square with a share for Dora and the children. Goats provided milk for cheese, honey was garnered from wild bees, and in small plots of soil between rocks the islanders grew beans, lentils and wheat. Herbs were the island's medicine, rheumatism was eased by a bee's sting, and bleeding cuts were dressed with a spider's web.

Alexis said, "We spent every morning in the sea, and some afternoons we'd visit our old servants. Dodo would gossip and we'd eat pomegranates and figs and grapes. In the evening when the men came in from fishing they'd bring out raki and tell stories of smugglers giving the patrol boat the slip. Usually there'd be someone with a bazooka for songs about robbers, shipwreck and love until we were nearly asleep. Then Dodo took us back, stumbling groggily through the orange trees."

One day a muleteer led them up and up into the mountains where cyclamen, crocus and blackberries grew wild, and vines were cultivated wherever possible. "It was very hot, toiling up the mountain," Alexis said, "and we were glad to stop when the islanders offered us figs and tomatoes. On the way up we wanted to rest in the shade of a forest of wild oaks, but the muleteer hurried us on, saying, 'It is a dead spot. Here a father killed his son.'

The magic of that summer on Ikaria seeped into my apprehension of the Greece Alexis offered me. For a short time we seemed to live in two worlds - our own enchanted one, and the grim Greek war against the odds of bitter cold and rugged terrain, wretched clothing, and above all, not enough equipment or men.

In early February the Greek army's plight became so desperate that the government appealed to Britain for troops. No decision was made until the beginning of March when Germany occupied Bulgaria. Obviously Greece would be next. Britain promised reinforcements, and when the British Expeditionary Force arrived in Athens, cheering crowds gathered outside the British Legation. In the legation my admiral growled that Greece was a forlorn hope, and it was folly to deplete General Wavell's forces in North Africa.

But the British had come and Alexis fulminated at being too young to join up. I wasn't very sympathetic, and when he turned up at the family apartment wearing a uniform, I felt he was making an ass of himself. His long legs were wrapped in khaki puttees, he was self-conscious and truculent, hoping we wouldn't laugh at him, especially Cy. I didn't laugh, but thought his long thin puttee-wrapped legs made him look like a stork. I was conscious of his youthfulness, and that I was five years older than him.

The uniform didn't seem to make much difference to Alexis' life, and in spite of sombre reports from the front we often forgot the war and, when I was free for a day, we took off to explore a new place. Thus Alexis gave me Greece.

On one of those days we walked for hours in the mountains and at last came in sight of the sea.

"Thalassa! Thalassa!" This from Alexis.

"What does that mean?"

"The sea! The sea!"

"What's the story? Tell me!""

So Alexis told about Xenophon leading a bedraggled army to safety after a bruising battle. "He was one of the famous 'Ten thousand,' Greek soldiers of fortune who went to Asia with young Cyrus."

"When?"

"Oh, around 400 BC. Cyrus wanted to conquer the Persian Empire. But the plan miscarried, the Greeks were isolated with only one commander. They elected new ones, including Xenophon who afterwards wrote his famous *Anabasis*. This tells how his discouraged troops were rallied to make an amazing five-months' retreat up the Tigris to Trebizond on the Black Sea. That's where they cried 'Thalassa! Thalassa!'"

The words came out in a shout, and right at that moment a shepherd began to play his pipes. The light was fading and soon the distant sea would be 'wine-dark'. The mountains were already deepening to purple and a few stars glimmered faintly overhead. The shepherd was walking behind his sheep along a track below, and each note from his pipe rose clear and sweet as the shadows darkened.

Another day we drove to Cape Sounion, explored the Temple of Poseidon on the promontory above the coast, pottered round the stones of Athene's Temple below, then scrambled down to the big deserted beach. We gathered sticks for a fire and got a good blaze going (against all orders) and sure enough an aircraft flew high overhead as the sticks crackled and flames announced our presence.

"Ours?" I asked.

"Let's hope so."

The aircraft flew away and we sat quietly watching the sun's great red ball of fire slowly slide below the horizon; but as if the gods had waited to balance its absence, the perfect silver disc of a full moon seemed to rise out of the sea. At such a moment, just being there was what life was all about.

There were many rapturous days, beginning with our first expedition together up the mountain where white marble was quarried and wild scarlet anemones grew amongst the gleaming white boulders. Another day we rode horses up Mount Hymettus. I fell off and pretended not to mind and Alexis teased me. Somewhere we picked armfuls of wild lilac and brought them joyously back for Dora. Years later she said, "You seemed to embody youth and hope in that terrible time." One day Alexis said I must see the Parthenon by moonlight, but we'd have to get past the sentry, for during the war the Acropolis was fenced in. After dark we walked within sight of the sentry box and waited until it was nearly midnight. Then we crept up, made sure the sentry was asleep, and after climbing the fence, went on, stepping carefully over the rough track so as not to dislodge any stones. At last we reached the soaring marble columns of the Parthenon. We were quite alone, the sky blue-black velvet, the perfect columns gleaming like captive moonlight. We stood unmoving until, simultaneously and without a word or sidelong glance, we fell on our knees.

Besides telling me the stories of Greece Alexis taught me rousing French songs which we sang, swinging along country roads:

> Il était un petit navire,
> Il était un petit navire,
> Qui n'avait ja-ja-jamais navigué,
> Qui n'avait ja-ja-jamais navigué,
> Ohé! ohé! ohé!

Alas, the ship founders and finally, food all gone, lots are drawn from a bundle of cut straws. The little sailor draws the short one, and is cooked and served:

> Avec des sal-sal-salsifis sautés,
> Avec des sal-sal-salsifis sautés,
> Ohé! ohé! ohé!

We sang another, rather bawdy song, about Jeanneton who went to cut wood and met two soldiers with consequences that were not, apparently, displeasing. "La-y-rette! La-y-rette!" went the lilting refrain.

We sang both these songs on what was our last long day together. During the afternoon we stopped at a cottage to ask for a drink of water. We were invited inside, and I saw for the first time a simple altar on which a loaf of bread was laid.

"Sacred bread," Alexis murmured, "The Bread of Life."

The lady of the house gave us fresh spring water, some bread and olives, and when we left Alexis tried to press into her hand a few coins of gratitude. This offering was impatiently rejected, and gesturing us to wait, our hostess disappeared. She came back with flowers cut from the garden which she pressed into my hands with a blessing.

As we walked away Alexis said, "I should have known better. We take hospitality seriously here. You give what you have, and are blessed in the giving."

Later we reached a village and went into an old church. Several village women were chatting to the priest while children played in the nave. We wandered round, and before we left paused to look a last time at the little group of priest and parishioners. Suddenly the priest consulted his watch and made a hurried gesture to the women. They straightened their shawls, quickly gathered the children together and prepared themselves for the evening service. Familiar words came into my head: 'When two or three are gathered together in my Name...' I thought that it didn't matter which Name, as long as the gathering was loving.

At the end of March Cy had an all-night party in his apartment. We lay about talking, and singing an occasional song. I can sing true, though am no prima donna, and that night I sang one of my favourite folk songs, right through. It begins:

> The river is wide, I cannot get o'er
> And neither have I wings to fly.
> Fetch me a boat that will carry two,
> And I will row my love and I.

The song speaks of the chagrin of love, and ends:

> I put my back up against an oak,
> Thinking to find a trusty tree.
> But first it bended, then it broke,
> And so did my false love to me.
>
> O love is handsome and love is fine,
> And love's a jewel when it is new,
> But when 'tis old it groweth cold
> And fades away like morning dew.

When the party broke up Alexis walked me, bug-eyed with lack of sleep, to the top of Mount Lycabettus to watch the dawn ("rosy-fingered dawn, Belinda!") flooding the city with light.

"At Easter," he said, "we process up here holding lighted candles, led by the priests and chanting choirs. It's very beautiful. You'll see."

But I never saw. On March 25, the Yugoslav Regent, Prince Paul, was persuaded to sign up with the Axis forces of Germany, Italy and Japan. Two days later there was a *coup d'état* in the name of Prince Paul's young nephew, King Peter. Cy at once took off for Yugoslavia, and in Athens news and rumours abounded. On April 3, Nazi troops invaded Yugoslavia, entering through occupied Hungary and Bulgaria. On April 6, Germany bombed Belgrade, and on the same day declared war on Greece.

The next evening Piraeus, the port of Athens, was in ruins.

∽ 25 ∼

The Kalanthe makes her last voyage.

Air-raid sirens were heard in Athens for the first time the night Piraeus was bombed. Illogically Alexis and I ran up to the roof. Beyond the city the night sky flamed with explosion after explosion, and when the explosions ceased the sky stayed red and menacing.

"It must be a massive raid on Piraeus."

"D'you think they'll bomb Athens?"

But no aircraft flew overhead. Finally the sirens wailed the all-clear, and it was then we heard a subdued babble from a little shed on the roof where the servants had built a makeshift altar with candles, and a vase, regularly replenished with fresh flowers.

"What on earth...?"

"Probably prayers to save us all."

He was right. Our small kitchen force was gathered on their knees before the candle-lit altar. They were absorbed, beseeching the protection of God and succour for the poor souls at the mercy of a new terror, unleashed like a thunderbolt from Zeus.

At the naval attaché's office next morning there was no sign of the admiral until around ten a.m. when he appeared, huge and mythical, as if he'd come from wrestling with giants. He was black from head to foot, his eyes red-rimmed, face grim, clothes in tatters. We stared, not daring to ask questions. All he said was, "I'll have a cup of strong tea, and bring your notebook, Belinda. We must get a report down at once."

As I took his dictation I realized he was in anguish. Ships loaded with explosives were routinely ordered to anchor at night outside the confines of the port. For once, this order had not been given. It so happened that a single bomb from a solitary German aircraft hit a train full of explosives. A flaming fragment fell on an ammunition barge laden with gun cotton, and flames touched off a ship carrying TNT: in a moment every ship in the harbour was set alight. Most of the buildings round the docks were laid flat, cranes were twisted out of shape, and great gaps were blasted in the quays. My admiral briefly noted that he had worked through the night to extricate people trapped in the ruined buildings, and I guessed his black face and tattered uniform were his sackcloth and ashes. That's the worst of being in command - if someone else slips up, it's your fault.

After the shock of this disaster following so swiftly on Germany's declaration of war on Greece, a strange sort of lull descended on Athens. One evening I plied Alexis and Shan with questions about what would happen next, what did the declaration mean right now?

Shan said, "It means Greece has to face the numerically superior German *Luftwaffe* in the mountains, as well as the logistic nightmare of mountain terrain and roads clogged with refugees from the Balkans. As for the Greek government, it's at sixes and sevens."

"Of course it is," Alexis exclaimed. "The Prime Minister had the misfortune of succeeding Metaxas - though his death in January was only the first misfortune."

"What's Metaxas got to do with what's happening now?"

Shan said, "Although he was a dictator, he was a tough nut with plenty of guts. He had the foresight to build up the Greek army and its equipment and when Italy invaded last October he got the country to close ranks behind him."

Alexis added that a dead dictator was about as bad as a live one, since they rarely left anyone capable of filling the gap. "Korizis is just a banker, not a war leader. What's the use of a banker prime minister, for God's sake, when the country hasn't enough men or equipment and the British can't help in spite of all their guarantees?"

Shan said, "D'you remember the crowds cheering wildly outside the British Legation when the Greeks checked the first Italian advance? That was a day! And again when the British troops arrived. There'll be no cheers when they pull out."

I asked why they would pull out and they both explained that the Balkans were lost and in North Africa Rommel was proving such a formidable foe that every soldier was needed there. Shan added that the evacuation of our troops was presenting the Greek government with tough questions. Should Greece capitulate? Should the government leave Athens? Should the British Expeditionary Force be helped to evacuate?

For ten days after Piraeus was bombed the questions hung in balance until, on April 18, Korizis met in conference with his ministers. After a long discussion he said he needed to reflect and left the room. The ministers sat in tense silence. Minutes passed, then a shot brought them to their feet and in the next room they found Korizis with a bullet through his head.

Swift changes followed on this suicide. The King took over as head of government and promised assistance in evacuating the British forces from Greece. The evacuation would also include everyone at the legation.

I always enjoyed walking through the streets of Athens. It was then a little city, or so it seemed, a city of people who loved to call greetings, to make welcome. It was very different the morning word spread that Korizis was dead and the British were leaving. That morning I walked through silent streets, absolutely silent, not because there was no-one about but because people simply stood in their doorways staring - at nothing, or briefly at me as I passed - and never a word. I wanted to cry out some foolish disclaimer that we had no alternative, we had to leave. But all I could do was meet their eyes and then glance away to save us embarrassment. This state of shock lasted the whole day. The next day was different. The greetings were back, nothing exuberant, but back, and there was a quiet demonstration of friendship in front of the legation. It was as though, with resignation and fortitude, understanding was offered. The new resignation was as painful as the earlier stunned silence.

The navy began evacuating the Expeditionary Force, rather more than half of which were destined for Crete, the rest for Alexandria and ultimately the Western Desert. British civilians were also being evacuated, including the majority of the legation chancery staff. I did not intend to leave so tamely, and had every excuse to stay in Athens for there was work to be done in clearing up the office. So I stayed and the legation chimney spewed a rain of charred paper on the surrounding streets.

Cy had returned to Athens after fleeing through Yugoslavia. Once he was only four hours ahead of the advancing Germans, another time only two, despite Yugoslav assurance that the situation was excellent. Twice he was suspected by the Yugoslavs of being a spy and told he would be shot. Cy kept us riveted, interrupted by bursts of laughter, but although he relished the telling he raged against the ruinous muddle and disarray, the shambles of blunders, contradictory orders and misunderstandings - and always the pitiful heroism. He told us of the Cretan colonel and his men who were all wiped out after every one of them refused the German order to surrender. He described the wounded Greek in a dressing station who cried out as the Nazis dive-bombed, "Listen men, we must hold them with our teeth!" In contrast was the bewildered group of Yugoslav cavalry wearing long grey cloaks with red facings. Cy said, "They seemed to have wandered out from a bygone and more chivalrous age." But the horseshoe nails they left behind were without chivalry. Cy had to repair his tires fourteen times, patching inner tubes by the faint light coming from slits in his blacked-out headlights while German aircraft 'slid' (his word) overhead.

All of us wondered whether Cy would now marry Marina. I write 'us', meaning this family which had welcomed and taken me into their home. Soon it would be dismembered. Shan and Roxane left on one of the naval ships, and Cy could have gone with them, but he was furious with the British. Through a bureaucratic muddle they had threatened to court-martial him for failing to secure proper accreditation to cover the fighting in Yugoslavia.

"I'm damned if I accept help from a bunch of nincompoops who picked a stupid quarrel in the thick of disaster," Cy expostulated, and proceeded to organize his personal escape route with a Greek sponge-fisher called Pantelis. Would he take Marina with him? I had to leave without knowing what happened.

As for Alexis, he was determined to get out of Greece so he could fight back in some way against the detestable invaders. There was no place for Alexis on my boat, which had been chartered by the Admiralty mainly for the remaining legation staff and their families. So I persuaded my admiral to sign several *laisser passées*, ostensibly for any last-minute stragglers needing to justify departure, one of which I gave Alexis on the chance it would be useful.

Then it was time to leave. I packed a minimum of clothing and precious items - a first edition of *Alice-in-Wonderland* and *Through the Looking-glass*, also a silver-trimmed tortoise-shell set of brushes, comb and hand-mirror. These were all christening presents I'd lived with all my life. I left the rest of my things with Dora and Marina, except my piano-accordion which at the last minute I slung over my shoulder. Then I went to say goodbye to the family.

Alexis wanted to know what sort of boat had been chartered and I said, "It's apparently a steam yacht called *Kalanthe*. Sounds rather posh. We're making for Crete. The minister's in Canea and that's where I'll go."

"I'll find you," said Alexis, "wherever you are."

In the early evening we piled on to the *Kalanthe*, and in spite of the sad ruins of Piraeus we generated a slightly festive mood, as if we were on an excursion. James, our good-looking Greek porter at the legation, contributed to this by borrowing my accordion.

"I will play you our songs," he said.

As there were about sixty of us there wasn't much room on deck, so we each claimed a spot and set about getting to know one another. I raised a guffaw from an American journalist who introduced himself as Earl Somebody-or-other and I asked, with polite interest, "The Earl of what?"

We were a motley collection which included the First Secretary Harold Caccia, and his wife Nancy, Doreen Blunt, wife of the military attaché, plus the children of both families, their two nannies, and a dachshund. There were two or three people from the chancery, a gaggle of British governesses, and a commando group which had been blowing up bridges to block the German advance. The commando leader was Peter Fleming, a well-known travel writer and adventurer whose books I had devoured with relish (his younger brother Ian Fleming later gained fame as the creator of secret agent 007). A small contingent of mixed nationalities included the Greek Minister of Information, a Greek merchant and his Jewish wife, a White Russian, and the Caccias' Chinese nanny. Finally, just as we were about to cast off, a man leapt magnificently from the quay, landing on a picnic basket and shattering two thermos flasks and a bottle of retsina. He was apologetic and explained he was an Albanian doctor fleeing from the Gestapo. After this minor drama the boat slid away from the ruins of Piraeus and sailed gently into the sunset with background music from James playing the songs of Greece on my accordion. It was April 24, 1941.

Very early next day, on a rosy-pink morning, the *Kalanthe* coasted in to a little bay at Paliaigos, a deserted island in the Cyclades. I leant on the side and stared down into the pristine sea, clear as spring water, the sandy bottom white as powdered pearls. It was a typical Greek island - sandy beach, rocks, the ground rising up through scrub and verdure. After we'd eaten our various breakfasts, Harold Caccia told us we were to leave the boat and remain on the island until dusk. Then we would board and continue our journey in the safety of darkness.

"German aircraft are everywhere," Harold concluded, "but we have the island and the beaches to ourselves, give or take a few goats. So forget about the war and enjoy yourselves for a day!"

That was easy. The sun shone from a cloudless sky, the blue sea was inviting, and I joined up with the oddly-named American and another young man to seek out a good beach for a swim. We took nothing with us but picnic food, and I also had in my pocket a book of Shakespeare sonnets and the British indispensable, a white linen handkerchief. None of us had swimsuits, so when we later found a perfect beach on the other side of the island we all swam naked. My two companions politely averted their eyes until I was in the water, a token gesture since the water was clear as glass.

Sometime during the afternoon an aircraft flew lazily very high overhead. The American said, "Doesn't seem interested in us," and we forgot about it. Around six, full of sun and well-being, we reluctantly left our beach and began strolling back to join the others.

There was no warning. Suddenly we heard the purposeful roar of an aircraft engine. We flung ourselves into a ditch, and as it screamed fast and low above us I looked up, and saw the pilot's head in a flying helmet. It was startling to see this human being, the same as me, yet intent on wreaking death, if not on us, then on the others scattered on the beach, and those on the sitting duck of the *Kalanthe* at anchor. This made me furious, too angry to be afraid, and my anger was directed at that long-unresolved conundrum, God.

"Look here, God," I shouted, "I don't know if you exist, but I don't propose to die until I've made up my mind. So just remember that."

The aircraft gone, we scrambled out of our ditch and began pelting up the rough goat path. We could hear machine-gun fire, an explosion, the stutter of gunfire and two more explosions, then silence. But as we ran up the hill a column of black smoke rose into the sky and soon we heard the wicked crack and splutter of burning wood. Breathless, we reached the hilltop and saw a little cluster of people on the beach staring at the blazing *Kalanthe* while men scrambled overboard into a rowboat alongside. They pulled rapidly away, rowing furiously from the stricken boat and as they grounded on the beach the watchers surged forward. There was a flurry of activity, and while we strained to see what was happening the *Kalanthe* exploded, and sank into the sea. This was when the American cried, "God, what about the kids?"

We couldn't see them anywhere and I began to run down the hill but the American stopped me. "Better wait here. We'll see what's to be done. Everyone's a dandy target down there."

I waited for a while, fidgeting, then unable to stand being idle, set off towards the beach. I didn't get far, for coming up the hill was one of Peter's commandos, and as we met I cried out, "What can I do?"

He said, "Get the nannies and children somewhere safe, over there'll do, behind those rocks. Stay until I come back. With luck there'll be help from Kimolos, that's the island over there. They must have seen what's happened." Then holding out his hand said, "I'm Norman Johnstone."

"I'm Belinda Lyons, the naval attaché's secretary." Calmed by these social niceties I went in search of the nannies and children. Before long I had the Caccia's Chinese nanny, children and dachshund herded behind the rocky outcrop with Doreen Blunt's children and their uniformed, very English nanny. Some of the stray English governesses joined us, also the Greek merchant and his Jewish wife. "I accompany her," he said. "She is greatly upset." The children seemed reasonably all right, perhaps soothed by the Chinese nanny who sat composedly knitting on a rock, the dachshund at her feet. The governesses were only a bit jittery, but soon the Jewish lady broke into a sort of running mutter, low at first, something like "What are we to do? What is to happen? Oh my God! All gone! All gone!" But the mutter gathered speed and volume until with a shriek she was off: "My jewels! My furs! All gone, all gone! Oh God, Oh God! My jewels..."

I didn't even think, I just slapped her cheek, hard. It startled both of us. She stared at me, silenced. Then her husband put his arm round her and they moved apart. I was rather pleased with myself.

From time to time I left my little herd to stare down at the beach below. I saw Harold and Nancy Caccia walking up and down, up and down, stopping often by the sea's edge to gaze fixedly into the water, then walking slowly on. I wondered what they were looking for, perhaps rescue? And sure enough it came at last, chuffing across the ocean, a little motorized boat, rather like a tugboat. I watched bodies being lifted into the boat and as it left another arrived. Before long Norman came striding up the hill and called out, "It's all right. You can bring your charges down now."

I asked him to come and reassure everyone first, and as we went back to our shelter he told me about the casualties.

"Two badly burned crew, and one of our chaps, Mark Norman, he's unconscious and full of machine gun bullet wounds. Peter's got a head wound, he's lost quite a bit of blood but it's not serious, and poor old Charles' leg is acting up." This was Charles Mott-Radclyffe who had been a military liaison officer with the British Expeditionary Forces in Yugoslavia. Norman added, "Nancy's brother, Oliver Barstow, is missing. He's one of our lot, was on board manning one of those ancient Lewis guns. Probably got blown in the sea when the boiler burst."

Poor Nancy, forlornly searching. I asked about the wounded and Norman said, "The women have torn up their petticoats to bind up the wounds. We never took any first aid stuff off the boat."

"Did they hit the boat straight away?"

"Not the first time. It was the second one that did it, two direct hits. That was when the boiler burst. All the dead, apart from Oliver and a couple of our other ranks, were crew who were trapped down below getting the engines ready. Eight of them, poor devils. Hadn't a chance."

We reached our shelter and Norman explained about the rescue boats and that the wounded had gone ahead with the three women who had nursing experience.

"That'll be my Mrs. Blunt," Doreen's nanny exclaimed. "Workin' 'erself to death she's been in that 'ospital in Athens."

"Indeed, Nanny, we're so lucky to have her and Mrs. Caccia; and our Greek friend, Joan Stavridis, is a trained nurse. Thank God there seems to be a hospital on Kimolos."

It took some time to get everyone to the island. The little boats took small batches in relays. I went in the last batch with the nannies, children and dachshund. It was quite dark by then, enormous stars glittering in the deep blue-blackness that is a Greek night sky. The ocean was still, no sign of anything unusual having happened, and so quiet, except for the chug-chug of the boat ferrying us across to Kimolos. It was wonderfully peaceful, and sparks from the little funnel showered out like fireflies into the night.

⊰ 26 ⊱

Kimolos. Santorini,
and a priest's blessing.

On Kimolos the nannies, the children, the dachshund and I spent the night in a cave at the back of a taverna on the quay. I was asked to keep an eye on my charges and wait in the cave for instructions in the morning.

In the morning I hung around until, impatient, I told the nannies I'd go and find out what we were supposed to do. We'd all had enough of the cave which was also the storage room of the taverna. The children, though shocked, had slept well enough, but the nannies and I spent a fitful night on heaps of very lumpy sacking alive with some active, biting creatures. The Chinese nanny retained a Buddhist calm, but Nanny Blunt was simmering about something obscure, inferred through innuendo, sniffs and tossing of the head.

The hospital was on a hill behind the quay and looked promising from the outside. But inside it was only a hospital in the making. There were numerous rooms, a collection of iron bedsteads and mattresses, and that was it. No pillows or bed linen, and more importantly, no doctors, medicines, or equipment. Nothing. In a big room upstairs Nancy Caccia, Doreen Blunt and Joan Stavridis had established some sort of order in a nightmare room of groans and blood and skin burnt black and raw. I told someone that the nannies and children were still in the cave, and then I forgot about them. They were forgotten for several hours and finally emerged from the cave, pale as mushrooms.

Free of my charges in the cave I asked what I could helpfully do in the nightmare hospital room. A bowl of water and a cloth were thrust in my hands and I was told to "try and clean up James."

"James? Our James?"

It was. Our handsome, accordion-playing James stared with frightened eyes, white against the blackened skin of his burnt face. I had no idea what to do, tried gently dabbing the poor face - and he screamed. I drew back, horrified, and seeing Nancy, begged, "Is there something I can do where I can't hurt anyone? I don't know a thing about nursing."

There was something. The islanders had brought oranges but there was nothing to squeeze them with. Could I work out some way to make juice, or perhaps cut them up small so they could be fed to the wounded?

I took the oranges thankfully and hurried away to the kitchen downstairs. There I found Jane, one of the chancery secretaries, staring around what could only be called the kitchen space. She said, "Where

219

do we begin?" and we laughed. The space contained a table, chairs, and some plates and cutlery. The stove was typically Greek, a sort of stone shelf against the length of one wall with several hollows for charcoal. But there was no charcoal and no matches, nor did either of us have a clue how to get the fires going, and anyway there was nothing to cook, nor anything to cook in. So we began with the oranges and earned much gratitude upstairs. For lunch we gathered remnants of food from the beach picnic and found a quantity of ship's biscuits, resembling dog biscuits in texture, which proved satisfying.

We found food in the village for supper, and during the meal some of the tension eased. I told Nancy about Nanny Blunt muttering and irritable in the cave, and when I asked if she had something on her mind, Nancy laughed. For a moment the laugh seemed strange, almost indecent - her brother was dead, upstairs three of six men's lives would be in balance unless medical help came soon. But it wasn't indecent. Nancy had a memorable spirit, and kept grief for her brother in some private place.

"I'll tell you what Nanny Blunt was muttering about," Nancy said. "As you know, the *Kalanthe* wasn't hit the first time round and one of the aircraft took a turn over the beach and dropped a stick of bombs. One fell quite close to a cave where all the children had been playing and so, mercifully, they were safe inside. Imagine, Belinda, the children, the nannies, Doreen Blunt and I, with all hell breaking loose and at that point Nanny Blunt turned on Doreen - really, like a tiger! - and said in her most disapproving voice, 'I have always told you, Mrs. Blunt, not to let your children play with the Caccia children, and unless you stop them now, I shall give notice straight away.'"

All hell had indeed broken loose, and gradually I pieced together what had happened when the *Kalanthe* was attacked. Four Lewis guns had been mounted on deck, three of them manned by officers and other ranks from Peter Fleming's commando unit. When the aircraft came over, Mark Norman and Oliver Barstow were on the bridge, Peter on the deck below.

The two aircraft made two separate attacks. The second time they came, as Peter described later, "at the height of a driven partridge" and dropped four bombs. The fourth hit the boat amidships and the boiler burst. A segment of the ship hit Peter on the head, leg and shoulder and while he staggered about looking for survivors, half-blinded by blood, two blackened figures came through the smoke and flames and the three managed to get lifebelts and the raft overboard. Meantime Norman Johnstone and Harold Caccia arrived in the rowboat and found Mark had been blown clean off the bridge to the deck below. He was an unrecognizable bundle, "a black man with black hair" Peter said, streaked from head to foot with blood, but alive. Oliver Barstow and the two other ranks could not be found.

I'd wondered why the *Kalanthe* had exploded and learnt that it was a floating explosive in itself, for Peter's commandos had stashed explosives and demolition equipment on board. That explained why Harold and Norman had rowed away so furiously after their final rescue mission, and had time to lug the wounded over prickly low scrub to safety. "They tried not to be clumsy," Peter said later. "Awful for them. One of the burned men screamed all the time."

On the second day a Greek boy, who'd been an assistant cook at the legation, was discovered in the village and brought to the hospital kitchen. Cooking pots were borrowed and by the evening we had a menu of a kind. The village provided what they could - fruit, eggs, some chickens - and we had the dog biscuits. I have a memory which seems unlikely, but here it is. A villager appears with two lambs and asks which lamb he should slaughter: I choose blindly, and flee.

Every meal had to be served twice since the table space and utensils were limited and we could only feed half the fifteen or so people gathered in the hospital. So we prepared the food, laid the table, served and washed up, then repeated the process for another serving. This pretty well filled the days. In between we sat in the sun, looking down to the harbour, chatting lazily, and wondering what was going to become of us. Peter Fleming's batman, Guardsman Tom Loveday, was assigned to help in the kitchen, and we often took a break outside together. He called me 'madam' at first, but soon we were both on first-name terms. Once or twice I thought this would not have happened in England, and how foolish our class divisions were. He was interesting, a good talker. It was quite a surprise.

At first the bedridden wounded remained upstairs. Peter quickly became a walking wounded, but Mark Norman was seriously ill with a cracked skull and fourteen machine-gun bullet wounds. James and one of the crew were dreadfully burned, Charles Mott-Radclyffe was much troubled by his leg wound, and the assistant naval attaché, who was on board when the *Kalanthe* was hit, had multiple leg injuries.

Once we got order into meal production, the badly wounded were brought down to a small room next to the kitchen where boiled water was at hand to dress wounds. Every day, morning and evening, the dressings were changed. It was the only way to avoid gangrene. At each dressing time some of the wounded screamed. The first day was awful. But we had our work to do, and quite quickly the cries became part of the day, not unheard, simply there, part of our kitchen routine.

Altogether roughly sixty passengers had been on the *Kalanthe*. On Kimolos everyone settled where they could. The hospital contained the wounded, nurses, legation staff, commandos, nannies, children and dachshund. A larger group organized themselves around the harbour; others slept somewhere in the village, amongst them two old and rather shaky naval men from the Royal Naval Volunteer Reserve who dug in to a steady daily routine of calming their nerves with retsina. The day Piraeus was bombed both of them were blown into the air and "that sort of thing takes it out of you," they said. I found one of them on my bed one night, dead drunk. I don't know how or why he had taken to my bed. He was insensible to polite requests to leave, so I hauled him off on to the floor where he flopped down like a full sack. I was too tired to care about him, and he was gone by morning.

In a very short time we slipped into an almost carefree routine at the hospital. After all, we were alive, the wounded so far were stable with no sign of gangrene and, a subtle point, we were all equal in having no possessions. In fact I was quite rich with my Shakespeare sonnets and pocket handkerchief. At mealtimes there was much laughter and telling of stories. Lost possessions were not discussed, but we were sorry for the Greek Minister of Information whose suitcase had included a metal box containing his wife's jewels. Their value was considerable and it was known that he planned to return after the war and pay a sponge diver to search for the box where the *Kalanthe* had gone down.

Our plight had been telegraphed to Crete and there was hope that not only rescue but medical help would materialize soon. Gangrene was a constant fear and there was no telling whether wounds and burns would heal simply with care - but unrelieved pain could inhibit healing and morphine would be a godsend. It was possible to send cables to Crete, but there were no means of receiving replies, and without rescue we were bound to fall into Italian or German hands. But there was nothing to be done, but wait. So day by day everyone did what they could. When German aircraft flew overhead (which they did regularly) Nanny Blunt pitched in to make sure God remembered whose side He was on. She herded the children, the Chinese nanny and the dachshund into a back room and soon we heard childish voices singing:

There is a green hill far away
Without a city wall...

or, more cheerfully,

All things bright and beautiful,
All creatures great and small...

The children's voices rose in lovely counterpoint to the ugly drone of aircraft, bent on wiping out things bright and beautiful.

For years after all these events I was sure we had stayed on Kimolos for at least ten days before there was any change. But on the third day something new did happen. Jane and I were preparing a meal, looking out of the window from time to time, on the chance of anything interesting happening down below. Suddenly both of us saw an unfamiliar fishing caique coming in to the little harbour, and without a word we dropped everything and began pelting down the hill, our passage perfumed with wild thyme as we crushed it underfoot. Breathless, we arrived at the very moment the caique bumped against the quayside, and then, in quick succession, a young British officer leapt impatiently on to land, Jane cried out - and flew to his outstretched arms. It was her husband. With him came a military doctor and three members from the Athens chancery. Jubilantly we took them up to the hospital and at supper that evening we learnt it was the three chancery men who had commandeered the caique and persuaded a doctor to sail with them. Goodness knows how Jane's husband got away from Crete, but here he was.

The rescuers brought food, medicine, and blessed morphine. The doctor lavished praise on how well the wounded had been nursed, and a huge sigh of relief went up that the wounded now could have pain-free hours and no fears of gangrene. Above all was gratitude and admiration that the four men had set off on an uncertain venture which they might never have completed. German aircraft could well have spotted the army uniforms and sent the little caique to oblivion.

For the next twenty-four hours the wounded profited from the doctor's ministrations, but he was anxious to leave for Crete as soon as possible. The island grapevine reported that the Germans were now not only in occupation of Athens but also taking possession of the islands. There was no way of checking this, but the threat of capture was real enough, and it was imperative to get the wounded, particularly Mark Norman and the burned sailors, into proper hospital care. So we busied ourselves packing up food for the journey to Crete. Personal packing was no problem; my Shakespeare was in one pocket, the handkerchief in another.

The evening before we were due to sail I went outside and looked at the bright stars, breathed in the peace of the night and was surprised by a twinge of regret that our days in the hospital, bonded by work and companionship, were nearly over. How odd, I thought, and then considered more practically that there was no telling whether we would sail confidently to safety. Crete was 76 miles away and with the caique capable of six knots - roughly twelve hours sailing. Even by starting at dusk there would be three and a half hours of daylight when the caique would be an easy target for German aircraft.

It was no simple matter to load us all into the caique. After supper on April 29, the wounded were manhandled as gently as possible into the depths of the hold and we piled in after them. But once we were settled the caique's captain refused to sail. He said the weather was too bad and the caique would make poor headway against wind and a rough sea. So the unfortunate wounded were taken from the hold, everyone trooped back to their temporary pads, and the following evening we embarked all over again.

We packed ourselves in the hold like sardines, each of us tucking into a personal crib between the wooden ribs of the caique. There was a lot of chatter with an undertow of excitement and anxiety, but a red-headed commando private, his hair flaming in the light from a hanging lantern, made us laugh at an unquenchable stream of

Cockney jokes. Peter's batman, Tom Loveday, put himself beside me and as we settled in I noticed that several large metal drums were stacked a little to one side above us.

"Ballast," Tom explained.

Sometime in the night I woke with a start. The caique was pitching a lot, and the oil drums were rolling about, making quite a racket. I'd barely registered that loose ballast in a rough sea might not be such a good idea when the caique jumped like a young colt and, with a sound like a drum roll, one of the barrels hurtled down to land with a crash, pinning Tom and me underneath. For a second I wondered why it didn't hurt, and then there were voices and hands lifting the barrel and I realized it had landed across the projecting ribs and we were all right.

I crawled out and was instantly overcome with nausea, cried dolefully, "I'm going to be sick!" and, as if I'd conjured a genie, a hand shot out with a small, white enamel basin into which, with exemplary timing, I threw up. After that everyone tucked themselves back in their cribs and there were no more shenanigans, at least not in the hold.

In the morning I went on deck as we approached the island of Santorini. The air was like a draught of fresh water after being battened down with a lot of bodies in not very clean clothes.

Peter Fleming was leaning on the rail looking like a pirate chief. He'd purloined an army blanket and cut a hole in the middle to put his head through, so the blanket hung round him like a cape. With his head dramatically bandaged he looked every inch the adventurer, just as I had imagined him from his first travel book, *Brazilian Adventure*, written in 1933 when he was twenty-four. I was seventeen then and pored over the photographs, thinking how handsome he was, and laughed at the tongue-in-cheek, self-deprecating way he wrote about his misadventures. Now I was sharing a major misadventure with him. It was wonderful! Callous? I was young and not dead.

Santorini was good to look at. The black volcanic cliff-face reared out of the brilliant blue sea, the village a cluster of dazzling white houses at the top. I said, "So we've got this far! Your Tom Loveday and I narrowly escaped being flattened by a loose ballast drum in the night. But we're all right," and I explained about the saving ribs of the hold.

"Glad to hear it," Peter said laconically, and with one of his sardonic smiles added, "We had our little drama too. A spot of trouble with the captain. Not long after leaving Kimolos he lost his nerve again, said the wind was against us, that he feared Santorini was in German hands, that the loss of his caique would be the loss of his livelihood, and ended with the logical reason that he'd never sailed to Santorini and didn't know how to find it."

Peter said that at this moment the two old RNVR sailors appeared on deck. "They were obviously well stoked up with retsina, which was probably why they volunteered to have a go at getting us to

Santorini. As the captain kicked up a fuss about this, there was nothing for it but take him at gunpoint to his cabin and lock him in. We cleared the old sailors' heads with a bucket of cold sea water, dried them off and sat them down with a faulty compass and a map of the Eastern Mediterranean (the captain obviously didn't believe in charts) and told them to get on with it."

Peter's rather saturnine face creased in a brief grin. "We stayed around for a few minutes and then left them arguing about which was north and which south. It was too late to change our plans and, as you say, here we are!"

The path up to the village was steep. Some of us walked, others hired donkeys. Ahead of me the Greek Minister of Information, wearing an elegant suit, polished shoes and panama hat, sat astride a diminutive donkey, his long legs dangling almost to the ground. At the last minute someone had thrust into his hands a child's chamber pot and he balanced this carefully on the saddle. In the village Jane and I, Tom and the legation cook took over the taverna and prepared a meal. I'm not sure why this happened, but that's how it was. Half way through our preparations there was a muffled explosion, and we all fell flat. Nothing happened, no falling masonry, no roar of retreating bombers. Cautiously we raised our heads and found the Greeks laughing at us. Santorini's modest volcano had just harmlessly blown its top, which it did every so often.

When the meal was done I sat on a small terrace covered with whatever climbing plant produces loofahs. I always used a loofah and was charmed to find them in their natural habitat. The Greek Minister of Information joined me and we sipped little cups of strong Turkish coffee, peacefully gazing out across the sea while he told me about his wife's jewels, and his plans to retrieve them. Little did either of us know that on his return he'd find his plans forestalled. Word of the jewels had got around, and an enterprising sponge-diver located the box. The jewels were unharmed, and the diver sold them to a German officer for a sum that seemed princely but was, in fact, a pittance.

Happily ignorant of this outcome, I wished the minister's venture well, and we talked of other things. As we wondered idly what would happen next, another of our Greek porters from the Athens legation appeared on the terrace. John was plump and good-natured and liked being helpful. He apologized for interrupting our conversation, but he had a message for me from his uncle.

"He is the priest here," John said, "and he invite you to take a siesta at his house. He wait to welcome you!"

Such kindness was not to be refused. John took me to his uncle's house, which was built on the edge of the black cliff fronting the sea. The priest stood at the bottom of a flight of white steps and all the way down red geraniums poked their bright flowers and green leaves between the white stone balustrades. My host was black-robed, his crucifix falling below a long black beard, cut square at the bottom, and he greeted me with a blessing.

We went inside where sweet wine was waiting and those delicious little round shortbreads sprinkled with icing sugar which melt in the mouth. Before long an elderly maidservant led me to a room where an enamel basin stood mounted waist-high on a graceful metal pedestal. Clean towels hung nearby, and a new cake of soap sat on a pottery dish. The servant returned with a jug of hot water, poured it into the basin, indicated a bedroom across the passage, blessed me, and left. Soap, hot water, a towel - these were luxuries beyond expectation. Much cleaner, I lay down on spotless, embroidered linen sheets, my head on a soft pillow, and fell like a stone into sleep.

Later the priest and I shared more wine and cakes and then went out together to the courtyard where John and the maidservant were waiting. I was just about to give a little speech of thanks when the priest turned and made a slight impatient gesture to the maidservant. She threw up her hands, disappeared, and was back in an instant with a bunch of red geraniums. Smiling, she handed them to me; we all smiled at one another and I thanked each one of them, the maidservant, the priest and John.

The priest blessed our journey and as we climbed up the white steps I really did feel blessed. I had red geraniums, Shakespeare sonnets, a handkerchief, and my life. There was no reason to desire anything more.

We left Santorini in the evening on a newly chartered ship, bound for Crete.

≪ 27 ≫

The Heraklion villa, escape from Canea, and the truth in Cairo.

A British army unit in Heraklion gave us what seemed a reckless British breakfast of bacon and eggs, marmalade and buttered toast, and coffee. We were told that a naval ship would take us to Alexandria, but inwardly deciding this was too tame, I asserted that my job was with the naval attaché and I must go to Canea. To my surprise this met with no opposition and I was able to hitch a ride on an army truck leaving for Canea in the morning. Probably I was given credit for loyally sticking to my post, but in truth Crete promised adventure.

Chaos was in the air, anything might happen, and I could be useful. That I might be a damned nuisance didn't occur to me.

After breakfast Peter said, "I'm going to see a chap about billets," and disappeared. We sat around talking in the sunshine and after a couple of hours Peter returned, having found a villa for the legation party. Nancy said, "This includes you, Belinda," and laughing added, "Trust Peter to pull a villa out of a hat."

We took possession after lunch. The villa was spacious, uninhabited, and fully furnished. There were beds and mattresses and a bathroom upstairs, and downstairs a dining-room with table and chairs, and a drawing-room with deep-cushioned armchairs and a sofa. We wandered round joking about easy living, and someone said rather scornfully that we were a decadent race. Tom Loveday was in charge of the kitchen, and before supper he came in with sherry and a tray of glasses. I thought what a treat it was to be waited on and smiled at Tom, then noticing we were a glass short, called him by his first name and asked if he could find another glass.

"Yes, madam," he said, "There's plenty where these came from."

Madam? I stared at his departing back not sure if I was dismayed or angered by a sardonic glint in his eye. Damn it, I hadn't invented social divisions. On Kimolos we'd been friends, or at the least talked as equals. Madam. I wrestled briefly with social ambiguities, but the problem was baffling, and Peter's stories were more fun.

There was a piano in the drawing-room and after supper Nancy played and we lazily sang the songs whose words we more or less remembered. One was the *Eton Boating Song* which Peter was unsuccessfully teased to sing.

"It's on record that I have absolutely no musical sense," he said, and this suddenly reminded me of a story in his second travel book, *One's Company*. On a long, slow journey from Moscow to China he had taught the *Eton Boating Song* to a young Russian who, rather improbably, was on his way to found a school of drama in Outer Mongolia. The journey lasted two weeks. The *Eton Boating Song* was a bizarre choice, being about Old Boys returning to their alma mater with a refrain beginning "Forty years on..." *One's Company* was published in 1934 and I'd forgotten the details, so asked Peter why the Russian wanted to learn a song, and why that one.

Peter said drily, "It was the only song I'd ever sung more than once in my life, and the Russian wanted the song for a play about English clubmen."

"Clubmen?"

"As far as he was concerned all Englishmen belong to clubs. In the plays, including the one about the clubmen, the characters always sang a song, but the only English song he knew was *It's a long, long way to Tipperary*. He was tired of it," Peter said, "and even had doubts about whether it was quite modern. Also he did so want to be reassured that it was customary for English clubmen to burst into song together. I hadn't the heart to disabuse him."

"Did he learn it?"

"We managed somehow. He was delighted. He wanted me to come with him to Outer Mongolia: I was tempted, but didn't. He was a good fellow."

The evening drifted pleasantly on until someone said, "Give us another song, Nancy, then we better sort out who's going to sleep where." Nancy's voice was clear and true. Her last song had a haunting tune which fitted the words: "Come, my love, come! for the wind is low/And the moon shines bright on the Ohio./Come, my love, come!..." I hear that last rising note, can feel the concluding pattern of the verse, but no words come. The fragment still sings in my mind, always incomplete.

Nancy played a last chord and we fell quiet until, in a desultory fashion, an effort was made to fit this and that person into the bedrooms upstairs. Charles had gone up early to ease his leg wound, and the arrangements became complex. Then someone said, "Don't let's bother!" and pulled a cushion to the floor. One after the other we did the same, disposed ourselves around the room, and slept on the floor through that last night together.

Before we parted the next morning Nancy said, "We're going to spend a little time recovering at the Mena House Hotel when we get to Cairo. If you aren't too long on Crete, Belinda, do join us there. You'll love Mena House. It's a splendid hotel on the edge of the desert and a stone's throw from the Sphinx." I said I'd come if I could, pleased to be asked, though never expected to leave Crete that soon.

The back of the army truck registered every bump, and at the end of a long ride everyone was very dusty. The legation was in a once elegant but now rather battered house and John, whose priestly uncle had entertained me on Santorini, opened the door. He greeted me joyfully, said everyone was out but he would make me a cup of tea. He led me to a room next to the kitchen saying, "This is the dining-room, not nice like Athens," and bustled off into the kitchen. He came back with a mismatched collection of tea things and laid a rough cloth on the table. "Not nice," he repeated, "but better than dead," and for a moment we silently remembered the dead.

John explained that Sir Michael Palairet (the minister), his wife, his daughter Anne, and my admiral were all staying at the legation. They came in one by one and gave me a great welcome, for I was the first survivor to bring a personal account of the shipwreck. At supper I told our story and at the end said (more or less truthfully) that I'd come to Canea hoping to be useful. Afterwards the admiral said he was glad to see me, but made no bones about there being no work to do. "It's unlikely we'll make a stand here," he said, "but now you're here, Belinda, stick around and we may get busy."

It didn't take long to realize that there was plenty of rather unpleasant 'busyness' going on all around. Every day the air-raid sirens wailed, though the main target was the naval base at Suda Bay across the isthmus from Canea. There were also frequent bursts of gunfire, and the nights were noisy with shouts and more gunfire. I was told that the Australian troops were trigger-happy. This proved very true.

I was having a siesta in my bedroom, which fronted on the street, when I was woken by someone calling my name, "Mrs. Lyons! Mrs. Lyons!"

I jumped up crying, "I'm coming! I'm coming!" and drew back the shutters. On the sidewalk below John and an Australian soldier stood face to face. John stared piteously up at me, and I saw that into his ample stomach the soldier was pressing the nozzle of a tommy-gun.

"He call me spy. Tell him no. He drunk. He kill me!" I said I'd come at once.

The legation entrance had tall double doors opening on a flight of steps. I threw the doors open, ran down the steps to be level with the soldier, said firmly that John was employed by the British Legation and there was no cause for an arrest. The effect was not as intended. The gun nozzle was redirected to my stomach and the soldier muttered impolitely something about "la-di-da...fuckin' spies," and wasn't quite steady on his pins. John was right - the soldier was drunk.

I wondered whether the safety catch of his gun was on or off, thought how ridiculous we must look, and having no idea what to do next, was thankful to see two young British officers coming briskly towards us. Just what was needed - except it had slipped my mind that the British do not speak unless introduced. With a courteous inclination of their well-groomed heads, the young men began to walk past, skirting round the Australian and his gun.

"I say!" I called out ('I say' was not quite the thing, but I was flurried), "Wait a minute. Could you please help us!"

At once they stopped and I indicated our problem. The young officer with the fair moustache exclaimed, "Oh, bad show!" and peremptorily commanded the Australian to put up his gun.

I was only slightly surprised when the gun swung to aim deliberately at the young officer's midriff and heard a truculent, "I'm not tykin' any fuckin' orders from a fuckin' British orficer!"

The young officer's pink-and-white complexion grew much pinker and I felt a detached interest in what he would do now. But I never found out, for just then a gentle voice behind us asked, "Is anything the matter?"

Lady Palairet stood in the legation doorway at the top of the steps. She was a beautiful woman (Augustus John had painted her portrait), slender, a little dreamy, tending to strings of beads and rather unconventional, loose clothing. Our quandary was quickly explained. Would she perhaps telephone...? The ugly words 'military police' were left unsaid.

She listened in silence, gazing mildly down at us. After a pause she said, "Perhaps the soldier would like a cup of tea?"

This novel proposal was so courteously made that I relayed it to the soldier without hesitation. "Lady Palairet has asked if you would like a cup of tea?"

The soldier didn't register the invitation at once for he was transfixed, gazing open-mouthed, at this vision on the legation steps. The invitation was repeated. After a rather tense pause he mumbled something equivalent to, "Don't mind if do."

I turned to go in, but the young officer was provoked to assert himself. "You cannot take your gun into the legation," he said, and commanded, "Hand it over!"

The reply was blunt. "I'll give my gun to the laidy!" and this the soldier proceeded to do. Lady Palairet took it bravely though without enthusiasm and, holding it at arm's length, led us between the cracked walls of the passage to the dining-room.

We sat round the table and John brought tea. While we spoke smoothly of this and that the Australian, his elbows bent spread-eagled on the table, sipped his tea cautiously, looking from one to the other of us with a mixture of disbelief and suspicion. I felt sorry for him, inexplicably in this unlikely scenario.

We did not have to keep up our fulsome conversation for too long. The other officer hadn't joined the tea party, and he reappeared expeditiously with a military policeman. The soldier submitted to arrest without a murmur and was led quietly away.

When I told this story it always raised a laugh. But at the back of my mind stirred a happiness that I had seen violence disengaged by the offer of a cup of tea.

A couple of days later I was walking across the central square in Canea when the air-raid sirens started to howl, and simultaneously heard someone shout, "Belinda! Belinda!" and turning, saw Alexis. As I ran towards him he cried, "You're alive!"

I laughed and shouted, "Why shouldn't I be?" as I tried to hug him, but his hands were on my shoulders, shaking me with exasperation as he exclaimed, "But I didn't know. Nobody knew! I was at the legation every day. They could only say that the *Kalanthe* had been sunk and there were survivors. But no names. It was awful, not knowing."

"How did you get away?"

"On a boat. I didn't use your paper." Over Suda Bay there was gunfire and the sound of aircraft and Alexis cried, "For God's sake, let's get out of this square." We ran to some kind of shelter and while we waited for the all-clear he said, "I want to hear everything. Let's have supper."

We ate at the only available restaurant in Canea whose sparse menu never changed - chicken or omelette with fried potatoes. Poor chickens, they must have been slaughtered in droves. We talked and talked, fending off the occasional drunk Australian who wanted to pick me up and became combative when I declined. Probably British soldiers got drunk too, but they didn't keep getting underfoot like the Australians.

I asked about Cy and Marina, and Alexis said that although Cy had proposed, Marina had refused. "Afterwards she wished she hadn't," Alexis said, "though she knew she was probably right. All Cy wants to do now is concentrate on the war and be where it's happening. And there's Dodo. Marina felt she couldn't leave her; it's going to be hell with Germans marching around, being in charge, damn their eyes!" He paused, then added fiercely, "I've got to get back there, Belinda, be trained for intelligence and go back. That's why I left. Now I must get out of Crete. The British aren't going to defend this island, it's a shambles here and it's going to be worse when the Germans invade. You'll be shipped off before long, but nobody's going to give me a berth. Do you have to stay?"

I admitted having nothing to do, and said that Anne Palairet was already talking about escape. "She's quite excited at the prospect of adventure."

"Belinda, let's you and me get out together. You're just one more person they'll be responsible for. You'll be doing them a favour."

Alexis had a point. I wasn't afraid of staying, but it did seem silly to hang about with nothing to do but wait to be evacuated. So the next day we set about finding a means of escape. Then Alexis heard that the consul from Piraeus had a caique he was going to sail to Alexandria, and we went off to Suda Bay in search of him. There was an air raid as soon as we arrived, and we cowered in a makeshift shelter until it was over. After that we started asking questions, and finally tracked the consul down.

His name was Hook. I don't know if his rank was really captain, but from then on he was for us Captain Hook - though he wasn't at all like that infamous villain in *Peter Pan*, shouting imprecations and threatening his captives with walking the plank. On the contrary, our Captain Hook was a man of few words.

"Just the two of you?" he asked. We nodded. He contemplated us in silence. "All right," he said, and we thanked him effusively. After we ran out of words he silently studied me with his sailor-blue eyes, and then remarked, "One thing, young lady, don't expect to have my cabin." I promised I had no such expectations. "Good," he said, "we're leaving tonight," and after noting a time and where we would find the caique, added, "If you're late, that's your funeral."

After this meeting I did not go back to the Legation. Everything I possessed, the little book of Shakespeare sonnets and my one handkerchief, were always in my pocket. It felt very free to have no possessions, no need to worry 'Shall I take this? Can I do without that?' But I should have told the Palairets I was sailing away from Crete in a caique. I should have left a note, but I didn't. It was, quite simply, unforgivable. I did nothing because they might have tried to stop me, and I did not intend to be stopped.

Alexis and I ate a last Cretan chicken with fried potatoes and left early for the harbour. We needed time to spare for blundering around in the dark, looking for the caique. There was nobody but us about, and dead quiet, just the sound of the water lapping against the quayside. We found the caique without difficulty - it was, of course, exactly where Captain Hook had said it would be.

"Good for you," he exclaimed and introduced us to the one other passenger, Wilfred, who explained he'd got separated from his regiment during the evacuation from Greece. Captain Hook then told us we could doss down in the hold. "There's a cargo of used army uniforms down there," he said. "Makes good bedding."

Right on time the caique slipped out to sea. The plan was to sail close to shore overnight, aiming for a small bay on the south coast. Here we would anchor until the following evening, then make for the open sea after dark, putting a good distance between ourselves and Crete before it was light.

"After that," Captain Hook said, "there's no refuge until Alexandria."

The three of us talked for a while before clambering down to the hold, but I was soon back on deck. The uniforms were flea-ridden. There was a bit of sail on the hatch which I wrapped myself in, and fell quickly asleep - it's handy to get used to sleeping hard.

I woke into quiet and stillness, and realized we must have reached the bay. The only sound was the tip-tap of the rigging as the caique rocked gently at anchor. Above my head the slender mast moved like a pendulum across the silver face of a full moon and, lying there, I thanked my stars for being where I was.

Captain Hook put me in charge of producing meals. The task wasn't demanding since our provisions were limited to a bag of onions and potatoes, a stack of 'doggy' ship's biscuits, and a generous supply of tins marked fiercely FOR EMERGENCY USE ONLY. After breakfast one of the Greek sailors, a merry little round man we called Papa, caught some fish after an excitable tangle with string and explosives. So Alexis and I prepared a fish soup, using the vegetables and, as we had no salt, we added a few scoops of seawater. The result was good.

The afternoon stretched ahead with nothing to do but wait until nightfall, so we asked if Papa might row the three of us ashore. There was a good beach and the bay curved at the end in an outcrop of rocks. It was perfect for a swim. Papa was willing and Captain Hook agreed, once again insisting on a punctual return, "Or you'll be left behind!"

"Sir!" we exclaimed, saluting idiotically.

We had the little bay to ourselves and swam naked for want of anything to swim in. The sea was warm, the sun shone and the war seemed an ugly chimera. It was only when it was time to begin making our way back that we noticed three small figures sitting cross-legged on the beach. They wore some kind of uniform topped by a brimmed hat and, disconcertingly, rifles lay across their laps.

"They look like local militia," Alexis said.

"Perhaps they're just having a rest," I said. "Ask them to go away, Alexis, or at least look the other way. We must get dressed. Tell them I'm embarrassed."

I don't know what Alexis said but after a few minutes of questions and answers Wilfred and I, impatiently treading water, asked for a translation.

Alexis said ruefully, "Believe it or not they think we're German spies and they're going to march us back to Canea under arrest."

"But that's absurd!" Wilfred expostulated. "Besides, it would take hours. There's a damn great mountain to scale. Tell them who we are."

"What d'you think I've been doing? I said Belinda was English and *they* said she had fair hair like all German girls. Then I pointed out that Wilfred was a British officer and his hair was black, but they said it was probably dyed. You'll just have to get dressed and we'll try and think up something."

The something we thought up was to persuade the soldiers to escort us back to the caique where, we assured them, we had papers to prove our identity. This was only partly true, but we were sure Captain Hook would impress them. After a bit of macho bluster, our captors agreed and lined us up with one armed man between each of us. We avoided one another's eyes, stifling laughter even though there was no knowing whether they might change their minds and take us in triumph over the mountain. On the other hand there was a good chance they had doubts and didn't want to make fools of themselves in Canea.

We reached the bay, hailed the caique, saw Papa wave his arms and give an answering shout before scrambling into the dinghy. We waited in silence as he rowed to shore, grounded the dinghy, and beached it before turning towards us - but then, with a roar, the leading militiaman threw down his rifle and rushed at Papa with arms flung wide. In a trice they were both bellowing and weeping and laughing, while the soldiers grinned and shook each one of us by the hand.

Above the turmoil Alexis shouted, "It's all right. That's Papa's brother. They haven't met for years!" Twenty years was bandied about at the height of jubilation, mutual apologies and congratulations. At last, as Papa rowed us back to the caique, a fusillade of rifle shots from the beach gave us a send-off in style.

After dark we left the protection of the coast and sailed into the open sea. Alexis and I talked for a while on the hatch until I rolled myself in the sail and he went down to the hold. Once again I was soon asleep, but woke abruptly into a wild, dark night. The caique was plunging like a bronco being busted, the waves tumbling on deck - and this time it wasn't ballast that rolled loose, it was me, pitched on the deck and sliding towards the scuppers. I crawled back to the hatch and, dripping wet, got down into the hold. Fleas or no fleas, it was safer and, in fact, positively cosy.

We woke to quiet seas, but the storm had broken all the instruments, including the ship's compass. "I've got my hand compass," Captain Hook said, unruffled. "We should make it, give or take a mile or two. Better not take more. We might land in unfriendly hands, so keep your fingers crossed." Alexis explained that the 'unfriendly hands' would be those of the Italian army in North Africa.

This danger seemed irrelevant as we continued our rather dreamlike voyage. We lay on deck talking endlessly about everything under the sun, particularly the world we meant to build after the war. Alexis and I were very intense about this. Not just ridding the world of Nazis, but building a better world. We waxed eloquent on beauty, truth and justice. We also argued inconclusively about war. I said it was crazy, as silly as trying to solve arguments with fisticuffs when the arguments were about all kinds of complicated things and couldn't be solved by punching each other on the nose. Alexis probably quoted the Greek philosophers, Wilfred said I was thinking sloppily, and they both asked what I'd do if the Germans invaded England. I replied by telling the story of Lady Palairet deflecting violence with a cup of tea.

"Oh, the English and their interminable cups of tea!" Alexis exclaimed. I said I didn't like tea much, but the argument was distracted by dolphins. We loved these visitations and would lean over the side to watch them leaping around us, exuding happiness. Another kind of visitor was a little owl who landed on the prow. The Greek crew were overjoyed "because," Alexis said, "she is the goddess Athene. They are very honoured and are sure we will now sail under her protection." The crew made a sort of altar with offerings of water and bits of food for the goddess. She was inscrutable, gazed at us with her big round eyes, a little thing, but very dignified. After about twenty-four hours she left us when we weren't looking.

Although the sun was hot the sea breeze kept us cool until the day we suddenly felt a great billow of heat as if a gigantic oven door had been opened.

"Africa!" Captain Hook said. "Shan't be long now," and with a grin added, "Seems we're on course." We were, and in mid- afternoon landed in Alexandria.

Alexis and I dined in style that night with Captain Hook. Wilfred excused himself, saying he must contact his regiment straight away, but I suspected he'd had enough of our conversation. We parted with goodwill and the three of us booked into an hotel, a table was reserved at the Officers' Club, and I went to my room and had three separate baths. Only then did I feel clean. I was a funny sight naked, my arms, neck, face and legs tanned so dark the rest of me looked pallidly white. I put on my grubby dress with a grimace, envied Alexis and Captain Hook who each had a clean shirt and pants, and hoped I wouldn't be barred from the Officers' Club. But this was no ordinary time and people were turning up from the sea in all kinds and conditions of clothing and cleanliness, so my ramshackle appearance was unremarkable.

Recklessly we ordered steak with new potatoes and little green peas, and a dessert of fresh strawberries and whipped cream. The strawberries stood on a nearby serving table, piled in a huge silver bowl beside an equally generous bowl of thick whipped cream. It was a wonderful sight.

We pitched into the steak with enthusiasm, but halfway through there seemed to be an awful lot of food on my plate. I glanced across at Alexis who was poking at his peas rather half-heartedly, and then caught Captain Hook's eye.

"Stuck?" he asked.

We both said we supposed so. Emergency rations and ship's biscuits, though sustaining, had not prepared us for gormandizing. Regretfully we had no room for dessert, and even now, after half a lifetime, regret lingers. No other strawberries and cream will ever match the tantalizing gleam of those berries or the velvet thickness of the cream we could not eat that night.

In Cairo the next day Alexis wanted to come with me to Mena House, but I said no. I felt mean and couldn't properly explain that I had something unfinished there, something to complete. Rather disconsolately he joined his aunt, Roxane, and Shan who had an apartment in the city - "with room for you also, Belinda," said Roxane, and I gladly accepted for later. I would have to find work in Cairo, but for the moment my salary had piled up during the weeks of escape, and I was going to blow some of it by staying at Mena House - which wasn't any old tacky boarding house.

Whatever sum I blew, it was worth it. Our lazy days were broken by only one outing to a party for the *Kalanthe* survivors, held at the British Embassy in Cairo. It was wonderful to see our handsome porter, James, his burn scars healing beautifully, and to learn that all the wounded had recovered, and poor Mark Norman was reported on the mend. But I got my come-uppance from Anne Palairet for so rudely leaving Crete without a word of thanks and explanation.

"We had no idea what had happened to you," she said. "My parents were desperately worried. You caused a lot of trouble. It was very wrong." I could only say I was truly sorry, and truly meant it, but could give no reasonable excuse. After upbraiding me she talked about her escape from Crete, which was exciting. But I thanked my stars for Captain Hook and his caique.

I stayed nearly a week at Mena House. We breakfasted by the pool, swam, slept in the afternoon, dined once in Cairo after the official embassy junket, and, of course, pottered round the Sphinx. It had been rather disappointing to find this huge winged figure, more than four thousand years old, crouched right across from the hotel. I'd expected to find her brooding over trackless desert, instead of lying at the end of a fine motor road built for the convenience of a visiting princess. At least the desert came up to the immense lion paws, and anyway, I'd not come for ruins.

So what had I come for? What did I expect from Nancy and Harold, Peter and Norman? They were people I hardly knew, most of them at least a decade older than me. Unless I married a diplomat it was unlikely we'd meet again. I wasn't even sure I wanted to be part of their world, yet I liked them, so self-reliant, taking such pleasure in each other's company, good-humoured, and easy in themselves. They had no doubts about who they were, and played their parts with conviction and pride. Why not? They belonged to the Establishment, the Ruck Keene world of people who *mattered*, though grandmother Birdie might have found obscure genealogical reasons for murmuring that some were "not quite out of the handkerchief-drawer, darling." Then I remembered Tom Loveday and his 'Yes, madam', and felt that Birdie's fine-tuned distinctions needed looking into.

But these were side issues to the main question of whether I'd put too high a premium on whatever it was we'd shared on Kimolos. Had I imagined its vitality? The answer was in fact, simple.

The evening of my arrival, Nancy and I were on our way upstairs to change for dinner. As we walked across the lobby a woman stopped in front of us and cried, "Good heavens! Nancy! My dear, I'm so glad to see you." She gazed dramatically at Nancy, began, "I'm so sorry, such a dreadful..." but jibbing at 'death', babbled, "What a terrible time you must have had! Such a dreadful..." She was all sympathy - and Nancy laughed.

"Oh no!" she exclaimed. "We had a wonderful time." Later, on our way upstairs, Nancy said, "I couldn't remember that woman's name. She'll probably tell everyone my mind is touched. Was I rude?"

I said slowly, "No, you were just...well, you were honest. It startled her. What's more, she wasn't there, and we were very much there, just being alive, even the sick ones – and that *was* wonderful."

We left it at that.

৵ 28 ৵

Major Wintle's 'toys',
and a spot of spying.

For all the enticement of its strangeness, Cairo seemed putrescent. I saw for the first time the degradation of poverty, and the bland indifference of wealth. Them and Us. The rich drove through the wide streets in gleaming cars, purring past the sick and the lame and the pitiful bundles of rags begging in the gutters. Every day I passed a woman holding a baby whose suppurating eyes crawled with flies. She wiped the eyes gently with a dreadful rag. I gave her some drachmas, but she was only one of a multitude, and the drachmas seemed more of an insult than charity.

One day, soon after I'd settled in with Alexis, Roxane and Shan, I was waiting to cross the road when Faroukh, the King of Egypt, drove past in a large limousine. Years earlier, when I was at school, Faroukh was being educated at a private school in England. His picture appeared in the *Tatler* and we exclaimed at his good looks, wondering what it must be like for him to wear regular schoolboy clothes instead of flowing Arab garments. Visions of Arab sheikhs galloping across illimitable deserts dazzled our senses with the promise of unspeakable passions. More primly we invested him with kingly qualities, born to rule wisely, beloved by his subjects.

So I looked with especial eagerness at a car approaching with pennants flying, for my companion had exclaimed, "Here comes Faroukh!" I saw a man with a heavy, expressionless face, his eyes hidden by sunglasses, his head turning neither right nor left. My companion remarked, "A rather loathsome chap, said to be hand-in-glove with the Nazis. According to gossip he has a huge collection of motor horns. Guess his favourite." I shook my head. "The one that sounds like a dog being run over."

So this was Egypt. Greece had been very different. Because of my avid, childhood reading of the Greek myths in *The Tanglewood Tales*, the country was so embedded in my imagination that being there was like walking into a territory already mapped, instinct with beauty. Egypt was harsh. The sun blazed unrelenting from a metallic blue sky, and the Cairo streets clamoured with the noise of people, so many people, shuffling under monstrous loads, hurrying with briefcases, sitting in cafés talking and talking, breaking off to clap their hands for another cup of strong, sweet coffee, poured from a copper pot with a spout curved like a toucan's beak. Amidst the multitude of sounds the juice man chanted his wares to the clitter-clatter of his little metal cups, until he paused to hold his jar of juice aloft and let fall into one of his cups a curving, expert thread of brown fluid.

The soukh had a contained, colourful life, common to all markets. Small, patient donkeys with loaded panniers neatly picked their way through the narrow streets, each street its own domain. There was a street for woven carpets and rugs, a street for leather, another for gold and silver, and one where men beat out delicate designs on brass or copper. There was a street of booths filled with glorious brocades, and another street just for sheepskin - the living background of *The Thousand and One Nights.*

This pulsating life provoked me to suggest to Roxane, Shan and Alexis that, instead of living in a commonplace, ordinary modern apartment building, it would be wonderful if we all shared a houseboat on the Nile. I took Roxane to see one advertised for rent and after we had cased the layout of rooms we went on deck. As we leant on the rails I expatiated on the pleasure of seeing the slender curving masts of the *feluccas,* the Nile fishing boats, outlined against blazing sunset skies, or floating past like a flock of monster birds, their wing-like sails filled by a morning breeze.

"Look at the space we'd have here," I cried, "and the view of the river and the coolness from the water!" But as I spoke the river current carried under our noses a very dead and bloated dog, his poor legs stiffly sticking up into the air.

"No, Belinda!" said Roxane. "That settles it. We'll stay on dry land with no corpses."

I accepted defeat and settled in with the others, though the word 'settle' is misleading, for each one of us was unsettled and fidgety in Cairo. Alexis was frustrated by inaction, his heart and imagination set on training for intelligence work. I wasn't much help to him. The four months in Greece had withdrawn into a limbo where we were young and carefree - and happy, despite the war. Now, in flight from Greece, Alexis had lost his country, and I had come face to face with war: I had seen the smoke rise from the doomed *Kalanthe,* watched Nancy search for her brother's body in the unyielding sea, and heard the burned men scream each time their dressings were changed. Above all, the agent of this carnage was the German pilot whose face I glimpsed, an everyday face, a face that could have been blown to bits had the Lewis guns hit their mark. So how come we perfect strangers were bent on slaughtering each other? There was no sense in the routine answers, and no others came.

Practically, Alexis and I needed jobs. Alexis had his sights set on regaining possession of his country; I had to get work in order to live. Sometimes I felt impatient with Alexis and his heroic dreams, and then was ashamed. He, Roxane and Shan, were all in anguish for their family in Athens, cut off from the world by the German occupation.

The war was, of course, discussed endlessly in the apartment. As usual I listened to the arguments and forecasts, and occasionally asked questions. Gradually I got a rough idea of what had happened and was now happening in North Africa. The pre-war Italian campaign in Ethiopia had given Italy a foothold in Somalia, Tunisia and Libya, convincing Mussolini that he could sweep the British out of Egypt. In 1940 the Axis partnership of Italy, Germany and Japan had been formed, and in April 1941, Italian and German forces captured Benghazi from the British. No wonder Captain Hook was nervous of landing on the wrong bit of North Africa. But only a month later the Italians surrendered to the British, the North African front was galvanized by Field-Marshall Rommel and German reinforcements, brought in to spice up the Italian troops.

In a way the discussions made the war seem rather academic, until, in an odd way, the North Africa front became very real. This was not due to bombs or immediate danger, but because of seven total strangers with whom I dined separately every day during that one week.

I had gone to a party without realizing it was a sort of farewell gathering for a number of young officers shortly due to leave for the desert front. At the party one of the officers asked me to dine with him the next evening; another invitation followed, and by the end of the party every evening was booked for the week.

My hosts were merry, and I took the first two proposals of marriage at face value, but not the third proposal. On this occasion my companion first laid on the table three antique books: Smollet's *Humphrey Clinker* and two volumes of Henry Fielding's *Tom Jones*. These were collectors' books, eighteenth century editions with leather spines and corners, gorgeous handmade marbled end-papers, and an elegant script in which the letter 'f' was often used instead of an 's'. The publication date was MDCCLXXXIV.

After I'd admired the books he said, "I'd like you to have them." I protested that he shouldn't part with them, but he repeated, "I'd really like you to have them, Belinda." He looked earnestly at me and added, "Then I'll know someone enjoys them if...that is...if I don't come back." He said this stoically, and then asked me to marry him.

Throughout that week I countered each proposal with the fact that I was married, but soon it crept up on me that my marriage wasn't the issue, nor even was sex. The books were the clue. These young men knew they soon might die, and suddenly the reality of death was the nothingness of obliteration - unless, by some miracle, they could leave behind a final footprint of their own. The books would be a footprint in my memory. The proposal was different, a wild bid to leave the indelible footprint of a child.

Had I been a different person I might at least have bedded them all for comfort; but sadly I wasn't a free enough spirit. Instead I listened, held their hands, hugged them and hoped the little I gave was better than nothing.

At the end of the week the batch of young men left for the desert. I went alone to the great mosque of *ibn Tulun* to wonder at the skill of human hands whose legacy of intricate designs was carved on the stone arches. Another day I spent hours in the Cairo Museum, considering the treasures buried with Tutankhamen, the mummified remains of a nameless Egyptian cat, and an ancient Egyptian human, also nameless. Pondering time and the collapse of empires I marvelled at the Tutankhamen treasures and how the nameless craftsmen assured posterity, "I was - and see, I am!"

Meantime I landed a job. I'd gone for a typing test with whatever organization listed job openings, and joined quite a crowd of other hopeful shorthand-typists in a big room full of desks and typewriters. A typing assignment was handed out which I completed and took to the lady in charge.

"You better start now, dear," she said. "The others have already begun." I pointed out that I had finished. She seemed surprised. I was no less surprised that everyone else was so slow. I left feeling rather smug. A few days later I was told a Major Wintle had an opening, and would interview me.

He wore a monocle and was very much the cavalry officer, producing the impression of having been born fully adult in impeccable cavalry boots and uniform. His face and features were lean, his expression slightly mad, but the glint in his eyes implied that he thoroughly enjoyed being mad and was ready sprung for decision and action. He worked in a small office of two or three rooms with a devoted sergeant and a couple of shadowy other ranks. He said the unit was dedicated to devising what he called 'toys'. I probably tried not to look bemused, but he didn't miss much and explained: "Booby traps - to fool the enemy," and producing a fountain pen, said "Here's our new little toy."

The sergeant quickly exclaimed, "Don't try 'er again, sir! She's not quite ready yet."

Major Wintle accepted this sardonically, and explained that in demonstrating the new toy to a visitor there was what he called "a bit of a snag." He ignored his sergeant's mutter about "bloody explosion" and went on, "Tricky little things, takes time to iron out the snags," and added enigmatically, "Good thing I was by the elevator shaft, so all was well!" I noticed that he missed one finger of his right hand, and though obviously long healed, I did wonder if he was prone to snags.

It wasn't very clear what work I might do in his office, but after a Wintle version of an interview, I was hired. Then he asked me most courteously if I would join him for lunch. His manner was slightly Edwardian. I did my best to reply in kind and hoped I could keep it up.

"Will Shepeard's suit you?" he said. "They give you a decent meal there."

Of course it suited me! Legendary Shepeard's Hotel was where characters in Somerset Maugham stories met and dined while living out their fascinating, trapped lives. As we sipped sweet Turkish coffee after an excellent lunch, it seemed fitting that Major Wintle should embark on an elaborate kind of courtship.

He put down his cup and looked me straight in the eye. "I have a question, Mrs. Lyons. I'm a betting man, but I never bet on a certain loser. I hope you will not think my enquiry impertinent. Are you married?"

A little flustered by this gambit I hesitated, then settled for being cool, and said that I expected to receive divorce papers from England.

"Thank you," he said.

He proposed about a week later and continued to do so off and on, accepting my refusals almost as though refusing was a proper move on my part, evidence of delicacy and appreciation of form. Occasionally I felt as though I was being conned into a performance. Fortunately I could distract him with questions about his life, a story which he told with panache. It went roughly as follows.

He was born in Russia. I believe his father was in the diplomatic service, and if he wasn't he ought to have been, for the diplomatic scene was Major Wintle's ambience. He spoke Russian and French fluently, had entered a British cavalry regiment and, as his sergeant told me, became a crack shot, able to hit a pin from some astonishing distance. This feat was remarkable because he had only one functioning eye. I never asked how he lost the eye or the finger, but liked his airy attitude towards their absence. "Always loved the piano," he said. "Still do. Took a bit of time getting used to being a finger short, but manage all right. Like to hear you play."

He knew people in high places, one of whom was General de Gaulle. Either when France fell, or was about to fall in 1940, Major Wintle decided that it was up to him to extract de Gaulle from France and bring him to England where he could build up a force of French patriots. So he requested an aircraft for this purpose. The request was denied. Convinced of the rightness of his cause he privately chartered an aircraft. Unfortunately the military got wind of this and, as he was about to board, he was arrested and taken to the War Office for questioning. The interview grew stormy and, as Major Wintle observed, "goaded by the ineptitude of a bureaucratic nincompoop" he pulled out his revolver and threatened to shoot if his plan was obstructed. He was subdued, arrested again, and rather romantically imprisoned in the Tower of London. This was appropriate to the Wintle style; anything less would have been an affront. It was also predictable that somebody must have urged leniency, for here he was, in Cairo, playing with booby traps and free as a bird.

I soon realized that Major Wintle's sergeant was jealous of me. The major was his baby and hero, and undoubtedly he disapproved of having the pure male preserve of the office messed up by a woman. Added to these unspoken feelings there was hardly any work for me to do, and before long there wasn't any Major Wintle. One morning his sergeant stiffly announced that the major was on a special assignment, that I was to stay on the payroll, but "there's no need to come to the office until further notice." This last was delivered with a stony face belied by a tiny inflection of triumph.

A day or two after the major's sergeant put me out to grass, a chance acquaintance put me in contact with another hush-hush unit. The man who ran it seemed quite old (at least fifty) and had the title of 'Bey'. This originated when Egypt was part of the Ottoman Empire. The title designated the governor of a province and gave the right to wear the Turkish fez. In due course the title became an honorary one, and later was often presented to long-serving administrators of the British protectorate. The red felt fez looked like an upside-down flowerpot, topped by a long black silk tassel. The fez made it easy to pick out a Bey in a crowd.

My Bey's manner to me was partly avuncular and partly secretive. His face, curiously featureless, gave an impression of a pink blob topped by a red felt flowerpot, plus tassel. He interviewed me in an apartment in a modern block, darkened by closed window-shutters. There was one bedroom with a narrow bed, side-table and chair, and the main room was his office, minimally furnished with a filing cabinet and outsize desk.

During the interview he pulled open one of the desk drawers and said it was wired to agents in the city and 'elsewhere', murmuring something about Baghdad. I was sitting across from him, separated by the expanse of desk, and had no way of verifying this interesting disclosure. But I found the whole set up so like a *Chums* spy story that it was hard to take seriously.

What he wanted me to do was work as an agent in Cairo where, he assured me, there were many Egyptians suspected of working for the Nazis. I was to pose as the chatterbox wife of a British officer, and to confirm the disguise I would be fixed up "with a nice little apartment." I said I wasn't cut out to be a spy, but this was brushed aside. I hesitated, for I was, after all, on Major Wintle's payroll, but his reappearance was problematic and any day I might be jobless. I told the Bey I'd give his job a try.

Before we separated he explained that he liked to get to know his agents personally and invited me to lunch at his house in Zamalek the following day, concluding, "My wife will be delighted to meet you." However, as we drove to Zamalek the Bey apologized for the unexpected absence of his wife. I said politely what a pity, and privately thought 'It sounds fishy, but good heavens, the man's old enough to be my father!' Aloud I admitted to being interested in seeing a house in this part of Cairo where British administrators had made themselves at home.

I expected the house to be fairly stylish, appropriate to British responsibilities and power, but the Bey's house, at least from the outside, might have been anywhere in boring middle-class suburban England. Inside it was no better. The standard lamps had hideous pinky-beige shades of pleated silk edged with dangling beads, the ornaments were deplorable, and there was little in the way of books. Then, a little ashamed to be such a snob, I murmured polite comments. I had to dish out more polite comments at lunch when the Bey revealed an enthusiasm for gazing into crystal balls, and predictably asked if I would do him the favour of holding the ball.

I said, "That will be interesting, but perhaps after the siesta?" and remembered someone saying that the Egyptians would be only too pleased to get rid of the British for good. No wonder!

Lunch over, I was led upstairs to a spare bedroom. Thankful for respite I'd just stripped off my dress when the Bey knocked on the door. After wrapping something round me, I opened it.

"My dear young lady, do forgive me! But perhaps...just a few a minutes..." and added something about vibrations. Thinking 'Drat you and your crystal ball,' I said I'd be delighted after the siesta and got rid of him. As his footsteps receded I gently locked the door. He tried it later and tiptoed away. When fully clothed I did hold his crystal ball. Maybe he saw something. I remember only acute embarrassment.

The next day or two I debated whether to extricate myself from the Bey. But Shan and Roxane were leaving for Jerusalem and Alexis had already gone somewhere for unspecified training. I reckoned I could keep the Bey at arm's length and there'd be an escape route if, or when, Major Wintle reappeared.

The Bey fixed me up with a small, charming apartment in Gezira. "We keep a few on hand," he said airily, then outlined my first assignment. I was to make an appointment with the owner of a very expensive hair salon in Cairo. She was suspected of German connections, and I was to chatter loosely about my husband, letting drop a few tempting insinuations about his work. I carried out the assignment feeling a complete idiot. Madame listened to my babble with a fixed smile, and asked not a single question. I was convinced she found my performance laughably inept, and reckoned it was a measure of her scorn when my elaborate hair-do fell apart within hours.

I reported to the Bey. He assured me I had the makings of an excellent agent, and should repeat my visit to the hairdresser every week. It's possible he proposed some kind of training, or at least an initiation into the elementary points of being a spy. Maybe he deserves the benefit of doubt, but I never repeated my fatuous charade at the hairdresser's. In less than a week I fell ill. My temperature soared alarmingly, but I managed to telephone the Bey to apologize for missing my hair appointment, but to my dismay he came round shortly after. When he insisted on transferring me to the bedroom in his office, I was too far gone to protest.

Perhaps I was no more than two days in that room, but the hours stretched interminably, measured by the chant of the juice seller in the street below and the rhythmic clanging of his little metal cups. I followed the rhythm with demented attention, while the pattern on the walls assumed huge significance as they constantly rearranged their alignments. From time to time the Bey appeared, featureless beneath his red felt flowerpot.

In lucid moments I was grateful that he kept the bedside table stocked with liquids. For his part I cannot have been an enticing proposition, sweating, sticky and sliding in and out of delirium. Very likely he regretted whatever impulse led him to put me in the office bed, and when I begged him to telephone Major Wintle he must have done so promptly, for suddenly there was the familiar immaculate figure, monocle, boots and all, bending over me and muttering, "Bad show, bad show!"

"Get me out of this place," I croaked, and later was vaguely aware of being wrapped in a blanket and driven through the hot streets to a bed in a quiet, cool room. I woke to find a nurse by my bed and asked where I was. She said, "In the hospital at Gezira, dear."

"What's the matter with me?"

"A nasty touch of jaundice. Settle down now and we'll have you right as rain in no time."

The hospital faced the Gezira golf course. When I was better my bed was wheeled on to the veranda with other recovering patients, and it was like heaven to lie and look at the green grass and palm trees and be waited on. Major Wintle made several visits during this time and by then I'd discovered the hospital was a private one. I asked how much my stay was likely to cost but he brushed that aside and said I wasn't to worry - and no bill was ever presented. One day the sergeant brought flowers and regrets that the major was for the moment unable to visit. No explanation. I hoped to see him again, if only to thank him for his kindness, so was really glad when the sergeant reappeared on the day before I was to be discharged. He said Major Wintle wished to see me and would I be well enough at the end of the week? A car would pick me up.

The sergeant collected me after dark. We drove in silence to somewhere in the suburbs, and stopped outside a pair of tall iron gates. Amongst shrubs and trees, a large house loomed without a gleam of light. Reality slipped into neutral as the gates opened soundlessly, and at the house a door was discreetly held ajar for our entry.

Once inside I could just hear a Chopin waltz being played on a piano. We began walking through rooms designed for splendour, but now in suspended animation with every piece of furniture and all the chandeliers shrouded in reams of white cloth. We walked on through the dimly lit rooms, the waltz grew gradually more distinct, and finally rose to full volume as we entered what must have been a ballroom. At the far end Major Wintle sat at a grand piano. From the light of a lamp on the piano I saw he wore black trousers, white shirt and a dazzling brocade dressing-gown of blue and gold, the gold threads gleaming in the lamplight.

As I walked towards the major he turned, and I saw he'd grown a beard. I decided to say as little as possible until I got a lead on my part in this performance. There was something about Major Wintle that made me feel protective, unwilling to spoil whatever this new scenario might be. Within minutes I learnt that he was off to Syria, then to Lebanon, with France his ultimate destination.

I asked why. "To pose," he replied, "as a Vichy French school teacher who wishes to be repatriated to France."

I said, "You'll have to explain. I don't know the background of what you're talking about."

"Of course, my dear, of course." He was a kind man, not given to making me feel my shortcomings, and he loved talking about himself. But first he launched into a potted history of how, after World War I, the Treaty of Versailles had awarded France a mandate in Syria and Lebanon. But the German occupation of France in 1941 meant that the French civil servants and administers of the mandate became the servants of the French government set up in Vichy by the Germans. This posed an immediate problem, for Syria adjoins Iraq and by 1940 Iraq was already a centre for German intrigue, and before long the Iraqis were openly collaborating with the Nazis.

Major Wintle said, "We knew that German pilots were being allowed to land at Syrian aerodromes and stockpile fuel in Aleppo. An impossible situation! The recent Allied campaign was undertaken to oust the Vichy French from the Levant and ensure its military security."

I wanted to ask what the Levant was, but he went on, "As you know, my dear Belinda, the campaign succeeded and the Vichy forces surrendered. Some have rallied to de Gaulle, the rest are waiting, with former administrators and their families, for repatriation to France." He paused, drew breath, then announced, "Here is my opportunity! I shall go with them and disappear into the bourgeoisie of France. It is an exceptional chance to gather valuable information."

I didn't dare ask who was sending him on this mission, suspecting it was another lone adventure. I murmured that the plan was courageous, but he wasn't listening. "I depart tomorrow for Syria," he said. "Forgive me for imposing on your time, Belinda, but I could not leave without bidding you farewell."

I played my part as best I could. We talked a little longer, then he kissed my hand and said, "*Après la guèrre, ma chère Belinda.*" I left him in the big, shuttered house supplying background music for my exit - a Chopin nocturne this time, a commendable minus-one-finger version. I did hope his plan would fare better than his bid to recruit de Gaulle, and wondered if I'd ever see or hear of him again.

Much later I heard that the proposed infiltration of the French bourgeoisie came to nothing. As soon as the ship docked in France, Major Wintle was seized and imprisoned. He could have languished in gaol for the rest of the war, but in one of the curious games played between intelligence organizations, he was exchanged for a Vichy agent being held in England.

I tucked his memory away thinking I'd hear no more of him, but a decade after the war ended I saw a short news paragraph in the *Times,* recording that a Major Wintle had been arraigned for disturbing the peace. Could it be...? I read on, seeking a clue - and found it. The major had encountered his wife's solicitor on a London street and, convinced his wife's affairs were being mishandled by the solicitor, tried to de-bag him. In other words, he attempted to pull off the solicitor's trousers - a traditional stratagem of British public school boys to show disapproval.

This was without doubt my Major Wintle. I noted that his wife was a pianist and was happy he'd found such a suitable mate. I was also glad he had enough fire in his belly to resort to that schoolboy prank, however ridiculous. Now, remembering his kindness and courtesy, I affectionately salute his improbable ghost.

✥ 29 ✥

The Cedars of Lebanon,
and a decision.

The train going north was crammed with soldiers, the compartments overflowing into the corridors. A doctor had told me to take a few weeks convalescence. "Jaundice plays havoc with your system," he said. "Get out of Cairo and take it easy somewhere pleasant," and recommended a rest-house on a lake beyond Cairo. A lake! I thought of cool lapping water as I stood in the corridor until I could stand no longer, and lay down amongst large army feet, bits of cigarettes and heaven knew what else, but didn't care.

The rest-house turned out to be a wooden bungalow which had seen better days. The air was as hot and heavy as in Cairo, the lake a dispirited scrap of water, and a few listless convalescents were sitting on the rest-house veranda. I made my way up the veranda steps and paused groggily, probably looking appalled, for an officer greeted me with, "Not exactly paradise, I'm afraid. You here for long?"

It was too much bother to pretend and said, "I'd like to be somewhere cooler. I've just had a bout of jaundice and don't feel very bright."

He studied me a moment. "I tell you what, your best bet is to get back on the train this evening and go on overnight to Jerusalem. Lovely place, higher, you'll even see a nice cloud or two." A cloud! Egypt was short on clouds. "I'll arrange for some chaps to meet you at el-Kantara. They'll row you over the Canal, save hanging about." I could have wept with gratitude, being in a state where tears sprang, easy as a baby's.

I was met at el-Kantara by what appeared to be a platoon of soldiers, and was escorted to a rowboat on the Suez Canal. As the rowers pulled away I looked back at the tired soldiers waiting for the ferry, and felt a spasm of guilt - rather token guilt, for there was no room for anything but relief. Even thinking was an effort. The boat was a haven; the slight groan of rowlocks and the regular dip of oars in the water were peaceful as a lullaby. I let my hand trail in the Canal and suddenly a magical cascade of luminous, phosphorescent drops rose and fell in the darkness. Drowsily I was filled with a surge of gratitude for unexpected kindness - and then, bang out of nowhere, a voice in my head said crisply, 'People do nice things for you because of the way you look. You'll look different when you're older. Better learn to be a really nice person before it's too late.'

I was in no mood to be hectored like this and stared up at the stars, willing back facile tears; but my thoughts were now out of control. The voice was silent, but instead Alice, the *Wonderland* Alice, took over. I saw Tenniel's drawing of her after she'd eaten the wrong bit of cake and grown nine feet tall. There she was, her neck like a giraffe's, exclaiming, "Curiouser and curiouser!" but soon beginning to cry because she couldn't get through the tiny door into "the loveliest garden she'd ever seen." My copy of *Alice* lay at the bottom of the Aegean Sea, but I knew chunks of it by heart, and remembered:

> "You ought to be ashamed of yourself," said Alice, "a great girl like you," (she might well say this), "to go on crying in this way! Stop this moment, I tell you!" But she went on all the same...

In the rowboat I did check the tears, but the next morning in the train I was mopping my eyes once more, this time at the sight of beautiful little white clouds floating in the blue sky over Palestine. The relentless burnished blue of Egypt's sky had no place for anything so tender as a cloud. Whoever heard of anyone weeping at the sight of a cloud? But, like Alice, I went on all the same.

In Jerusalem a taxi took me to the King David Hotel. As I walked unsteadily into the lobby, a voice called, "Hallo, Belinda! What are you doing here?" I recognized an English journalist, met casually in Cairo, couldn't remember his name, and collapsed into his startled arms. The next day I was in better shape and gladly accepted the journalist's invitation to go with him to Beirut.

"You can relax at the *Hôtel St. George,*" he said, "it's right by the sea, and the view's unbeatable. They're still mopping up after the Syrian campaign and only the press are allowed into Lebanon. At the border just keep mum and I'll say you're my assistant."

During our drive I asked why he used the French *Hôtel St. George* instead of St. George Hotel, and he said because French was a second language in Beirut. "Syria and Lebanon have been locked in a French mandate since the end of World War One. There's a French University and French mission schools all over the place."

"So what are you looking for in Beirut?"

"They're still getting the country untangled. With luck I'll dig out a story or two about some of the little games going on."

"Games?"

"Human nature games. Various generals are at odds with each other, the Vichy and Free French are at loggerheads, and the Arabs are scrambling to stake out their claims. It's quite a circus. They say that fur's flying already between Wilson and Spears."

"Who is Spears?"

"General Louis Spears, heads the British Military Mission, a brilliant man. Quite a tiger. But you needn't let any of this bother you."

Beirut was indeed much too beautiful to bother about power squabbles I didn't understand, though the divisions were reflected in the clientèles of the *St. George* and that of the only other hotel of any size, the *Hôtel Normandie.* The *St. George* was full of British and Free French officers; the *Normandie,* which was out-of-bounds to the British and Free French, contained only Vichy French officers.

My hotel room looked out across the sea to the coastal mountains, and for the first little while I swam in the sea, slept, pottered along the beach past the *Normandie,* and poked happily around the town and market.

It was hot and quite humid, but the sea was there, and the people were different from the Egyptians, more lively and friendly. The market smelt of spices and the stalls were piled with fresh fruit and vegetables, goat cheese, a delicious sort of spread called hummus, sesame halvah, trays of fat, sticky dates, Turkish Delight, and baklava stuffed with nuts and dripping with honey. A pedlar slipped a garland of sweet-scented jasmine over my head and when I paid the full price his white teeth gleamed in a delighted smile. The price was so small, and I was never any good at bargaining.

Slightly drunk with the languorous perfume of jasmine, I wandered through affluent parts of the city, trying to imagine what the big stone houses were like inside, furnishing them with sumptuous divans and priceless carpets in rooms lit by flames in hanging brass lamps. I caught glimpses of pink oleanders, dahlias and roses in the gardens, saw date palms and fruit trees rising above the surrounding stone walls draped in tumbled cascades of purple, cream and deep red bougainvillaea. There were flowers everywhere, and in the midst of these delights I gave silent thanks to the kind person at the rest-house who sent me on my way, and to the journalist who brought me here - and for the happenstance of jaundice.

By the time the journalist went back to Cairo I was ready to explore further. I saw him off after breakfast and was touched when he gave me a little six-sided box, made of wood and hand painted. Each side was quite crudely decorated with a deer, a hare, and a few birds, and on the lid were two Arab figures, a man and woman in close converse. At least, that's how I saw them at a quick glance, for the journalist thrust the box into my hands as he said goodbye, brushing aside my thanks. Only later, looking more closely at the two figures, I noticed that 'close converse' was a euphemism: 'close embrace' was nearer the mark. It was hard to tell whether the lady's upflung arms indicated passion or protest, for both figures were fully clothed. Did this carry a message - regretful, exasperated or nonplussed?

No answer came, except that many men took for granted that a single, attractive woman was in an almost permanent erotic fervour, ever-ready to oblige the passing stranger with a toss in the hay. Maybe I should loosen up? I stared out of my bedroom window at the incomparable view. But there was no way round it: I needed a slower process, and to be in love, whatever that meant. Anyway, for now the mountains waited to be explored and it was enough to be in love with Lebanon itself.

Beirut lies on the curve of a bay. To the north the range of mountains rise from the coast to the snowy peaks of Mount Lebanon. I was told that 'Lebanon' derived from 'Liban', the Aramaic for white. Pockets of snow lie all year round on Mount Lebanon, as well as the westerly ranges of Anti-Lebanon and Mount Hermon, whose crests make a natural border with Syria. I decided to go north along the coast and then find a mountain village where I could stay.

In 1941 the only way to reach mountain villages was by shared taxi. The passengers were varied. On this first trip I squeezed in with several women and their chickens. By the time we parted I had become fully initiated into the ladies' uninhibited curiosity about my private life - that I was English, alone, so young, no husband, no children. We had no common language, but warmth of heart and pantomime were just as good.

The driver turned his taxi north somewhere by ancient Byblos. The road climbed up through olive groves to a village where half the inhabitants seemed to be harvesting apples and apricots, plums and pears. The taxi stopped by a small hotel shaded by walnut trees. There was a café nearby, and the taxi driver smiling said, "Here the food is good." I noticed they were serving the kind of Arab food I'd begun to enjoy - hors d'oeuvres of hummus with thin Arab bread, and delectable slices of cold, fried eggplant. I asked the driver to wait, and finding that the hotel had a free room, decided to stay.

The taxi-driver was right. The café served a delicious lunch of chicken kebab, a salad of tomatoes and cucumber sprinkled with mint, followed by fresh fruit. There was an abundance of fruit everywhere, and each morning, as I set out to explore, the harvesters pressed fruit into my hands, smiling as they cried, "Take! take!" I took, giving back smiles and thanks, but no money: these were gifts of hospitality.

My first walks began unadventurously, wandering through the olive groves and up through umbrella pines, stopping to drink from a spring, cooling hands and face in rocky pools fringed with delicate maidenhair fern and the blade-like leaves of harts-tongue. Soon I climbed higher, following rough paths, tantalized by tinkling goat bells ahead. One afternoon in an upland meadow I sat by a stream and was joined by a shepherd, three little boys and a flock of goats. After exchanging smiles and sitting in companionable silence the shepherd got up, took a small metal dish, washed it thoroughly in the stream, and filled it to the brim with milk from one of the goats. He carried it with care and, with a beautiful courtesy, presented it to me.

I had been warned never to drink unboiled milk, but flung this caution to the winds and drank the warm frothy liquid slowly, pausing to smile and show my pleasure. Meanwhile the little boys were giggling and pushing each other around, glancing back to see if I was watching. Then, with sudden bravado, one of them stripped off his pants and shirt and jumped into the water. In a moment the others were naked, shouting and splashing together. The shepherd smiled, gesturing with his hands. It was a golden moment.

Every day I explored a little further until, inevitably, I got lost. The sun beat on my head, I upbraided myself for tramping along in the midday sun, but plodded on and on. At last, feeling rather queer, I found myself walking unsteadily into a camp of Australian soldiers.

The commanding officer sat me down, called for a strong cup of tea with plenty of sweetened canned milk, and summoned the medical officer who said, "You shouldn't be wandering around alone."

"Why not? Everyone's so friendly."

"They're A-rabs." That's how he pronounced it, A-rabs. "They're all right in their way, but a gal like you...'sides, jaundice is real crook, takes time to get over. You need good food, moderate exercise, and after a quiet week or two somewhere out of harm's way in the mountains you'll be dandy."

"Righty-ho!" said the commanding officer. "The place for you is the hotel at the Cedars. Beaut. Just your style. We'll have a bite to eat, go and pick up your stuff and I'll drive you there this evening. No, not a word. That's an order!"

It was quite late by the time we got to the hotel. I was too tired to take in much, except that it had a rambly old charm and felt good. "Get well and enjoy yourself," said the Australian as I tried to thank him.

250

I went straight to bed, woke early the next morning, dressed quickly, went outside and stood very still. Far away, beyond the descending tree-covered mountains, I could see a gleaming strip of silver that was the sea. Below the hotel the mountain slopes were terraced, every patch of ground cultivated, and two men in baggy pants, collarless shirts and the invariable head-cloth were already winnowing their harvest of grain. They tossed it rhythmically with long-handled wooden forks, the light chaff falling aside into one mound, the heavier grain dropping in a separate heap. It was a scene straight from the Bible.

I walked round to the other side of the hotel. Two handsome cedars grew right beside it and a little way off was a grove of cedars, huge trees, surprisingly enclosed by a wall. Then it hit me that I was looking at the remnants of King Solomon's cedars in lovely Lebanon, the land of milk and honey - and suddenly ravenous, went in search of breakfast.

The dining-room was large and in it were only two young British officers. One of them hailed me to join them, which I did, and learnt that the hailer's name was David Barrow, the other Robert something-or-other, and that both were on leave after serving in the Syrian campaign. I was still full of the grain harvest outside the hotel and told them I was trying to remember just what the Bible said about sinners being winnowed like chaff.

David, who wore round his neck a red cotton kerchief with white spots, laughed and cried, "Never mind about the sinners, what about Solomon: 'Thy navel is like a round goblet which wanteth not liquor; thy belly is like a heap of wheat set about with lilies.'" He grinned (he had a most engaging grin) and added, "Nothing personal. All we need is a Bible, and we'll find sinners galore and Moses going on about 'a good land and a large, a land flowing with milk and honey,' to say nothing of figs and vines, dates and olives, sheep and goats. Also shepherds with their flutes - you'll hear them higher up."

I told them about the shepherd milking one of his goats for me, about the children playing in the stream, and how it seemed that the mountains were their home, the milk a gift of welcome.

David quoted: "'For he was at one with the stones of the field, and the birds and the beasts were at one with him.' That's it, isn't it?" he said. "What a country for poets! Imagine the Bible written from the deserts of Outer Mongolia! Wouldn't be the same at all."

"Where is Outer Mongolia?" This from Robert.

"Definitely well beyond Inner Mongolia," David retorted. "You're a schoolmaster and ought to know."

"I teach science," Robert said, "and have to keep my students' minds on their test tubes. Regular soldiers like you should have a clear grasp of geography even if they do write poetry and paint pictures." He added affectionately, "God knows why the army puts up with you."

I looked at the cotton kerchiefed David with interest. He was fine-boned and lean, with clear-cut features and an open, candid gaze – 'a very parfit gentil knight,' though his fair hair was untidy and his feet were shod in rather scruffy desert boots. I liked the way his mouth and eyes smiled together, and the red kerchief was a nice touch; I was sure it wasn't worn to mock the army, but because he liked wearing it. He was an engagingly irregular regular soldier.

After breakfast we walked to the grove of magnificent royal cedar trees, their heavy, dark green branches spreading a deep shade. Robert said the grove contained about 500 trees, centuries old. "And around a dozen are said to date back a thousand years."

David said, "The local people believe they're sacred trees endowed with perpetual life."

One old giant had a circumference, so Robert said, of 36 feet. We held hands, trying to encircle it, laughing at our presumption. Robert said the wall had been built to protect the trees, which give or take a few smaller clumps, were the last of the ancient forest.

"Done in," David said, "not only by Solomon and the timber trade but by goats. They're insatiable nibblers, can't resist tender young shoots. But here's a bit of history. Queen Victoria contributed to the cost of the protecting wall. Good old girl!"

We strolled back to the terrace and I asked about the hotel and if it hadn't once been rather grand. David said, "Very popular with the French for winter skiing, but now a little faded. The food's all right though. They serve chicken and rice, eggs, and a good dish with green beans, tomatoes, garlic and bits of lamb. The salads are delicious, and so's the fresh yoghurt and local honey, and the Arab bread's excellent when it's fresh." Robert said the bread was made outside by the women, who were probably making a batch now, and they were. We exchanged greetings and smiles and sat watching them. Crouched on their haunches, the women began with a knob of dough which was kneaded into a sort of pancake until thin enough to throw to-and-fro, to-and-fro, gradually stretching the dough to a paper-thin circle with a diameter from fist to elbow. At this point it was ready to fling over a curved metal dome, blazing hot from a wood fire underneath. When the big flat circle of dough bubbled it was ready, crisp and at its best. After a day or two it became limp and, "D'you fancy half a yard of bread?" became a silly joke as one or the other of us pulled off a flabby strip.

The three of us passed each timeless day together, exploring, enjoying leisurely meals, telling stories and laughing at idiotic jokes. The day before David and Robert had to leave, we hired donkeys and a donkey-boy for an excursion into the mountains. The little creatures had harnesses of scarlet wool mesh covered in bobbles and beads and bells. They picked their way sure-footed over the roughest ground, and even a narrow path with a daunting drop to one side posed no terrors.

At noon we found shade and stopped to eat our picnic lunch. The donkeys drank from a nearby stream and stood, patient and drowsy, twitching their big ears against troublesome flies. With each twitch the bells on their tasselled harnesses jingled melodiously. After lunch the donkey-boy slept and we lay contented, rather sleepy ourselves, idly talking. The war seemed a million miles away but it was there, putting a premium on time. We might have known one another for years and a look or a laugh spoke volumes - akin to the astonishment of love. But David was married, so it wasn't that. Which, I told myself, was lucky, remembering my vow on leaving Budapest that never again would I let myself grow too fond of a married man.

As we said goodbye the next morning, and I was wondering if we'd ever meet again, David gave me a piece of paper saying, "We'll be at this address for a while, waiting for our new assignment." He smiled, and added, "Let me know when you're back here in Beirut. I don't think it'll be long."

After our goodbyes I drifted back to the hotel expecting to be the sole inhabitant, but by lunchtime it had been invaded by a cheerful company of Australian soldiers. Their commanding officer said they'd come for the night. After supper the bottles of beer circulated, the soldiers grew ever more cheerful, and I went early to bed.

Instinctively (and for the first time) I locked my door and, sure enough, before I fell asleep someone knocked and, without a word, tried to come in. This was succeeded by a frustrated muttering, and then the door was kicked by what I guessed was a large Australian boot. I asked who it was. The answer was muzzily ingratiating, "I'm gonna tuck you up, li'l gal."

I thought of the Frenchman trying the very same ploy in the train to Salonika, thanked the voice politely, assured it I was quite comfortable, and in my best nanny tones called out, "Sleep well!" There was a trenchant silence, then followed a curious litany.

"You's a real beaut li'l gal! Sure thing. I love li'l gals, all li'l gals - li'l aunts, li'l sisters, li'l cousins, li'l grannies. All the li'l gals. I tuck 'em up, God bless 'em!"

I didn't reply. "You there, li'l gal?" I said nothing. He fumbled at the door again, and then must suddenly have been overcome, for I heard a heavy thump and a few last words, "...sleep...li'l gal...safe...them A-rabs..." Not long afterwards there were footsteps and the commanding officer's voice told the body outside to get up. Nothing happened. Footsteps receded and shortly after a heavier tread suggested reinforcements, followed by sounds as of a sack of potatoes being dragged away down the corridor.

The Australians left soon after breakfast and at lunchtime two young British medical officers turned up. At supper they said they had only a few more days leave and were going to visit the great covered soukh at Aleppo. They described what they knew of this enormous market, and how it was fed by caravans from the desert.

"It sounds wonderful," I exclaimed, and was overjoyed when they invited me to go with them.

Unfortunately, as the road dropped down towards the coast, a very large hornet (it really was a dragon of a hornet with long, dangly legs) fell on my lap and stung my thigh. By the time we reached the coast road at Bécharré my ears were hot and swollen, and welts were coming up on my head which itched like mad. The driver stopped alongside the beach and I ran down to the sea and poured handfuls of water over my head. One of my companions said, "You've had a reaction to the sting, it's called urticaria. It shouldn't last too long. D'you think you're fit to come on to Aleppo, or would you rather stop here?"

I rashly promised I'd be all right. But after little more than an hour at the soukh I collapsed in the street of goldsmiths. Back at the hotel the doctors told me to eat nothing and drink lots of bottled water for twenty-four hours. I apologized for being such a nuisance and told them to go back to the soukh. They apologized for having to leave the next morning and said they'd tell the manager to keep me supplied with bottled water. All next day I drank the bottled *gazooza* in a darkened hotel bedroom, feeling very odd, but the urticaria subsided.

I didn't go back to the soukh; instead I went back to Cairo with a plan of action. I meant to get a job in Beirut, and return to Lebanon as quickly as possible.

Decisions do have a life of their own. Less than a week after returning to Cairo I learnt that General Spears, the tiger at the head of the British Military Mission in Beirut, needed a shorthand-typist. I was interviewed by someone called John Hamilton, and when he seemed disposed to take me on I admitted to knowing next to nothing about Lebanon or the military mission, and added that I'd heard General Spears was quite a tiger.

"Quite a tiger?" He seemed amused, said, "Well, you could say that," but added more properly, "He's a brilliant man, served honourably in World War One, and wrote two good books about it. Winston Churchill thinks highly of him. He brought de Gaulle out of France in 1940 and worked with him to set up the Military Mission to the Free French in London." I gave a passing thought to Major Wintle, but undoubtedly Spears had clout and official backing. John Hamilton continued, "Spears is on a difficult wicket now. You'll soon find out all about it. The General gets a bit hot under the collar when he's hard pressed, but don't let that intimidate you. I'm sure you can handle him," and added an afterthought. "He can be charming."

A week later I was back on a train to Beirut - 'and Damascus!' I thought, savouring the word, hearing muezzins calling the faithful to prayer from a hundred mosques. As for this tiger, General Spears, I'd no intention of being intimidated by him.

❧ 30 ☙

Beirut. General Spears, Kassab,
and lighthouse territory.

At the St. George Hotel there was a message from General Spears to 'come up' for an hour's work after supper, and a car would be at the hotel at eight. So much for a leisurely supper and early bed. Obviously General Spears was a tiger for work. But 'come up' where?

The answer was literal, for the car drove out of Beirut on the mountain road to Damascus. The Lebanese driver explained that General Spears had a summer house at Aley. "Many rich people have houses there. We drive half an hour from hot Beirut and *voila!* it is cool." He shrugged his shoulders. "It is good to be rich." The air grew pleasantly cooler as the road mounted. I hoped the general would be equally pleasant.

If anything he was a little over-pleasant. He had probably been good-looking when younger (I guessed he was quite old, maybe fifty) but now he was heavy set, his features thickened. He rolled his 'r' like a Frenchman, smiled a lot, asked a few polite questions about my journey, and mentioned his wife and something about her 'unit', which meant nothing to me. After this exchange we went to his study and got to work.

Halfway through his dictation all the lights failed. I laughed and had just asked, "Does this often happen?" when I felt a hand up my skirt. For a split second I feared that my "Does this often happen?" might sound like tarty coquetry, but fury took over. I shoved his hand away, saying sharply, "Don't ever do that again!" As if on cue, the lights came on.

Smoothly Spears remarked, "How charming you look when you are angry," but he was displeased, and that pleased me. 'Bad cess to you, you insensitive old satyr,' I thought. But this archaic curse was only slight relief. For the next half-hour my shorthand wobbled, and worse, I wanted to weep. What was the matter with me? It wasn't the first time some old fool had tried to fumble. It was all tediously in a day's work of being young, personable, and available.

On the drive back to Beirut I remembered a pre-World War One story about Rosa Lewis when she was young and merry, all set to become the legendary owner of the Cavendish Hotel on London's Jermyn Street. One day a guest at the hotel, a not so young Frenchman, invited Rosa to dine out with him. She accepted cheerfully and, as was customary at the Cavendish, she ordered champagne to start the evening. But the Frenchman grew amorous and tried to embrace her. Briskly she shook him off, and as she stood glaring at him, pulled her skirts up to her knees and said. "Take a bloody good look at these, for

255

you're not going to see the rest of me tonight, or any other night. So if you don't think it's worth while taking me out for a meal, you'd better go and find a nice clean tart in Piccadilly."

'Good for her!' I thought, envying her wit and spirit. At least I'd been firm with this general who was presumably a tiger for more than work. But he'd been a bore, and I suddenly felt very tired indeed.

At the hotel I had a bath and fell into bed, telling myself I'd be all right after a good sleep. But I wasn't at all better in the morning. I wrestled with wobbly shorthand at the Spears Mission, hoping to make sense of Spears' report, and when it was done I went to consult the mission doctor.

"You've got a dose of sandfly fever, young lady," he said. "Nothing to worry about, it's common here, and you're a bit run down; jaundice takes some getting over. I'll give you something to scuttle the fever and tell Spears you should take a week in the mountains."

I went back to the hotel wondering where to go, and was pleasantly surprised by a message from General Spears that a car would be at my disposal after lunch. Where to go was resolved by the young Lebanese manager of the St. George, who recommended a small hotel beyond Aley.

As the car drove past the turn to Spears' house I gave him a passing thought. Did he simply believe that all secretaries were good for a touch? Perhaps he expected me to be gratified? Well, I wasn't, but the car was worth a nod of thanks.

The small hotel was a simple stone house standing in a clearing amongst aromatic pine trees. I got out eagerly - and then stopped short, thinking, 'I can't live with this!' 'This' was a penetrating, shrill sound that seemed to drill into my head. I put my hands over my ears and, seeing the driver laughing, cried out, "What's making this noise?"

"Cicadas, they rub their little legs together and sing. Very happy. See, on the trees." Of course! There were hundreds of happy little winged insects about an inch long clinging to the tree trunks, and exulting. I made a pantomime of covering my ears again but the driver shook his head. "Tomorrow, no noise!" And within twenty-four hours the happy cicadas were part of the dry heat, the scent of pines, and peace.

The cicadas weren't the only surprise. From the hotel came, not the usual mountain Arab in baggy pants and headcloth, but a grizzled figure in checked shirt, Western pants held up with a leather belt worn well down on the hips, and on his head a gangster style fedora.

"Hiya!" he cried, "Welcome, ma'am. Hussein, at your service. You like cold beer?" I nodded and he walked to a stream that ran past the hotel, pulled out three bottles, and holding them aloft said, "Best little old icebox ever!" In confirmation I saw a large watermelon also keeping cool beside bottles of *gazooza* - and more beer, for this was Christian Lebanon where beer was permitted.

The driver and I drank companionably with Hussein, and his wife Mariam brought olives and goat cheese and thin Arab bread. Soon I learnt that Hussein had made his pile in America, and come back to build his own house and live where he belonged. "Our guests pay a few liras," he said, "and we are happy." Later I found that the cost of my airy bedroom, and three meals a day really was "a few liras." Best of all, I was the only guest.

Every morning Mariam brought breakfast on a tray and I lay in bed, sipping coffee while the cicadas sang outside in the pine-scented air. The days passed idly and I took the prescribed week, fed up with being ill and weepy. Tears were no way to deal with tigers of any stripe.

On the drive back to Beirut I decided to try and like Spears. But the next day, while skipping through a backlog of un-filed papers, I read a letter of his with mounting irritation. "My new secretary left for the mountains the day after taking up her job, and is still communing with Mount Ida." The quote was from one of Tennyson's more tedious poems, with a lot of carry-on about "O Mother Ida, many-fountained Ida" and "Dear Mother Ida, hearken 'ere I die." Dammit, I was getting well from a fever, not mooning around putting on an act. But another letter revealed that as soon as Spears was appointed to head the mission in Beirut he had begun pulling strings to get his long-time secretary, Nancy, sent out from England. This was a relief. I was a stopgap, and Spears and I could put up with each other until his Nancy came to save him.

One evening, a few days after I'd returned to work, a bellboy came to my room at the St. George and said that someone was waiting to see me in the lobby. It was David, with a dog on a lead.

"I got your letter," he said. "That was quick work, getting a job so soon. But I knew you'd be back." Then handed me the dog's lead. He spoke cheerfully as if we'd parted a few hours earlier. "He's for you, Belinda. He's a saluki and his name is Kassab."

The sight of David brought such a rush of joy that all I could do was take Kassab's lead, and smile. He was an elegant, handkerchief-drawer dog, a little bigger than a greyhound, biscuit-coloured, with decorative fringes on legs, ears and tail. He wore a leather collar, studded with blue beads and white cowrie shells.

David said, "The blue beads protect Kassab against the Evil Eye, and the shells are for good luck. Salukis are excellent gazelle hunters and a prized possession. I found him in the soukh at Damascus. Very unusual, Arabs rarely part with their dogs." He grinned, and added, "I hate to tell you, Belinda, that a Bedouin is said to rate in importance his horse, his hound, and his wife, in that order. Perhaps it's easier to get another wife than a hound or a horse of first quality."

"Oh dear!" I exclaimed. "Galloping across the desert flung over the saddle of an Arab sheikh always seemed the height of romance."

"Dear Belinda!" David said, his blue eyes holding mine briefly. "But now listen to what you must do with Kassab. Keep him all day on a lead for a week. At night he'll sleep in your room. Unleash him at the end of the week, and he'll never leave you."

David stayed a couple of days and though he didn't let on where he was going next, I guessed it was North Africa. He talked about Rommel dislodging the British from earlier gains, and how he was aiming for Tobruk. "If Tobruk falls the way is clear for a German thrust through to Alexandria. Thank God for Germany's invasion of Russia; that's taking off some heat."

"War is very odd," I said. "One minute Russia is an enemy and now they're a godsend."

"It'll be a godsend if they can hold the Germans off until the winter. Then it'll be the story of Napoleon all over again. Did you know that Hitler began this invasion one day exactly before Napoleon invaded Russia?"

"1812," I said. "That's one of the few dates I do remember, because of Beethoven, not Napoleon. Our history was nothing but English history, mostly battles and coronations, as if ordinary people didn't count, were just playing bit parts. Lots of bits in bloody battles." This thought prompted, "Have there been a lot of casualties in North Africa?"

"I don't know," said David. "What's a lot? 2,000, 200, 20? My father was a general and believes it is glorious to die for your country."

"That's what my father believed. On the night of his last leave my grandmother put her arms round him and said she'd pray God to protect him. And he said, 'Why Mummy, to die for your country is the finest death any man can die.' She never saw him again. Do you agree with him?"

David smiled (his smile turned my heart over) and said, "To be honest, Belinda, I don't. It's more important to paint a picture, write a poem, love, and till your garden, like Voltaire's Candide. Should be so easy. My father, dear old boy, would be shocked to hear such heresy from a career officer. The difficulty is how to stop people like Hitler happening long before they happen. Just now we're in a ghastly happening and have to sort it out with guns and tanks and bombs. Things must, absolutely must, take a different way after the war."

We were sitting on a beach somewhere, just the two of us. He got up suddenly, exclaiming, "Look at the water, pure cobalt blue," and chucked a stone to splinter the surface into a myriad sparkles. Then he turned and said, "It's going to be exciting after the war. I want to be there."

The day before David left we took Kassab to the mountains and hallooed him away to do what he did best, which was to run like the wind with effortless grace.

"He ought to be chasing gazelles," I said.

"Don't worry, he'll be happy looking after you. And don't forget, keep him on a lead for a week and he'll be no worry to you."

David left, and I kept Kassab leashed until the week ended and, with some trepidation, unleashed him. He shook himself, sat down and looked hopefully at me. From then on I never had to cry "Heel!" for he was always there. He came to the Spears Mission every day and lay beside me in one of his many languid poses, the fringed paws crossed just so, the fringed tail lying in an heraldic curve. The soldiers who worked as clerical assistants at the Spears Mission called him Sir Kassab, like a knight protector of old. One day he did put on quite a show of being just that.

Someone lent me a car and driver one weekend and we went up into the coastal mountains to see one of the few remaining clumps of cedars. The driver was happy to sleep for a while in a shady spot while Kassab and I climbed up to the cedars. I sat down with my back against a tree and Kassab padded off to case the territory. It was very quiet, so a sudden rattle of stones made me look up and there, a few yards up the mountain slope, was a wolf, pursued by Kassab - or, more truly, in slow motion pursuit. It was quite obvious he wasn't trying, even though he could have run rings round the wolf. Both wolf and pursuer disappeared, and shortly afterwards Kassab returned to flop beside me, somewhat out of breath, his tongue lolling.

"You're a bit of a humbug," I said, "but sensible. Better chase than fight." I told him he was a fine dog, and ruffled the fringe on top of his head. He thumped his tail languidly, and we sat peacefully under the spreading branches of the cedar tree. I thought about David, and wondered what his wife was like. After a while I told myself it should be possible to love without coveting.

It soon became urgent to find somewhere affordable to live, which the St. George Hotel was not. So I asked the helpful young hotel manager if he knew anyone who had a small apartment to rent. "An Arab house," I said, "not a modern block of flats." He said he understood and wrote down some addresses.

The first house seemed promising. A servant took Kassab and me to a pleasant room full of plants and divans where we waited for the owner. The divans were definitely Arab but, turning to rearrange a cushion, I saw it was embroidered with a horseshoe, a sprig of white heather and the words 'Good luck!' This was rather a comedown and I was relieved when the owner regretted she could not accommodate Kassab.

After seeing several impossible rooms I took my problem to Edward Mayne, one of the officers at the Spears Mission. He was a gentle, middle-aged man who had been a Shell representative before the war, first in Egypt and later in Beirut. I told him about the cushion and he said, "Many of the upper class women had Scottish nannies when they were young. The cushion is probably the legacy of dear old nanny. You must get used to not being surprised at anything in the Middle East."

"What I want," I said, "is to live in an Arab part of Beirut. Every time I explore beyond where the British and French live I'm fascinated by...well, it feels so different, like another territory. A sort of territory of the mind. Does that make sense?"

Edward said it did, and that he'd also searched for a house in the Arab quarter when he was first in Beirut. "It caused a bit of disapproval from my European colleagues, and warnings about the murderous, thieving Lebanese. But I took no notice and found just what I wanted, a lovely old house." He laughed, added, "It was quite an experience." I asked why, and he said, "I'll tell you another day. I've got work to do. Good luck in your search."

I did find what I wanted. It was on the headland where the coast turns south from the sweep of bay that cradles the city like a curved arm. An old lighthouse, striped a faded blue-and-white, stood above a big house which was a little dilapidated but still elegant, the exterior plaster washed by time to a delicate strawberry pink. Below it, and quite separate, my small house was tucked into the hillside. A little terrace led into a living room, a middle room ("for your servant," said my landlord) and a bedroom; off the middle room was a kitchen and a bathroom. Altogether it was unpretentious, the floors tiled, and the furniture minimal - but the terrace was a little paradise, a butterfly place, for all around poured a tangle of purple bougainvillaea. From this terrace lay a vista of sea and mountains. I couldn't have asked for anything better.

My landlord lived in the pink house. I only met him once, the day I was taken to settle my tenancy. He got up from a divan in a very large room and greeted me courteously, but all I did was stare. Magnificent carpets hung on the walls, draped over divans, and spread underfoot. This truly was the Arabian Nights. Then I remembered my manners and made my apologies. They were brushed aside, and we sat down to exchange the requisite pleasantries and sip strong, sweet Turkish coffee (deliciously laced with rosewater). My landlord talked happily about his carpets and seemed pleased when I picked out an exquisite collection of small prayer rugs, woven in silk.

The rent was modest, we parted amicably, and key in hand, I went back to my house to take stock of its humble furnishings. There was a bed and chair in my bedroom, a divan in the middle room (for the servant who was promised for the day I moved in), and in the living-room a big table with a couple of rush-seated wood chairs, and a divan. There wasn't much in the way of crockery, so I would have to buy more, and a few more chairs. The kitchen had a cupboard, a table and two Primus stoves. This seemed inadequate, but Marie, the young Lebanese girl who came to look after me, cried enthusiastically, "Two is good!"

She proved right, cooking delicious meals, and even baking light-as-air cakes in an old biscuit tin perched on top of one of the stoves.

The lighthouse territory was quite rural which perhaps accounted for the presence of spiders, cockroaches and one scorpion. The spiders had bulging, revolving heads and hairy jointed legs and were at first disconcerting, but not deadly. The cockroaches lodged behind the kitchen cupboard where they kept quietly to themselves, but if I was late home and turned on the kitchen light there'd follow a moment of frenzied rustling. The scorpion steamed into the living room one afternoon, pincers erect, and was firmly crushed underfoot by Edward Mayne. I protested but he said the bite could be fatal. There were no more scorpions, and after a while I reckoned that the cockroaches and spiders had been in occupation long before me, and were part of the territory.

"Don't you mind living out there on your own?" I kept being asked, and realizing I was thought odd, pointed out that I could always seek company at the *Bain Militaire*, a swimming place barely ten minutes walk down the hill from my house. In pre-war years this good sandy beach, protected by a rocky headland, had been groomed for the French who were administering their mandate in Syria and Lebanon. Now it was popular with the Free French and British officers, and civilian employees like me. The blue paint on the bathing huts had faded and the little restaurant was past its prime, but there were striped umbrellas and date palms, and even a brief stretch of cracked cement promenade. Overall it breathed a ramshackle, *fin de siècle* charm.

So my lighthouse territory combined solitude, and a place for friends to visit. In contrast, I didn't lack invitations to dine and dance, being one of the few young women at the Spears Mission. But I was glad to be a little outside the territory of jolly social rounds. It was only eighteen months since I'd left England in 1940, but now, in the autumn of 1941, the war and the killing made it feel like a lifetime - especially the killing, because of Alexis and David.

I didn't know where either Alexis was, or David, though from David came an occasional letter, presumably from North Africa. Sometimes he sent a poem, and always drawings to make me laugh - once it was a bewildered penguin, hurtling over a row of camp beds towards a recumbent soldier, from whose mouth a balloon encircles the words, "Someone chuck me a Penguin!"

There were letters from England about London ravaged by bombs, of Home Guards and rationing, and children evacuated from the East End who were deeply shocked to find milk came from dirty cows, instead of thick and sweet from nice clean cans. My mother had been living in Hampstead with my two young stepsisters, but moved to the safety of Devon after a frightening air raid. She wrote, "Normally I let the children sleep during air raids but this time, when the sirens howled, I just went straight into Joy's room, yanked her out of bed and hurried her, crying, into the passage. I held her tightly, listening to the aircraft pass overhead, heard the thump of a bomb quite close, and felt the house shake. When the 'all clear' sounded we went back into her bedroom, and there was a great chunk of ceiling coping where her little head would have been."

I went out on the terrace and wondered if our different experiences would be a kind of no man's land we'd never quite share. For my mother the war must be a boring slog of making do, plus that one moment of gut-wrenching terror. For me, the war was a mix of adventure and voyage of discovery. Though uncertain of what I was discovering, one certainty was becoming insistent - that nothing, but nothing, justified war.

Two envelopes bearing distinctive English stamps were memorable for different reasons. The first was postmarked November 22, 1940. It had been addressed first to the cottage in Hertfordshire - Hog's Hill, Church End, Albury. From there it went to the Westminster Bank in London, then successively to the British Legation in Budapest, the British Consulate-General in Alexandria, and to the (non-existent) British Consulate in Beirut. This had been crossed out and 'Spears Mission' scrawled across the last available space. OPENED BY EXAMINER #1917 was printed in heavy black letters on the envelope which, as another sticker noted, had been damaged and repaired. I was touched that this small missive had been so kindly eased on its way, and opened it eagerly. Inside was a diminutive sheet headed THE NORTHMET POWER COMPANY, Electricity House, Ware, Herts. Below was a brief note:

"We regret to have to inform you that owing to non-settlement of outstanding hire purchase instalments to the value of £2. 6s. 5d., we have taken the necessary legal steps for the recovery of the debt."

The other communication had greater significance, though not without an element of farce. It had not been entrusted to the mail, but was delivered to me personally at my house by a jolly young Lebanese representative of Cook's Travel Agency. He cast a slightly comic-opera flavour on what should have been a moment of some import. Yet, on consideration, Cook's seemed quite an appropriate messenger, since the package underscored a kind of journey. Inside were the divorce papers from Arthur's solicitor.

The following evening I dined with Edward Mayne and told him about the Cook's messenger. He laughed and said they did all kinds of jobs throughout the Middle East. "Once they got me out of a fix in Cairo," he said. "An elderly Shell colleague sent his wife back to England at the outbreak of war, and before she left she made me promise that, if her husband died, his body would be cremated and the ashes shipped to her in England. Actually the poor old boy died not long after she left, and in that heat the cremation had to be quickly arranged. But to my consternation there wasn't a crematorium anywhere in Cairo. So I turned to Cook's. 'No problem, sir,' they said, 'we will arrange.' In parting I insisted on being present at the cremation, and after a slight hesitation, this was agreed."

With a chuckle Edward went on, "In due course a hearse arrived, adorned with wreaths, and a separate carriage for me. The cortège trotted sedately through the city and suburbs, but as soon as the houses thinned out they got up to quite a gallop.

When a couple of wreaths flew off I became anxious about the coffin, and kept an eagle eye on it until we stopped. I'd not noticed where we were going, so was dismayed to step out into desert, nothing but sand. There wasn't a crematorium in sight, only a huge pile of sticks and branches and miscellaneous wood."

Edward shook his head, and concluded, "Before I could demand an explanation, a very small chair was placed on the sand for me, considerately a little distance from what promised to be quite a bonfire. So I sat down, the coffin was balanced on top of the faggots, and hour after hour the flames were fed and the old gentleman was gradually consumed. Finally, when the stars glittered in the night sky, all that remained were ashes of some kind and these, as promised, I sent to the widow in England."

As for my divorce papers, Edward assured me that Cook's would transmit them safely to England. I delivered them the next day, and also wrote a letter of apology to the Northmet Power Company. The letter and papers were signed Thelma Lyons. 'Thelma.' It seemed odd, almost like a forgery, for by now I was signing everything 'Belinda Lyons.' Belinda belonged to Budapest and Athens, Cairo and Beirut. Thelma, though the recipient of divorce papers and an unpaid bill, was a trifle insubstantial.

Belinda. For now that was me and, however uncertain the future in this new territory, one thing was certain - she'd never regret having been there.

∾ 31 ∾

A river of blood,
and war in the Middle Eastern briar patch.

During the last months of 1941 the Spears Mission was evolving from a military to a political mission, with much coming of new staff, and going of the military. Edward Mayne was due to be transferred elsewhere and I was really sorry; he'd been a good friend, someone I could talk to.

He came to see me a few days before he left and, pausing on the terrace, exclaimed, "This was a real find - couldn't have done better myself!" He gazed out at the view and said he hoped Beirut wouldn't get too sophisticated after the war, he liked it the way it was. Then Marie brought tea, and with a shy, *"Bon appétit!"* laid a cake on the table. "The walnut cake?" I asked, and she nodded. I told Edward it was a masterpiece and she went off to the kitchen smiling broadly.

"I do enjoy her," I said. "She's opening up my mind territory. Recently she assured me that every spring the Adonis River above Byblos ran red with the blood of Adonis. 'Red, red blood. All the world can see it!' she cried, determined to convince me. She's a good Christian girl, educated at one of the French mission schools, but I bet the river of Adonis' blood is as real, maybe more so, as Christ's on the cross."

Edward said, "Byblos began celebrating the festival of Venus and Adonis roughly 3,000 years before Christ was born of a virgin. Adonis was also miraculous - he sprang, not out of a virgin, but a tree. A vegetative god."

"Vegetative?"

"Like plants," said Edward. "The seed grows to maturity, is cut down, and resurrects. There are lots of Adonis version stories; Marie's sticks to the one of him dying in the arms of Aphrodite (or Roman Venus) after being speared by a boar."

"And Christ was speared on the cross!"

"Quite so. But Adonis isn't the only pagan/Christian look-alike. There's Tammuz and Ishtar in Sumeria, Isis and Osiris in Egypt, and the Canaanite Baal and Astarte. Baal was called the Rider of the Clouds - and sometimes Yahweh."

I cried, "Yahweh was an Old Testament name for God." and added, "This is a good game - you do make me think!" Then I told Edward how I'd lain in a ditch on Paliaigos when the German aircraft came overhead, and shouted to God that I didn't intend to die until I knew if He existed. "Now here I am, alive, but still not sure about God."

"Take your time. The idea of God has been much abused."

"I wish you weren't leaving," I exclaimed. "The Spears Mission is like a railway station just now."

"It's taken time to clear up after the Syrian campaign," Edward said, "and war breeds chaos. As for thinking, don't be lazy. You can read all about gods and goddesses and think for yourself."

"I will, indeed I will. At least this lighthouse territory is Arab enough to put me in the right frame of mind. There's my Arab landlord, steeped in precious Arabian carpets, and when I walk to work the Arabs in the little houses scattered along the road greet me with friendly nods and smiles. I like to think of them all leading their Arab lives, so different from the buzz of Spears Mission parties, and politics, and generals."

"War is a bore," said Edward.

And I said, "I'll make a confession. It's been an adventure for me. I suppose lots of people find war an escape, or just less boring than their own lives. But I wouldn't have missed anything that's happened so far. For one thing, I wouldn't be here if it wasn't for the war."

"Pity about the killing."

"Yes," I said, feeling I'd been flippant, and thinking of David said again, "Yes, and someone I'm fond of is in North Africa and the killing is very real. It was real enough when the *Kalanthe* was bombed, but on Kimolos the proximity of death made life more wonderful - like Nancy Caccia saying, 'We had a wonderful time!' It's a paradox I haven't thought through yet."

"You will," Edward said. I poured another cup of tea, and with a grin he took more cake. "Tea and cake, the reassuring English ritual."

"And a good moment to forget the war," I retorted, "and tell me about your old house, and why it was 'an experience'."

"All right," Edward said, finished his cake and began, "When I found my charming house I was surprised to learn it had been empty for some time; but the landlord gave no explanation and I saw no reason to make an issue of it. However, as my colleagues thought I was crazy to live amongst the Arabs, warning of thievery and murder, I made the concession of sleeping with a revolver under my pillow."

He paused, reflecting, then went on, "Not long after I moved in I woke suddenly, my heart pounding. Was it a nightmare? But I couldn't remember one. I lay trying to shift the panic, staring around the now-familiar room, moonlight falling in strips through the slats of the window shutters. It was very quiet and I stayed very still, not wanting to move, telling myself, 'There's nobody here,' but it felt as though there was - and then I saw him, a man wearing a long *galabyeh*, standing in a corner on the edge of moonlight. I didn't move a muscle, kept staring, thinking it must be my imagination. And then the figure made a slight movement, and the moonlight gleamed on a knife blade."

"Now," said Edward, "I was wide awake. Very slowly I slipped my right hand under the pillow, grasped the revolver butt and decided to aim at the floor. I steadied myself - and then in quick succession whipped out the gun, pulled the trigger, threw back the mosquito net and was out of bed shouting, 'What the hell are you doing here!'"

Edward paused, and with a gesture said, "The room was empty. Absolutely empty. Afraid I might have hit the man I ran through the house, checking doors and shutters, but there was no trace of blood or sign of a break-in. Yet I swear, Belinda, that man was as solid to my eyes as you are now. I went into the kitchen and brewed up some tea. After a while I calmed down, did a bit of thinking, and had a rather fitful sleep. The next day I got hold of the landlord and asked him point-blank, 'What's the matter with your house? Why was it empty so long before I took it?' I had to listen to a litany of compliments to my wisdom and compassion as defender of the weak and protector of the poor, but I got an explanation in the end. A few years back a man had slit his wife's throat in the room where I slept."

"It must have been a ghost! Did you ever see him again?"

"No, and I don't have an explanation, only the thought that certain happenings might leave prints on a house and insinuate themselves into the mind's territory."

"Did you stay on in the house?"

"Oh yes," Edward said, and laughed. "The landlord was convinced I'd exorcised the ghost."

There were no ghosts in the dull cement apartment block that housed the Spears Mission, but the balconies faced out on snow-capped mountains and the sea. In spare moments I'd go out on my balcony to take a great gulp of view, and because I was reading about the pagan gods, the view rang with Time. Temples to the gods had been built when Beirut and Byblos, Tyre and Sidon were busy Phoenician trading centres. Byblos, from *byblia* (a Greek word for book) was one of the oldest inhabited towns in the world, and grew famous for its papyrus exports to Mycenae. Over the years shiploads of cedar and glass, gold, wine, fish, salt, and cloth dyed with Tyrian purple were dispatched to Phoenician colonies all over the Mediterranean. Byblos withstood turbulent centuries of tribes founding independent city- states, which in turn were swallowed up by the empire-builders of Assyria and Babylonia, Persia, Macedonia, Rome, Egypt and the Turkish Ottomans.

Edward had told me that somewhere on the rocky coast north of Beirut an Assyrian soldier had carved a triumphant message for posterity:

"We, the Assyrians, came and conquered,
and washed our weapons in the western sea."

The proud rhythm of this translation sent prickles up my spine, but in counterpart was Edward saying, "Pity about the killing." Roughly 2,000 years after the Assyrians washed the blood of Byblos citizens in the western sea, the Crusaders, in the name of God, continued the bloody business of killing until Byblos was finally razed. Now, more than a thousand years on, we were at the same game - an endless river of blood.

The Crusaders had always seemed so romantic, marching forward to regain Jerusalem from the wicked Infidel. But now the Infidels were the Arabs I knew, and my reading revealed that the mixed bag of people marching on the Crusades had very mixed objectives, from peasants with only a hazy idea of Jerusalem, to great princes who were more concerned with gain than God. It was amazing that this muddled migration dragged on and on for 200 years (*two hundred!*) until the Mamelukes of Egypt overran the last of the Crusaders' castles in the 13th century. One of the most magnificent was the *Krac de*

Chevaliers, only a few hours drive from Beirut - that was on my list of 'Must visit.'

It was a wry business that the Crusaders' rivers of blood had left, not a predominant Christian God, but a river of religions. I made a list of the current faiths in the Levant, beginning with the Infidels, i.e. Muslims. They were the most numerous though weakened by quarrelsome divisions like that between the Shi'ia and Sunni, who were at loggerheads about the rightful heir to the caliphate of Muhammed. The Druze were a tantalizing group, neither wholly Christian nor wholly Muslim, with a secretive and flexible creed dating back more than a thousand years.

As for the Christians, diversity proliferated. The oldest and most numerous were the Maronites who originated in the 4th century. After them came a motley crew, including Catholics of various stripes - Chaldean, Greek and Roman, Orthodox Syrian and Greek Armenian - and various brands of Protestants. The Hebrews were mostly in Palestine, where a scattering of Jewish settlers from Europe lived a sort of co-operative life on (or was it in?) *kibbutz*. I was vague about the Jewish element, and the numbers seemed insignificant.

My reading was very intermittent and not at all scholarly, fitted in to a work routine that began every day before sunrise when Kassab and I walked in the cool of the morning. Work at the Spears Mission started around eight in the morning and stopped at mid-day. Sometimes I lunched at home and had a siesta, or went to the *Bain Militaire* for lunch and a lazy swim before returning to work until seven-thirty or eight.

In leisure hours there was no want of company. I was a commodity in short supply - young, female, personable and single. General Spears had attracted interesting people to the mission with whom it was agreeable to dine and dance. There was also a clutter of uninteresting people - ambulant uniforms with the insignia of captain or major to whom war had given a taste of rank, and they made the best of it. Peace would likely be a harsh comedown, peace casualties.

I loved to dance and enjoyed the sociable evenings, but was thankful for my lighthouse territory where friends could come for supper, to talk and sometimes to sing, for I had hired a piano. At first singing was a problem because I couldn't play by ear and though I found Bach and Schumann and Chopin in the music store, there were no English songbooks.

To Mark Lubbock, who came from a family of musicians, I bemoaned the lack of sheet music and my inability to play by ear. He said kindly, "It's easy if you begin young. As soon as my children's hands were big enough to pick out a tune on the piano I'd show them how to transpose it to every key. It was a game for them, and they loved it." Mark laughed, and said, "One day a visitor joined us for tea. He didn't know the family and when we'd eaten he asked the children if they would sing a song, adding patronizingly, 'Perhaps a little nursery rhyme?' The children, all four of them, nodded politely, looked at one another, murmured 'Three blind mice?' and then, without further ado, sang it in four parts. The youngest must have been just five."

Mark offered to write down some songs, so I bought two manuscript notebooks and he filled them with folk songs, rounds, a hymn or two, some Scots reels and Irish jigs, carols for Christmas and even added a short Elizabethan poem set to his own music.

Mark's song was a favourite with a young Welshman (another David, but spelt Dafydd) who had fought in the Syrian campaign. One evening, shortly before he left Beirut, he sang the lovely words in his light, warm tenor:

> Come my Joy, my Love, my Heart,
> Such a Joy as none can move,
> Such a Love as none can part,
> Such a Heart as joys in Love.

Dafydd sang it twice and afterwards wandered over to the door to the terrace and stood looking out at the view. He asked suddenly, "Would you be shocked if I told you I loathe war and killing and I can't see how it's ever justified? And I hate it because it has to turn ordinary, gentle people into blood-lusting barbarians."

He paused, then said, "I'd like to tell you something I haven't told anyone else," and turning his head, spoke to the sea and the mountains. "It happened during the campaign. We had to attack a Vichy gun emplacement up a hill. There weren't many of them and not many of us. I don't remember quite what happened, only that we began pounding uphill, howling like savages and flourishing our rifles." He made an odd noise, almost derisive, said, "Five of us had bayonets," and added flatly, "bayonets are very sharp." He was silent, then in a rush, "I must have swung my rifle like a club, for the bayonet split the head of quite a young boyo. Easy, like splitting a melon." He repeated, "Quite a young boyo," and burst into tears.

We talked about war for some time that evening and after he left I remembered a quote, the author forgotten: "Music alone with sudden charms can bind/The wandering sense, and calm the troubled mind." I hoped music would always help Dafydd, though he would have to live with that young boyo forever.

I was left with a discordant chorus in my mind - "Quite a young boyo" with 'We, the Assyrians...' and Edward's "Pity about the killing." How many more weapons would be washed in how many seas, and to what end? The question kept recurring and I, in the middle of a war, couldn't see the wood for the trees. Come to think of it most of the trees were people, and in Beirut General Spears was one of the largest.

General Spears was a puzzling, complicated, unpleasant but interesting man, and working for him was no sinecure, not least in keeping calm when he was explosive about something or someone (though not me). During the first month at the Spears Mission I despaired of ever untangling all the interconnected Middle Eastern crises let loose by the war, or what was behind the climacteric clashes between General Spears and General de Gaulle: they reminded me of the pagan gods and their infinite capacity for disruption.

I couldn't like Spears, but he was impressively at the centre of discordant interests fuelled by ambitions, antipathies and intrigues. I should have been impressed, but often his passionate outbursts seemed too much like a performance, bound up with himself. It was tempting to think he sometimes inflamed the difficulties, as if, being unsure of himself, the greater the difficulty, the greater he deserved acclaim. Yet he was brilliant and powerful, and apparently Churchill was his devoted friend. 'But he's such a cad,' I thought, remembering the predatory hand up my skirt. Grandmother Birdie would most likely have brushed him off with, 'Not out of the handkerchief drawer, darling.' Perhaps he wasn't, and this irked him. I couldn't judge, knowing nothing of his background, and was too ignorant of the problems he was grappling with. Then, one day my ignorance came home to me, and I could no longer ignore it.

General Spears often spent a day working at Aley, his mountain retreat from the humid heat of Beirut. A staff car would fetch me, and sometimes I'd stay to lunch with him and whoever else was around. One morning I'd just settled down to my typewriter when half a dozen young officers turned up to pay their respects to Spears. They were new arrivals, prospective district officers who would be assigned to maintain security throughout the Levant, keeping an eye on local events and people.

Spears told me to look after the young men until he was free, so we went out to enjoy the view from the terrace, poised several thousand feet above Beirut. Below us the forested mountainsides fell in green folds to the coast, and shifting clouds threw shadows across the valley separating Aley from Broumanha. I mentioned casually that General Wilson had his headquarters at Broumanha. This bit of information elicited an almost perceptible pause, followed by a cautious barrage of rather too-eager questions. Obviously I was being needled for insights. Everyone knew that Wilson and Spears did not always see eye to eye, and it was a fair bet that I, being Spears' secretary, would be a mine of information, even game for a pinch of gossip. I smiled, murmured a few irrelevancies, and stared at the view, hoping to look inscrutable.

Next morning, when Kassab and I took our pre-breakfast walk, I had a distinct vision of my head as a paper bag full of random information, all jumbled together to no purpose. It was ridiculous not to understand what was going on all around me. I needed an informant, and the best person for that was Brigadier Stirling.

I liked Brigadier Stirling. He was a sturdy, grizzled soldier, blunt and straightforward, with a background touched by romance. He had been a friend and colleague of the legendary Lawrence-of-Arabia (T.E. Lawrence) who had fought alongside the Arabs in World War One, and described it all in a very long and rather turgid book, *The Seven Pillars of Wisdom*.

I told Stirling that I was ashamed of my ignorance and needed help. He said comfortably, "Come to dinner and ask me questions. I'd like that."

I began with T.E. Lawrence, and Stirling talked about the book and how Lawrence had written the first draft in 1919 and mislaid most of it in a taxi. "Imagine losing 250,000 words! The worst of it was that, as he worked on the first draft, the silly fathead had destroyed his wartime notes. But he set to immediately, wrote from memory and had a fresh draft done a year later. He sent a copy to all of us who were with him in the Hejaz so we could comment."

"What did he say about you?"

Stirling grinned. "He said I was tactful and wise and my passion for horses was a passport with Feisal and the chiefs. Yes, those horses!" He reminisced about the horses and then started on the British and their broken promises, but that involved the Arab revolt against the Turkish Ottoman Empire, and I was at sea, and said so.

"All right," he said amiably, "here it is in a nutshell. For 600 years the Ottoman Turks dominated territory spreading from Asia Minor to the Balkans, and including Syria, Lebanon and Palestine. By 1914 the empire was falling to bits and the Turks, making a bad bet on who would win the war, aligned themselves with the Germans. Early on in the war a Turkish force, led by Germans based in Damascus, attacked the British at the Suez Canal. Obviously we had to get the Germans out of Damascus, and Arab support was vital. Ever heard of Feisal?" I hadn't. "Never mind. At this time, in a part of Saudi Arabia called the Hejaz, a body of Arabs, led by Feisal, had risen in revolt against the Turkish Ottomans. Their aim was to establish an Arab nation."

Stirling gave an ironic snort and said, "The revolt was just what the British needed. The High Commissioner in Egypt promised the Sheriff of Mecca that, if Arabs would help the British capture Damascus, the territory they liberated could be the nucleus of a pan-Arab State. The Arabs jumped at the offer, a series of letters confirmed the deal, and Lawrence, including myself and a handful of British officers, joined Feisal in the Hejaz. Together we succeeded in blowing up part of the desert rail link between Medina and Damascus. The British were then able to sweep north, capture the city, and also occupy Palestine. With the British promise in mind, Arab hopes for an independent Arab state were high."

Stirling gave another snort and said, "Some hope! Another promise came to light, but this one was made in London, and to the Jews. The Jewish factor in World War One had many ramifications, but a major part involved Britain's post-war security in the Suez Canal and the approaches to India. A friendly Jewish presence in the Middle East would be invaluable. So James Balfour, Britain's Foreign Secretary, formally declared that the British government 'favoured' a Jewish national home in Palestine."

I exclaimed, "But the two promises cancelled each other out. What a mess!"

"Can't trust politicians a yard," Stirling said. "It wasn't surprising that by the war's end Lawrence felt betrayed and was utterly disillusioned. And a fat lot of good came of all that broken faith. After the war the Treaty of Versailles awarded France a mandate in Syria and Lebanon, and the British got Palestine. The mandates were intended to ensure future security in the volatile Middle East."

"Did it work?"

"No - the Arabs had lived for 600 years under the Turkish yoke. The mandates were simply another yoke. The British mandate in Palestine has become a nightmare, and in Syria and Lebanon the Arabs are playing the British and French off against each other for all they're worth. After all, Belinda, where might they stand if the Germans win? I expect you know that de Gaulle has promised Syria and Lebanon independence and freedom from the French mandate. But he's just a rebel general speaking in the middle of an uncertain war, and the promise can turn out to be no more than a scrap of paper. And when, as we expect, the Germans are defeated, what kind of government will there be in France? And where will de Gaulle be?"

I said, "Spears is heart and soul for Arab independence."

"He's dead right, and good for him," Stirling said stoutly, "though it's a bad show that he and de Gaulle can't get along. Spears has enough trouble keeping a hold on his bailiwick here without de Gaulle having tantrums. Look at Palestine. In 1937 Britain attempted to partition the country between the Jews and Arabs. But it failed miserably, and left a can of worms. As the barbaric Nazi treatment of Jews in Germany worsened, a safe Jewish homeland became an obsession. Equally, the Arabs were obsessed with their broken promises of statehood."

Stirling growled, "A can of worms, with extremists on both sides making the British position untenable."

We ate in silence for a while as I tried to piece together my personal dislike of Spears and this view of him struggling with problems affecting millions of people. Then Stirling asked, "Have you read *The Arab Awakening* by George Antonius? You should. It's the voice of pan-Arab nationalism, a hot topic with the students at the American University, and not only the young. It's stirring stuff."

I bought *The Arab Awakening*, read it from cover to cover and ended firmly on the side of the Arabs. I also thought better of General Spears. But why were he and de Gaulle such a combustible pair?

Once again I dined with Brigadier Stirling who said we should start with the surrender of France to the Germans in 1940, and the arrival of de Gaulle in London.

"There are two stories about how de Gaulle got out of France," Stirling began. "Spears asserts he engineered the escape: de Gaulle claims he got out on his own. But whoever did what, in centre stage was de Gaulle, bitterly humiliated by the French surrender, convinced it was a national dishonour which forfeited the world's respect."

He paused, said, "So there they were, a rather ill-assorted pair. But together de Gaulle and Spears set up a headquarters in London for the Free French movement, and de Gaulle called on Frenchmen, wherever they might be, to rally to the Free French cause. He was full of zeal. But the numbers of those who rallied (the *ralliés*) were not impressive. It was humiliating, and combined with the unpalatable fact that the Free French movement owed its existence to Britain who, damn them, had not surrendered to Germany." Stirling shook his head and observed drily, "de Gaulle doesn't like the British much - and French defeat at the battle of Agincourt probably still rankles."

"But that was hundreds of years ago!"

Stirling shrugged, said, "Four hundred, to be exact. What's worse is the bitter civil war which began when France collapsed and Pétain collaborated with the Germans to set up the government at Vichy. Civil war makes bad blood between brothers, and in the Levant it made additional complications, because the army and administrators of the French mandate here unavoidably remained answerable to the government in France. As far as the Allies were concerned Syria and Lebanon were a hotbed of Vichy French who were not only on the wrong side, but dangerously friendly with the pro-Nazi Iraqi government - and Iraq bordered on Syria."

Remembering Major Wintle's potted history of the Levant, I exclaimed, "Which meant that German troops could sweep through Syria and Palestine to Egypt."

"That's it!" said Stirling. "So the campaign was mounted. Within a month the Vichy force were defeated and 3,500 Vichy military and civilians had to be repatriated. Meanwhile they were variously confined to barracks and camps, and the *Hôtel Normandie*. This concentration of Frenchman was, for de Gaulle, a golden opportunity to secure more *ralliés* to the Free French. Once again the call went out - and only 500 responded. Another slap in the face for de Gaulle, another humiliation for France. That's why he's obsessed with maintaining French influence in the Levant."

"What do you mean by 'influence'?"

He laughed and replied, "This time you need only go back to the 19th century when several thousand Christian Maronites were massacred by the Druze. Without getting in a swamp of detail, the massacre happened because the Druze suspected the Maronites were being manipulated by the Turks, to the disadvantage of the Arabs. The

272

French government, in the name of God, intervened effectively, thereby gaining prestige and influence for France. Therefore de Gaulle now insists that a French presence in the Levant is essential to stability - and, of course, essential to regaining respect for France."

I said, "But Spears is obsessed with Arab independence."

"Just so," said Stirling. "And at the end of the Syrian campaign the Commander-in-Chief of the Free French Forces in the Levant, General Catroux, released Syria and Lebanon from the French mandate, and declared their independence. Of course de Gaulle didn't like it, but it was the agreed Allied policy."

Nearly sixty years later de Gaulle was in Canada, and from a balcony in Montreal shouted to a cheering crowd of Québecois, *"Vive le Québec libre!"* (O God, O Agincourt!) And in Beirut, sixty years earlier, Spears exclaimed, "I have created a Frankenstein. Shall I strangle it before it strangles me?" They were quite a pair.

Brigadier Stirling was given another posting away from Beirut, and on our last dinner together he touched on the friction between General Spears and General Wilson. Spears, as head of the Military Mission to the Free French in the Levant, was responsible for political stability. General Wilson, who commanded the Syrian campaign, was the head of military security.

"Apart from their incompatible personalities," said Stirling, "Wilson distrusts the *ralliés*, and before repatriation there were difficulties between the British and French soldiers."

These difficulties were very human. While awaiting repatriation the defeated Vichy French soldiers remained in their old barracks which had leisure facilities, but the victorious British troops continued to swelter in tents with no facilities for passing the time. There were unfortunate incidents when the British soldiers vented their feelings forcibly on the bloody frogs, exacerbating friction between Spears and Wilson.

"People," concluded Stirling, "are a problem."

I laughed, said the mission soldier clerks still complained of having no place to go in the evenings, adding vaguely that maybe I should do something about it. He gave me an amused, quizzical look, but said nothing. I remembered that look when I later did do something about it.

Stirling left Beirut in early December, and one cool night I was sitting on the terrace with Kassab when a searchlight suddenly picked out a vessel on the water. The light held it briefly, brilliant as a jewel in the dark night: equally suddenly it disappeared.

In the same way had the bright vision of a pan-Arab state disappeared. People said Arabs could never agree long enough to create anything permanent, and blood feuds were part of their culture. Recently a man had been shot dead in a sidewalk café, and nobody intervened. This was Old Testament stuff, 'Life for life, eye for eye, tooth for tooth, hand for hand, wound for wound, stripe for stripe.' The killing could go on forever.

I stroked Kassab's silky head, and he thumped his tail. Suddenly I could think no more. "It's time for bed," I said. "Tomorrow we'll plan for Christmas. We've got a holiday."

❧ 32 ❧

The Cedars, Christmas 1941,
New Year in Damascus. A marriage.

For various reasons everyone at the Spears Mission was jubilant as Christmas approached. An obvious reason was the American declaration of war on Japan, announced on December 8, one day after Japan bombed Pearl Harbour. On December 11, Germany and Italy declared war on America. There was much indignation about the unspeakable Japanese not playing war by the rules, but jubilance was natural, since the war in North Africa had taken a desperate turn. Field Marshal Rommel's troops were battering the small British garrison of Tobruk and, if it fell, Rommel would have a clear run of only 100 miles to the Egyptian border. In Tobruk British naval ships were contriving to unload supplies at a makeshift jetty to keep the garrison alive, but the contrivance was chancy. For all I knew, David was in Tobruk.

The other reason for everyone's jubilance was that General Spears was leaving for London. The prospect of his absence produced a pleasantly light-hearted atmosphere at the mission, and I dithered happily over whether to spend my week's holiday exploring Damascus or go south to Jerusalem. Then someone said, "Why not go to the Cedars? There's plenty of snow, and you can hire skis at the hotel. It'll be a change from humid Beirut, and make your cheeks tingle."

That sounded good, and the Cedars under snow would be...well, beautiful, and different from the hot, pine-scented days with David - and Robert. So two days before Christmas, Kassab and I were jammed into a crowded taxi, listening to the driver warning us that the mountain roads were deep, deep in snow.

One passenger, a businessman from Beirut, hinted that I might have to turn back. I said I'd do no such thing, and he shrugged his shoulders, turning up the palm of a hand in a typical Arab gesture. Like many Lebanese, he spoke French, and though my French was rough, I got him to promise that, if our driver's nerves failed, he'd find me another driver.

The road was very snowy. When we reached the mountain village which was the destination of everyone but me, the driver said he would go no further, and walked off. So I held the Beirut man of business to his promise. Twice he returned to say, "Madame, it is not possible. The road is not safe." But I shook my head, and after raising his hands and eyebrows he went off to try again. At last he reported success. I gave him quite a speech of thanks, to which he listened politely.

When I finished he said, slowly, and with emphasis, *"Madame, vous êtes formidable, mais je suis tout à fait content que vous n'êtes pas ma femme!"* What could I do but laugh! So did he at last, and we parted mutually content: I had a driver, and he could give thanks I was not his wife.

On the road to the Cedars we passed a lot of abandoned cars, and my driver was not happy. When the car slithered to a halt at the edge of a nasty drop into nowhere, I agreed there was nothing wrong with walking. Luckily we were close to a cluster of small houses and a sturdy Lebanese was willing, for a modest fee, to lead me to the hotel.

He shouldered my bag and set off at a brisk pace along the road, but soon he struck off onto the terraced mountainside. He loped along with the steady stride of a mountaineer, with Kassab bounding after him. As it was already dark and hard to keep both of them in sight, I did wonder what I'd do if he disappeared into the night with my belongings. But at last the lights of the hotel shone faintly above and beyond us and, after a final slog, we were there. Rather ashamed of doubting my guide, I paid him a little more than bargained for and he left, smiling cheerfully.

Inside the hotel I stood for a moment, remembering David laughing and teasing Robert. Then I realized it was very quiet, and as there was no-one in the lobby, I went into the lounge to see who else had finished the journey. There wasn't much to look at - just two English officers, and as I stared in surprise one of them cried out, "You must be Rucker's niece!"

"Well yes, I am," I said. "But how on earth...I mean...do I know you?"

He broke in with, "Must be ten years." He got up and introduced himself, "Tom Paisley." I looked blankly at the tall, lanky officer, and he smiled. "We met at Sandhurst. Your uncle Phil Ruck Keene was on a course, and you came for the weekend."

"Good Lord! I remember. I was sixteen. I'd just left school. How amazing!"

"You look just the same," he said.

The other officer left after breakfast, saying he wasn't amused to ski in a blizzard. Tom Paisley said he was game, so we went together out into a whirlwind of blowing snow, and the deep, soft snow which was heavy going underfoot. When we stopped to draw breath Tom shouted what seemed to be a question. But the wind blew the words away and I mouthed, "What did you say?" He tried again. I shook my head, so he leant forward, and with his lips practically in my ear, he roared, "Will you marry me?"

I tried hard not to laugh. Not much more than twelve hours earlier a stranger had been thankful I wasn't his wife. Now this nice lunatic, as old as my uncle, was bawling a proposal. I bit my lip and shook my head yet again.

He took the refusal philosophically, and in the hotel insisted on giving me a length of exquisite gold brocade. After another day the blowing snow really was too much, and Tom offered to drive me back to Beirut. He drove cautiously down the empty, snow bound mountain road, past the abandoned cars, now buried in snowdrifts. We dined in Beirut, and after Tom had left the next morning I hitched a ride to Damascus.

At dawn on January 1, 1942, I was woken by the first passionate, high-pitched cry of the muezzins calling the faithful to prayer. I was out of bed in a moment, and flung back the window shutters to a sky streaked with the yellow light of pre-dawn. I knelt at the window as the calls to prayer multiplied, one by one by one, until the whole city rang with them and blended into a wild fugue. This chant, which was almost a song, had no familiar concluding cadences, and the voices seemed to fly up and away, imploring "Come!" but leaving the outcome unresolved. The fugue rose to a great crescendo before, one by one by one, the voices died away.

I went back to bed and watched the sky gradually flame into the daylight of a new year, wondering who might come out of the limbo of war. Beirut was a sort of magnet, drawing all manner of people. Maybe Alexis would come, even David, in this new year.

Kassab and I spent the whole morning in the Damascus soukh, and I even tried to buy a small length of brocade. The price seemed reasonable and I smiled, nodding willingness to purchase. But the vendor simply folded the brocade and put it out of sight. I waited, but nothing happened, and as we couldn't communicate, I gave up. When I told friends in Beirut about this peculiar behaviour they laughed and said I hadn't played the bargaining game.

"But the price was fair!"

"On the contrary, he hadn't asked enough. Bargaining is how you reach the market price."

At least I was allowed to buy a roughly made peasant jacket of sheepskin and a tasselled donkey bag. The winter day in Damascus was cool, so I wore the jacket and slung the donkey bag over my shoulder. Kassab and I wandered happily through the market, standing aside respectfully to let a camel pass on his big, soft feet, his head held high, disdainful of the small fry below. Along the way I exchanged smiles with passers by, until I suddenly realized that I was gently being laughed at. But why? Then one man accompanied his laughter by a shaking of one hand with thumb and third finger joined, and I recognized the familiar, ironic gesture. It made me laugh - of course, I was both shocking and comical, a young lady, wearing a peasant's jacket and shouldering the saddle-bag of a humble donkey. No Arab woman would be seen dead in such a get-up. I shared the joke laughing, but gave thanks for not being a Muslim lady, shrouded in black veils and black garments down to my toes.

General Spears was still absent when I got back to Beirut, and I learnt that the military mission would soon become a British Legation, with Spears as Minister Plenipotentiary (he was going to like that). I foresaw that his secretary Nancy would most likely come from England, and I'd be out of a job. But I wasn't worried. A legation would mean an influx of under-secretaries and attachés needing shorthand-typists.

Meanwhile I kept track of letters and reports and hobnobbed with the soldier clerks, who enjoyed complaining about being hard done by.

"There's nothin' to do of an evenin', miss," one of them said, "'cept go out and get drunk." Brothels and the occasional brawl with the Free French other ranks were not mentioned.

"So what do you do in your free time?"

"Oh, we jaw an' play cards an' that's about it."

I liked the soldiers and felt they deserved better. Then I remembered Brigadier Stirling's amused glance when I'd casually said I should do something about their plight, and thought, 'Bother you, I will do something. I'll invite them to my house and...' And what? I'd no idea what they might like to do. I'd never spent an evening with working-class men. Into my head floated a memory of grandmother Birdie at Copford Green arranging jolly evenings in the village hall, with songs and games and Scottish reels. Perhaps that sort of thing would go down well? I had my doubts, but told myself not to be silly, and decided to invite them the very next morning.

But that evening two visitors put the clerks right out of my mind. Roxane and Shan Sedgwick appeared unannounced on my terrace with the wonderful news that Cy Sulzberger and Alexis' sister, Marina, were to be married in Beirut the following morning.

The wedding was held at the home of a gentle English Protestant missionary. He'd raised no objections to joining a young American Jew and a girl of Greek Orthodox faith. After the ceremony there were tears mixed with the joyous embraces - tears for Dora and the beloved grandmother locked away in Greece, and for Alexis, whose whereabouts were obscure. The missionary and his wife had prepared a delicious lunch, and afterwards the five of us went to my house for Marie's walnut cake and cups of tea. Then I insisted on hearing the whole story of how Cy and Marina were so unexpectedly in Beirut, and together.

Marina began, "After the German and Italian troops had occupied Greece, it took time to sink in that we were cut off from the rest of the world. It also took time to realize several other things - that we had very little to eat, or could at any moment be deported as labourers. Food was a real problem, but little by little we learnt how to make bread from broom seeds and sugar from carobs and how to eat cat and donkey." She wrinkled her nose, "Also we learnt how to fight the enemy, quietly."

Cy had, by this time, left Athens, but not with the British with whom he'd clashed in the Balkans. Instead a sponge fisherman, Pantelis, rowed him to Turkey. It was a very slow journey, and no sooner had it begun than Cy knew for sure he should never have left Marina behind and must immediately go back for her.

On arrival in Turkey he hired two boatmen to row him to the Greek island of Chios. Halfway to the island they wanted to turn back, fearing that Chios was already occupied by the Germans. But Cy brought out his revolver and, in silence, began to clean it. Reluctantly the brothers rowed on. In Chios he telegraphed Marina that he was coming for her and she must get ready.

"It was wonderful, Belinda," said Marina, "and I got ready. But he never came." He didn't come because nobody would take him to the mainland. He sent more telegrams. "But they didn't come either," Marina said.

Cy returned to Turkey and, in Istanbul, chance intervened. The antiquated Turkish telegraph system had caused endless delays in sending despatches to the *New York Times*. This happened every day, driving Cy to such a fury of exasperation that he rented time on the government radio. From then on, at two o'clock every morning, he spelled out his reports, not every word, just the difficult ones, using habitual alphabetic symbols like R-for-Robert, E-for-Edward and so on. Then one day he made a change. He was longing for Marina, and switched to M-for-Marina instead of M-for-mother, and for good measure used D-for-Dora, A-for-Athens, and G-for-Greece. He continued doing this in the slender hope that Marina might hear him, and would at least know he was thinking of her.

On the first of May Marina was twenty-one, and sitting late with the family and some friends she began to twiddle the radio knobs, hoping to pick up information from somewhere beyond German censors. Suddenly Cy's voice was there in the room, dictating his report and spelling every M-word with M-for-Marina.

"Imagine, Belinda, hearing that voice without any warning!" said Marina. From then on she listened every night at two a.m., and every night it was M-for-Marina, D-for-Dora, A-for-Athens and G-for-Greece. But very soon it wasn't enough. She wanted to answer back. But better still, why not devise a code so Cy could spell out...well, whatever he wanted to say.

First a messenger had to be found to take the code to Cy. Luckily America was still neutral and, by good fortune a friend at the American Embassy in Athens was leaving shortly for Persia. The code was entrusted to him.

Marina said, "I worked out the code very carefully. It had to give Cy every means of escape. So E-for-Edgar, meant 'I love you very much but don't think it a good idea you should come just now.' E-for-Ernest meant 'I don't care for you any more.' The key word was A-for-Alexander." She laughed and said, "It meant 'I adore you, try and come at once.'"

The waiting period was excruciating. Night after night Marina heard the same old spellings - and then came the night when Cy's voice spelled every A-word with 'A-for-Alexander.'

"Of course, Belinda, this was only the beginning," Marina said. "I couldn't leave without a travel permit, and you'd never believe what difficulties there were. I even toyed with secret ways to escape. But one day I got fed up, and decided to take the bull by the horns and just ask the German authorities if they would let me leave the country. So I put on my best hat and my last drop of scent, and with my heart in my boots, started off for the *Stadt Commandandt's* office."

Some time earlier Marina had been arrested for speaking English in the street. She was taken to a *commandandt* who must have been in a genial mood, for he asked her with an amused smile why she didn't speak in German. "It is a beautiful language," he said, "a language for poets!"

I could see Marina, slender and young, standing with her head held high, staring back at the *commandandt* with her beautiful dark eyes. Her reply was firm. "Why should I speak a language which will soon be obsolete?" Maybe the German didn't know what to do with her, for nothing happened. But as she hurried away to get the travel permit and leave Greece, she did hope no-one had put a black mark against her name.

She was led into an immense baroque room where a German official sat behind a huge, polished desk. Marina, determining not to be intimidated, soulfully begged for his help so she could leave Greece and join the Turkish carpet dealer who was distractedly waiting to marry her. This hint of thwarted love worked wonders. The German smiled and murmured, *"Ach, wie schön!"* and shortly afterwards the travel permit was issued.

The next hurdle was transport, for no civilians were allowed to leave Greece. Again she investigated improbable routes of escape until she managed to bribe a seat on a plane leaving for Bulgaria. Triumphant and wildly excited, she began to pack. Then, two days before departure, a stranger telephoned. He wished to meet her, said it was important, and suggested a café rendezvous.

The next day Marina met an elderly Greek colonel who had somehow got wind of her leaving the country. Solemnly he pointed out that it was her patriotic duty to serve Greece, and this she could do by carrying secret information to Allied headquarters in Egypt. Marina said, "I rather enjoyed this Hollywoodish touch and said I'd do it. He then discretely passed me a paper which he said contained a list of troop dispositions and other sensitive facts. He emphasized that I must memorize the facts and burn the list, and added, very severely, 'If you are caught with it you will most certainly, and quite properly, be shot.'"

Marina memorized the facts, packed her small case of necessities and left Greece. The aircraft flew first to Sofia where she stayed overnight. Another night was spent in Salonika. At each stop her papers were minutely scrutinized by German military and Gestapo officials, though neither at Sofia, Salonika, nor on arrival at Istanbul was she asked to open her case.

"I didn't bother to unpack at the overnight stops, simply pulled out my toilet things and," this with a grin, "my second-best nightdress."

But at the hotel in Istanbul she unpacked everything. Her best nightdress was at the bottom of the case and she took it out to give it a shake.

"I had to sit down very quickly," Marina said. "The secret document for which I would 'quite properly' be shot, had all this time been folded in my best nightdress."

Cy snorted and said she'd packed the document with fine feminine absent-mindedness, but Marina exclaimed, "That's nonsense. In the excitement of preparations I forgot all about it, and probably some helpful person put it into my bag together with photographs of the family."

This was not the only shock. She expected to be met in Istanbul by Cy with, as she said, "orange blossoms, rings and priests all together." But she'd overlooked the fact that on June 22, the Germans had launched their invasion of Russia. The Americans were still neutral and Cy had taken off immediately for Moscow. So there was no Cy, no orange blossom, rings or priest.

Luckily there were friends to stay with, who also had charge of Cy's terrier, Felix. After a while, with Cy still in Russia, she and Felix moved to Jerusalem, where Shan had been accredited the *New York Times* correspondent to British army headquarters.

In Jerusalem Marina light-heartedly began making wedding plans. Shan recommended a civil ceremony, Marina being Greek Orthodox and Cy Jewish ("though a thorough-going atheist," he growled). Unfortunately, Britain's mandate in Palestine ruled that only British subjects were permitted a civil marriage - "Typical!" Cy interposed. So Marina turned to the Greek Orthodox Patriarch, who was charming but regretted the impossibility of marrying one of his flock to a Jew. The Grand Rabbi seemed more open-minded, but Marina was abashed to find his willingness depended on her conversion to the Jewish faith, and that involved a year or two of studying the Talmud. Shan next proposed finding a friendly Muslim to officiate, but

Marina said, "I'd be damned before I was blanked out behind a veil for anyone."

So this was why they came to Beirut.

Towards the end of the story Cy and Shan got caught up in one of their impassioned wrangles about the war. When Marina, Roxane and I had talked ourselves to a standstill, Cy and Shan were still hard at it. I wondered if Cy had forgotten it was his wedding day, and Roxane began to fidget. I glanced at Marina, who smiled and shrugged - it was a familiar replay of gatherings in Athens. But Roxane was never a one to sit like patience on a monument.

"Come on you two!" she said, "Time to go." So we said our farewells, and I watched them drive off past the lighthouse and out of sight.

That evening Kassab and I sat on the terrace and watched a glorious sunset fade into half-light. The first stars twinkled demurely overhead until they were glittering and brilliant in the night sky. Kassab lay companionably beside me, giving his fringed tail a languid twitch of thanks when I remembered to scratch behind his ears. I was absent-minded, wondering if, or even whether, I would see Cy and Marina, Shan or Roxane again. I wished I knew what Alexis was doing, and thought about Dora, who had hoped we would marry. I loved Alexis, but not as a life companion; I didn't know why, only that it wouldn't do. I wished it would do, for I knew that a part of me would stay forever in Greece, a luminous place which Alexis gave me.

What I did know was that I wanted a travelling companion. I heard David exult, "It's going to be exciting after the war. I want to be there!" But I couldn't be there with him, because he was married, and had his own life to get back to.

I went indoors and played *Home, sweet home,* on the piano. It wasn't much help since no-one in particular was keeping home-fires burning for me. I propped open the one book of Bach I'd found in Beirut (24 of the 48 preludes and fugues) and played the first quiet prelude. That was better. Good old Bach, calmly moving through his universe where each note and part had its place. He didn't fuss about who he was, he was just there, making music.

'And I'm here,' I thought, and remembered my plan to invite the soldier clerks to my house. "All right," I cried aloud to the glittering stars, "I'll invite them tomorrow, before I get cold feet."

The Spears Mission clerks.
Also a potter, a poem, and a Princess.

The soldier clerks accepted my invitation with disarming enthusiasm. Touched, and stifling misgivings, I decided there must be plenty of tea and buns to see us through the evening, and told myself not to be in such a flutter. Every day I talked and joked with these men, yet I was in a jitter that as my guests they might be disappointed and uncomfortable.

We were all a little uncomfortable at first, but they liked the little house and the view from the terrace and dutifully gathered round the piano to sing. They even managed a Scots reel, but as they thumped around the living-room in their large army boots I knew this part of my plan was absurd, and it was time for tea and Marie's delicious buns.

They drank tea copiously, with plenty of milk and spoonfuls of sugar, and finished off the buns. We were still a little on our best behaviour when they said it was time to go, but I took courage and asked if they would like to come again the following week. To my astonishment they chorused, "Yes, miss. Thanks a lot, miss! Just like home, miss! See you again next week."

The next week I gave them tea straight away and under its homey influence they began to talk. It didn't take long to understand that this was all they wanted to do, just talk, mostly about their wives and sweethearts. Were they being faithful? How would it be when the war was over? Would they be strangers? Already those damned Yankees were all over the place with pocketfuls of money and treats from their PX stores.

"Choc'lits, silk stockin's - 'cor, miss, it's not fair! 'ere today and gone tomorrer, back to the U S of A where the streets are paved wiv gold - I don't think! As for us, we'll be in our civvy suit issue, and no job most like."

Another exclaimed, "Bloody Hitler! 'scuse my French, miss, but what a little squirt to give so much trouble! And the Frogs walkin' around 'ere as if they owned the place. I dunno, wars don't make things much better, do they?" He added, "My best buddy caught it at Dunkirk. Just married, and his girl with a bun in the oven. Wot's it all for, I ask you?"

In the visits that followed, the phrase, "no job, most like" came back again and again in various forms as they talked about how it had been for them as children. One came from a family of Welsh miners in the Rhondda Valley, and as he talked I remembered the day Arthur took me to see one of those forlorn villages, the pithead machinery stilled, a great black slag heap looming over the desolate, deserted row houses. This was the breathing reality of his world, and I could only peer into his territory, not share it.

A couple of soldiers were from the Midlands. One said, "Never 'ad no shoes 'til I went to school."

"No shoes?"

"Honest, miss. Lots of us runned barefoot 'til school. Then Mum got a pair from somewhere, stuffed 'em with newspaper 'til me feet grew bigger. Gave me bleedin' great blisters."

I asked about school and another soldier said he won a scholarship at the King Edward grammar school in Birmingham. "One of the oldest in England," he said proudly, "founded by Edward VI. I liked it there, but me Dad lost his job and walked all the way south before 'e got another. There weren't no grammar school at the new place, just the local one. I left at fourteen and got a job to help out. Not much of a job. The war were a bit o' luck you might say." I noticed that sometimes he dropped his H's and sometimes didn't, and thought with a twinge of disgust of Birdie's "Not one of Us, darling. Such a deplorable accent."

From time to time Marie made a fresh pot of tea and piled up her buns which vaguely resembled standard English rock buns, but much less rocky and generously filled with raisins. Tea and buns loosened tongues and I listened, hardly believing I'd lived most of my life in England and knew such a little part of it. When I was a child Abbie and Emma had always felt like friends, and I'd loved our Irish servants, Mary and Peggy, who looked after us so cheerfully in London. But had I ever known them?

On one of the last evenings the soldiers spent with me, they were bubbling with excitement about a programme set up for them at the American University by President Dodge and his wife.

"We can use the library," the scholarship soldier said, "and there's gonna be music programmes and talks on all kinds of subjects." These soldier clerks had been selected for office work because they were better educated than many of the other ranks, and they seized on this scheme as if it were manna from heaven. I wasn't surprised when their visits to me petered out, though not before one memorable evening when they were voluble about this new world the university had opened up, and the kind of world they wanted after the war.

"I'm not gonna to let my kids grow up like I did," one of them said. "The only music I ever 'eard was when we got tipsy in the pub. And books! Not a one at 'ome, just the Sunday rags and the more shockers the better. Nothin' to make you think. Easy game this makes us, don't it? Keep us amused, get our votes and don't ask questions!"

With an exclamation of disgust, the grammar school soldier exclaimed, "Those old men at home, been around too long, makin' everything tickety-boo for their lot, and the devil take the rest of us. Labour's the party for us."

I asked what they thought of Churchill. The answer came out raw. "When all's said and done 'e's just one o' them. When the war's over it'll be time to say 'Thanks chum, and goodbye.'" The others nodded and one muttered, "and good riddance!"

I was surprised. Churchill didn't mean much to me, but then I wasn't being bombed in England and in need of stirring speeches to keep me going. I knew next to nothing about socialism and the labour movement, but the soldiers had laid open a new territory with a view of what it meant to be English and working class, simmering with resentment and impatience.

That night, after they left, I remembered J.M. Barrie's play, *The Admirable Crichton*, in which the upstairs conversation waxes indignant about how servants are getting uppity and will soon want to take tea in the drawing-room with their betters. Then disaster strikes, and it's the butler, Crichton, who takes command and saves the day. Was that how England was going to be, the class structure cracked open and men like my visitors in the leadership? That was an odd thought. No wonder David said the system had to change; no wonder he was excited and wanted to be there.

In February we learnt that Spears had been knighted in London and would be returning in March as Sir Edward Louis Spears, His Majesty's Minister Plenipotentiary to the British Legation in the Levant. The change to diplomatic status had already begun with a flurry of departures and preparations to accommodate new arrivals. I was kept very busy and was glad to get away one Saturday for a trip into the mountains to buy crockery.

I'd seen the pottery in Beirut and put off buying anything else until I could get a ride to the potter's studio a little way beyond Aley. Several times the trip had been put off because Spears had something important to dictate, but Spears was out of the way and we set off, light-hearted, on the lovely road to Damascus which rose gradually through forests and plunging gorges. Like all the mountain roads it was untrammelled by road signs or protective barriers to halt an unwary skid into a gorge. Often clouds lay low and the road would be slippery until burned dry by the sun, and there was always the human hazard of a demonic Arab driver, hurtling flat out with accelerator down to the floor and one hand on the horn.

We turned down a rough road and found the potter's studio behind a typical stone house, out of which the potter emerged with a woman he introduced as his mother. He was a young man, with liquid brown eyes, slightly built and fine-boned, a little shy at first, but in his studio he grew animated about his work. He had a good supply of everything I needed except small bowls. These were waiting to be glazed, so I asked him to keep some aside for me and I'd pick them up later. He packed up my purchases in a couple of boxes which we put on the back seat beside Kassab. Both the potter and his mother spoke good English, and together they saw us off with smiles and thanks.

"An interesting pair," I said, "tucked away in the mountains," and my companion remarked that the Middle East was full of surprises.

Just then we turned on to the main road and he said, "The brakes on this car need adjusting. If I jam them on it throws the car to the right. Not a good idea with the road a bit slippery still. It's easy to forget."

It was too easy. We came round a bend too quickly, my companion rammed on the foot brake, and the car slewed straight off the unguarded road towards the gorge below - and everything went curiously into slow motion. I noted with a certain satisfaction that I wasn't screaming or flailing about, but was sitting with hands folded on my lap, thinking calmly, 'I hope it will be quick and not hurt too much.' The thought was clear, and the end very quick.

A violent jolt threw the car back across the road towards the rocky mountainside, but instead of crashing into the rock face, it bumped up a little goat track, as if magically conjured for us. We got out and, a little shakily, walked back to the main road. What the front wheel had hit was a very small heap of stones. There seemed no reason for the heap on that spot, nor was there another heap anywhere in sight. The car was all right, though Kassab was a little rattled by being catapulted from the back seat to the front.

When the boxes were unpacked, only one cup was broken and my companions said, "This potter is full of surprises," and we laughed, not knowing how right he was.

Just before Spears returned I was loaned a car and military driver so I could return to the studio for my bowls. The potter and his mother greeted me with much friendliness, and while he packed the bowls in the studio, the mother led me into the house for coffee. She told me she was widowed, that she and her son were Christians, and both had been educated at a Protestant mission school. This accounted for the book of Moody & Sankey hymns lying open on a harmonium in the living-room. I'd glanced at the music when I came in, and noticed that the score was printed from right to left. Arabic was sometimes printed that way, but music? The mother saw my surprise and smiling asked if I played? I admitted to playing the piano, but never the harmonium, and she urged me to give the music and the instrument a try. So after the potter joined us I sat down with the right-to-left score, had a tussle pumping air into the harmonium with my feet, but got it going and then was surprised to find how easy it was to read the music back-to-front. I played some of their hymns and rounded off with *Country Gardens*. We had a happy time.

When it was time to go I bade the mother goodbye, was invited to return, and the potter came to see me off. But before we reached the car he stopped, and began a long speech about how well his pottery was selling and how he would like to work for me and then, very formally, asked me to be his wife.

I stared at him, wondering why such wildly improbable people insisted on proposing marriage. What had I done and what could I say? My silence provoked another spate of words, including a picture of our married life and the touching avowal, "I will make you beautiful pots." It was too much. Quickly, so he couldn't say any more, I thanked him for the honour, said firmly it was impossible, and left.

Three days later he appeared on my terrace. He wouldn't come in, and I heard him out with rising disbelief. He said he had come to offer himself as my bodyguard, and would sleep on the terrace so no harm came my way. When he stopped I must involuntarily have shaken my head for his big brown eyes filled with tears. I had to be straightforward, and when he left I felt miserable. Had I encouraged this young man? All I had intended was to be friendly.

After a few days of finding no answers I poured out my dismay to Dick Usborne. He was an imposing person, four years older than me, very tall and dauntingly intellectual - a Classics major from Charterhouse and Balliol. I was fond of him, even though he called me a cloth-head once after I burst into his office and insisted that he "come at once, and be prepared to shoot a horse."

"My dear Belinda..." he began, but I wasn't listening.

"It's fallen down and nearly dead and being kicked by the driver who wouldn't stop, so I kicked him and he was very surprised. The horse is all skin and bones and it's just given up and so would you if you were skin and bones. It simply must be shot."

Dick pointed out that one couldn't go around arbitrarily shooting other peoples' horses; but he came with me to where the horse still lay as if unwilling to make any further efforts. My attack was smoothed over with baksheesh and apologies, and after the wretched horse was given water and feed, it staggered to its feet. It was a heart-rending sight, but reluctantly I admitted that Dick was, at least in.... some ways, right. Nothing would have been served by shooting the horse, except to take it out of its misery. I knew by now that animals in the Middle East, unless thoroughbreds, were simply a means of livelihood, not much different from a beat-up old truck. To shoot the horse was to shoot the means of a meagre livelihood. Dick was right, but unsatisfactory.

When I told Dick about the potter, he said, "Dear Belinda, you are a dangerous combination, distractingly pretty and given to spreading sweetness and light."

"What am I supposed to make of that?" I cried. "I was just being nice to the potter, I liked him, and his mother. Should I go around being English and patronizing?"

A few days later Dick presented me with a poem, saying "You know I'm devoted to you, don't you, Belinda?"

"That sounds like one of your double-edged compliments," I said, saw the title of the poem, *BELINDA, in war and peace an example to us all,* exclaimed, "Really, Dick!" and between laughter and exasperation, read on:

> Belinda Lyons never could
> resist the chance of Doing Good.
> She much preferred a person who
> gave her a lot of Good to Do
> to one who managed on the whole
> to run his own immortal soul.
> Show her some loneliness or sadness
> or some nice meaty case of badness.
> She'll roll her sleeves, spit on her hands
> and ripple her adrenal glands
> and, with no thought of quid pro quo,
> start Doing Good like billy-ho
> with blankets, bowls of soup and miles
> and miles of sympathetic smiles...

The dots indicate editing. It's a witty mocking poem, but long. So I've trimmed a chunk about malingerers feigning sickness to win smiles and soup, and continue:

> Belinda heard (an Army chaplain told her,
> laying *his* sorrows on her shoulder)
> that British troops, on leave or duty,
> without a thought for Truth or Beauty...
> were going out at night to cruise
> around the low-class bars and stews
> to find bad women in Beirut
> and try to take them on the toot;
> or, drinking arak neat, get tight
> and look for Free French troops to fight.
>
> Well, said Belinda, they can use
> my flat instead of bars and stews:
> for Shakespeare-readings, guessing games,
> charades (in teams) with Bible names
> and other healthy spurs to laughter
> with hot, delicious cocoa after...

Here Dick mercilessly invents my hopes for a better world *where people laugh, and play and sing/ and Good is simply The Done Thing.* Then the poem ends:

> So there she stands, a russet-hued
> lone, lovely, live Beatitude...
> and one man said the other night
> he'd danced with her and, with his right

hand decorously on her torso
felt little feathery sprouts, and, more so,
though quite unpractised in such things,
could swear that she was growing wings.

Of course it made me laugh, even though I cried, "How dare you tell such barefaced lies! We didn't sing madrigals or play guessing games or charades, and they drank gallons of cha, not cocoa." Glaring at him I added, "What d'you mean about lovely smiles and soup?" But not waiting for an answer, I hugged him and said, "Dear Dick, I'll never have such a poem written about me ever again. I'll keep it forever." But I was irked by 'lovely smiles and soup'. Was he referring to Kemal?

Kemal, like Dick, had been one of the young men who, in 1941, came to take up posts as district officers and other intelligence jobs. Kemal worked up north as a 'wheat officer'. Proper distribution of wheat was one of Spears' major preoccupations. The Lebanese were skilled in spiriting away charitable shipments of grain which they hoarded to sell at inflated prices on the black market. As starving peasants meant political instability, obstructing the hoarders was a political priority.

I met Kemal when he was recovering from some Middle Eastern infection in Beirut. He was rather sorry for himself, and it seemed a pity to have my house empty all day, so I offered him the use of it. He was soon spending every day there, and he stayed his last weekend with me before returning to Aleppo.

He was a sturdy young man with curly fair hair, had a ready wit, and wrote quite good poetry - as David had said at the Cedars, "This is a land for poets." Kemal, despite his Arab name, was English. He was born in Egypt, where his father had been a British civil servant to whom the Egyptian government had given the title of Bey - like the spy Bey I got mixed up with in Cairo. Kemal was fluent in Arabic and French, possessed an infectious dynamism and was fun to be with. Sometimes I didn't much like him, but he'd leave and I'd forget the irritation.

He usually stayed with me on his intermittent trips to report at the Spears Mission, and through him I made a return visit to Aleppo. I'd always wanted to explore the great covered soukh in that city after my visit in 1941 was ruined by a hornet sting. So when Kemal came unexpectedly to Beirut I jumped at his offer to give me a ride to Aleppo. Spears was expected at the end of March, after which no more impromptu jaunts would be possible.

Just before we left somebody gave me an introduction to a Princess in Aleppo, saying, "She lives in a fine Arab house right in the city. You'll find her interesting. She's a Muslim, but educated in America." I took the introduction eagerly, with no thought of causing any kind of future trouble.

I spent a long absorbing morning at the soukh. After a siesta, I took my letter of introduction to the Princess's house where a servant showed me to the women's quarters. It was a very fine house indeed, and the Princess was a very beautiful young woman. She was dressed in graceful Arab clothing, her golden skin and glossy black hair set off the fine modelling of her face and sparkling brown eyes. After going through the formal courtesies she sent for her little son, "my great joy," she said. We spent a while with him before he was taken away, and then she began to talk about her life in America.

It was a curious anomaly to hear her speak of the wonderful freedom, the stimulus of study at a prestigious university, and the widening of a world-view that sent her home an ardent pan-Arabist. This conviction she shared with her husband who, she told me, belonged to a prominent Muslim family and had an important post in the Syrian government.

She said, "We married for love. I knew I'd have to live in traditional seclusion, but when you're in love everything's possible, isn't it? But here - what irony! I live so close to Beirut where, as everyone knows, the ladies of Damascus go for a breath of freedom. Off come the veils and on with tennis shorts, swim suits, party dresses - whoopee! - then back to Damascus and veils and seclusion."

Whoopee? It sounded incongruous in these very Arab surroundings. Her intelligence and commitment was stirring, but I was anxious to do the right thing, so tried to be sympathetic, encouraging and non-committal all at the same time. We parted with expressions of friendship, and she urged me to come and see her whenever I was in Aleppo.

Back in Beirut I forgot about her in the flurry of Spears' return, as Sir Edward Louis Spears, and the transformation of the military mission to a British Legation. Then one evening I was reading on my divan, and hearing light footsteps outside, switched on the terrace light. It illuminated the Princess.

I got up quickly, invited her in and, after formal greetings, she presented me with a head scarf of pearly-white, handspun silk, embroidered rather roughly with broad bands of gold leaf. Overwhelmed by such a gift, I was glad that Marie brought tea, and the calming ritual of pouring and sipping got the Princess settled quietly on the divan. Then at last she explained why she had come to me. The reason was no surprise - she had decided she must escape from the stifling confinement of her life in Aleppo. She did not explicitly admit that she had run away, but said firmly that she wished to work in Lady Spears' hospital unit in Beirut.

Lady Spears was an American, a wealthy and remarkable woman. In World War One she had funded and recruited a mobile hospital to serve at the front in France. She and Spears had met, and after a passionate *affaire*, were married. When de Gaulle and Spears created the Free French movement in 1940, Mary Spears recreated her mobile hospital unit for the Free French in North Africa: she also ran a small hospital in Beirut.

The Princess's expectations seemed doomed to failure, but I took it quietly. She was very sure her offer would be warmly welcomed and brushed aside my hesitant warning of possible difficulties. It was a long evening. Finally I promised to arrange a meeting with Lady Spears, if possible the next day, and the Princess let me make her comfortable on my divan. She was fast asleep when I left for work, and I told Marie to have coffee ready when she woke up.

By good fortune Lady Spears was in Beirut, and she agreed to see the Princess straight away. A car took me home, and carried the Princess away, apparently confident of her reception. I hoped to see her later, but she didn't return. Instead I got an earful from Lady Spears.

"I am sure you understand, Belinda," she said, "that this is a very volatile part of the world and our position is delicate. A false step, like harbouring the troubled wife of a local dignitary, could lead to a major political scandal. It's the sort of thing that can spread like wildfire here and jeopardize all the minister's hard work."

Abashed, I said I'd been careful not to rouse the Princess's discontent, and then, disinclined to do further penance, asked, "Did you dissuade the Princess from working at the hospital? Whatever did you say?"

Lady Spears replied drily, "I made her come down to earth, Belinda. There's truth in the saying, 'Sometimes we must be cruel to be kind.' I asked about her training as a nurse, suspecting rightly that she had none. So I pointed out that her work in the Unit would therefore be limited to cleaning the rooms and the bedpans, making tea for the patients and nurses, and running errands when necessary. She was," Lady Spears said, "quite insulted. She is a Princess and very conscious of it. But she behaved well. She's good material and should be able to work out a way of living in two worlds and not fail her husband. They will have to survive great changes together."

I was impressed by Lady Spears' adroit handling of a potentially explosive situation, and heard no more from the Princess. I kept her gift - its return would be an insult, but keeping it bothered me. An Arab gift anticipates some return, and all the Princess got was a diplomatic slap in the face.

I loved Lebanon and the responsive, warm Arab people, but I knew very little about the codes of behaviour and speech, or the loaded implications of their gestures and glances. It was unmapped territory and finding a way through it was by no means a piece of cake.

I vowed to do better and, dosed with optimism, went to bed, feeling already on my way to wisdom and forethought.

↰ 34 ↱

Comings, goings, decisions,
and a happiness.

The metamorphosis of a military mission to a British Legation got going in earnest as soon as Sir Edward Louis Spears returned. An influx of diplomatic staff began arriving, including Spears' secretary, Nancy Maurice, and I pitched in to work with whichever newcomer needed secretarial help. They all did, so I was glad to learn that another shorthand-typist was on the way to Beirut. She had an interesting name, Taqui Altounyan, and came from Aleppo, where her father was a doctor.

Taqui arrived dramatically bereft of all her belongings. On the train she got a place by the door, and tucked her suitcase safely under the seat. The carriage was full, the journey slow, and she was half asleep when the train stopped at a station halfway to Beirut. People got out and others got in, drowsily she registered doors slamming and the whistle blowing. But just as the train groaned into movement, the door was suddenly flung open and Taqui's suitcase was whipped out from under her feet. As she cried out the door slammed, the train gathered speed, and there was nothing to be done - the train had no alarm system.

Her case was full of new clothes and now she had only the dress she'd travelled in. I took her on a modest clothes-buying spree, very modest, for the stolen clothes had been a gift from her parents and she refused to ask them for money. She was a very independent person, and was the first young woman whose company I enjoyed in Beirut.

She was half Armenian and half English. Her face was striking, shaped by the kind of strong bones that last, her expression a little shy, but her brown eyes twinkled below thick dark eyebrows. She said her eyebrows were inherited from her Armenian 'Black Gran'pa', Dr. Aran Assadour Altounyan. Black Gran'pa had long ago brought his English wife from Turkey to Aleppo where he founded the hospital. Now he was in his eighties, but still hard at work, and Taqui said proudly he had become a legend of wisdom and skill throughout the Levant. He was also a great storyteller, and Taqui introduced me to the folk hero, Hojja Nasr-ed-Din - sage, clown and free spirit whose ingenious stratagems did not always succeed but always ended with a witty, pungent aphorism. He was a favourite of the market storyteller whose audiences sat cross-legged around him in rapt attention, spiked with bursts of laughter. Later, after Taqui had left Beirut, I suggested to the press attaché that these stories might be given a propaganda twist. It was a silly idea to which Taqui, with her instinct for Arab sensibilities, would have given short shrift; but unfortunately she was no longer around.

291

Taqui did not enjoy being a secretary. "I'm naturally inefficient," she said, deprecating with amused detachment the confusions she got into. After a couple of months she left to join her parents in Jerusalem, but during her brief stay we laughed a lot, shared enjoyment of books, and I listened entranced as Taqui talked about her childhood.

The family lived in Aleppo, but there were routine summers in England at her mother's family home in the Lake District.

"There were five of us," she said, "my brother and three sisters, and we loved the lake. We swam and sailed, dreamed up adventures, and camped on the islands. One of them, Peel Island, we felt belonged to us for the place where we made our camp fire was blackened by generations of family fires." What gave her stories an added interest was that each of the five children became one of the five characters in a classic children's book, *Swallows and Amazons,* whose author, Arthur Ransome, was Taqui's uncle.

By contrast to this very English world was the life in Aleppo. There the children chattered Armenian with the servants, stared down from the battlements of their old house at the comings and goings at the hospital, and at home there was a steady flow of visiting writers, artists, and travellers. Outside the house were the delights of soukhs and busy streets, and beyond lay a countryside of plains, desert and mountains. It all sounded wonderful, and I would have had no problem in changing places with her.

One day we took Kassab for a walk in the foothills. Wild purple cyclamen grew in profusion on the terraces, and the little black figs were already ripe on the vines. A couple of girls were gathering figs and when we greeted them they cried "Take! Take!" which we did. As we bit into the delicious soft fruit, the youngest girl bent forward and lightly touched Kassab's head. He had been gazing absent-mindedly at nothing in particular which was why, quite out of character, he gave a startled yelp and nipped at her hand.

I cried, "Kassab, how dare you!" and quickly asked to see the hand. Mercifully the skin was unbroken, but the girls drew aside. I looked at Taqui, who said quietly, "Wait a minute." After a muttered conversation the older girl came shyly forward with the oddest request, she wanted some of Kassab's hair. Seeing my bewildered face Taqui said, "It's all right - it's the hair of the dog that bit you."

Kassab, conscious of misdemeanour, meekly yielded his hair which the older girl carefully applied on her sister's hand and, reassured, they parted from us with smiles. When we were out of earshot I exclaimed, "So the hair of the dog isn't a joke about having another drink when you're already drunk. Is this a common practice?"

Taqui said, "Not with everyone by any means. It's folk medicine, a kind of 'vaccination', and real vaccination was being done in these parts hundreds of years ago." She told me about Lady Mary Wortley-Montague who, sometime in the 1700s, was caught in a smallpox epidemic in Turkey, and had her own children vaccinated. "That was brave," Taqui said. "Back in England she told everyone about this wonderful treatment and even got some doctors to try it. It didn't always work, not until Jenner found the right source for the virus, but that was much later."

As we walked on I saw that Kassab's long tail hung dejected as a flag at half-mast, and realized he wasn't happy. I never spoke sharply to him, and with a twinge of guilt bent and patted his head murmuring, "You're the best dog!" At once the end of his fringed tail curled upwards, and a moment later he was off up the mountain path chasing gazelles - phantoms that were plentiful in the territory of *his* mind.

By the time Taqui left Beirut I was working for the Counsellor, John Hamilton, and the legation had settled into a new diplomatic ambience. The legation staff of first and second secretaries in their well-cut civilian clothes were a different lot from the military mission colonels, captains and majors. A few of the military remained, but the smooth cream of the Foreign Office was evident.

The difference made me wonder whether all that barking out of orders and saluting all over the place created a character change. I couldn't imagine the Second Secretary, Tony Lambert, or the First Secretary, Dan Lascelles, barking out orders. Dan, highly intelligent and sensitive, had the sort of grave features one sees in portraits of Elizabethan aristocrats, and his unfailing good manners were unobtrusive. He was definitely not the barking kind. Tony was lanky, rather elegantly languid, and educated at Harrow. Dan could well have been at Winchester, and gave credence to an old joke about a cricket match attended by boys from Eton, Harrow and Winchester. An Etonian notices a lady without anything to sit on and exclaims, "We must get you a deck chair at once." The Wincastrian runs to fetch it; and the Harrovian sits on it. Churchill was at Harrow. There's a smidgen of truth in all stereotypes, but Tony was not at all boorish. He and Dan were gentlefolk who knew who they were, what they were doing, and why. It was interesting that Spears, reputedly not a gentleman, had a taste for collecting 'quality'.

John Hamilton, the Legation Counsellor, was a gentleman of the old school. He had been seconded from the High Commissioner's office in Cairo to ease the transition from military to diplomatic status. He was a dear man, wise, a little stiff and British, but he would no more have put his hand up my skirt than come to work without collar and tie, even in humid Beirut.

I soon discovered John wasn't having an easy time. Churchill was a great supporter of Spears and his outspoken championship of Arab independence, but it alarmed the Foreign Office people in London. British government policy was to treat de Gaulle and his ambitions with kid gloves, as he would be a key player when the Allied armies re-entered Europe and liberated France. John had spent years in the Sudan, spoke Arabic and was alert to the intricacies of Middle Eastern diplomacy, so he had to walk delicately amongst the various protagonists. I never heard him criticize Spears, but I sensed he didn't personally like him much, and didn't much like the French either.

One day he got quite wrought up about how the French had cynically ruined the silk industry during their twenty-year mandate in the Levant, and said, "The valuable political constituency of the silk industry in France resented competition, so the mulberry trees were cut down or allowed to languish and, of course, without the trees the silkworms died." I put in a word for Spears' hard work to revive the industry by importing fresh trees, and securing orders for silk parachutes.

"Of course, of course," John agreed, "but the French were culpable, and betrayed their mandatory responsibilities."

I rather suspected John believed the French to be innately depraved, setting up mistresses in a most ungentlemanly fashion. I wondered about the rather tight little kisses he sometimes gave me. It seemed churlish to refuse and I hoped he took them lightly. He was kind enough to make no comment when I refused to attend a garden party for the Duke of Gloucester.

The Duke's visit was a royal acknowledgement of the new legation and the minister's knighthood. A garden party was planned so all the legation staff could rub shoulders with royalty. I was wondering what to wear and asked Tony Lambert's advice. "Oh, one of your pretty dresses, Belinda," he said, "and by the way, we've decided that a hat and white gloves are *de rigueur* for the ladies."

"But why? I hate hats and who wants to wear gloves in this heat! Besides, it's a waste of money on something I'll never wear again."

"You know very well why, Belinda - etiquette."

I liked Tony, but the soldier clerks had sharpened my resentment of English social inequalities, and I replied impatiently, "What little I've heard of this Duke doesn't inspire me. In fact he sounds rather a clod."

Tony murmured something deprecating but I ignored him. "If I can't come bareheaded and gloveless I'll give the party a miss. I'm sure the Duke won't miss me." Tony tried gentle persuasion but I felt obstinate. "I'm sorry, and I know, *I know* - it's the royal family and all that. But I'll have a nice swim while you're all sweltering it out in gloves and hats on the legation lawn."

I knew I was being excessive, and actually felt rather dispirited when everyone was junketing with the Duke, but less so the next day when I heard what followed the formal dinner party. Spears took the Duke to his study where they were joined by the secretaries, attachés - and John - for the usual 'informal exchange of views'. They came into the room one by one for individual introduction to the Duke who stood by the fireplace, opposite a long leather-covered sofa. He had dined well, and was merry.

Dan Lascelles came in first and had barely begun his courteous salutation when the Duke gave him a rough push and roared with laughter as Dan went sprawling onto the sofa. This prank was played on everyone. I imagined Dan struggling to hide disgust at this unseemly horseplay. I asked John if he'd also had the sofa treatment, but he shuffled papers on his desk, murmuring something about being spared on account of his grey hairs. I didn't press him, but was glad I hadn't bought gloves or a hat for such a silly fellow, however royal.

Quite soon after the Duke's visit a much more interesting, and in her own way more illustrious person, arrived from Baghdad. I knew Freya Stark through John and Diana Murray, and John Murray had published Freya's first book, *The Valley of the Assassins*. This account of her journey in the Hadramaut had made her famous. When Arthur and I were married Freya gave me a pair of beautiful gold filigree earrings from the Hadramaut.

Freya made more journeys to places in Arabia where no Western woman had been before, and described them in classically simple, riveting prose. To be honest I had always been a little alarmed by Freya. She was a scholar, of the kind that would read philosophy in Greek and Latin while prostrated by sickness, miles from anywhere in a tent pitched on blistering desert sand. This seemed to happen quite often. In one of her books she had been sharp about women who didn't match up to her standards of toughness, mental and otherwise.

We lunched together at the St. George Hotel and as we ate and talked I kept thinking she was like a knowing and disconcertingly intelligent bird, her almost black eyes peering through a frizz of feathers. Actually it was a frizz of hair, worn low to hide the scars of a gruesome childhood accident when her long hair was caught in machinery and she was nearly scalped. Freya was wonderful company, and flattered me by wanting to hear my adventures, clucking sympathetically when I said that her earrings now lay bedded on pearly sand amongst the wreckage of the *Kalanthe*. I got quite carried away about how much I loved living in the Levant, and even told her about the potter and the Princess.

In her turn she described her work in Cairo where she had created the Brothers of Freedom, an association of pro-British Egyptians. Now she was in Baghdad gathering together a group of women who would work with her to build an Iraqi Sisterhood of Freedom. Her assistants would develop friendly contacts with the wives of prominent Iraqis, and it was hoped that the wives would influence their husbands to promote Anglo-Iraqi friendship.

I listened with interest, but was taken aback when Freya put her head on one side (just like a knowing starling) and after remarking that I would fit in very well, asked me to come to Baghdad and work with her. "It will be a wonderful opportunity for you to get to know the Arab people more intimately," she said.

For one giddy moment I nearly accepted, excited by the compliment and the prospect of new territories. But against this rose a clear conviction that she misjudged me, just as the Bey had when he said I was cut out to be a spy. I wasn't; nor would I fit in with Freya's ladies. Moreover, after the Princess episode I felt allergic to the idea of manipulating anyone, particularly the *élite* ladies of Iraq. So I refused.

Forty years passed before I saw Freya again. She was on her way to Asolo, her home in Italy, and I lunched with her and Diana in London. After lunch we drove together to the airport and Diana went off to find a wheelchair, for though Freya was mobile enough, she was a bit rocky on her pins. We talked about many things as we waited until, after a pause, she laid her hand on my knee, and looking into my face said, "You know, my dear, I do believe my travelling days are over."

She was 89 when she made that admission. Four years earlier she sailed on a barge up the Euphrates wearing a picture hat and accompanied by a television crew. In May of 1993, aged 100, she set off alone on her last definitive journey.

I went through a brief agony of regret after refusing Freya's invitation to Baghdad - but not for long. One afternoon, without a word of warning, my uncle, Philip Ruck Keene, appeared on my terrace. He was dressed improbably in a rag tag of off-white garments, and on his feet a pair of black, patent leather shoes.

"Phil!" I cried, "How marvellous to see you! But what are you doing here? And why are you wearing such peculiar clothes?"

Typically he replied, "What a lovely place, and you look wonderful! Not a day older!"

We did not embrace and I thought, 'This is a very Ruck Keene meeting' and aloud said, "You look splendid as ever, but I didn't know you were in this part of the world. Why didn't you tell me you were coming?"

Phil told me that my ignorance was due to Dan Lascelles' kindness. The legation knew that Phil's submarine base ship, the *Medway*, had been torpedoed and sunk in the harbour at Alexandria, but as there was no list of survivors, the news was kept from me.

Marie made tea and brought slices of newly-baked cake. She was excited by this visitor, and whispered, *"Il est très beau!"*

In his turn Phil remarked approvingly, "That's a pretty girl you've got!" beaming at her. Marie spoke no English but she got the message. She tripped away to the kitchen and began to sing. Phil had that effect on women.

He sat on my divan and I sat at the table so I could pour cups of tea and ply him with cake. I kept looking at him as he told his story, thinking how pleased I was to see him and how odd it felt to be Thelma Ruck Keene who wasn't Belinda nor, with the divorce soon to be absolute, really Lyons. I heard myself slipping into the Ruck Keene intonations of speech, recounting the past years light-heartedly to imply that it was all enormous fun. Doubts and fantasies about mind territories would spoil a good story, and the Ruck Keenes, bless them, loved a good story.

Phil's account of the *Medway* sinking was true to form. "I did the proper thing, y'know, not leaving my ship until everyone was safely off and all that. So when (as I thought) everyone was off the *Medway* she was lying almost on her side, which made things easier, except for the barnacles. There were a hell of a lot of them, great big crunchers, and about halfway down it struck me I was wearing my best shoes and barnacles wouldn't do them any good. So I sat down gingerly on the barnacles and began to untie the laces. The chaps in the water must have begun shouting to me for I suddenly thought, 'You fool! the ship's going down, you better get off,' which I did, at the double. Don't know what happened to the shoes. These were the only ones that fitted, couldn't mess around trying to find a pretty pair of whites. We've got to get our base re-established and carry on fighting this war."

He held out his cup for more tea and said with a grin, "In the water everyone behaved splendidly, and when a sailor offered me his lifebelt I waved it away. Seemed the proper thing to do." I said it sounded like a story in *Chums*. He got up, took another piece of Marie's cake and ate it standing by the door looking out at the incomparable view. He didn't speak for a moment, then quite unexpectedly said, "When a ship sinks it upends at the last, stays for a second or two like a great sea-beast, and then goes straight down. It did this just after I'd refused the lifebelt, and that was when we saw a sailor sitting high up on the prow, a tiny mannikin, screaming. Nothing to be done. Poor devil, and I thought I'd got them all off."

I didn't say anything, and Phil suddenly exclaimed, "I hate this bloody war. All we can do is get it over, fight the war properly and get down to something worthwhile, like woodcarving. That's all I want, a workshop with lots of tools." He stepped out on the terrace and then turned to say more cheerfully, "Look at those marvellous mountains! Y'know, as soon as we were on the deck of the destroyer that picked us up I knew what we'd do, and startled Bill King (remember him at Harwich?) by shouting, 'Beirut, that's where we'll go.' Now I've got to find a house that'll do as a mess and operation centre." He smiled. "When we're settled we'll have some good hikes together, what!"

He found a fine house not far from the old port, and before returning briefly to Alexandria he came to say goodbye. I guessed what he was going to ask, and wished he wouldn't, but he did.

"What d'you say to moving in, help with the secretarial work, play hostess?" I said it might cause difficulties at the legation, that I'd have to think about it, and knew he was surprised and not a little hurt. How could he understand that working with him would be slipping backwards, Harwich all over again? No doubt he'd rate my current job well below that of working for his sailors. Of course he would. But my job had its purpose, and was mine, sought and taken without help.

When Phil returned to Beirut he repeated his offer and I refused. He said gamely, "All right, old thing. You know best. But keep some free time for the mountain hikes."

Phil soon encountered just the right person to work for him. Anita was a young woman, the daughter of a well-known Irish writer, Shane Leslie, and was herself witty, intelligent, highly competent and lovely to look at. He took her on as a driver and in no time she moved in to the base house to act as hostess. So it worked out fine, and after the war she married the submariner, Bill King. This goes to show it's foolish to do the wrong thing for the 'right' reasons – though it's not always easy to disentangle which is wrong and which is right.

I shouldn't have been surprised that the next few months were rather flat. I'd refused two new opportunities, and by the end of the summer my friendship with Kemal had cooled – provoked funnily enough by an octopus, a very small one.

Kemal was a splendid swimmer, which I was not, but he liked trying to make me more adventurous. On the last but one of his visits we'd spent hours in the water catching fish for a bouillabaisse, and as we lazily swam back to the beach Kemal spotted an octopus. He was a minuscule octopus, and hung on to a rock squirting purple ink at Kemal in a fury of indignation. I didn't want him caught, but Kemal became obsessed with getting the better of him, and finally killed the little creature as if it had no business to defy him.

"Don't be so squeamish, Belinda," he said, "he's only an octopus."

I didn't like 'only an octopus', and after he left I admitted there were too many times when I didn't like Kemal either. He was an odd mixture of sensibility and a sort of boisterous crassness. I wondered why I was letting him come and go so casually? None of the obvious answers pleased me: then everything changed when Kemal was back for a quick visit in October.

Nothing very dramatic happened. We'd dined with a friend - Havard, a delightful Scotsman, happily married, of course, whom I liked very much. He was another district officer, not a poet, but a painter of colourful, rather childlike scenes of Beirut. The three of us were walking back to my house as Kemal gave a lively description of investigating the storehouses of an Arab landowner suspected of hoarding wheat.

"I was wearing Arab dress," he said. "I like to think it gives me an advantage, and tends to confuse them, which is all to the good. I insisted on poking at every sack of grain in every shed and barn, sure the bastard had got a heap of wheat stashed away somewhere. Finally I saw a small, suspiciously windowless shed. Without asking I pulled open the door, stepped out of the sunshine into blackness, and damn me! walked slap into a cess pit right in up to my bloody crotch. God, I was angry! I clambered out, pulled out my revolver and fired a half circle in front of that damned Arab's feet. Frightened the daylights out of him. Then I demanded fresh clothing."

At this point Kemal gave a shout of laughter, whipped out his revolver and demolished a couple of streetlights. We were in the countrified approach to the lighthouse and the lamps were dim. They tended to be poor stuff in the humbler Arab quarters of the city.

"You ought to replace those lights," I exclaimed. "The Lebanese haven't got money to chuck around to amuse you." But Kemal wasn't listening, he was making Havard laugh with the sequel to the shoot-up.

General de Gaulle turned up just as Kemal emerged in his clean Arab clothing. "He asked my name, and enquired sharply what I was doing playing about disguised as an Arab. When I said I was a wheat officer from the British Legation he angrily asked by whose authority I assumed that title." Kemal guffawed and shot off another light. "The pun was too good to miss, even if Spears no longer sported his rank, so I replied, *'Mon Général, mon Général.'* The old man wasn't amused, glared at me, and left without a word."

Of course the double pun was a neat retort, but I was vexed. Havard hadn't backed me over the lights, and I thought Kemal's behaviour to the Arab was arrogant and provocative. The Wheat Commission, jointly controlled by the French and British, was fragile. The Syrians resented the Free French presence on the commission, and de Gaulle resented that the commission was not solely under Free French control. As John Hamilton remarked drily, these petty jealousies were ridiculous but one had to remember that starving peasantry in the Levant could be a serious hindrance to winning the war.

I walked on in silence to the house and knew I was finally disenchanted with Kemal. He had qualities, but they weren't for me. He slipped his arm round me, saying "Dearest Belinda, don't be stuffy!"

But I went early to bed, leaving him talking with Havard. From then on Kemal did not stay with me when he came to Beirut.

The last visitor in 1942 came barely a month after Kemal's departure. It was early evening and one minute my terrace was open to the wide view of sea and mountains, then suddenly it framed a familiar figure, wearing battered desert boots, and a white-spotted red bandanna round his neck.

David coins a phrase.
The Press Attaché, and Palestine.

"David! It's you!"

I met his lucid gaze, felt I could fall flat from pure happiness, and sought equilibrium in a prosaic, "However did you find me?"

He laughed, the skin crinkling at the corners of his blue eyes. He was thinner, very tanned. "It was easy. I asked the way to the English girl who lived near the lighthouse. And the answer was, 'Ah yes, *es-bint* in the sheepskin jacket who walks with a saluki.'"

"But where have you been all this time?"

"Tobruk. I thought you'd guess."

"I sort of did. How did you get out?" Silly questions, perplexed by joy.

But David, gently matter-of-fact, said, "After El-Alamein the Eighth Army kept chasing Rommel, hot-foot for Tunisia. On the way they had the goodness to relieve us." He smiled and added, gently mocking, "May I come in now?"

"Oh David, of course!"

I called to Marie for tea and she whispered, *"Pas de gâteau!"* and when I introduced her to David she promised, *"Gâteau demain, monsieur."* He smiled in response and she murmured in my ear, *"Comme il est gentil!"*

I poured tea, gave him a cup and said, "You will stay here?"

"I would like that."

He stood looking down at me. Once again that absolutely open gaze was clear as spoken words, so clear that without intention I must very slightly have shaken my head, watching his face, longing for him, fearing to lose him, and foolishly unable to explain the vow made in Budapest when I left Ted.

For a fraction of a second we looked at one another, and then David said quietly, "This is where I want to be."

He stayed nearly a week.

At first he talked a lot about Tobruk, of how they lived in foxholes dug into the sand, of the flimsy jetty made of old planks and barrels which the navy used to keep supply lines open. Adrift in happiness I listened and thought I would remember everything. Now only one story remains, and I'm not even sure whether it happened in Tobruk or simply somewhere in the area - only that David was there.

Once the siege was relieved the journalists poured in, eager to see everything. David took a couple of them to visit wounded soldiers who were being cared for by a few nuns and a British sergeant. It wasn't a hospital, just a building with bare rooms, all spotlessly clean. The sergeant led them from room to room, stopping in the last where a soldier, his head bandaged, was talking to a nun. She turned to greet us and with a smile said, 'Take a good look at our showpiece. He had to have a trepan, and he's well on the mend. We're very proud of him!'"

One of the journalists exclaimed, "Good God, that's a very delicate operation! I'd like to meet your surgeon!"

The nun looked at the sergeant and after a silence he mumbled, "In a manner o' speakin' sir, we 'aven't got a surgeon."

"But the operation, this trepan thing...?"

"Well, you see sir, I 'ad to do it meself. Not much alternative you might say. We 'adn't nothin' in the way of instruments, so I used me penknife. Made 'er good an' sharp. It were a bit o' luck, really, seein' it was just an itty-bitty bone, and come out nice and clean."

David said, "A penknife and a bit 'o luck. Marvellous. You know, Belinda, for all the unspeakable waste and horrors of war, you never know when you'll stumble on this sort of thing, pure gold."

David had arrived early in the week and I had to work every day, but when John Hamilton knew about my visitor he told me to take Friday off. With the bounty of a long weekend we planned a trip to places we wanted to see together. David said he could get the use of a car, and meanwhile he bought canvas, oils and brushes for an orgy of painting, and chose my 'basket' boy for a model. These boys, aged between ten and fifteen, made money carrying peoples' purchases of fruit and vegetables from the market. My purchases had to be carried further than most so my boy got paid more and was always delighted to see me. He would stride along with his basket on his head, barefoot, cheerful, and beautiful, his skin golden, the dark eyes soulful beneath a mop of thick black hair. He was a terrible model, naturally bemused by what David was doing because Muslims were forbidden to paint portraits, for this would be an infringement of Allah's prerogative to create the human form. David said it was like trying to paint an eel, and the intervals between letting the boy stretch and walk about got shorter and shorter. But a likeness was caught. Now the portrait hangs behind my bed in Vancouver.

It was good to be away from cosmopolitan Beirut and feel the country belonging to itself and its own people. At our first stop there was no-one about but ourselves. The massive Crusader castle called the *Krak de Chevaliers* had been built by the Knights Templars in the 12th century, and as Kassab bounded ahead through the towering main gates we felt like midgets entering a village built to accommodate giants. We picked our way over fallen stones along wide ruined passages that took us gradually up into a great vaulted chamber. It was as long as a football field and David said it had probably housed the men-at-arms.

"With their horses?"

"It's big enough."

In the chapel where the knights had chanted Latin mass we stood enveloped in silence and the light breath of ghosts; then we toiled up to the outer fortifications and stood gazing out at the plain which stretched north-east towards Homs. David said there'd have been another castle over there, yet another to the south and two more strung along the coastal plain. "They were badly short of men and had to be visible to each other so they could give warning of Saracen attacks."

It was very quiet; just us, Kassab nosing around, and hawks wheeling overhead.

We drove to Hama expressly to hear the giant wooden water wheels which had been turning since the time of the Crusaders. They gave great groans like deep organ notes as each circuit poured water into a network of channels. Though set in the desert, Hama bloomed with gardens and fruit bearing orchards, and had flourishing textile mills. At one of the booths in the central square I bought a length of heavy white handspun cotton, block printed in bold black on white squares. Tables were scattered about the square, and we sipped strong sweet coffee lightened with a dash of rosewater, sat listening to the organ voluntary groaned out by the water-wheels. The only other coffee drinkers were men. They clicked amber beads through their fingers as they talked, occasionally glancing at me out of the corners of their eyes, for I was the only woman, and unveiled, in Muslim Hama's public place.

Baalbek in the Beka'a valley was our last stop. The valley, lying between the mountains of Lebanon and Anti-Lebanon, is part of the Great Rift which starts in Syria and ends at the Gulf of Aqaba on the Red Sea. I'd made a quick visit here before returning to Cairo in the summer of 1941, when the valley had been green and fertile and the irrigation channels winked in the sunlight under whispering poplars. Now the harvests had long been brought in, and snow lay thick on the high mountaintops.

As we drove towards the village the six great rounded columns of the Roman Temple of Jupiter dominated the valley, and I asked David if the first settlement was Roman.

"No, the first were Canaanites and Phoenician traders," he said. "Then the Roman colonizers used the Great Rift as a highway, followed by Christian Byzantines and the Crusaders."

We left the car and picked our way towards the Temple of Jupiter, skirting round great chunks of stone, the scattered entablatures carved with garlands and acanthus leaves, and the heads of lions and bulls. As we stared up at the temple's tremendous columns David said, rather tartly, "Emphatically wealth and power; I wonder if Romans had any doubts about themselves?' Then added, "But what flawless craftsmanship!"

The smaller Temple of Bacchus was altogether more delicate, "Perhaps," said David, "because it was actually dedicated to Venus."

Suddenly I giggled and he asked, "Are you mocking my relentless potted history?"

"No, of course not, you're the best ever ambulant guide-book. I just remembered something that happened when I made a lightning visit here after we first met. There was hardly anyone around, just a few Australian soldiers, and one was standing alone right where you are now. He was staring up at this temple, a stocky little chap, legs apart, big brimmed hat on the back of his head. He was frowning, looking kind of puzzled, and I asked what he thought of Baalbeck, and wasn't the temple beautiful? Well, he gave it a final once-over, turned to me and said, very firmly, 'Wot I can't make out, miss, is why they 'ave to go and build all these 'ere ruins?'"

David was laughing as we strolled back to the car, but when we stopped for one last look he exclaimed, "You know, Belinda, that bit about 'these 'ere ruins' was inspired. Wealth and power - wouldn't you say they're programs for ruin? Ruin builders, that's what we are. I wonder if your Aussie has given a thought to how bombs build ruins quicker than anything."

On the way back to Beirut we stopped off in Damascus and mooned around the soukh. David bought me an antique copper coffee pot and a splendid square carrier bag woven in black, red and white wool, sturdy as a carpet. He said with a grin, "Just the thing when a sheikh throws you across his saddle and gallops away with you across the pathless desert. He'll appreciate your domestic foresight."

"I'll settle for stuffing the bag to make a monster cushion," I retorted, "and every morning Marie will serve breakfast coffee in the pot."

"And you'll remember me?"

Looking into his clear blue eyes I said, "And I will remember you."

On our last evening we talked about the war, particularly what Japan had done since the beginning of 1942. I said, "At the legation people are saying Japan aims to control the Pacific from the Aleutians to the Solomon Isles. But I don't know where the Aleutians are, or the places the Japanese have taken."

"I'll draw a map for you, Belinda," he said. He took his sketch-pad, made a rough outline of continents, and filled in Manila, Malaya, Singapore, the Burma Road, Java, Timor (I'd never even heard of Timor), and in Australia added a dot for Darwin which the Japanese had bombed.

I said, "The Pacific's always been a sort of dream place, the Faraway East, except for Australia, and particularly Tasmania because my cousin Elizabeth's grandfather was Bishop of Hobart. But none of it's as real as Hungary and Greece, Egypt, Syria and Lebanon. I've been there and verified them."

David laughed and asked if North Africa was real, and I said, "Of course. You were in Tobruk and I was in Cairo."

He drew North Africa and the coast of Spain, added the long boot of Italy and Sicily, and talked about the North African campaign that went so badly until the battle of El-Alamein. He ran a finger along the coast going west towards Tunisia, and pointed to the African coast below Spain. "Look, the Americans and British are landing already in Morocco and Algiers, and the Eighth Army is on its way to Tunisia. When they meet, North Africa will be the jumping-off ground for an Allied invasion of Sicily - and that, my love, will launch the Second Front and the end of the war!"

I thought, 'You hate this killing, but you're a regular soldier and your father is a general. I shouldn't be surprised that your eyes are sparkling.' As often happened, David picked up the thought.

"Belinda, you know how I hate this war, but all we can do now is fight it well." I said Phil had used almost exactly those words. "Of course, he's like me, trained to defend by fighting. What matters though is what happens when it's over. It's injustice that has to be tackled, I mean the imbalance of poverty and great riches. We ought to be able to make life worth living for everyone. Killing each other is primitive, makes for more anger, more misery, more...more panic, so people can't think calmly. So much to be done," he said, "and I want to be there!" Dear David.

The morning he left he gave me an address in England. "I don't know where I'll be from now on and I don't suppose you'll stay here for ever. This address will always find me." In exchange I gave him my little volume of Shakespeare sonnets, sole relic of the bombed *Kalanthe*.

That night four lines by another poet ran in my head:

Joy & Woe are woven fine,
A Clothing for the Soul divine;
Under every grief & pine
Runs a joy with silken twine.

Yes, oh yes, but no answer to why, oh why did David have to be married? And why was a triangle so impossible?

In the new year of 1942 I was transferred from working with John Hamilton to being assigned full time to the new Press Attaché, Sandy Mitchell-Innes. I wasn't displeased; John was a dear, but Sandy was, in Spears' words, "a live wire of the American advertising industry."

I knew nothing about the advertising industry or about Americans (except through the movies) and couldn't imagine all that fast-talking nervous energy fitting in with the sober ways of a British Legation though, come to think of it, Spears didn't fit in all that well either.

Sandy was not quite all-of-a-piece, combining the nervous energy of a live wire with being very much the English gentleman. One day I asked him what his initials, A.P., stood for.

"Alexander and Plantagenet," he said. "Quite a mouthful, isn't it!"

"The real, true-blue Plantagenet?"

Sandy let out his rather high-pitched laugh, and said, "Oh absolutely. Alexander was King of Scotland in the 13th century and brother of Edward the First. The family goes back."

"Edward, the Crusader king?"

"That's him. And now we're here again. Maybe we'll do better this time."

Sandy worked me hard, and the day often ended by having dinner together. Gradually I learnt about his background - Eton, a wartime commission in the Rifle Brigade (a very gentlemanly brigade), and several pre-war years in India. I guessed he must be about forty as the India he described sounded like Kipling's India of big game hunting, polo, that sort of thing. He was proud of having been the only Englishman to ride in the Delhi Derby, adding, a little sadly, "I didn't win." Sandy had the neat build of a horseman, the fine-tooled features of unbroken gentry breeding, and a wide, sensitive mouth, which he kept disconcertingly half-shut when he talked, as if he might unwisely let out something untoward. He didn't confess to his passion for painting until I invited him to supper.

When he saw my house, tucked beneath the lighthouse and the landlord's faded old mansion, Sandy exclaimed, "It's beautiful! May I do a painting?" To my surprise he did a really good sepia water-colour of the whole grouping.

Altogether I wasn't sure what to make of my new boss, or why, as I went upstairs on the first day of work with him, a voice in my head said clearly, 'Better get on with it.'

'Better get on with what?' I thought impatiently. I went on up the stairs, and no recollection surfaced of the evening, seven years earlier, when I had taken a canapé from a plate offered by Arthur, and a voice in my head said clearly, 'Oh well, too late now.'

The main tasks of the press attaché were to put out effective propaganda about the Wheat Commission and a future Allied victory, as well as to discourage the local journalists from inflammatory distortions of gossip and hearsay. Sandy brought to the job a conviction that advertising techniques would enliven the rather lacklustre civil service approach. I wasn't so sure, and one day we got into an argument about manipulating people's minds.

"Facts are one thing," I said, "but manipulating opinion with technical tricks is immoral. How can the gimmicks that sell toothpaste or Pears' soap make any impact on Lebanese and Syrian mistrust of us and even of each other, and what about the Arab dream of a pan-Arab state?"

I was feeling strongly about the Arabs, having just read a report from Glubb Pasha, an English officer who had joined Jordan's Arab Legion after World War One. He became famous throughout the Middle East for building the legion into a formidable fighting force. Glubb wrote passionately about Arab pride in an empire dating back to the 8th century, and the magnificent legacy of their art, architecture and learning.

"He says their empire lasted longer than the British Empire has to date. He talks of Bedouin warriors and Arab pride in that heritage, and if that pride isn't appealed to, Allied propaganda will be a waste of time."

All Sandy said was "Go on!"

His attention rather went to my head so I did go on, and remembering Taqui's stories of Nasr-ed-Din said, "What about laughter?" and tossed out the idea that some of the stories might be adapted. "They could have a derisive sting about the Germans or Italians."

Sandy's response to this flight of fancy was, "You're very creative, Belinda. Why not work out one or two adaptations, give your idea a run."

I had yet to learn that Sandy believed in encouraging his staff of copywriters to play with ideas. This was all right when he was working with a staff of expert advertising scriptwriters in London. In Beirut his staff was just me. So I laughed, truly surprised. "I couldn't begin to, Sandy. I haven't the wit or the knowledge or writing skill." Sandy said something complimentary but I was wishing people wouldn't give me credit for talents I didn't possess. What Dick called being 'distractingly pretty' carried the penalty of distracting people's common sense into inventing wildly unsuitable roles for me. It was very tiresome.

For a while I heard no more of Nasr-ed-Din as Sandy was preoccupied with various propaganda projects, but he did expect more from me than just reproducing his dictation. Instead he'd hand over a rough outline and tell me to get it into shape. This was challenging but there wasn't much let-up, and I was touched when he said, "You could do with a rest, Belinda. Take a car and spend a few days in Jerusalem, lovely country. Get the feel of what's happening in Palestine."

Nobody had ever before asked me to get the feel of a country, but I said I'd try, and my heart lifted at the prospect of getting out of Beirut. It was little more than a year since that first visit to the Cedars Hotel, but it felt like a lifetime.

I decided to take the road through the Rift Valley. It was spring, and I'd been told the valley would be full of wild flowers, and that route would take me by Lake Tiberias and the Sea of Galilee. I still hadn't made up my mind about God, but Palestine was bible country and I wanted to get the feel of *that*.

At the first sight of a stretch of deep blue I cried "There's Tiberias!" In fact it was not a lake of water, but a mass of blue lupins along the lakeside, and in amongst the lupin sea were migrant storks. Against a background of black basalt hills they stood motionless on slim pink legs, big birds, white-feathered with touches of black. I asked the driver to stop, got out quietly and stood gazing at this dreamscape, beautiful as a medieval tapestry. The big birds were still as statues, except when they bent to the water and caught a fish in their long yellow beaks.

We drove on down the Jordan Valley, lush with citrus groves. The surrounding hills were sun-dried and covered with scrub, old hills, wrinkled like the skin of an old tortoise. Olive groves were plentiful, the tree trunks and branches gnarled and twisted with age, as if frozen in a moment of intricate motion. The feel of it was so old and timeless that the sight of some young men and women in bright blue shirts and brief blue shorts was a shock. The brilliant colour and briefness of the shorts seemed an affront to Arab etiquette, and I asked my driver who they were.

"Jews from a kibbutz. More and more they come." He shrugged. "They do not belong here."

Obviously I was going to need someone to talk to if I wanted to get a true feel of Palestine, and in this I was lucky. A friend in Beirut had given me the address of a guesthouse not far from the city centre. "It's run by an old Englishwoman," I was told. "She's a character. Get her to tell you some of her stories."

I cannot remember her name, and see her simply as small, elderly, grey-haired and featureless, offset by a sense of her presence. The guesthouse stood on a hillside amongst olive trees, and luckily the old lady was at home, and invited me in. The first thing I saw was a Welsh dresser of dark oak, the shelves ranged with familiar blue-and-white willow-pattern china. It might have been the living-room of any charming English cottage. There were no other guests and, after drinking tea with my hostess, we went together through an olive grove to a chapel, which she explained, was built to her design.

The chapel was small, cool and full of soft light, the floor completely covered by a woven carpet of rain-washed blue. Each of three corners carried a different symbol - the Arab Crescent, the Christian Cross, and the Jewish Star: the fourth corner was empty. The Englishwoman said, as if speaking for an old friend, "God does not require a name and address, or identity papers, and this is a family place where everyone belongs."

Over the next few days I sought answers from the Englishwoman, particularly after wandering into a side street in Jerusalem which was thronged with intimidating men wearing long black garments and wide-brimmed black hats with low, flat crowns.

Their long side-curls were very black against their pale skin, and they stared at me as if I was some kind of abomination. For a moment I had a nightmarish feeling of being trapped. Then I realized they must be a special Jewish sect, though vastly different from the young settlers in their bright blue shorts and shirts.

At the guest house I asked what kind of Jews they were and admitted to finding them menacing. "Not really menacing, dear," was the reply, "you just stumbled on a quarter of the Hasidim, very strict Jews of the Orthodox faith; it includes plenty of 'It is forbidden to...' When people have a mission to forbid, they tend to become, in themselves, forbidding." She picked up the teapot, said "For you, dear?" and when I shook my head poured herself a third cup of tea.

I asked, "Haven't the Jews and Arabs lived more or less peacefully here together for a long time?"

"Once they did, more or less. But contradictory promises during the Great War were made by two different British statesmen. How, I ask myself, could any statesmen in their right minds think that one country might be a homeland for the Jews, and at the same time an independent Arab state? Jews and Arabs. Each, believing the promises, had such high hopes - and what did they get? A British mandate, which from the first was nothing but a packet of trouble."

In Beirut there was much talk of Arab unrest in Palestine, and I asked whether this was serious. She exclaimed, "I am often flabbergasted by how little the English know. Yes, it is serious. The British can barely maintain order, and now they have the Jewish Stern Gang as well as the Irgun to grapple with."

"I've heard of the Irgun, but the Stern Gang...?"

She said, "Pay attention to those people, dear. They mean to build Israel in Palestine, if necessary through violence. British Intelligence thought to make use of the Irgun against the Arabs. Very foolish that was, to play politics with Jewish obsession and misjudge the extent of Arab disillusion."

The worst of learning something new is realizing how little you know. I was saddened by what this Englishwoman told me, for I'd fallen in love with the countryside, and the beautiful old city - except, that is, for the Church of the Holy Sepulchre. It was more like a battlefield than a place where the peace of God passed all understanding. Different religious groups had jurisdiction over different parts of the church, which wasn't aesthetically pleasing and the interior was darkened by candle-smoke. Out of the gloom emerged priests - Coptic and Armenian, Greek Orthodox and Roman Catholic - begging for alms. The chapel built by the Englishwoman was a great deal more serene.

The night before I left we talked about the quarrelsome nature of religious bodies and the Englishwoman told me a story. "Shortly before the war," she began, "and at the height of a new burst of violent unrest, I woke to find an Arab standing by my bed. I asked who it was. He didn't answer, but when my eyes grew accustomed to the night gloom I recognized a young man who did occasional work for me. I called him by name. He still said nothing. I asked why he was in my bedroom at this hour of night, and at last he spoke. 'Lady, I am sorry, I have come to kill you.'"

"I thought, 'He is very nervous and has got in with foolish young men who have a list of British enemies to be done to death.' So I spoke quietly, said I too was sorry, but as this was a grave act he contemplated, as well as a grave moment for me, we should first visit the chapel to make peace with our God. I asked him to turn aside while I put on a robe, and this he did. Then we went up the hill together to pray."

She sat in silence for a moment, and in my mind I saw the young Arab and the little Englishwoman walking through the olive grove, silent in the soft Mediterranean darkness. She went on, "In the chapel I led him to his corner of the carpet, crossed to mine and knelt beside the symbol of the Cross. I prayed for reconciliation - or resignation, if that was how things turned out. It was very quiet, and God was with us. I rather forgot about time, for the peace of God does pass all understanding. However, I came to myself, stood up, and said I was ready."

She paused, said, "He got up and stood still for a moment. I couldn't see his hands, though when he turned and came quickly towards me I was sure he held a knife. But when he reached me he threw himself at my feet, his empty hands spread out on the floor. He wept, begged forgiveness - and was gone." With a smile she filled up my teacup and said, "So I am here, my dear, very glad to be drinking this good English tea with you."

On the way back to Beirut I remembered the day in Canea when Lady Palairet offered a cup of tea to the drunk Australian who had threatened us with his loaded tommy-gun. I paired her with the Englishwoman deflecting violence in her way. How predictable violence was, the perpetrators convinced of success, yet the outcome, as David said, was more fear, and anger, and violence.

That was all very well but, as if to mock me, the words on the rocks above Byblos came unbidden:

"We the Assyrians came and conquered,
and washed our weapons in the Western sea."

As always, my spine prickled, and angrily I thought, 'So you get a kick out of spilled blood, do you!' Then I heard David ending his forecast of the Allied invasion of Europe with the triumphant "and that, my love, is the beginning of the Second Front and the end of the war!" The second front, and probably David would be there, spilling the blood of strangers, his red bandanna tucked away out of sight.

And afterwards the war would end. The war would end, and what then?

⤝ 36 ⤞

Changes.
I shake on a deal.

Early May 1943, German and Italian troops were trapped between the Eighth Army and contingents of British and Americans advancing from Morocco. On May 10, Rommel's troops surrendered to Eisenhower in Tunisia. In Beirut, Sandy held a press reception to alert local journalists that Italy's collapse was imminent. David had been right: this was the beginning of the end of the war.

The press reception was held in a large room divided by double doors shutting off the half where a table was loaded with refreshments. The briefing over, the doors were rolled apart and I watched with consternation as the journalists rose in a body and, without a word, bore down on the table like locusts. In very little time the food had disappeared, and for the first time I saw the pity of these hungry men in worn suits, wretchedly paid to toe their editorial line.

The plight of ill-paid journalists was only one of many new perceptions which came my way throughout most of this restless year. The focus of war had shifted to Europe, and change was in the air. Sandy had so much to deal with that he kept handing me the jobs he hadn't the time for or didn't want to do anyway.

The first job came up soon after I was back from Palestine. "This'll interest you, Belinda," Sandy said. "A Muslim school has invited me to attend a concert given by the children." He added with a grin that the concert was possibly to keep the kids' minds off food as it was Ramadan, and everyone would be fasting from food and drink from dawn to dusk. "So don't expect refreshments."

"What am I supposed to do?"

"Just look appreciative and thank them gracefully. They'll love you."

The school, tucked away in an Arab quarter, was obviously a poor one. I was welcomed with touching fervour and led into the sun-baked central courtyard where a lot of children were already crowded on rows of benches. My place was in the front row of chairs set aside for the teachers. I wished I was more important, hoped they weren't expecting a donation and that my being there was enough.

Groups of children mounted the makeshift stage to sing their songs or repeat poems, each one with many verses, and in Arabic. Hours seemed to pass until all the children had taken their moment of glory and then, to my surprise, I was invited to take refreshment. I thanked them and waited to be led somewhere, but no move was made, the children remained on their benches, and the teachers engaged me in conversation. Though vaguely aware of activity on the stage, I did not put two and two together until I was courteously ushered to where, at centre stage, one chair was set beside a small table, laid for one.

I sat on the one chair while, with kindly smiles, the bearded teachers seated themselves in a half-circle of chairs at a respectful distance from me. I was then served a sequence of simple dishes. I ate in silence, watched by the teachers and some fifty hungry children anchored to their benches in the courtyard below. At least I knew the etiquette, and ate everything to demonstrate my appreciation.

Sandy found this ordeal entertaining, said it had been a good way to get the feel of Beirut and I'd enjoy the next outing he had for me. "The British Council has sent out a young historian to give a lecture in Aleppo. He's an Oxford don and the lecture's titled 'The Mother of Parliaments.'" I said it was a ghastly title and supposed this was the Ministry of Information's idea of giving the British a good name.

"Westminster is a model all over the world, Belinda, and if the chap's any good he'll make the lecture amusing."

But he wasn't any good. Worse, the invited audience was made up of educated Syrians whose minds were lively and perceptive. The don was a plump young man, and pleased with himself. Barely five minutes into his so-called lecture I suspected he hadn't bothered to prepare it. My toes curled with discomfiture as he rambled on and on, making little academic jokes which he punctuated with patronizing snorts of amusement. When, mercifully, he stopped, the audience clapped politely, their faces frozen into unconvincing smiles.

"I only hope none of the guests were insulted," I expostulated to Sandy. "Talk about 'getting the feel', I got the feel of embarrassment. Who on earth chooses such second-raters? What a waste of money to send him all this way!"

Sandy agreed it was all a frightful bore, but he wasn't running the British Council. "Never mind," he said, "here's something really interesting lined up for you," and handed me a package of photographs. "Take a look at these. Jolly good aren't they? Taken by *The Times* photographers. Should make a good impression." The black-and-white pictures were of English cities and countryside, and they were beautiful. "Pick out the ones you like. I've arranged for a showing of them in Damascus next month. Set them up and run the show for a week."

A week in Muslim Damascus was something I'd been longing for, it was such a different city from free-and-easy Christian Beirut. In Damascus the big houses of the well-to-do proclaimed a fiercely-guarded privacy, the few apertures obscured by dense latticework, the carved wooden doors massive and uninviting.

But the intense heat of inland Damascus was a shock after sea-girt Beirut which was sticky and humid, but the sea was there to swim in, and at night the air cooled slightly. In Damascus, to step outside from the moderately cool gallery was to step into an oven. My clothes stuck everywhere they touched, and something cool to drink was paradise.

The show, in terms of attendance, was a great success and there was even a morning for ladies only. They came heavily veiled, but as soon as they were safely inside the veils were lifted and they passed from photograph to photograph, twittering like a flock of little birds. They had a happy time - but did these black-and-white pictures of unfamiliar places really mean anything? The old man who came next day posed no such question. He was a simple old man, rather poorly dressed, but he spoke a little English and was full of goodwill, raising his hands in delight as I told him about London or the bits of country I knew well. Before he left he took a photograph from a few lying loose on a table, and with an exclamation of pleasure held it upside-down. "Good! good!" he cried, smiles creasing the lines of his old face, and together we admired the print, wrong way up.

A very different person was the elderly Arab lady on whom I called to thank for arranging the ladies' morning. She was striking - fine dark eyes, a beautiful voice and an impressive presence. She received me in a room shuttered against the voracious sun, and when I sat down on the divan with a sigh of relief she clapped her hands and gave a brief order to a servant.

"He will bring you a refreshing drink," she said.

He returned with a copper pot and a tall glass nearly full of crushed ice. From the curved beak of the pot he poured a ruby-red stream of liquid on the ice. I took the full glass eagerly from him, but my hostess said, "Now wait for the juice to cool." So I waited. When the ice had crimsoned she said, "Now sip it slowly."

I sipped slowly, and with a sigh of pleasure said, "It's nectar. What is it?"

Smiling she said, "Mulberry juice."

"Thank you!" I said. "I'll never forget it."

Memorable at another level was her response to my account of the Princess's visit (no name mentioned). With emotion she spoke of the restricted lives imposed on Muslim women, and the painful changes that were inevitable. "Your visitor from Aleppo demonstrates the difficulty of combining Muslim codes with Western education. So that you understand where she comes from, I will arrange for you to visit a relative of mine who is waiting and hoping for betrothal. She is young, but already time is catching up on her. Her education has been limited, and you will see how great a gulf there is between your life and hers."

The young woman's house was built round a large inner courtyard, tiled underfoot, planted with flowers and shady trees, the ear soothed and the air refreshed by water lightly falling from a central fountain. It seemed an oasis, a sort of paradise, but after an hour I wondered if the gentle chatter of water might become insistent as a spell, for the courtyard and her quarters were her whole world. Her visitors were confined to women friends and relatives, and selected male relations. Even the male cook had to pass her meals through an aperture in the wall, the opening discreetly turning a corner to keep his mistress out of sight.

Most Arab women were married off when still slender gazelles in teenage bloom. This lady was plump, round-faced and probably well into her twenties (she looked older, but I didn't ask). She showed me every item in her two painted marriage chests which almost overflowed with beautiful embroidered garments and household linen. Surely she must despair? Yet oddly enough, though she might have been pathetic, there was something game about her, bubbling discreetly out of sight.

The bubbling provoked me to ask if she ever went shopping. Demurely she said her personal maid shopped for her. Daring a little I tried another question. "Have you ever seen a movie, a film?"

At this she gave me an unexpectedly bright glance and I held my breath. So far her expression had been friendly, but a touch shy; now the big brown eyes suddenly twinkled. In little more than a whisper she said, "Sometimes I borrow the clothes of my maidservant and we go..." she bit her lip, nearly giggled, "we go together to the cinema!"

Damascus left me ruminating on the extraordinary systems human beings have devised to enforce violent restrictions upon groups of people trapped in compliance by the imperceptible spider webs of their particular tradition, a fine network of race and culture, family, superstition and a pantheon of gods. I thought, 'If you exist, God, you have much to answer for.' Yet the idea of God in all his various constructs had created beauty in the craftsmanship of music and literature, art and architecture and, thinking of my Quaker friends, there were some good Godly people.

I'd never known any Quakers personally until meeting the little group of young men who took their mobile clinic to villages on the desert plains of Syria or buried in the Lebanese mountains. From time to time they returned to Beirut for supplies, and I looked forward to their visits. They had great stories to tell, and I was moved by how, without fuss, they and their Quaker colleagues resolutely refused to take part in the killing demanded by war. Instead they offered their services to succour life - on the battlefield or wherever needed.

"Don't think we're afraid of death," they said, "we simply reject taking life. That's murder. Whether you're in uniform or the priests tell you the cause is just and God's on your side, killing is murder." They told me of Quaker friends in North Africa working as stretcher-bearers and ambulance drivers, and I asked why they had chosen to operate their mobile clinic.

The answer was unhesitating. "We felt we could improve life in places where people are ignorant of simple facts about health. In wartime everyone is too busy with killing and winning to bother about unimportant Arab villagers and their needs." One of the Quakers smiled and added, "From the politicians' point of view, humanitarian help creates a good impression, though it's not always easy to offer good medical advice effectively." Then he talked about trying to get some village elders to clear their swamp.

Swamps are a breeding ground for anopheles mosquitoes, carriers of malaria which was chronic in the village. Sober explanations failed, so a new approach was tried, using cartoons. The first cartoon showed the swamp swarming with mosquitoes, each carrying a spear tipped with the poison of malaria. In the second cartoon the swamp had been drained, and the mosquito corpses lay very dead on the sun-baked soil.

The cartoons were shown to a gathering of elders. They nodded their heads, muttering approval, and promised that the swamp would be cleared when the Quakers came on their next visit.

But on the next visit the swamp was still there. The elders were asked why. They replied with that familiar shrug and lifting of the hands, "Allah gave us the swamp. Allah will take it away."

"Oh dear! Do you ever despair?"

"Not really. We just keep plugging away. It was a Muslim village and the drawings were probably meaningless. Anyway, you can't expect people to jump several centuries in a flash. Change is frightening, and a long process." Then they told me about the old man and his bottle of medicine.

The clinic made routine visits to their villages, arriving in the evening and opening for business early in the morning. People lined up for diagnosis, or for bottles of medicine which carried labels with dosage instructions. The old man had been pleased to be given a bottle and, as he couldn't read, the daily dosage was explained. On the clinic's return visit the old man was last in the line of patients. When his turn came he held up his bottle, and with a broad smile cried triumphantly, "I am well, thanks be to Allah and the Saviours of the Sick!"

"Naturally we said his news made us very happy, and took the bottle, assuming it to be empty, but the seal on the cork was unbroken and the bottle full - the only thing missing was the label. He seemed surprised when we questioned him gently about his cure, but, as if to children, he explained that he had boiled the bottle and its label, inscribed with sacred words, and drunk the water. "The water was blessed," he said, "and see! The sickness has gone!"

"Actually he was much better!" my friends confessed, "so we and the label shared the glory of the old man's recovery."

I envied the Quakers their sense of purpose. From time to time I'd toyed with the idea of staying in Lebanon. But it wasn't enough just to love the country and the people. The Quakers had a skill and a purpose, whereas I was just a secretary. The Levant was a singular mind territory, volatile, warm, and subtle - very un-English, and liable to end in disappointment, misunderstanding and muddle. I had no romantic wish to become another Lady Hester Stanhope who, in spite of her talents and brilliance, ended in the mountains alone, sick and rather batty.

So I carried on working for Sandy, which was never dull, and to my relief he seemed to have forgotten about my idea of utilizing the Nasr-ed-Din stories for propaganda. Currently he was absorbed with a new idea. He had become friendly with Stuart Dodo, Professor of Sociology at the American University of Beirut. The two of them shared an interest in market research techniques which Sandy felt could be adapted to gathering reliable information on such tricky matters as wheat distribution. This made some sense, as sources of information were either local and often unreliable, or depended on hard-pressed district officers (like Kemal) with an impossibly large territory to cover.

Stuart was a brilliant mathematician, and a decent, honest man. His wife and two boys were in America and he missed them badly, but he was always good company. I liked his square, homespun face, and the way he looked you straight in the eye. I knew nothing about market research and Sandy was a bit harebrained, but if Stuart was behind their scheme I felt it must be sound.

The summer of 1943 was an odd one, as if change was inevitable and there was nothing to do but wait. The passage of days was punctuated by small, oddly memorable occasions, like a visit to my dressmaker. She and her husband were a neat little pair - at 5' 6" I felt a giantess beside them. She was a good dressmaker, by no means *haute couture*, but she always received me in a most elegant long black dress, Paris salon fashion. Her husband was an artist, and being Christian he was free to paint what he liked, mostly landscapes. They weren't very good landscapes, but the triumph was their size. I would be taken to see the newest canvas, its proportions identified with pride. But this was not all. Their daughter played the piano, and once, speaking of her prowess, I was assured, with breathless emphasis, that she could play Chopin's three-minute waltz "in two-and-a-half minutes exactly. Madame!" As ever I was suitably amazed and, as ever, they were delighted.

I related this to Dick Usborne who said the East/West fusion could be charmingly unexpected and told me of a first meeting with his Lebanese friend Khouri. "He asked if I was related to a man of the same name who was killed at the battle of Waterloo. I was about to disclaim the connection when suddenly I managed some quick literary footwork, and realized that Khouri had confused me with Thackeray's George Osborne in *Vanity Fair*. Remember?"

"Of course I do," I exclaimed. "I read the book at school and learnt that sentence by heart." Hesitatingly I began, "'The darkness came down on the field and city...'" paused, then the words came back, "'and Amelia was praying for George, who was lying on his face, dead, with a bullet through his heart.'" We smiled at each other and I exclaimed, "It always sends shivers down my spine. No wonder Khouri remembered it as history. It's as good as."

"And we're as good as living history now," Dick said, "about which people will write books, and we'll tell our stories and be boring old buffers."

"Well, I love your stories, they're never boring and there's such charm in East/West confusion."

But a few weeks later I discovered that the confusion was not always charming; in fact it could be downright unnerving.

Now and again my uncle Phil took me off on hikes in the mountains, each expedition infused with his exuberant delight in finding new places to explore. I loved these daylong times with him, but secretly what I loved even more were the mountain walks Kassab and I took on our own.

The charm of these solitary walks was never knowing what or whom I'd encounter. It might be a profusion of wild oleander shrubs covered with fat pink flowers in full bloom; once I came upon a young goatherd playing a reed flute while his flock ate everything in sight; another day, way above sea level, I kicked an odd-shaped stone and stooping, saw it was the fossil of a fat spiral sea shell. Could it be from the Flood? Not that it mattered; there was magic in simply finding a seashell on a mountainside. People asked if I wasn't afraid to walk alone. "But I have Kassab," I said, "and what should I be afraid of?"

Towards the end of summer, I took a long-intended walk that followed the Dog River to a spring reputed to gush spectacularly from the hillside. It meant leaving Kassab behind as the river had to be forded, and even though it was the Dog River, Kassab wasn't keen on water.

The walk began near a hospital where my friend, Havard, was recovering from jaundice, and I planned to pay him a visit after my walk. I left my driver content to drowse in the shade by the hospital and set off downhill, past bamboo groves and through an orchard to the river. A young Arab lay fast asleep on the riverbank, and skirting past him, I found a place to ford the river. Halfway across I climbed on a flat rock to sit in a dapple of sun and shade and listen to the river rippling past. It was very peaceful, and I unpacked Marie's pita and humus and fruit, ate contentedly and afterwards dozed a bit until, with a glance at my watch, saw I'd slept too long and better get going.

About twenty minutes later I came into a clearing where a wood-cutter was at work. I returned his greetings and asked about the spring. My Arabic was rudimentary and his English non-existent, but he got the drift of my query and I got the drift of his intention to be my guide. I wasn't too pleased about this, but he was all smiles and, after laying down his small, sharp axe, he courteously gestured me to follow him.

The river now ran deeper and faster than at the ford and the narrow path seemed very private, one side walled in by high ground and overhanging trees. I began to wish I hadn't come. It seemed a very long time indeed before my guide stopped and with a flourish indicated the spring as if, like Moses, he'd struck the rock and lo! water gushed forth. He gave a small speech in Arabic. I admired the spring, smiled my thanks and saw nothing, for by now I had a single purpose - to return the young man to his clearing, and leave him. I tapped my watch and, turning, led the way back at a brisk pace, wishing I was a porcupine with sharp quills sticking out all over my body. Lacking quills, I willed every inch of me to proclaim, "Keep off!"

He did keep off. At long, long last we got back to the clearing. Vastly relieved I thanked him and would have left if he hadn't made gestures indicating another expedition. I shook my head, he persisted, miming what seemed to be an even greater flow of water, and concluded with a stunning smile. Suddenly I was fed up with the whole performance and, holding out my hand, said firmly in English, "Goodbye!"

I might as well have thrown off my clothes. He seized me in what promised to be a passionate embrace - but oh! I was angry. I banged him on the chest, let fly a startling volley of abuse, and struggled with such determination that he let go. I would have run, but for once that voice in my head didn't mess about, and said sharply, "Walk!"

So I walked, holding my head high, feeling as if the backs of my legs were made of jelly. I turned once, but looked away quickly - his pantomime was unmistakable and hardly genteel. When I was well out of his sight, and only then, I took to my heels, and rounding a bend nearly collided with a couple of Maronite priests.

The sight of their amiable, bearded faces was so ordinary and reassuring that I began, in bad French, to pour out a disconnected account of what had just happened. But not for long: they didn't understand a word. One of them remarked gently, *"Vraiement, ma'mselle, c'est une bonne journée pour votre petite promenade, n'est-ce pas!"* and the other chimed in, *"Regardez le ciel!"* in case I hadn't noticed it, *"comme il est bleu!"* Perhaps they thought I wasn't quite all there which, in truth, I wasn't.

We said goodbye and I pressed on until, not five minutes later, I heard a cough and stopped short. With heart thumping I looked up - and into the face of a goat. He stared down at me from an outcrop of rock, his long face sober as a statesman, his rather mad yellow eyes considering me with detachment.

"Hallo, goat!" I said shakily and walked on, feeling sick.

Once across the ford I told myself that, after all, nothing terrible had happened and walked confidently along the path through the orchard. Then I saw him. He stood some way from the path, shadowed by fruit trees, the little sharp axe in one hand. I realized, with a stab of panic, that he must have been the sleeper on the river bank, that he'd probably seen me sleeping on the rock, and knew I'd come back this way. Then panic exploded in a burst of rage. I shouted at him to stay where he was, had a fleeting impression he was disconcerted, and stormed on along the path, walking, not running, until I was sure he couldn't see me. Then I lost my head. I plunged off the path and within seconds was hopelessly tangled up in a dense thicket of bamboo. Terrified, flailing about, I crashed on and on, making a great deal of noise as I fought the bamboo as if it was in league with what must be the pursuing Arab. At last I broke through to open ground, the hospital only a hundred yards away, and nobody was chasing me.

Havard said I looked rather wild. "Have you been tumbling in the hay?" he asked. I told him what had happened, making light of it, hoping for the cure of laughter. But it didn't work. I took Kassab for a few more solitary mountain walks, but I was frightened. What galled me was knowing I couldn't have been more idiotic if I'd tried - holding out my hand so polite and English. What an ass! And no more solitary walks.

It was not a good moment for Sandy to revive my idea of using Nasr-ed-Din stories for propaganda. I thought he was happily away on market research, but one day he produced a Nasr-ed-Din cartoon and said, "There you are, Belinda, try your hand twisting the script."

I protested, but it was no good. Once again I was being invented, this time as a keen scriptwriter. Cross and reluctant, though touched by Sandy's desire to develop my talents, I took the cartoon, wrote an abysmal script and laid it on his desk where he would find it in the morning. In fact I doubt that he ever saw it, for in the morning he opened an envelope whose contents put everything else out of his mind.

The letter had been misdirected. It was a criticism of Sandy, written by someone with the distasteful job of reporting regularly on the personal qualities of people working closely with the Arabs. The report was astringent and unflattering, implying that commercial advertising techniques were irrelevant to the sensitive tasks of a press attaché, that Sandy's understanding of the Arab mentality was limited and could lead to unfortunate repercussions. Sandy took the letter to Spears, who was outraged at not having been consulted about his staff. But a copy of the letter had already gone to one of the Intelligence groups in Cairo, and the harm was done. There was a row, but no redress, and Sandy was, in diplomatic no-speak, "recalled to London to take up other duties."

As it happened I knew the writer of the report. He explained that the misdirection had been made by a careless orderly. "This is wartime, Belinda," he said miserably, "when nobody trusts anyone in the desperate business of winning. I hate my job, but one can't refuse to obey orders." I had to admit that Sandy laid himself open to criticism, but his creative approach had been stimulating; and he'd been good to me. I'd grown fond of him, and knew he'd be disappointed that the market research idea would come to nothing. On this score, however, I'd underestimated my boss.

On September 22, after Sandy left Beirut, the Italian troops in North Africa surrendered to General Eisenhower. A week later the Allies invaded Sicily, and set up military headquarters in Palermo. We followed these events avidly in Beirut, I always wondering whether David was one of the invaders. This shift of focus in the war made me restless for change, and the temporary press attaché was boring after Sandy. Although I often disagreed with his opinions, it was interesting working for what Spears' called 'a live wire of the American advertising industry.'

It was early in October when Stuart Dodd called me at the legation. "Can you get away for a few minutes in your coffee break?" he asked, "I've a letter from Sandy that'll interest you. I'll meet you outside." He sounded unusually excited. I promised to meet him in an hour, and went back to my office feeling I was ready for almost anything.

At coffee break I ran down the stairs and found Stuart outside, the letter in his hand. The gist of it was that Sandy had got backing in England for an experimental unit to explore the value of market research techniques in collecting information for military administrators.

Stuart said, "Sandy wants me to head a unit, based at Allied Military Headquarters in Palermo, Sicily. He asked if I can get a six-months leave of absence from the University, and Bayard Dodge has agreed. The job involves training Sicilian interviewers, overseeing their work in the field, and writing up a full report of the findings and the process." He paused, added, "Sandy says he'll engage an interpreter, thank goodness, and two or three assistants with a background in mathematics." Then he smiled. "He also suggests, Belinda, that you come with me as my personal assistant. Will you?"

I didn't hesitate, said simply, "I'd love to go with you," and laughing, we shook hands.

❧ 37 ❧

Adieu Beirut.
Palermo and the Sicilian circus.

There was no way I could take Kassab with me. He had become so much part of my life that the realization was a shock, the only comfort being that a saluki would always be valued in the Levant. There was no time to start seeking a suitable Arab owner, so Kassab was given into the care of the corporal in charge of the soldier clerks. He loved Kassab dearly, and said solemnly, "Sir Kassab is an institution in the legation. He'll be all right, miss, and I'll do what's best when I have to leave." The corporal was a good fellow and I trusted him; but the parting was - and is still - a heartache.

At least some unexpected comedy made me laugh. Probably during one of the press receptions, I had mentioned to a guest that I was interested in folk music. Exuberantly he exclaimed, "Our dancers are very fine. You have seen?"

I had seen the whirling Dervishes, spinning in their white robes, one hand upraised, the other pointing downwards to transmit grace from Allah to the Faithful. Their ecstatic whirling had been accompanied by the hypnotic chanting of seated Dervishes. This was not exactly 'folk' (remembering English folk dancers with bells and be-ribboned legs prancing innocently about to piping melodies on the recorder). So I shook my head. At once an evening of Arab dancing would be arranged, "An evening," I was assured, "to remember! You will see!"

The invitation came out of the blue a few days before Stuart and I were due to leave. Music and a dancer had been specially engaged, and it was impossible to refuse. To be on the safe side I asked if I might bring a friend. "Of course, of course!" was the reply, possibly in expectation of another young woman. But I brought Stuart instead, and was glad of his solid presence, for I was the only female guest.

Arab hospitality takes a long time to get going. We sat around the room on stiff little chairs, exchanging courtesies until refreshments were offered. We did the proper thing and ate with evident pleasure. More conversation followed, and the room grew sultry. At last the musicians trooped in. They were a rather dispirited group, implausibly clothed in battered black tuxedos enlivened by Old Etonian ties - the bands of light and dark blue were unmistakable.

It had taken me a while to appreciate Arab music. Songs with dozens and dozens of verses seemed, at first, more of an onslaught than a pleasure, but after a while I began to hear sophistication in the complex structure and the versatility of decorative phrases. The reward

320

was suddenly to hear, not caterwauling, but music. The dancing would, presumably, be a new dimension of the music.

The dancer's entry was greeted with enthusiasm. She was unexpectedly a lady of considerable dimensions, and though not all that young, her fruitful charms were lightly clad. As the room was not very large we had a close-up view. She was undoubtedly flexible, and revolved her not inconsiderable stomach and various parts of her body with skill. One dance followed another, the room grew warmer, and the male guests who wore European clothing began removing their ties. Around one in the morning the heat and close proximity of gyrating flesh became overwhelming. I murmured to Stuart that we must leave, and when the dancer disappeared for a breather I began our apologies. They were met with exclamations of distress. Surely we did not mean to leave? I explained that we had much to do before our journey to Sicily. Our host assured us that the evening had only just begun. I assured him we had been royally entertained, and the evening was unforgettable.

"But madame," he cried, raising protesting hands, "you cannot leave now. In a moment the lady will return to dance quite nude!"

Outside we didn't dare speak or laugh until well out of earshot. Then we laughed, though not without a sort of pity - for the dancer, a little past her prime? or maybe the musicians in Old Etonian ties? It was hard to say. As we walked through the soft night of early fall I said, "They'd taken off their ties. Was it to be an orgy?" I quoted from Edward Lane's *Modern Egyptians* in which he wraps up his description of a dancing party with, 'The scenes which ensued cannot be described.'

"When was that printed?" Stuart asked.

"In 1895," I said. "Lane says the songs and dances were licentious and the men encouraged their womenfolk to watch through the lattice on an upper floor to 'increase the libidinous feelings of their wives.' Were my libidinous feelings meant to be aroused?" I asked. "Can you imagine what was anticipated?"

Stuart said firmly, "No, I can't imagine anything, not here in 1943. We'll never know, and just as well maybe. At least we'll be spared similar entertainment in Palermo." So he thought.

The first leg of our journey was to Morocco, and our aircraft flew over what had been the battlefields of North Africa. We looked down on empty desert, miles and miles of yellowish sand grooved by war, littered with wrecked army tanks and broken trucks, still as death. This desolate detritus seemed irrelevant, accidental, offering no clue to 'Why?'

Our aircraft was a DC 3, basic spartan army transport. We were glad when it was over, and looked forward to meeting with the interpreter and other unit staff Stuart had requested. But the only person waiting to greet us in Morocco was the interpreter, Hubert Howard. I was delighted to meet him for I had waltzed memorably in Cairo with his brother, Henry. He'd been a dream partner, tall and assured; with his hand lightly but firmly on my back, I'd spun like a top beneath sparkling chandeliers, free as a bird, our steps perfectly synchronized. That dance, wherever it was in Cairo, had been the first and last of our meetings; all I remember of our conversation was learning that Henry's mother lived in a 'grace-and-favour' apartment at Hampton Court Palace. In explanation he said, "It sounds very grand but when Queen Victoria was faced with 1,000 spare rooms in the palace she sensibly assigned them to widows whose husbands had worthily served the royal family."

Hubert was very like Henry, tall, slender, naturally courteous, and fluent in Italian. "Thank the Lord!" Stuart exclaimed, "he's the perfect choice - and he's here."

The others gradually turned up, but were not perfect. In disbelief Stuart exclaimed, "I clearly requested at least one statistician and preferably two, and hoped that a third would be familiar with market research techniques."

Instead he had a pleasant professor of history from an English university, a very brash American advertising man whose experience was in sales (even Stuart found his breezy hyperboles hard to stomach), and a cheery old-school British officer with no particular expertise. Later he revealed a talent for making shoe-leather shine brilliantly, and explained that the trick was to do a final working over with a piece of bone. "Takes time to get a bone just right, nice and smooth," he said. "This piece belonged to me pater." Neither the professor nor the advertising man stayed the course, and we were left with the officer, a kindly man who became a sort of nursemaid, clucking after our well-being and polishing our shoes.

When this unlikely crew was assembled and we were at last assigned a flight to Palermo, Stuart called Hubert and me for a conference.

"We've got quite a little challenge here," he said. "First, we have to select and train a body of Sicilians, who speak no English, and will not understand the purpose and method of our techniques. They must be left in no doubt that it is forbidden to manipulate interviews, and the answers must be truthfully and accurately recorded. I've planned a series of short lectures which I'll give through a translator - your first job, Hubert. As soon as possible we'll get the boys out into the field for a trial run and that'll weed out the ones we can't trust. We may have to get new recruits, do a second training session and practice run. After that we can get down to the serious business, depending on what information's wanted at headquarters. Secondly, you two have to learn how to formulate the answers statistically. I can't handle it alone, and the others are not promising material."

I stared at Stuart in disbelief. "But I'm useless at maths. Really a dolt."

Stuart said cheerfully, "Well, I'll be darned, Belinda!" Hubert murmured that he'd studied classics himself, but Stuart laughed at us both. "Your mothers must have read you the story of *The Little Engine that Could.* Don't worry. Once we've settled in, the three of us will do an hour's maths every morning before breakfast. You'll soon get the hang of it. Honest Injun! Isn't that what you English said as kids?"

"No, Stuart. We said, 'See it wet, see it dry, cut my throat if I tell a lie.'"

"I'll stick to honest Injun," Stuart retorted, chuckling about 'you Brits!'

An American officer met us at Palermo airport and we were driven straightway to what was to be our office and my apartment. He said I'd be tickled to bits when I saw it. Actually it left us all speechless. The previous tenant had been mistress of some prominent Italian - a general, or the mayor, or maybe a mafia boss (even all three). Her taste in interior decoration was bold - the furniture was brilliantly upholstered in scarlet leather, and the floor covered in large black-and-white tiles. The overall impact was powerful. Even Hubert was at a loss for words. The officer obviously felt it was a snappy, European-style pad, so I managed to say feebly, "It's very bright and...and jolly."

"Sure is! Plenty of space, ain't there?" He apologized for the absence of heating or hot water and said one of the boys would bring a bucket of hot water each evening from the mess across the road. "Anything else you want, ma'am, just ask the boys. We got plenty of everything right there."

I said hot water would be wonderful, and most nights for the next six months I stood in the bath and poured teacupfuls of warm water over myself. It was a chilly exercise on cold evenings in an unheated apartment. But it was all right. I hadn't expected Beirut comforts, and a bitter, slogging war was being fought across the strip of water separating us from the mainland. For all I knew, David was there.

On the night of our arrival we ate supper in the mess. As the city was occupied by American troops, and the Allied headquarters was commanded by an American general, the mess was full of American soldiers. I sat next to one, hoping to get into conversation, but in no time was flummoxed by their peculiar English, and what Stuart later explained were wisecracks. Not being versed in wisecracks I ploughed on, hearing my polite, cool English voice affecting my companions like a dousing in cold water. The food was equally strange - there was plenty of it but meat, vegetables, salad, and stewed fruit were all sloshed together into a compartmented mess tin with huge slabs of bread which the soldiers (and Stuart) spread liberally with peanut butter. The accepted thing seemed to be to fork up the fruit with meat, vegetables, or whatever. Fork only, mind; knives were laid on one side after everything was chopped up, like you did for a baby in England. How were you supposed to push the food on the fork without a knife?

"Is this how you all eat in the States?" I asked Stuart, "I mean, with a fork only and everything mixed up?"

He grinned. "The fork alone is our way, and we mix sweet and sour quite a bit." At breakfast the next morning he said, "The waffles are good, aren't they. Just like home." The crisp slab of little squares on which butter was melted and then covered in syrup was more like a pudding than breakfast, but I agreed that yes, they were pretty good, though I never remembered eating them when I was in Texas.

"You know, Stuart, I expected to be easy with Americans after living in San Antonio. But I can't remember how it was. And it's funny how everyone speaks English, but it isn't English. Your English," I added, "is quite normal."

Stuart laughed, said amiably, "That's good," and added, "You probably sound funny to them."

Discomfited, I decided to ease up on being the frightfully polite English gentlewoman when talking to Americans.

Stuart lost no time in hiring the first batch of Sicilian would-be interviewers, and started the training sessions a couple of days after our arrival in Palermo. In contrast to my brothelish apartment, Stuart was assigned a huge ballroom in a palace of faded magnificence. The ceiling, supported by fat little plaster cherubs, was painted with fluffy clouds in a blue sky where nymphs frolicked in flimsy garments. But the palace was unheated, and damp had flaked and cracked the plastered walls.

There was a lot of ballroom, and not many of us. We - the Sicilian students and our unit - clustered in overcoats on little gilt chairs ranged below the dais from which Stuart lectured. The Sicilians, in worn suits, their faces pinched with chill and hunger, reminded me of the Beirut journalists and I wondered how on earth, under these unpromising circumstances, Stuart would create a body of competent interviewers. But on the first morning he mounted the dais and greeted us as cheerfully as if we were all in a comfortable lecture room at the American University of Beirut.

For the inside of a week Stuart patiently, in brief sentences, explained what they were going to do, and why. After a few sentences he would pause, his square, friendly face exuding good humour, while Hubert translated. Each session lasted an hour. Then came a break for hot coffee and something to eat (as in Beirut the food vanished in a trice). In the breaks we 'socialized' (Stuart's word, presumably American), all of us grappling with minimal common language, and thankful for Hubert who floated around, making connections and conversation.

The unit staff - the historian, the leather-polishing expert, the advertising man and myself - attended every session. To my surprise I wasn't bored, despite the chill and the laborious process – Stuart speaking in English, then Hubert in Italian, over and over in small sections. I was fascinated to learn that replies to questions from a small sample of people would yield a pretty accurate picture of hundreds of opinions or actions. I didn't quite believe it until, working on the first survey returns, I found it to be true. And irritating. Apparently I was nothing but part of a mass, not unique.

I complained about this to Stuart who said, "Keep your hair on, Belinda, what we're measuring are actions or opinions at a given moment. Quantity is measurable; the variable of quality, where your uniqueness comes in, is much harder."

One big surprise was discovering I wasn't a mathematical dolt. Every morning, sharp at six o'clock, Hubert and I were up and ready for a maths lesson with Stuart. He not only made the sessions fun, I could soon handle the calculations.

"You must have had a poor teacher," Stuart said, and I remembered my tears over arithmetic tests involving men painting rooms or collecting apples. "Manipulating figures is simply a matter of solving problems. That's something kids enjoy unless they get scared or thoroughly muddled. Figures are simply another dimension of communicating ideas." He also taught the importance of framing questions very clearly and ensuring that interviewers made no attempt to manipulate the replies. "This is essential," he said. "The technique relies upon integrity all round. Without that the answers will be unrepresentative and the results open to misuse. Dangerous. Here we'll keep the questions very simple."

The first batch of interviewers were sent out to get an answer to the simple question of whether sugar was being fairly distributed. If the interviewers could be trusted, we would go ahead with a priority survey of wheat distribution. Wheat hoarders were, just as in the Levant, a major problem, exacerbated in Sicily by intractable poverty and habitual corruption, for we were in Mafia country. The Americans appeared confident that they were going to break the Mafia in Sicily. Hubert observed drily that the American expectations were touchingly innocent.

Stuart seemed not at all surprised when nearly half the first trainees were found to have fudged or invented the replies. "But how do you know they've cheated?" I asked.

He said, "Remember I'm an old hand at this. I'd almost take a bet on which answers were filled in by their kids and which they invented when drinking *vino* with their buddies. Must have thought they were on to a good thing. But there's plenty more hungry guys where these came from, and by getting rid of so many this time they'll reckon it's no cinch trying to put anything over us. The next lot should be a good bunch."

Stuart was right. But he was such a truly modest man I don't think he realized how much the goodness of the bunch was in large part due to the way they felt about him. When the time came to leave they hung around, offering to do errands without pay, begging him to come back, and it wasn't just for the money. Stuart was someone who gave a great deal without making a point of it. For him, everything in the universe was connected, and beautiful.

But even Stuart's equanimity was shaken when, early in December, we attended a dinner party given by the American general commanding Allied Headquarters in Palermo.

Our invitation came from a Major Panotti. On the night of the party we made our way through ill-lit streets and stopped short to stare up at a huge palace whose entrance was guarded by a laconic American soldier. All the American soldiers seemed congenitally loose - they wore their uniforms loosely and carried their rifles loosely. Americans were certainly another breed. Stuart showed our invitation to the guard who, after giving it a perfunctory glance, handed us over to a soldier inside the palace, who gave us directions to the major's room.

The passages were dimly lit, the high ceilings lost in shadow, and I soon felt we would be lost forever, but Stuart assured me that, as a seasoned hiker, he could find his way to most places. He confidently turned right and left until he stopped outside hefty, glass-fronted double doors. They were thickly curtained and a faint glow showed through a crack in the folds, but there wasn't a sound of life from inside.

"Here we are, Belinda," Stuart said, and read a card taped to the glass, "Major Panotti. That's him."

"D'you think we're early? Maybe he doesn't expect us yet."

Stuart, a stickler for punctuality, shook his head, said, "We're right on time!" and rapped firmly on one of the glass doors.

Nothing happened. He tried again. Silence. His third knock was the sort that gets attention.

"Aw'right, aw'right! Can it, can't ya." The voice was peevish, "I'm comin'."

We heard footsteps, a key turned and the door was pulled open by a young officer, still doing up his fly-buttons. Behind him a young woman was applying lipstick, perched on a very large and tousled bed.

Major Panotti pulled himself together and invited us in. As both Stuart and I were so obviously square, what might have been an embarrassing situation became at once wildly formal. We introduced ourselves, were presented to "my sweetie Maria," and led to where drinks were laid out on a low table. The usual queries about "What'll you take?" saved us from thinking up any conversation, and within a few minutes other guests arrived - three or four officers with a complement of shy Sicilian girls. This was fine, except I heard myself being introduced to each person as "the Lady Lyons." I quickly disowned the title but this was ignored, the guests perhaps thinking my disclaimers were an example of weird British humour. After a couple of drinks I decided not to disappoint everyone, and remained Lady Lyons for the rest of the evening.

Our next move was to the *piano nobile*, and a very noble main floor it was, including the reception room of the general's apartment. From the painted ceiling hung twinkling chandeliers, and on a table loaded with wine and aperitifs was an array of exquisite crystal wine glasses engraved with an elaborate family crest. Stuart and I were introduced with some ceremony to the General, a big man with a craggy face, that could have been designed in America for the movies. He was seated on a handsome carved chair, slightly raised on a sort of podium. Beside him stood a raven-haired lady of uncertain years, very done up in ruby satin. Draped around the edge of the podium were three young girls. They wore long evening dresses in different jewel shades of taffeta. It was quite a tableau.

The General greeted us boisterously, putting quite an emphasis on my title. "Delighted to meet the *Lady* Lyons," he said and presented "The *Contessa*" (the raven-haired lady) and, without explanation, "my little girls." He shook Stuart's hand and said something about "great to welcome a fellow-American." I glanced at Stuart in his sober party suit, looking normal and unassuming, and saw us both as extras in a rather mad charade, or guests at the Red Queen's party in *Alice in Wonderland* - a few frog footmen wouldn't have seemed anything extraordinary.

I was escorted to dinner on the arm of a tough, stocky little Texan. He was, he said, "something in oil." To be on the safe side I said cautiously, "That must be interesting."

"Booming!" he exclaimed vigorously.

To avoid having to make sense of this exchange I told him I'd lived in San Antonio when I was a child. "Well, wad'ya know! Little Lady Lyons lived right in my home town!" He was delighted. I would have followed this up, but was distracted as we entered the first of several interconnecting rooms. They flowed one into the other through a sequence of archways, the perspective narrowing to the dining room where the last arch framed part of the table on which, as if in a classic still-life, stood a gleaming silver vessel filled with a glorious arrangement of flowers. But most stunning of all were the shelves of books. They lined each room we walked through, row after row of old and probably priceless books, bound in tobacco-coloured leather.

I exclaimed with pleasure at such a collection, and my companion, acknowledging the shelves with a nod observed heartily, "Fine buncha books!" and steamed on.

The long table was set with snow-white napery, gleaming silver cutlery and yet more delicate crystal wine glasses. The crest had been woven into the napery and engraved on the silver as well as the crystal. I wondered whether the owner had fled and what would he have made of the company at his table, who were best described as duplications of Major Panotti and his sweetie. I was puzzled by the women, none of whom had quite the poise of *contessas*. They were either uneasy or noisy and their clothes were either flashy or pathetically tawdry. Perhaps the uneasy ones had little English, and party clothes were probably hard to get in wartime. As the wine circulated and voices grew louder I was going to question Stuart discreetly about the female guests, but a voice suddenly shouted from further down the table, "Hey buddy, what sorta whore you got tonight?"

I glanced at Stuart, saw he was looking decidedly square, and murmured, "Wine and women, but where's the song?" He seemed about to answer when a chubby 'other ranks' soldier appeared, carrying sheet music. He sat down impassively at a grand piano and began to play. Throughout dinner he made his way manfully through a programme of 'Best-Loved Tunes', and ended with a florid transcription of the famous *Samson and Delilah* song. He gave us plenty of runs up and down the keyboard with much crossing over of hands. This mightily impressed my escort.

"Just lookit!" he exclaimed, "Lotsa talent!"

After dinner we returned to the General's apartment and did some of Stuart's socializing. The General, by now in a mellow mood, brought out photographs of the wife and kids back home.

"Great little guys, eh? And the lady wife, one o' the best." Meanwhile the *Contessa* and the little girls looked the other way.

The evening ended with more music, this time a choir, and a remarkably good choir with a black base singer whose voice was rich and velvety. He stood foursquare and easy to let the sound pour effortlessly out of his barrel chest. The absolute ease of it was beautiful - he might have been saying, "Please pass the salt, ma'am," but actually was singing:

> Oh, a-rock-a my soul in de bosom of Abraham,
> A-rock-a my soul in de bosom of Abraham
> A-rock-a my soul in de bosom of Abraham,
> Oh, rock-a my soul.
>
> When I went down in de valley to pray,
> Oh rock-a my soul,
> My soul got happy an' I stayed all day,
> Oh rock-a my soul.

The voice and the simple, heartfelt words rang true, the only true thing in that evening of fustian. As Stuart remarked afterwards, "War isn't exactly ennobling, is it?"

To cheer him up I said, "After the Arab dancing party d'you remember saying we'd be spared anything like that in Palermo?" But for once Stuart was put out.

"It was a dinner party with prostitutes, and you were invited! Unforgivable."

"I really didn't mind, Stuart. Maybe they expected you to bring a whore, and got Lady Lyons instead." That at least made Stuart laugh and then he began talking about the war. He said it was crazy, and contrary to every value we pretended to believe in.

To provoke him I asked, "What do you do about someone like Hitler?"

"Ah, the sixty-four dollar question! When we've got some time I'll tell you about one way we might avoid wars in the future. War's a bad habit, Belinda. There's nothing wrong with differences, we wouldn't get anywhere without them, but we need to find a sound method of looking ahead, be aware of trouble brewing, look at the causes, plan action in time instead of acting too late and getting sucked into killing and violence and blustering. We have to grow up, we really do."

I asked him about his idea and he said, "My wife Betty calls it Dad's Barometer. I'll tell you about it another time. We must get some sleep now."

The next few weeks were very busy with a stack of returned questionnaires to work on. We had just thankfully completed the calculations and were wondering what Christmas in the army mess would be like when Sandy suddenly appeared out of the skies - "to see how you're all getting on," he said.

He stayed over Christmas and, before he left, asked me to be his wife.

✀ 38 ✀

Unanswered questions.
England.

Sandy said, "I planned this market research experiment so I could get you out of Beirut. I was sure you knew, my darling."

"I didn't," I said, though I should have done. I knew Sandy's marriage was at an end; but I hadn't expected a proposal of marriage. I tried to take it in while feeling a sort of psychic flatulence, as though I'd not digested the recent years of adventure and misadventure, and wasn't ready for decision. I'd left England determined to take my life in my own hands, make my own choices, belong to myself. Now without warning I had become an involuntary player in a script which was already written. It was very queer.

Only two things were clear. I didn't know what to make of this engaging, volatile, and often exasperating man: nor did I know how to deal with loving David, who was married, and would live his own, separate life.

Sandy spent nearly a week in Palermo, and I bent to my task of trying to see him as a person who, for a start, was fourteen years older than me. So when I was born he was already at Eton, almost set like a poached egg, while I was wobbly, just out from the shell. Eton.

Grandmother Birdie would like that, and Alexander (Sandy) Plantagenet Mitchell-Innes was definitely out of the handkerchief drawer, darling.

I did seem to be dogged by Etonians - John, Arthur, and now Sandy. Stuart said Eton gave an outstanding scholastic education, but I found the result was an odd mix of assurance and lack of it. I'd often noticed that men from the great English public schools - Eton and Harrow, Winchester, Rugby, Charterhouse - tended, in moments of unease, to finger the knot of their old school tie as if it was a talisman. Not a very scientific observation, but over and over again I'd seen the hand stray up to the knot and fiddle with it. Idly I wondered if Englishwomen had a talisman of their own, perhaps the invariable string of pearls, or even better, pearls mated with a cashmere twin set?

'Oh dear!' I thought. 'Will I feel at home in England?' No answer to that. Meanwhile, every evening in Palermo Sandy and I dined and talked, dined and talked, playing our curiously scripted parts.

One evening he talked about his parents. "My father was a fine man, y'know, very much one of the old school. My mother is a darling, you'll love her, very different in her way, but...well, of course, she'd never be disloyal, though she didn't always see eye to eye with him."

"Like what?"

After a pause he said, "There was the time when I wanted to learn the piano. I was a youngster and Mother was all for it, but my father was adamant. He said it wasn't a manly hobby, all right for the ladies, of course, smiling at my mother who played beautifully. Instead of piano lessons he gave me my first gun and taught me to shoot. I was a good shot and he was pleased. I admired him a lot."

Remembering the water-colour Sandy made of my house in Beirut I asked, "Did your father know you had a talent for drawing and painting?"

Sandy shrugged, and said, "I share that with my mother who is an accomplished water-colourist. Actually shooting and riding took up a lot of time in the holidays. Like everyone else, I went off to prep school when I was seven and holidays were the only time I was at home. Rode every day, rain or shine, loved it." He told me again about riding in the Delhi Derby and became quite poetic about the beauty and elegance of well-bred horses, and the exhilaration of being a part of their matchless movement and speed. He said all this while gazing at me with his ingenuous blue/green eyes. Only a stone would have been unmoved.

Another evening Sandy told me about his first visit to Paris. "I was twenty and spent three months there. God, it was wonderful, being on my own and in Paris! The lilacs were in bloom and I met a girl. I wrote to my parents about Paris in the spring - not mentioning the girl, of course - but waxing pretty lyrical about the lilac." He paused, gave his bark of a laugh, and went on, "I was surprised to have a letter from my father by return of post. Was my mother ill? But it wasn't anything like that. He simply desired me to know immediately that he hoped never again to receive from his eldest son another letter of such unmanly sentimentality."

"Good Lord!"

Sandy said, "At least you knew where you were with the old boy," adding rather inconsequently that he still wore one of his father's old shooting jackets. I must have looked astonished, and he explained, "He believed in quality and not wearing clothes out. His suits were made by a tailor in Sackville Street and his shoes, of course, by Lobb's of Bond Street. He had a pair of shoes for every day of the week. Still have a couple of pairs, perfectly good."

I didn't know whether I was more touched than angry that Sandy was still wearing this dominating old boy's shooting jacket and walking in his shoes. Nothing wrong with quality and continuity, but really...! Yet Sandy had gone into advertising, and that must have shocked his father. Maybe the choice was a spark of rebellion, and I asked Sandy what he liked about advertising. He repeated what he'd told me in Beirut - he enjoyed working with creative people, and he knew he had a nose for the right approach. Then he added, "It's a challenge to beat the other fellows at their game."

Suddenly exasperated, I exclaimed, "How can you get excited about making people buy this or that, when this is not vastly different from that? It's all right to advertise what's available and what's it made of, but not all that stuff about how wonderful it is. Like Pears' soap - surely you don't have to go on and on advertising it? Is it any better than other soap?"

Sandy grinned and said, "As it happens the Pears' soap people are one of our clients. Before the war they thought like you, decided they were paying us lots of money for nothing and closed their account. They said Pears' soap was a British institution, and the English public would buy it until kingdom come. Quite soon the sales started going down, and went on down until their top man came, cap in hand, and asked us to take them on again. We did, of course, but it was nearly three years before the sales climbed back to where they'd been."

"And that's true?"

"Absolutely."

"It's depressing. Makes everyone into sheep. Anyway, advertising soap doesn't seem a very inspiring way of earning a living, even if you do earn lots of money." Thoughtlessly I warmed to my subject, just as I'd warmed to the idea of Nasr-ed-Din, and Sandy said I was adorable and agreed I might have a point. I said impatiently that being adorable wasn't at issue, building a different world after this horrible war was what mattered. Didn't he agree with Stuart's idea of putting in place a system that would circumvent budding crises before they blew up into war? Then I fell silent while David soundlessly cried, 'It's going to be exciting after the war, Belinda, and I want to be there!'

After a moment Sandy asked, "What would you think of my going into politics?" and added vaguely, "It's been suggested..."

Surprised, I said, "Well...yes. Why not? if you felt excited about what you could do." Perhaps we were interrupted, and nothing more was said of politics. But on our last evening together he brought up something very different - the loss of an inheritance he always assumed would be his.

The inheritance was a family estate in Scotland with a handsome, old stone house set in acres of splendid shooting. It was owned by an aunt whom he'd met only when he was a child. Before making her last will she asked Sandy and his brother to visit her separately. Sandy said, "I had just turned twenty-one and tried desperately to make a good impression but I was nervous and felt she didn't take to me. My brother is a great chap, very different from me, always solid and calm. She chose him, even though he didn't care a jot for the place."

"That was a shame!"

"Yes," Sandy said, "it was."

I felt so sorry. Before he left Palermo I accepted his proposal.

Stuart was delighted about Sandy and me, and both he and Hubert went about looking pleased, as though vaguely responsible for a desirable outcome of our rather loony experiment in Palermo. The sense of being successfully scripted into my part roused an unexpected nostalgia for England - the England of my cottage in Albury and the harvest of Cox's Orange Pippins that would be picked in the fall, the England of old Copford Rectory which was forever. The memories were inviting and I pushed aside queries that kept sidling up asking 'Do you know what you're doing?' and 'Do you love Sandy? Will you make him happy?' and 'What about David?' which was foolish, as he was married.

The unanswered questions lay in a lump somewhere between my heart and stomach, making me cranky - very cranky now and again, but luckily I was usually too busy for crankiness. As our stint of six months drew towards its end there were final statistics to record, and Stuart's summaries and comments to be typed. Sometimes we wondered, idly, whether our work would be followed up.

"That's the army's problem," Stuart said cheerfully. "We've tackled our problems and done the best we could. You and Hubert have been a fine pair to work with, and it's been mighty interesting to see an army at close quarters. Convinces me the only drawback to armies is giving them a license to kill. Take that away, and you can redirect all that discipline and commitment and energy to keeping the peace."

I asked how peace could be 'forced' on people if they were angry and determined to get what they wanted. Stuart said, "It's a matter of rejecting violence, and that's as simple - and difficult - as saying 'Love your neighbour as yourself.' But violence is literally a dead end. There'll always be differences of opinion and conflicts about power. We have to learn there's no real solution in killing each other and laying countries to waste. It doesn't tackle what's really wrong, just adds another wrong."

I told Stuart about the Australian who, amidst the ruins of Baalbek in Lebanon, said, 'Wot I can't make out, miss, is why they 'ave to go and build all these 'ere ruins,' and confided David's comment, 'Ruin builders, that's what we are, Belinda.'

"He hit a bull's-eye there," said Stuart, and with an engaging grin, which always made him look much younger, added, "At least I'm dead sure there's a place for Dad's Barometer. We need statistical measurement of unbiased, informed observation that clarifies our understanding of contentious issues the world over. We have to understand the reality of other cultures and find common ground from which to deal with recurrent, underlying problems. As you say, Belinda, peace can't be 'enforced', it can only grow from a willingness to go slow, build up trust and not expect instant solutions. Deadlines are false. They're a threat, which is violence." He laughed and said, "You've got me going, Belinda, reminds me I've got work to do when I get back."

'Back' meant Beirut. It was hard on Stuart to be in Europe, so much closer to America yet with no chance of seeing his family until the war's end. At least he had a 'back' to return to, enviably rooted in family and Dad's Barometer and worthwhile work at the university. The only cloud on this future was that much had gone wrong in Lebanon since we left. The trouble erupted the previous August, following the election of a new government.

Stuart had kept in touch with friends in Beirut, including the university president, Bayard Dodge, and his wife. Their letters had brought intermittent, up-to-date news about the government in Beirut, formed after Syria and Lebanon were declared independent of the hated French mandate. As expected the Lebanese government voted in a radical constitution. The first hint of trouble came when Stuart heard that legislation had been passed to end French influence in Lebanon for good. Stuart commented, "Let's hope the French accept the changes - de Gaulle won't like them."

Then came a letter telling of the draconian response from the unpopular M. Helleu, the Free French representative in Lebanon. "I can't believe it!" Stuart exclaimed. "Helleu arrested all but two of the elected ministers and shut them up in an old mountain fortress. To compound the insult the arrests were made by the detested Senegalese troops. Worse still, around midnight a French officer led a contingent of Senegalese straight to the President's house and, getting no answer, they broke down the door and rampaged through the ground floors in search of the President. As they couldn't find him they burst into the bedroom of his young daughter - only thirteen, poor child! Apparently the officer ripped the mosquito net off her bed, demanded to know where her father was, and when her brother intervened, he was abused and manhandled." Stuart was deeply shocked. "Have the French gone mad?"

At least the Lebanese had not been cowed. There was no reason to doubt the next letter which came from Mrs. Dodge, who had worked with Lady Spears to forge friendships with a number of women amongst pro-nationalist Lebanese families. Her letter recounted how a small, stalwart band of these women set off to seek support against the French action. They went first to the British Legation and then to every other diplomatic representative in Beirut - American, Egyptian, Turkish, Iraqi, even the Grand Mufti himself.

Stuart said, his eyes sparkling, "As the women walked towards the city centre other people fell in with them until a huge, motley crowd of Maronites and Muslims, Catholics and Presbyterians, gathered in the *Place des Canons*. Marvellous! Apparently the French had tanks out and rumour has it that some people were run down. Thank God the French troops wouldn't fire on the crowds and the local *gendarmes* refused to turn their hoses on them. But nearly a hundred people are reported killed or wounded. It's outrageous."

"What about Spears? What did he do?"

"He stood up for them, as you would expect - he's a good man, Belinda! - and insisted that the ministers and President must be reinstated. Even so, it took ten days before they were released and the government back in place. Of course they promptly voted in the new constitution and the French had to swallow their pride. Extraordinary how they've misunderstood the Arab mood all along."

Hubert said, "The French tend to be a touchy lot at the best of times, and this is the worst of times for them, with de Gaulle the touchiest of them all."

"I wish we'd been there," I exclaimed.

"Sure thing, Belinda," Stuart said. "We've missed out on a bit of history."

We couldn't kid ourselves we were making history in Palermo, and even though we spent six months there, it remained curiously unreal. The work was real enough and fairly concentrated labour, keeping us confined to the unlikely scarlet leather furnishings and over-large black-and-white tiles of the apartment - a set for some flashy drama of passion and murder. Occasionally I broke out and went dancing with American officers, but Americans generally remained foreign, more so even than Arabs or Greeks or Hungarians who spoke another language. Americans spoke English, but I kept having to do a double take on their language - and attitudes.

After one of the dances I grumbled to Stuart that Americans seemed obsessed with being liked.

Stuart asked mildly, "On what do you base that sweeping generalization, Belinda?"

"Well, take yesterday's dance. The last partner I had was fairly drunk, and without preliminaries he suddenly mumbled, 'Let's get outa here, sweetie. I got the hots for ya!'" I ignored Stuart's brief frown and went on, "I said 'no' quite politely after a quick translation of 'the hots', but as we went on shuffling round the dance floor he laid his head on my shoulder and rather weepily said, 'Don't you *like* me?' Really, Stuart, what a baby! I'd never met him before and didn't want to go to bed with him. Was that too difficult for him?"

Stuart said, gently mocking, "Your premise is unsound, Belinda. You are young and attractive, and regrettably your partner was drunk and assumed you were fair game. But I agree, we do tend to be overly concerned about other people's opinions. Not like you British!"

"All right, I'm being over-critical. But this is what happened on the way back from the dance. I shared a taxi with a couple of officers I'd met for the first time that evening. There was no moon and about midnight we came to a quiet square with a statue in the middle. The taxi slowed down to circuit the statue when right away there was a crackle of rifle fire. Instantly the two officers slid to the floor and hunkered down, hands covering their heads. I was curious about what was going on and stayed on the seat as the taxi roared away with a screech of tires and another burst of gunfire. The officers got up off the floor, and after swearing about god-damn Palermo thugs they ticked me off for being crazy, sitting up on the seat like an Aunt Sally."

Stuart laughed, but I said crossly, "They were very ungentlemanly. For all they knew I was paralysed with terror. They could at least have pulled me down with them. Wouldn't you have?"

"My dear Belinda, they've probably been under fire when it's each man for himself, and assumed you'd have the sense to do the same. Who fired at you?"

"Who knows? Bandits, perhaps? We didn't stay to find out."

Later we heard it had been a bunch of over-eager *carabinieri*. The local police had been tipped off about a midnight Mafia assignation at the statue to collect misbegotten loot or liras, and we just happened to arrive at exactly the expected moment. Luckily the *carabinieri* aimed at our tires and were rotten shots. It was interesting to be shot at, but as far as local colour went I preferred hearing men at work lustily singing scraps of Mozart and Rossini. The music sprang from joy, a blessed antidote to the hatreds of warfare.

As the time of leaving Palermo came nearer I made efforts to look hopefully at the future, tried to think seriously of life with Sandy and keep David in his safely married place - a dear friend, just that. Sometimes I went to the outskirts of the city for a dose of serenity in the 12th century cathedral at Monreale. Greek craftsmen had been brought from Constantinople to fill the interior with wonderful mosaics. In the domed apse above the altar a huge head and shoulders of Christ Pantocrator stared down from a sky of gleaming gold. The face was strong and compassionate, the large eyes dark and thoughtful (a very Greek face). In one hand he held an open book, the other was gracefully uplifted, the two first fingers bent to join the thumb, the other two raised towards the heavens. The gesture reminded me of the whirling Dervishes, one hand upraised, the other pointing down to earthbound souls in need of grace. In their different ways the Dervishes and Christ Pantocrator sought connection - cosmic, divine, no matter what. How foolish it was to fight about the differences.

In the peace of Monreale I thought of Paliaigos where I'd shouted at God that I was not going to die until I knew whether or not he existed. That was nearly three years ago. Well, here I was, not a bit dead. Should I grovel, convinced and grateful for life? Certainly not. If God was Person who had chosen to give me the power to think, it would be daft if he didn't want me to use it. So it was up to me to answer conundrums like why war should kill one person and not some other one. Alternatively, if there was no God and no divine justice then life and death happened and were part of the mystery. Sometimes - maybe often - they happened because of yourself; sometimes the happenings were beyond control, like earthquakes. With or without God life went on, because life was so strong and amazing and whatever happens we have only one life, a sort of journey, and you can't just pack it in because the things that happen seem to break your heart. 'I'm part of all life,' I concluded, 'and whatever the wrong turns it's possible to find your way back to life - unless you're dead.'

Christ Pantocrator gazed down at me with great kindness. It was soothing to sit quietly ruminating in the cathedral.

In April our unit disbanded. Hubert was flying to Cairo and as we parted I thought how much I liked him and was a little sad to know this was another wartime hail-and-farewell connection.

Stuart and I flew together to Rabat in Morocco, and were stuck there for several days. Faced with delay Stuart insisted on hiring bicycles. "We can explore and keep fit at the same time," he said. We did both, some of it painfully, for though bicycle tires were in short supply, the Moroccans ingeniously strung rubber washers on a length of thick wire which they twisted as tightly as possible round the wheel frames. It looked deceptively all right, but as the wheels turned the washers were individually slightly displaced, and we progressed in a series of thumps - *ker-plunk! ker-plunk!* Every bone in our bodies ached, but we laughed a lot, and for a short while the problematic future took care of itself.

We said goodbye on the Rabat airfield and Stuart stood waving until he was only a speck below. As the aircraft soared into the blue sky I murmured to his vanished figure, 'It's been a privilege to know you.' And that was, quite simply, true.

The aircraft landed before dawn somewhere in the West of England. It was early May, and perishing cold. I'd forgotten how England's chill zapped straight into the bones, and that wasn't the only thing I'd forgotten. As the train rumbled along in the half-light of a misty morning I was confused by the total absence of conversation in our carriage, even eye contact seeming to be deliberately avoided. Was England always like this?

No answer came so I stared sleepily out at very green fields neatly packaged by hedges, no sign of life at this time of the morning. I dozed, woke, dozed again - and on next waking stared out of the window in disbelief. In a field, under a clump of trees, stood three huge statues of shire horses. They were amazingly lifelike, magnificent creatures, their rumps well-fleshed and muscular, manes and tail silky-thick, the generous fetlock fringe making their great hooves look like rather classy boots. I peered through the window, astonished at the extent of British devotion to horseflesh. But why erect these statues in a lonely field? I had to know, and was about to ask, 'Who did these sculptures?' when one of the statues shifted a massive hoof.

Biting my lip to stifle a giggle, I thought ruefully, 'I'm out of touch,' and covertly reassessed my fellow-travellers who would never starve their livestock. We sat facing one another on the familiar bench seats (probably stuffed with horsehair), luggage racks overhead, and below them were screwed faded black-and-white photographs in wood frames. One showed a sunless sky and a stretch of beach peopled with adults in very pre-war clothing, the solemn children holding buckets and spades. In another photograph sheep gazed moodily from a bleak moorland landscape. The overall effect was grey and more like a warning than an invitation. My silent companions seemed no less grey and with a touch of nostalgia I remembered the Arab travellers and their cries of 'What is your destination? You are alone? Aiee! And your husband?...Ah!...No children yet?...but soon soon you will be blessed!' And etcetera, etcetera.

After a while it occurred to me that the silence was my fault, and I might possibly have given offence. Perhaps my shirt was indelicately unbuttoned? Maybe I was showing too much leg? I pulled my skirt lower and ran a hand down the shirt buttons. All were closed. Then I had the gumption to suspect that everyone was probably just tired out by the war. Poor things. Anyway, didn't the English like to keep themselves to themselves? Whew! England was going to take quite a lot of getting used to.

Gradually daylight spread and, as sometimes happens on a railway journey, I seemed to have lived in the train for years. Meanwhile the sounds and smells and a myriad details belonging to Budapest and Athens, Cairo, Beirut, even unreal Palermo, withdrew into a very private part of me. The withdrawal left a sort of loneliness, as if that part of me was - might always be? - elsewhere.

At a level crossing the whistle blew, at a station the engine slowed and stopped, huffing and puffing clouds of steam. People, with their newspapers, left the compartment, bestowing no farewells. Other travellers took their seats, opened their newspapers, and did not speak - a dreamlike sequence. At least my cottage was no dream, and I dearly hoped the tenants would leave soon, and the evacuees in the garden studio would go back to London. After all, London wasn't being bombed - or was it?

❦ 39 ❧

Sandy and London. David.
D-Day, Doodle-bugs, and Dartmoor.

There weren't any bombs falling on London in late April of 1944, which was all for the best; but there were times when bombs would have been something definite to deal with. Sandy and I were, indefinably, not quite definite. Sandy's divorce was in process, and I was a wife-in-waiting, feeling rather like a fish just landed in a weird element, even though I had agreed to be landed, and Sandy was a gentle fisherman.

Work would have been firm ground. I told Sandy I was used to earning my living, said there was a war and it seemed wrong to be idle, adding vaguely that I felt rather like a ghost returned to old haunts.

"Darling Belinda," he said, "you've come back here to be my wife. You need a rest, and there must be many people you want to see again. Your mother will be coming soon, and there are your relatives and friends. Take your time, find your feet in England, feel at home."

So I, who was now both Belinda and Thelma, tried to feel at home. Sandy had furnished a flat in a part of London outwardly untouched by war. The furniture was his own, nice furniture, the kind that's been around for generations, reminding me of Copford Rectory and the England I'd nostalgically mused about in Palermo. Well, here I was, not sure what to make of it all, and even dithering whether to write to David. But I had to, if only to verify him, make sure he wasn't just a figment of my imagination. I'd know at once: maybe then I'd stop feeling like a landed fish, or a ghost.

So I wrote to David, told him I was engaged to Sandy, and hoped we could meet. I had no idea where he was, couldn't even be sure he was in England, and prepared to wait.

So began a restless waiting period, with a bright point at the end of July when my cottage would be free of tenants. Before long my mother was coming to London, bringing my two young stepsisters so they could all meet Sandy, and meantime I wrote to friends who might be in England, but could be anywhere. It was the same with relatives; I wasn't sure where my cousin Elizabeth was, and wrote to her mother for direction. Phil Ruck Keene was still in Beirut, but my aunt Dick was in London. We had lunch together and she made me laugh about a visit she and Phil had made to see my youngest uncle Hugh, when he was still a postulant in a Benedictine monastery.

Dick said, "Phil and I were taken on a tour of the monastery grounds by a dear little fat monk, who suddenly embraced me warmly behind a bush." She laughed, and said, "He was very sweet and meant no harm. But Hugh has been asked to leave because he's too contentious, asking questions which upset the monks." There were few laughs about my poor aunt Dorothy, still confined to her 'home'. "But," said Dick, "she sometimes escapes for wild spending binges. It's a bit trying as we have to return the purchases, and explain." At least Abbie was happy in her cottage the family had bought for her at Copford Green, and Emma came every day on her bicycle for a chat. I remembered the big tree on the Green and the encircling bench where old men had sat, and pulled forelocks when my grandmother, Birdie, stopped to pass the time of day. Now there was no Birdie, and no family centre. So much for Copford Rectory nostalgia.

The Garsia relatives were, as usual, thin on the ground. My uncle Marston was out of London, but Willoughby and Yedra were still in their little South Kensington house. It was a touch shabby outside, but unscathed by bombs, and I soon learnt that Willoughby was making a quiet name for himself as a chiropractor, particularly after discovering a way of treating what was then called a 'slipped disc'.

"It was all because of me," Yedra said. "I fell down some steps in the blackout, and was in agony. The doctors said I might never walk again."

Willoughby said, "I called in a couple of doctors. One wanted to put Yedra in traction, and the other proposed a plaster cast." After a familiar, quiet chuckle, he went on, "I was not impressed, and went off to browse through the second hand medical books in the Charing Cross Road. One of them simply fell open at a page which had exactly the information I needed."

After a pause he said, "I went to Regent's Park and sat for a while, thinking carefully what I must do. Back home I prepared Yedra for her daily massage, and when she was quite relaxed I gave her a swift, firm adjustment."

"I let out a yelp," Yedra exclaimed. "But next morning I was on my feet, sore, but walking."

"What about the doctors?" I asked.

Willoughby smiled and said, "I rather hoped they might be interested in what I'd done. But what they said was, 'That was a lucky fluke, my dear fellow.'"

We laughed, and I thought there was no-one like my uncle. With Yedra around I had no chance to talk alone with Willoughby, but when he came outside to see me off he said gently, "Did I ever tell you that when I am in difficulties, I rest in the arms of the universe?"

"Yes, you did," I said, "but I don't think I've got the knack. At the moment the inside of my head feels a bit like a railway station - a lot of running about trying to find the right platform, and nobody to ask."

Willoughby said, "Try sitting and thinking of nothing. It takes a bit of practice, but it's worth it. The universe is busy, but orderly." I loved Willoughby for being the same as ever, but this advice was no help. I needed someone to talk to, though wasn't even sure what I wanted to talk about. The need to talk was stronger after Sandy took me to meet his mother.

Mrs. Mitchell-Innes was indeed a darling. Sandy left us alone for a while, and we soon got on to books, and Thackeray. I told her Dick Usborne's story about his friend, Khouri, who confused him with George Osborne in *Vanity Fair*, which led to Thackeray's marvellous description of George Osborne's death. At this, Sandy's mother memorably said, "I knew an old lady who knew Thackeray, and he confessed that it had taken a week before he was satisfied with those few sentences."

I exclaimed, "Your saying that makes me feel that, just a moment ago, Thackeray walked out of this room."

Before we parted she gave me a pair of little Victorian gold earrings, studded with tiny pearls and turquoise, and taking my hand said, "You have a great capacity for happiness, Belinda." Our eyes met and I knew that Sandy was precious to her, and she hoped I would give him what he needed: but we said nothing.

Shortly after this visit I heard from Elizabeth. She was in London, working at the War Office. This was close to St. James' Park, so we arranged to have a picnic lunch there the following day. I thought, 'Liz is someone I can talk to.'

As soon as I saw her I cried, truthfully, "You look blooming!" and laughing, she told me she was engaged. Of course I had to hear all about him, that he was a Canadian in the British navy, that his name was George Whalley, that he was brilliant and handsome.

"He writes really good poetry," she said, "plays the piano beautifully, and paints lovely water-colours." I said he must be a paragon, and with a laugh she retorted, "You're not going to meet him until our wedding day!"

I surprised us both by exclaiming, "Good heavens, Liz, am I such a man-eater?" Then, vexed to have let on I was hurt, I said quickly, "Tell me more about him," and she needed no prompting.

When we'd talked our fill I asked, "Tell me about the blitz. You were here all the time, weren't you? It must have been terrifying."

"Actually I got so tired I just slept through the raids," she said. "They came night after night and I couldn't stand the shelters. Then one morning I was woken by a man shouting, "Blimey, there's a girl 'ere!" He was staring into the bedroom and my window hadn't any glass in it. He said, 'Sorry, miss, you give me quite a turn. You can't stay 'ere. Building's not safe. Better get going.' So I got going. Luckily there was a vacancy in the Chelsea house I'm in now. That's where I met George."

"Tell me what the raids were like."

"Well...they were terrifying, but everybody was in it together, people being helpful and kind and cheerful - British grit and all that. Lots of jokes, of course, and the barriers down."

I said yes, it had been like that on Kimolos. We talked about barriers, amongst other things, but even with Liz, who was almost as good as a sister, there was a gulf. For four years she'd carried on and on in London, making do or doing without. It must often have been boring, as well as frightening - but, as she said, there was sharing, and the barriers down. My four years were rarely boring, and though there was sharing, it happened in intermittent bursts with different people under changing circumstances. In four years we had lived two distinct lives.

This separateness kept turning up. I met old friends and exchanged stories, but I was sure we didn't hear half of what either of us was saying. After telling friends about escaping from Crete with Alexis and Captain Hook, one of them remarked, "Well, Thelma, either you are very brave or have no imagination." What the devil did she mean? I had no idea, didn't ask, and decided that she was, after all, very British - which left me wondering whether I would ever be truly British.

Partly because I had time on my hands with so much waiting to do, I began picking my way around London, looking for landmarks in streets transformed by ruins. I was truly shocked by the ruins, and kept hearing David murmuring 'Ruin builders, that's what we are, Belinda.' To that I would silently answer, 'I know, I know! But what can be done about it?'

Meantime the ruins were a queer landscape in their own right. Sometimes a row of houses would have a neat gap, as if excised by a surgeon's knife. Then there were the big, empty spaces strewn with tumbled building blocks and rubble, mixed with homely paraphernalia, and sometimes a kitchen sink, or complete toilet, would hang, like an art exhibit, on an exposed wall. I'd stare, trying to remember what had been in these spaces before they became ruins, and was touched that already green shoots sprouted from the desolation.

"Be a nice show of willowherb come the summer," a passer-by remarked pleasantly.

Smells could give me a jolt. As I stood at the top of the stairs leading into Green Park underground, a familiar wave of warm air, redolent of dust and bodies and train oil, rose up like a greeting. I almost cried aloud 'Hallo London! so you're still here!' Taste had the same effect. Baked beans on toast in a Lyons Corner House whisked me back to days on a lean Foreign Office salary. In a railway cafeteria I bought a rock cake, rockier than ever when made with dried egg powder, as if announcing, "We are England, firm as a rock!" I couldn't swallow mine, and wrapping it discreetly in my handkerchief, consigned it to a waste bin.

In contrast St. Paul's Cathedral, apparently unharmed, sailed magnificently on a sea of rubble. It was almost jaunty, and I laughed, remembering a quirky Clerihew:

> Sir Christopher Wren
> Went to dine with some men.
> He said, "If anyone calls,
> Say I'm designing St. Paul's."

'Good for you, old boy!' I thought, and scoured other city streets for more Wren churches. Two were badly damaged and one demolished, but others remained, serene and lovely. Then I made my way to the courtyard in the Temple where, on a foggy night so long ago, John and I stood together under lamplight. Then the trees had been bare; now they were covered with the fresh green of spring. It was very quiet, just as it was when I was green, and stood in the centre of the universe.

Some days I sought out the perennial icons of London, beginning with the Houses of Parliament and Big Ben. They were solidly present and correct; so was Buckingham Palace and Pall Mall. At the Cenotaph I paused to connect with the dead of World War I, but instead of pain there was outrage. 'What can I do about it?' I asked David. As no answer came, I left the nameless dead to keep asking the question.

Other days I tracked around the hotel icons and found Claridges and the Dorchester still intact, but the friendly, elegant old Berkeley Hotel was simply a hole in the ground. The Berkeley was where John and I first dined and danced together: it was where Peter Harmsworth threw a birthday party for me when I was seventeen, and I was shocked by the wad of notes he brought out to pay the bill - naturally, for I was earning fifteen shillings a week at Liberty's then. So many ghosts!

At least Hyde Park and the Round Pond were in place, and Peter Pan still played his pipes in a quiet corner of Kensington Gardens. The parks were green and pleasant, but seemed surprisingly spacious until - why, of course! the iron railings had vanished. In older wars scrap iron was used to make canon-balls. Maybe the railings were melted into some part of whatever British pilots dropped on Germany in tit-for-tat ruin-building raids. In Regents Park I tried to locate the lovely Georgian house where Arthur's parents had lived, and failing, struck off down Portland Place for a visit to the Queen's Hall. But it was only another empty space. I'd been at the last promenade concert in that space, must have been the fall of 1939. As usual we sang *Land of Hope and Glory* at the end, but the tears which ran unchecked down many cheeks were not usual. Queen's Hall had been special, just the right size, wonderful acoustics, the audience a gathering of companions. I'd never felt the same about big old Albert Hall. I found it untouched, and so was German Albert's statue across the road. He stood in grave contemplation under his gothic stone canopy, Queen Victoria's anguished memorial to her darling. What would Albert have thought about being bombed by the *Luftwaffe?* Definitely not amused. How utterly ridiculous war was.

Rationing, however, was not ridiculous. I'd lived for four years in countries without rationing, and Sandy seemed able to pull extra food and clothing coupons out of a hat. So I didn't come to grips with rationing until I sat down with friends who welcomed me with a basic English tea - bread, butter, jam, and a cake. I chattered away, buttering my first slice of bread liberally, but as I reached for the jam something made me look up, and there were four pairs of eyes (two adult pairs, two young ones) staring at my plate. I pulled my hand back as if the pot was a live coal, and cried, "Why didn't you stop me? Is this your week's ration?" Of course it was, and the youngest child said solemnly, "The cake's got two real eggs in." Everyone was nice and understanding, but I was ashamed of myself.

Unfortunately I was also a terrible cook. I'd never learnt to cook, and throughout my marriage and the war, I'd had servants. However, I now made an effort to produce some simple meals to please Sandy, but when I burnt to a cinder a rare gift of mushrooms I had to confess that I'd never cooked, even when I was working in London before the war.

"What did you eat?" Sandy asked.

"Lord knows. Boiled eggs, toast, cheese, jam and tea, Campbell's baked beans, fruit when it was cheap, buns. I went out a lot." So for the few weeks I was in London, Sandy and I also went out a lot.

But I was very glad of Sandy's extra food coupons when my mother came with Felicity and Joy. I was nervous of this visit. I'd never felt part of my mother's new family, but Sandy's food coupons made it possible to produce a lavish tea for them. I was touched when both the two girls rushed at me with open arms, heroine-worshipping the long-lost older sister from far away. I hugged them awkwardly, hoping the treats would make them feel welcome, and was truly glad to see my mother. Sandy stayed briefly and was himself, kind and hospitable, but I knew my mother was disappointed.

"You look tired, darling," she said before they left. "Do come and stay with us when you can get away. We've got lots to talk about." Indeed yes, and maybe we could talk together. I said I would come soon, but after they left I felt tight as a drum, and knew that nothing was going to be right until I saw David.

All through May the restless waiting days continued, and I began to feel a fierce longing for the end of July when I could take possession of my cottage. I shut my eyes and saw the Cox's Orange Pippins neatly racked upstairs in the studio, smelt their sweet, clean smell wafting down to the big room as I played the Blüthner, the glass doors open to the orchard and valley beyond. Poor Blüthner! now only ash, blackened ivory keys, and a tangle of wire amongst the ruins of a city warehouse.

Thoughts of the cottage provoked an even greater longing for the countryside. Budapest, Athens, Cairo, Beirut, Palermo - a four-year feast of cities: but now I wanted country quiet, the space of sky, the smells of earth and dung, and hedgerows. I remembered Phil, gazing at the view from my terrace in Beirut, saying fiercely, "I hate this bloody war. All I want is a workshop full of tools." And the workshop was tucked beside his thatched cottage on Dartmoor, backed by wild moorland, and overlooking a valley where the Swincombe River chattered over rocks. The river formed deep pools, and Phil loved tramping across the moors to where a trout might be hooked for supper. The silence of Dartmoor was full of underlying moorland sounds - lambs bleating, wild ponies making those huffing noises peculiar to horses, the ripple of running water, light winds soughing through clumps of trees, and larks, catapulting into the sky, trilling paeans of praise above the heather and bracken and the huge stones, called tors, standing like relics of ancient monuments.

That was when I knew it was Dartmoor where I absolutely should be - should, not just wanted to be. Phil's cottage was let, but not far off was Brimpts Farm, and the Mudges might still let rooms. Being wartime they probably would not serve breakfast porridge with thick Devon cream, but they might have a room.

I asked Sandy if he'd mind my going away for a week or two and Sandy, always kind, said, "Of course, Belinda, it would do you good, get some colour in your cheeks. Too many years in the Middle East has run you down."

So I wrote to the Mudges, and yes, they did have a room. Their reply came the day David telephoned, and two days later he came to see me.

There are certain facts I remember about our meeting. The first, was simple: David was not a figment of my imagination. The second was the inscription on the book he brought:

For Sandie and Belinda
from
David
May 1944

'Sandie and Belinda,' another fact, alongside the first.

I read the title, *Monkey*, and seeing that it was translated from the Chinese by Arthur Waley, smiled and said, "I remember we both like Arthur Waley. But who is Monkey? I love the cover."

David said, "Duncan Grant did the cover; he's good, isn't he? Waley's translation is excellent, and he catches the legendary magic of the story. Monkey's a typical mythological character, mischievous and wise, and the story's a mix of folklore, Buddhism and poetry. I know you'll love it, Belinda - and Sandie too, of course."

Of course.

The third fact was not simple. I asked David about his wife, and he said quietly, "She's been writing a lot. She's very good and wants to be free, be on her own so she can write." He paused. I said nothing. He added, "We've known each other most our lives, more like brother and sister really." I still said nothing, unable to ask, "Are you still together?"

So we caught up on what we had done since we last met, but underneath everything we said ran what was not said, like a river that, for me, was dammed by 'For Sandie and Belinda' which could have been another couple, but wasn't.

I asked David where his regiment was, and quickly added, "That was a silly question. Of course you can't tell me."

"It's not silly, Belinda, and I can't tell you though wish I could, only that it's tremendously important."

"Of course."

It seemed no more than the blink of an eye before David looked at his watch and said, "I've got to get back. We're on a short lead just now." As we stood up he smiled and said, "I mustered surprising powers of persuasion for a few hours off to see you."

Even then I said nothing, we walked together down the passage to the front door and, pausing there, David looked straight at me, his eyes unguarded. Neither of us spoke. He seemed to be imprinting the whole of me into his being, and I was pierced and stamped by that look and a longing and tenderness that, whatever the future, could not be gainsaid. Then he walked down the front steps to the street, turned, raised his hand in a little formal salute of farewell, and went away.

Five days later, on June 6, 1944 to be exact, the Allied armies launched their invasion of Europe from the south of England. This was D-Day, David's 'tremendously important' destination. Meanwhile there was already in the mail a letter I'd written to David in which I'd cast aside all the prescribed virtues, those invisible spider's webs which can tie up lions.

I remember only the gist of this letter, which was that I loved him, and believed he loved me. I don't know what I said about Sandy, but I told David I'd loved him ever since we first met, and one day I hoped to explain why his marriage was such a stumbling block. At the end I gave him my address on Dartmoor.

I didn't leave at once for Dartmoor. Before David came, I'd promised to spend a weekend with old friends in a village outside London. This is why, a week after D-Day - June 13 - I was in the flat in London when a small aircraft droned overhead. It flew slowly and steadily, as if having a look round, which was a little spooky. As there was no anti-aircraft fire it presumably was one of ours. But what was it up to? Then the engine cut out. Was it going to crash? For a moment nothing happened, and then there was a violent detonation somewhere ahead.

I ran outside and found people in the street looking up and asking questions. There was a general agreement that it was Hitler's 'secret weapon', launched from pads on the coast of France. Sandy confirmed this more specifically: it was a robot missile and the launch pads had been known about for some time and steadily bombed. On the radio an official called the robot a V-1. The newspapers referred to them as 'flying bombs', but soon they were dubbed 'doodle-bugs' - trust the British to come up with an ironic put-down of something powerfully frightening.

The doodle-bugs kept coming. Their leisurely drone was unmistakable. Everyone's reaction was to be still, hoping the engine wouldn't cut out overhead. When it flew on to drop its deadly eggs elsewhere, thankfulness was unashamed. The blast was mainly on the surface, slicing buildings off at base and zipping round corners. Despite their nickname the doodle-bugs were altogether sinister, masquerading as an airplane, ghost-driven. They bugged the Londoners who had stuck out the blitz, and now here were these damn-fool robots - enough was enough.

I felt a bit guilty about leaving for Dartmoor, as if I was running away, but Sandy said, "Of course you're not. Get your weekend visit over, and be off with you."

So I made my visit, and enjoyed it. The weather was lovely, and I took the opportunity to wash some clothes and hung them out to dry. "They'll smell of country air," I said, "and they'll be dry in the morning." I meant to be back in London before lunch, but the clothes were still damp, and I was easily persuaded to catch a later train.

In London I took a taxi to the flat, and stepping out on broken glass I saw the front door hanging drunkenly on one hinge, and all the windows blown out. In the flat, glass and plaster was everywhere. I telephoned Sandy, and as I was wondering what to do first, a neighbour came to see if help was needed.

"What time did this happen?" I asked, and when she told me I cried, "Well, I'll be damned. If I'd caught the early train I could well have been unlocking the front door just exactly then."

"A lucky coincidence, dear," she said, and told me about a coincidence of her own.

She and her husband had lived in a Victorian row house, and a shelter was set up in the basement of one of the houses, with connecting doors to all the others. "I hated the shelter," she said. "It was smelly and we never used it. But one night, after the air raid sirens wailed, my husband insisted on going down there to the shelter. I was brushing my hair, getting ready for bed, and said. 'Stuff and nonsense. Whatever's come over you?' But he wouldn't take no, kept saying 'Hurry, hurry!' So down we went."

They'd just dusted off the shelter benches and made themselves comfortable when a deafening explosion brought down showers of plaster and bits of ceiling, but the shelter held firm. When the all-clear sounded they found the passage to their flat was blocked, so they went through the neighbour's flat to the street.

"Our house wasn't there," she said. "The other houses were all right, but ours was gone." She shook her head. "Don't you wonder why some die and others live? Doesn't seem any reason to it."

"No," I said, "there doesn't. It just happens."

I helped Sandy clean up the flat, but we couldn't live in it without immediate repairs, so he arranged for the windows and door to be boarded up, and by good fortune his advertising firm offered storage above their offices in Berkeley Square. Sandy fixed up a room at his club, and after an uneasy night amongst the debris in the flat, he saw me off on the train to Devon.

"Stay as long as you like," he said. "Wait till things settle down, and in another month your cottage will be free. I'll keep you posted."

❦ 40 ❧

David.

Brimpts, the Dartmoor farm, had only one other guest, an eccentric lady who - like the Bey in Cairo - was an ardent crystal gazer. We ate our meals together, but otherwise I saw little of her, and settled into a writing routine. I'd decided to record some of the stories of the last four years, and wrote diligently every morning. After lunch I walked for miles, came back to read, sleep - and wait to hear from David.

During meals the crystal gazer told me stories about what she had seen after this or that person held the little, gleaming sphere of solid glass. "Once I saw a Roman centurion," she said triumphantly. "He was standing by one of the tors - as you know, there were Romans here. Wasn't that wonderful! I saw him clear as anything, looking out across the moors, his helmet and garments just like the drawings in my history book!"

"How amazing!" I said, not believing a word.

Inevitably she asked me shyly, "Would you mind...it wouldn't take up much time...you just have to hold the ball quietly..."

She was painfully eager, her pale eyes anxious, her thin faded hair escaping from a nest of long, old-fashioned hairpins. Poor old thing, I couldn't refuse her, and said I'd be glad to hold it, adding lightly that she mustn't be disappointed if she saw nothing.

The weather was beautiful, and we sat outside in the sunshine, a faint breeze moving gently through the trees. I wondered idly whether anything was ever truly seen in a crystal ball and, as I took it in my hands, was surprised how cold it was. For some time my companion gazed into its cloudy surface until, after taking it from me, she murmured, "Yes...oh yes, there is someone. Not quite clear yet...getting better..." After a pause she breathed, "Ah, there he is," and more sharply, "He's in bed." She peered intently, muttering, "A young man I think, but his head...his head is bandaged. I can't see his face very well." Another pause, and then she looked up and quite firmly said, "He is very ill." I didn't speak and she asked tentatively, "Perhaps...a relative?...a friend?"

As from a distance I heard myself replying that it was hard to say, one didn't always know where people were. "Wartime secrecy," I said. "You know how it is." I told myself that young men with bandaged heads were likely to be two a penny just now.

No other session was proposed and the crystal gazer left Brimpts a day or two later. I kept busy writing my stories, explored new walks, and every night, before going to bed, stood alone outside and listened to the incomparable silence. Then I read, slept, and the morning was another day of waiting for a letter from David.

A letter did come. In the envelope was my letter to David, and also a brief, formal handwritten note:

> *I regret to inform you that Major David Barrow died of head wounds received during the invasion of Europe.*

It seemed important to decipher the signature, but it was just a squiggle. Then, slowly, I read the message again.

In the following days I tramped through the heather and bracken, sat by rippling streams to watch the water dimple in the sun, listened to the bleating lambs, to the wild ponies whisking their tails, and marvelled as the larks breasted the heavens to sing for joy. Life and purpose was everywhere, but David wasn't here at all, not at all.

One particular anguish was not knowing whether he had held my letter in his hand. Maybe it came too late, and a stranger opened it to check the return address. I'd never know, and it didn't really matter, now that David was elsewhere, the other side of time.

After a while I spared a thought for David's father ("dear old boy, how shocked he would be to know what I feel about war"). Gently he merged with Birdie and Ted, mourning for my father and for Ben and young nephew Ralph - and my mother. So many tears. Did David's father believe his son's death was 'glorious'? Did Birdie and Ted ever doubt that God snatched the best and bravest to be with him (Him?) in heaven? Did it help my mother to have me?

Perhaps no ends were absolute, each end leaving something for a beginning. David had given me love, and the sound of his voice saying, "Things must, absolutely must change after the war." Also, "I want to be there. It's going to be exciting." Also, "Killing each other just makes for more anger, more misery." Also that triumphant, "Ruin builders, that's what we are, Belinda!" And always, "I want to be there."

I cried aloud to wherever David was, "I can't see my way without you, not at all. We had so little time, and I have so much to learn. Did you know what you were going to do after the war?" No answer came from that intangible presence somewhere beyond time.

But there were tangibles. Dear Kassab had been very tangible. If only I could have kept him - but that hurt, and I turned to unfeeling tangibles, listing them slowly. There was the antique copper coffee pot David bought in the soukh at Damascus; the big red and black saddle bag, the tassels a bit scrappy, but woven to last a lifetime; and a heavy leather trunk strap (what had that been for?), its massive metal buckle also contrived for a life span. There was that last gift, *Monkey*, chosen for me despite the inscription, and best of all his oil painting of my basket boy from the Beirut market. But the memory twisted my heart; that was the time I denied us both the mercy of lying in each others arms. How could I have been so prissy, so tied up in misbegotten precepts? I saw David as he had been the day he arrived from Tobruk, heard myself ask, 'You'll stay here?' and himself, teasing, 'I would like that,' and myself saying, 'Of course,' with that slight involuntary shake of my head, and David's gentle, "This is where I want to be."

That night I wrote a memoriam for David's painting:

Portrait of my basket boy, painted in Beirut in 1942 by David de Symons Barrow, my dearest friend, who died in France of head wounds received on D-day, June 1944.

There was a small fire in my room, and in it I burned the letter I had written to him: it was his alone. Then I went outside.

Under the blazing stars I leant against a great tree, solid as a monument. The bark was rough against the palms of my hands, and slowly I gave myself over to the breathing universe, and a silence that was almost a song.

At last I said aloud, "All right, here I am," and walked through darkness to the farm. I felt quite light, almost carefree - except it was more like feeling-free. This would have to do for the moment.

∾∾

PART THREE

Everything is difficult,
but everything is possible.

Persian proverb

1944 – 1966

England – and to Canada

41

The end of World War Two.
Marriage. And Alexis tells his story.

In August I gained possession of my cottage and thankfully lost myself in making it habitable. Ivy came from the village to help sweep and scrub the studio, which was a bit smelly after housing the evacuees from London throughout the war. We left the double glass doors open for days on end, and when the fall harvest of Cox's Orange Pippins was stored in the racks upstairs, their scent would drift down and fill the studio.

The cleaning done, I bought a piano, and for company adopted Jess, a black-and-white border collie. We went for long walks together, though I tired easily, and Sandy insisted on my being tested for any lingering Middle Eastern bug. There weren't any bugs, but the doctor said country air was the best way to get back my strength - get it back, as though my strength had gone off on its own and needed coaxing. So I settled thankfully at the cottage with Jess.

Sandy was still working at the Ministry of Information in London, and we made a flat for him above the offices of his advertising firm in Berkeley Square. This was where he had stored his furniture after the doodle-bug trashed our flat in Kensington, and when he was offered the use of the whole floor as a flat, he at once accepted. That was when I knew he was going to stick with advertising. The casual remark he made in Palermo about entering politics had never been repeated, and probably hadn't been serious. So we made the Berkeley Square flat comfortable, and Sandy lived there during the week, coming to the cottage on weekends: sometimes I spent a few days with him in London.

Did I ever speak to him about David? Probably not. Though inexcusable, I couldn't, not then. I wasn't able to talk about anything to do with feelings, not even with my mother, whom I visited after leaving Brimpts. It had been a good visit. I'd forgotten what fun she could be, and she made me laugh, re-telling old family stories. But I clammed up when, over a cup of tea, she said, "I do like Sandy, he's charming and obviously adores you. I don't want to interfere, darling, but...well, do you really love him? Will you be happy with him? He's so much older."

It was an opening, but I shied away, said I was really fond of Sandy, and not to worry. In truth I wasn't worrying. Sandy wanted to marry me, and why not? David was dead.

The war dragged on for nearly another year until, on May 9, 1945, eleven months after D-Day, the Germans surrendered. At Albury the village celebrated with a huge bonfire. The flames were blazing up

353

to the sky as I ran down the hill, and people were already dancing round the fire, shouting that Hitler was dead and Britons never, never would be slaves. When the smoke made my eyes run, one of the old village women said, "They old smoke do get in the eyes, don't it!" and her smile was kind.

For three months after Germany surrendered, the war against the Japanese continued in the Pacific. It was so far away it seemed unreal, until Sandy brought a newspaper with Phil Ruck Keene on the front page and the caption, "God! that one nearly got my nose!" This had been roared by Phil from the bridge of his aircraft carrier *Formidable*, and 'that one' was a Japanese kamikaze pilot, diving at the ship to crash on deck like a human bomb. The attack happened on the day of Germany's surrender and a second followed, but apparently Phil was all right and the ship still in action.

Sandy said the Japanese were trained never to surrender and the suicide attacks were greatly honoured, "which," he said, "is why they are such a formidable foe, utterly ruthless."

Sandy also brought sickening details about German concentration camps, and gradually unknown place names became fearful and portentous - Auschwitz, Dachau, Buchenwald, Treblinka, Bergen-Belsen.

In a nearby village a friend's husband returned from Germany after liberating Belsen. "He won't talk about it," his wife said, "and he keeps having these awful nightmares. The barbarians!" she cried. "At least there can be no question now of whether this war was just."

I didn't say that many Germans I'd met were sensitive, intelligent human beings. They couldn't all have been transmogrified into barbarians - and it was very likely that the Germans and Japanese called us barbarians too. I thought of Shakespeare's *Henry V* shouting. "Cry havoc! And let loose the dogs of war!" and saw the dogs like Conan Doyle's hounds of the Baskervilles, hideous, their teeth bared - except it wasn't dogs that war let loose.

Then, on August 6, 1945, the first atom bomb obliterated the heart of Hiroshima. Three days later Russia declared war on Japan and that same day, August 9, the city of Nagasaki was trashed by a second atom bomb.

Sandy brought a report of thousands, literally thousands of people killed instantly in both cities, and many thousands horribly injured. Numbing facts and figures emerged, but I couldn't grasp the obscene reality of it until, a year later, I read John Hershey's *Hiroshima,* and understood the full outrage of radiation on human bodies.

But early reports of the atom bomb attacks had already sparked one of our recurrent arguments after I exclaimed, "Sandy, those people were just civilians. That's not war, it's wholesale murder!"

Sandy retorted, "The German bombing of London was also murder, wasn't it?" and insisted that these fearful new bombs were the only way to end the war and save lives.

"Whose lives, for heavens' sakes?"

Less than a month later - September 2, 1945 - the Japanese surrendered. After almost exactly four years, the Second World War was over.

In Albury a second celebratory bonfire was lit, not quite as big as the first. Hiroshima and Nagasaki somehow made the gilt on the gingerbread of victory a bit tarnished. But there was much hatred of the Japanese as ugly tales of their prison camps emerged. The husband of another friend had been a prisoner of war in one of these camps, and after he came home she confessed that he seemed a little crazy.

"He insists on eating off one plate," she said. "He carries it around with him and won't allow anyone but himself to wash it. He explains that plates were very precious in the camp, and I do understand, but it's like living with a stranger. It breaks my heart, and I'm afraid...I'm afraid he'll never be the contented, gentle man I married? Damn the Japs and all their works."

Once again a contrary inner voice argued that the Japanese were doing what they believed was their duty, just as the British pilots were when they bombed Dresden, and the Americans when they dropped the atom bombs. 'Ruin builders, that's what we are, Belinda,' and 'we' meant all of us. I longed to talk with David, and when I tried out my thoughts on Sandy he floored me with the usual, "So what would you have done about Hitler?"

I had no solid argument, only a wild, "I think war is just as bad a crime as anything Hitler did, or the Japanese for that matter. And look at the cities we've destroyed. What's the use of everyone laying waste? Don't you remember Stuart's barometer idea, measuring danger points long before they blow up into big problems and war?"

Sandy said patiently, "Of course that's a wonderful idea, Belinda, but sometimes there's no alternative, and isn't it the business of diplomats to keep an eye on danger spots?" He added rather dismissively, "Stuart's a fine man, but a bit of a dreamer."

"I thought you were his friend!"

"There's a time and a place for everything," Sandy said vaguely, and switched the subject to the new United Nations' Charter. "It declares that the United Nations are determined to save future generations from the scourge of war. The old League didn't work," he said. "Let's hope this new idea will. Does that make you feel better?"

"Well, yes. It's wonderful! Don't you think so?"

"I'm not as optimistic as you. It's natural to fight, and in spite of all the deaths, war does stir up all kinds of new inventions, and you must admit, Belinda, that war makes life seem very worthwhile."

"It's not very worthwhile to be dead," I said with a pang, then letting myself be irritated by Sandy's, 'it's natural to fight', I added,

"Once it was natural to be cannibals." But like many similar discussions with Sandy, we got nowhere.

From now on the cottage was our base. I spent hours playing the piano, and made a study of English folk songs, which unexpectedly came in useful more than fifteen years later. I also began to read, gobbling up anything that might shed a light on the violence of our world. I read with little discrimination and no discipline, not even sure what questions I wanted answered. In between piano and books and looking after the garden I went for long walks with Jess.

On one of our walks Jess and I took a short cut through a friend's farm, and I stopped to chat with one of the farm hands, a little old whippet of a man with a brown pippin face and lively brown eyes. He said he remembered me as "a slip of a girl" (was I really 'a slip'?) and after telling him where I'd been for four years, he said, "My war were the first one. Passchendaele, 1917."

"You're lucky to be alive! Weren't there terrible losses?"

"Four 'undred thousand on 'em, us and the krauts, poor buggers - beggin' your pardon, miss."

"Not something you'll ever forget."

He hadn't forgotten. Slowly and simply he described that waterlogged plain in Flanders where the struggle for Passchendaele was just one battle in the three-months long Ypres campaign. As he talked I heard men cursing as they stumbled through mud and human guts, past disembowelled horses and bodies of men who'd choked to death in mud. At the end he said, "Didn't do no good neither, all that for a bitty ridge we never did capture."

I said feebly, "What a nightmare!"

"Yes, miss," he said politely, and then, looking me straight in the eye, added firmly, "But y'know miss, it's a funny thing, I wouldn't 'ave missed it, not for nothin'."

Startled, I stared at him, then remembering, said slowly, "I know what you mean. After our ship was sunk life was simple - just life and death and being together."

"Yes, miss. Friendly, in a manner of speaking. Different."

We shook hands. I called Jess and we went on with our walk. I'd been reading *Goodbye to All That,* Robert Graves' book about World War One. He described how he and most of his peers rushed to enlist, fearful that the excitement of a scrap might be over in six months - which, of course, it wasn't. Then, as the toll of dead mounted, and the war went on and on, patriotism was engulfed in disillusion and anger.

I stopped to lean over a gate and watch Jess set off after a crop of rabbits. She always made me laugh because her chase was really a round-up. The rabbits naturally ran straight to their burrows so she never caught one, but seemed satisfied to have done her duty in getting them home. People were like this too, rushing off to act in set ways that weren't appropriate, but were the ways they had been taught and must,

356

therefore, be right. Would my father have been disillusioned if he'd survived his war? Or would he have said he wouldn't have missed it for anything?

The grave released no answer, but it was confusing to know that I also wouldn't have missed the past four years, not any of it - the excitement of discovery, the fear as well as the laughter, and joy and heartbreak. All of it was intensely, vividly real: and if it wasn't for the war I wouldn't have known and loved David. Or lost him.

I climbed over the gate, feeling I'd been jolted out of the vaguely peaceful limbo I'd been in since David died, and was back in that other limbo, the vivid war limbo when I wasn't a hybrid, Belinda/Thelma, but just Belinda, and very much alive. Suddenly I thought of Alexis, and was ashamed that he'd been so long out of my mind. Affection for Dora and the family came back in a rush, and especially for Alexis, who had given me Greece. Whatever had happened to him in the last four years?

That night I wrote to Dora in Athens and asked her to give Alexis my address. I mailed the letter in the morning, but didn't hear from him until after Sandy and I were married in the spring of 1946.

We went to Norway for two weeks. Sandy fished happily for river salmon, and I went for walks. We stayed in an old farmhouse, every inch of it painted inside and out in different cheerful colours - apparently this was a regular winter task. I liked Norway and the straightforward Norwegians, and the magical nights of dim half-light. Sometimes after midnight I'd slip outside to the orchard and sit a while on the middle seat of the outhouse (newly painted and clean as a pin), not because of need, but for its peaceful location. The long wooden seat had three holes, large, medium and small, as if for the three bears. I left the door wide open on to the orchard, heard birds stirring, and sat in the half-light as if in a spell.

Back in England we took up the same pattern of life, the cottage our summer base where Sandy joined me at weekends. Then, one summer weekend, Alexis came to the cottage with his wife Diana.

Sandy and Diana got on splendidly. She was attractive, clever, and very rich, and as they chatted about mutual friends Alexis and I slipped off for a long walk together.

It was a lovely day. We found a dry patch and sat, bathed in sunshine, not speaking for a while. Then I said, "First of all I want to know why you couldn't come to Beirut for Cy and Marina's wedding?"

"I was training for intelligence work."

"Just what you wanted!"

"Yes, Belinda, just what I wanted. But I could have done without the next bit."

'The next bit' started in 1942 when he and Frank, an English captain Alexis had trained with, were sent to collect information from Greece. They landed on one of the islands for a rendezvous with Greek contacts, and here trouble began. The late-night rendezvous turned into a party, retsina flowed, and Alexis said, "I kept telling everyone to be quiet, but they were sure there was nothing to worry about. It was very stupid, for somebody ratted on us, and we were caught, sent to Athens, and imprisoned. We were there for five hundred days, I counted."

"You were interrogated?"

"Oh yes."

"Tortured?"

"Kicked around. I'll tell you something funny - I would imagine my head was a football and get absorbed in trying to keep it from being kicked. That way the pain...." He shrugged and went on, "Koestler wrote about pain reaching a ceiling, after which it's - well, just happening. I suppose that's why people can have fingernails pulled out and so on and not give anything away. Thank God they didn't do that. Anyway, there was a trial, and we were condemned to death."

"Alexis! It can't have seemed real. What *did* it feel like?"

He laughed and said. "Roxane asked us both that question one evening after the war. She was receiving on the terrace, and several friends were there. Quite truthfully I said it was frightening, but infuriated her by comparing it to being summoned to the headmaster's study for a caning. You know what Roxane's like - she said I was being facetious, that I was aping Frank's English understatement which, for a Greek, was simply affectation. Frank intervened loyally, said 'Honestly, all you have to do is grit your teeth and take your medicine like a man.' But Roxane would have none of that, called it childish nonsense and said both of us deserved to be shot."

Alexis and I laughed; it was Roxane to the life. Then he told me about the trial.

As an English officer and a Greek civilian were involved it was a show trial and open to the public; so Alexis' mother, Dora, and other relatives were in court. Alexis said, "When I saw Dora my first thought was, 'She can't let me be shot.' Then I remembered she hadn't been able to stop my father dying, and after controlling my knees, I waved and smiled at her. Believe it or not, I felt a sort of fatalistic calm, almost light-hearted, and went on feeling calm, even when Frank was '...*condannato a la pena di morte mediante fucilazione al petto*.'"

"What's '*al petto*' and why in Italian?"

"The judge and our jailers were Italian, and *al petto* meant he'd be shot 'in the chest'. Then it was my turn. I drew myself up - I'm sure I could have died quite well at that moment - and then...oh then, Belinda, I heard the judge say I was condemned to be shot *al schiena*. That means in the back. You see, Frank was captured in uniform and as a soldier honourably serving his country he merited the honourable death of being shot in the chest. But I was in civilian clothes and a Greek spy, so would be shot in the dishonourable manner reserved for spies."

He paused, said, "I confess, Belinda, my knees began to tremble violently then and went on trembling till the day we escaped."

"Was it the dishonour that was so bad?"

His answer, so typically Alexis, made me want to cry. He explained that he and Frank knew it was likely they'd be sentenced to death. So during the long nights before the trial, Alexis came to terms with death by creating a detailed scenario of his execution. In it he faced the firing squad dressed in a white shirt open at the neck, a scene borrowed from a movie about the execution of the Emperor Maximillian. Imagination played the rest in slow motion, concluding with bullets travelling visibly toward that white expanse of carefully preserved, ritual shirt.

But this sequence was shattered by the verdict, for now he would face a blank wall. He would hear the sounds of preparation behind his back, words of command, the shuffle of feet, the clank of breech-blocks, the crash of the volley, an agonizing interval of suspense, and then a searing pain in his back as the bullets tore through his lungs.

"I replayed the scene over and over, and how I would look down and the bullets would pucker my shirt outwards, rip through the cloth and crash into the wall before me. I saw the blood pouring out from the ugly gashes in my chest, and, for that moment, I was living after death."

"Dear God!"

"It was like a film. It ran through my head night after night, turning on automatically."

Wanting to shift from this replay I asked about his treatment in prison, and if there was enough food. "Barely enough to keep alive," he said, and pulled down one side of his pants. "See that scar? It's where my hip-bone cut through the skin. I couldn't stand for long towards the end, and lay on the concrete floor most of the day. It was very hard." He tucked in his shirt and grimaced. "One day the relatives of another prisoner in our small cell sent him a dish of spaghetti covered with tomato sauce. It smelt delicious. I watched him spoon in every mouthful. After he'd finished it all up, Belinda, he farted and, my God, that fart also smelt delicious; I sniffed every whiff of it."

It was too real. I shut it out of my mind and asked how they got away. "The gods were with us," he said. "Italy surrendered to the Allies on September 8, 1943 and the Italian guards celebrated by letting us both slip away across the roof."

But Alexis didn't escape scot-free. The effect of being kicked about, of starving and anticipating death for five hundred days, took its toll. "I fell ill with tuberculosis," he said. Then added, "When I got to Cairo I didn't know why I felt so terrible, and I came to Beirut to find you. But you weren't there."

"Dear Alexis," I cried, "I'm so sorry. I didn't know what you were up to...had no idea..." But he said of course, it wasn't my fault, and anyway, the hospital in Cairo cured the TB, he met Diana - and, well, it was all right. He said he was working for the new United Nations organization, but dampened my enthusiasm by saying that already the usual jockeying around for power had begun, and he didn't expect to last long there.

As we walked back to the cottage Alexis said, "After I was passed fit and left the hospital, I fell ill again with a return of the TB. I went back to hospital feeling very depressed, but the doctor told me this often happened. In hospital you don't have to make decisions and face life. It was after I was discharged a second time that I met Diana. She was very good to me, and knew a lot of the interesting Cairo intelligentsia - artists and writers, all that. She was sure I was a poet. I suppose I was rather a romantic character in her eyes. Strange how we tend to invent the people we live with."

"Yes," I said, "I suppose we do." Maybe I talked a little about Sandy. I'm not sure, for what was uppermost in my mind was Alexis fruitlessly going to Beirut, feeling so ill, and I not there. That really hurt, but beyond the pain was a furious certainty that war was utterly disgusting, puerile and a disgrace. I could only hope that Alexis was wrong about the power struggles in the United Nations, or at least that the idea of it would be greater than the power play. As for the two of us, we both had been pulled from rough waters, but were still adrift. I think we both knew, that in our different ways, we had a bit of a muddle to sort out.

<h1 style="text-align:center">✑ 42 ✑</h1>

Contentious issues, a lunch in Milan, and post-war Germany.

Alexis' visit was short, and our walk together no more than two hours, but it was a reminder of the expansive ease that came from sharing a common ground to toss ideas around on. It wasn't Sandy's fault that we couldn't talk about things that were, to me, important. He'd listen patiently, but after a while I'd feel I was knocking my head against a wall, unsure whether I was more vexed with myself than him. But as the arguments, which should have been discussions, were about everyday things, they kept turning up. One began because of an advertisement for toothpaste.

I'd come to London and, being short of toothpaste, went to buy some. The store clerk asked what kind I wanted and I said absent-mindedly, "Maclean's, please." But when he put the tube on the counter

I exclaimed, not very politely, "Oh not Maclean's!" Then I had to apologize. The right kind was produced, I made the purchase and went outside, wondering why Maclean's had popped into my head as if a button had been pressed. Then, as I waited to cross the road, a red London bus lumbered past, and on the back was a large advertisement asking, "Did you MacLean your teeth today?"

"It made me cross," I told Sandy, "that a stupid ad has no business getting into my head, like a worm. It's sinister."

Sandy said it was 'subliminal' and we got into a wrangle about the danger of manipulating minds. "All that stuff about Horlicks preventing night starvation," I said. "You told me how a bright copywriter discovered a word in a German dictionary, and shouted 'Eureka!' because the English translation, 'night-starvation,' was a sure-fire advertising gimmick. But it's dishonest to purloin a phrase, which had quite another meaning, and make it sound scientific, so you can tell people their lives can be happy and successful if they drink Horlicks at night. It's absurd, and unkind, for the people who believe it are probably losers anyway."

Sandy said, "My dear Belinda, there's nutrition in Horlicks. Is it wrong to encourage a healthy drink in a way that appeals to people?"

"Milk would be just as healthy," I retorted, "and not so expensive. Anyway, the reasons for drinking Horlicks are misleading. Horlicks won't change their lives, so they'll end up mired in disappointment, frustrated and angry and...and probably vote Labour forever, which won't please you."

Sandy laughed, and so did I. "Dear Belinda, I love your vehemence!" he said.

And I said, "But Sandy..." Our arguments mostly ended like this.

We weren't always contentious. We had country friends and friends in London, and I tried to share in rituals that gave Sandy pleasure, even when some of them stuck in my gullet.

One country ritual I particularly detested was the shooting weekend. Sandy had what was termed 'a gun' on the estate of friends near Albury - this meant he paid a fee, shot all the birds he could, and took home a personal ration of little carcasses; the rest were sold to help maintain a steady supply of game. Sometimes I'd walk with the beaters and pretend to flush birds from the undergrowth, or I'd walk with Sandy and his black retriever bitch. He so loved this dog, though she didn't live with us but was kept in kennels, a working dog only. She was a beauty, her short coat shiny black, her breeding impeccable, and she was much more satisfactory than I at doing just what was expected of her. I felt sick when pheasant after pheasant fell from the sky in a scatter of gorgeous russet feathers; but Sandy's bitch ran off joyously to do her retrieving. It seemed a pity she couldn't cook, I'd have gladly relinquished to her my job of producing succulent little roasted birds for dinner parties. Actually I did learn to cook them well - and oh dear! they were delicious.

The birds were delicious, and so were the expensive meals in London. From time to time I joined Sandy for ritual cocktails and meals, often at the Connaught Hotel near Berkeley Square. This was a favourite rendezvous of advertising executives, and Sandy liked having me around to meet his friends. There's nothing wrong in a fine glass of sherry and a good meal, but no-one ever questioned it: and I couldn't forget the soldier clerks in Beirut talking about the constraints of poverty and the ever-present fear of it. Meanwhile I, privileged by being 'out of the handkerchief drawer, darling', was living at ease. I didn't know what to do about it, except not to forget that once I'd been young and short of cash. So sometimes I'd slip away from Berkeley Square and order baked beans on toast at a Lyons' Corner House, just to remember that this basic dish was once a treat. Except Lyons' Corner House wasn't the sort of poverty the soldier clerks had talked about. Then, on one of my ritual visits to London, I got a chance to experience poverty - only at second hand, but at close quarters.

Sandy and I went to a party where I met Mark Abrams. He was the young director of a market research group, and I told him about Stuart and the surveys in Palermo. To my surprise he asked if I'd like to be an interviewer on a couple of upcoming surveys. "One is about housing in Holborn," he explained, "the other is for the big bugs at the War Office; they want to know why young men aren't keen to enlist in the army."

'Bully for them,' I thought as Sandy said, "Why not, Belinda?" So I took up the offer.

During the next two months I learnt that I knew nothing about poverty. The first survey in Holborn (a badly run-down London district) aimed to establish whether low-income housing was a greater need than commercial development. As an interviewer I had to keep an open mind, but I wasn't blind to bug tracks on the filthy walls of the old houses, and there was no avoiding the smells.

In a miserable room with one small, grimy window, a woman of unfathomable age crouched at a table cluttered with candle ends, bits of stale cheese, mouldy crusts of bread, and God knows what other domestic detritus. In another house I walked up rotting stairs to a windowless room with a bed on which, an unseen body under a heap of rags, groaned and mumbled. There was no-one else in the house and all I could do was report it to Mark Abrams.

Some of the interviewers had to be de-loused. I was lucky to escape this, but didn't escape the shock of seeing the degradation of poverty, and the impoverishment of spirit. These people had been robbed of will or hope, and I'd leave each interview railing at their hopelessness. But on the last interview in Holborn an elderly lady confounded me.

362

She also lived in an awful house, but I stepped into a miracle of cleanliness and order. A pot of geraniums flowered on her windowsill, and a little yellow canary sang in a cage. She made tea for me and poured it into a pretty little porcelain cup with a matching saucer.

"My lady gave this to me when I left her service," she said, and told me she'd been a lady's maid in a big house. "I was an orphan, you see, and my lady was very kind, and taught me how to keep things nice."

After I left her I thought about Abbie and Emma who had been happy at Copford Rectory. Though my grandparents were dyed-in-the-wool conservative gentry, they did care for their servants, and everyone in their parish. Perhaps living in a village made a difference, it was a community, and if you were lucky, you served people who linked 'keeping things nice' with self-respect. Even so, this did not justify a society that tolerated and upheld great wealth and abysmal poverty.

The army survey was in Liverpool. Sometimes I interviewed young men in factories, though more often after work in a cramped row house whose front door opened straight on the sidewalk of a drab street - no trees, no green grass, no flowers. What was it like to live in such houses, tramping to work every day through the cheerless streets, trapped in a job with little prospect of change? The answers were not to be found in the interview routine, so when we were done I lingered to talk, as one human being to another. Then they spoke of their longing to get away, find a better job in a place that was good for the kids to grow up in - an echo of the soldier clerks in Beirut.

I asked one bright young man why he didn't apply for other jobs, and was rebuked when he pointed out, politely, that he had a wife and kid to support, and if he didn't work every day there'd be no pay, see? As for jobs away from Liverpool - where'd he get the money to travel to the interview? Not by stopping work, not by a long chalk.

So I learnt that poverty was not only a prison, it was a society of its own. The gentry had the freedom of cash and connections and time - luxuries they took for granted. I remembered how shocked Sandy had been when the July election of 1945 brought in a Labour government and the downfall of Winston Churchill. The soldier clerks had said, "The old stuffed shirts have to go," and vowed that Labour was the party for them. Many of Sandy's friends said the working-class were traitors to ditch Churchill who'd saved the country from disaster. But I told Sandy that politicians should serve a six-month stint of working class life in Liverpool or Holborn or wherever they would repeat the same deadening ritual, day after day after day.

One marriage ritual, in which I failed entirely, was to settle down with a brood of Sandy's children. He wanted that, but I remained un-pregnant. He didn't talk about it, but I felt badly for him; he was a kind man and deserved better.

It was at this juncture of our lives that an odd thing happened during a lunch in Milan. Sandy had to make a business trip to Rome and took me with him. From there we went on to Milan, mainly to see da Vinci's *Last Supper*, but also because Sandy had another business meeting there. After their meeting I lunched with Sandy and the business contact, who also brought his wife.

Conversation with the wife was a bit heavy-going until she told me she'd been in Cairo during the war and I mentioned having been in Beirut. At this her face lit up.

"I went to Beirut for a break," she exclaimed, "it was the best few days I spent anywhere in the Middle East. I had an introduction to an English girl - I forget her name. Maybe you knew her. She lived in a marvellous little place by the lighthouse." I listened to a description of the view from my terrace, of Kassab and Marie, and even a reference to my rough sheepskin jacket. With a smile she concluded, "I'll always remember that visit."

I managed to say lightly, "I remember you now. You were in uniform. People look so different in uniform, don't they?" and added, "Of course, I wasn't in uniform." Then we stared at each other while I thought, 'Have I changed so much in four years?'

She said in a small voice, "How silly of me. I didn't recognize you." But I felt I wasn't quite there, or was fading away, like the Cheshire-Cat in *Alice-in-Wonderland* who left its smile hanging briefly in the air before fading out entirely.

On our return from Italy a letter was waiting for me from a Beirut friend, John Barraclough. He was a quiet, sensible man whose view of human nature was habitually gloomy. In Beirut his invitation to dine usually included "I need a dose of your incurable optimism, Belinda." The letter explained that he was the military governor of North-Rhein Westphalia with headquarter in Essen, West Germany. "I have a comfortable house here," he concluded, "am waited on hand-and-foot and could do with cheerful company. Do come and spend a few weeks. You will find it interesting here, sad, but interesting. I hope Sandy can spare you."

Sandy said, "By all means, Belinda. Keep some notes; you might write about what you see." He saw me off at the station and when the whistle blew he called, "Give my regards to John. Keep me posted!"

The train rumbled through the depressing streets of south London as I brooded about love, and not-love, and what I myself meant by 'love'. Was it only the tumult of sex? Absolutely not. It was part of love, but not the whole thing. I liked St-Exupéry's 'Love is not looking in each other's eyes, but looking together in the same direction.' On the other hand, the meeting of eyes could speak more than words. Then remembering David, I sat very still, and let him go.

I had to change trains at Cologne and, having an hour or two to spare, walked to a point overlooking the city. I don't know what I expected, but I stared in disbelief. A huge area of the city had been rubbished, except for the cathedral which sailed, apparently intact, like a galleon on a dead ocean of wrack and ruin. Now and again a loose sheet of corrugated iron banged against the gravestone wall of a shattered building. I was quite alone and, surprised by tears, cried out to the graveyard below, "How can we do this to one another?"

But Cologne was only the beginning of dismay. John was busy during the day, and I was free to pick my way through Essen. John told me his first task had been to get bulldozers recreating the map of city streets, so people could get about. Amongst the detritus I found people living wherever a shelter could be patched up from bits of buildings, bits of furniture - all kinds of bits. I talked with many people, but an old lady and her young grandson especially moved me. They welcomed me into a cupboard of a space, the earth floor smoothed and swept clean. It was an honourable cleanliness, claiming order out of chaos. As I talked with her I thought of the cartoon German enemy, invariably subhuman and bloodthirsty, and felt that cartoons were as false as the advertisements for Horlicks.

After a few days prowling around on foot, John gave me a car and driver and told me to go out into the countryside and see another offshoot of chaos - the slow stream of stateless refugees. Even in 1948 a human tide was still flowing nowhere in particular, away from fear, or total loss. Some were fleeing from the Russian occupation of East Germany; others had fled when advancing armies overran their homes; some were the remnants of roughly 10,000 non-Germans from captured territories, forced to work in places like the huge armaments complex of Krupp's in Essen. John told me that these workers were chained to their factory benches during Allied air raids to ensure that production continued.

One night my driver took me to a field, and we lay watching dark figures slip like wraiths across the border of East Germany. In daylight the refugees were like poor scarecrows, plodding along with pathetic bundles of possessions until they reached some kind of sanctuary - one of the burgeoning refugee camps, or a church, or a school, or community hall. Inside these makeshift ports of call each family made a little home with a blanket, and perhaps a teapot and a plate. I did not know that, a few decades later, this kind of scene would become commonplace on television screens the world over. In 1948 the enormity of pain and loss and despair that war lets loose was like a first look into hell. But one sanctuary was different.

The large house stood in extensive grounds on the edge of a forest, and children were everywhere. This haven was run by a priest and some helpers. In the closing days of Germany's collapse the priest had pulled children out of the mayhem of war. Some he took from trains where they'd been thrust by parents distraught with fear; other children were culled from cities where they'd banded together to rove

365

the streets like packs of starving animals. Too many children had been forced to watch their parents murdered, even tortured. The priest said that the sight of a man in uniform had sent some of the first batch of children screaming into the forest.

"They need much love," he said. "We do what we can, but we are few amongst so many."

Of all the horrors, the worst was Belsen. A miasma of despair and death pervaded this terrible place, even though the huts were empty and the surroundings clean and tidy. At first I was puzzled by the mounds of earth, some very large, others quite small, over which a kindly blanket of green grass had grown. Each mound had beside it a small, unobtrusive metal plate, and bending to read the words, found they briefly recorded how many dead lay heaped in each monstrous grave.

If Belsen had been a relic from the time of Genghis Khan any of the numbers would have been a sickening reminder of ancient barbarity. But this was the twentieth century. Was this insanity, or possession by evil? Years ago, when I was at St. Agnes' school and we were caught being naughty, Sister Catherine would cry, "You are all possessed!" (meaning 'by the Devil'). We thought her silly. In Belsen it did not seem so unlikely. But what was evil? Could minds be manipulated for evil? If so, what became of choice?

I wandered around, haunted by spectres of terrible jailers and pitiable victims, until pity for the wretched victims spilled over to the grotesque jailers who, with bent minds and spirit, undertook their unspeakable daily tasks.

That night I bombarded John Barraclough with talk of mind territories and guilt and the iniquity of war as well as hopes for a changed world. John listened patiently as I grew incoherent about alienation and hatred, and the need to think differently about practically everything.

Finally he said, "You should visit the Krupp's armaments complex in Essen. It's a huge area, and includes a village for the workers - charming little Austrian-type houses. The Air Force missed them, though otherwise our chaps did a fine job here - crippled the place. But many buildings are intact and full of undamaged machines. They're being dismantled now and sent as reparations to countries which suffered most acutely from German occupation. The man in charge of dismantling and packing will take you round; a likeable chap, brilliant in his way. About your age. He's got a big job and doing it well. His name is Harry Edge. I'll set up an appointment for you."

I didn't visit Krupp's for nearly a week as I was offered a seat on an airlift flight taking supplies into West Berlin. I wasn't clear why the airlift was happening, so John explained that Berlin and its surrounding districts had been divided into four zones, and each zone was separately administered by American, British, French and Russian military commandants. Unfortunately the Soviet zone contained part of the West Berlin sectors, so in order to get supplies to these sectors the Western Powers arranged transit through the Soviet zone. This worked all right until March of 1948 when a decision was made to merge all four zones into one economic unit. The Russians didn't like this, and blocked all road, rail and river access to West Berlin through their zone. But they couldn't block air space. So in May the airlift of essential supplies to West Berlin began.

I sat with the pilot, and as we flew over the ruins of Berlin he told me that some 76,000 tons of explosives and incendiaries had been dropped there during the four years of war. A further 40,000 tons of shells had been fired into the city by the Russians in the last ten days before surrender.

The Western sector was a desolate place, but I had been assured that the Russian sector was worse. I was also warned about the Russians. "It would be madness to go into their sector alone. If you aren't nabbed you'll probably be stripped of your watch and those pretty gold earrings of yours." I disregarded this fuss and bought a subway ticket to East Berlin. However, the warning had not been an idle one. When I got off the train I saw passengers from another train being frisked by Russian soldiers, so I didn't linger.

East Berlin was pathetic, and made West Berlin seem quite a hub of sophistication. But a poster advertised a performance of Tchaikovsky's *Eugene Onegin* in the evening, so I bought a ticket and got there early to snap up a seat in the second row of the stalls. The stalls soon filled with Russian big-wigs and their wives, the men covered with medals, the women wearing rather awful dresses. The performance was marvellous, and when a troupe of Russian dancers raised a roar of approval, I clapped and shouted with everyone else. But the most memorable moment was just before the performance started. The lights dimmed, the conductor lifted his baton, and light from the orchestra pit softly illuminated the rather grim Russian faces on either side of me. I was taking a good look at them when somebody in the audience gave a prodigious sneeze - a real, bellow of a-tishhoo! - and all the Russian faces burst into enchanting, childlike grins.

Back in West Berlin I went, on an impulse, to the Press Club and asked if Ted Howes was in the city. The last time we met was when I abruptly left our shared apartment in Budapest, so I was delighted to be directed to "the redhead over there. She'll tell you where Ted is."

The redhead was chatting with a group, and readily gave me a telephone number. "He'll probably be there now," she said, and added, "What's your name, in case you miss him?"

"Belinda Mitchell-Innes," I said, and was about to say he'd remember my first name, when our eyes met. We stared at one another in a silent instant of recognition. There was nothing to be done, so I said lightly, "Thanks a lot!" and walked away, kicking myself for forgetting that Ted's wife was a redhead.

Ted and I lunched together, and I apologized for being so stupid. He said it didn't matter, though added ruefully, "I got into rather hot water."

We caught up on news of ourselves and mutual friends, and at last I learnt that Basil Davidson's news agency in Budapest had been a blind for a very different assignment from SOE (Special Operations Executive). His real task was to prepare for the inevitable Nazi occupation of Hungary. In order to frustrate Nazi river traffic on the Danube, Basil was training Hungarian divers in the art of affixing explosives to the hull of ships.

Ted said with a grin, "In sardonic SOE parlance the explosives were referred to as 'toys'. Basil amassed a considerable stock of toys which he hid in the basement of the British Legation. Very sensible, the safest place, though against Foreign Office policy. Inevitably someone blabbed to the minister, and you know what he felt about anything 'irregular'.

"Did he give Basil hell?"

"Oh yes, sent him off with a flea in his ear after telling him that the military attaché had been instructed to chuck the entire stock of toys into the Danube."

"Whose side was the minister on?"

"The Foreign Office," said Ted.

This got me on to a tirade about the idiocy of war until I said, "Don't let me go on. I don't know enough to be convincing, and so much has happened to me in eight years." We looked at one another across the divide of time, and I thought how fond I was of Ted, remembering the Christmas sleigh ride in 1940 when I'd wished he was with me. I said, "What news of Joan and Otto and Margit? Margit must be ten years old, same as your Emily."

Ted hesitated before saying slowly, "The Jews didn't have too bad a time until Eichmann took over in '41. He got the Hungarian Fascists to co-operate in searching out Jews, especially those with property, and they were all packed into the ghettos of Budapest. An awful lot of them died there, but not everyone. Then just before Germany surrendered Eichmann stepped up the deportations. It's not an exaggeration to say that about 400,000 Jews and gypsies were shipped off from Hungary to Auschwitz and Dachau and Mulhausen."

"Gypsies?" I exclaimed, remembering Sandor Veres and his tiny wax disc of an old gypsy violinist playing a wild czardas. "But why? What had they done?"

Ted said, "Nothing, except be 'social deviants'. Something like 30,000 gypsies were rounded up with other deviants - homosexuals and anything likely to contaminate the purity of the German *Herrenvolk*." Then he said, "I've tried to find out about Joan. All three of them were taken from the estate, but we don't know what happened. We presume they died, maybe in the ghetto, or in a concentration camp."

At dinner with John I told him about Otto and Joan and young Margit, and said it was hard to think straight about what the Germans had done. John said I might look more kindly on what the British had done during their air raids on Krupp's, and that he'd arranged for me to go the next day.

⤚ 43 ⤙

Krupp's and unmapped territories.
A decision.

The Air Force had certainly done a thorough job on Krupp's. As my driver made his way past crippled factory buildings and heaps of rubble and twisted steel, I was raging about the hideous game of war and its huge waste. There was no condoning Krupp's chaining workers to their benches during air raids, but it could be argued that army conscripts in any country couldn't get away from their assigned tasks, and if they tried, they were shot. There wasn't much to choose between a bench or a trench when there was no choice.

The car stopped at the Reparation Centre and an orderly took me to the office of Harry Edge, the young man who was to be my guide. He got up to greet me from behind the barrier of an impressive expanse of polished desk, and I had the fleeting impression of a lithe, tall figure, thick dark hair and a striking but odd face (Roman nose commanding a reticent chin). But the impression was at once overlaid by two things happening in quick succession - I met his glance, and immediately a blow like a strong electric shock, hit me between the shoulders.

Neither of us moved. Then we both broke into civilities and introductions. I sat down, listened to, but did not take in a word of his brief run-down of Krupp's history. Finally he left the sanctuary of his desk, took his hat from a stand, said, "Let's go," and walked to the door. He held it open with rather a flourish, as if making some sort of point. Curious, I looked him full in the face and instantly my improbable inner voice remarked rudely, 'Look out, he's an oik!'

'Oik'. This was a word I never used, a hateful word, crudely reflecting my grandmother Birdie's, 'Not out of the handkerchief drawer, darling.' 'Oi' instead of 'I' betrayed your class origin and damned you as one of 'Them'. Indignantly I rejected the unregenerate inner voice, but couldn't stop an instinctive satisfaction that this disturbing person didn't say 'Oi' - and then thought, 'Not that such nonsense matters.'

The tour of Krupp's remains mostly a blur of desolation, except for the startling Krupp's mansion. In the bathroom all the water faucets were made of gold, and a large room lined with massive cupboards turned out to be where Frau Krupp kept her clothes. I remarked lightly that war was a paying proposition, but Harry snapped, "Bloody bastards!" I didn't like that, nor did I like him twice kicking open the door to rooms where Germans were working.

"Doesn't the door open properly?" I asked, and was disconcerted when his answer implied a fury of hatred for all Germans. Yet he seemed sensitive, even a little shy, was very intelligent and had a disarming ironic humour. An interesting person, and I was glad when he asked me to dine with him the following evening.

After the visit I asked John what he knew about Harry Edge. "Not much," he said. "He's a skilled airplane technician and during the war was working on Spitfire prototypes, so he wasn't called up. Obviously a very bright working-class boy who's made good. He was sent to Germany after the war to winkle out top scientists willing to have their brains picked by the British. Did you like him?"

"Yes. He's rather unknown territory, and his hatreds are quite violent." I described the doors being kicked open, and John said, "That's bad manners, but remember what it was like to come face to face with the horrors of the concentration camps. Not easy to forget or forgive."

"Yes," I said, "I can understand that now, after Belsen."

Over the next couple of weeks Harry and I often met. We talked about his job and books and music and, of course, ourselves. I learnt that he came from Birmingham - a city I'd never been to, but matched it with the dreary streets of Liverpool, and tried to imagine life in a working-class household where if you had a job it was all right, but if you didn't, it was very bad. Harry said his father was a skilled panel-beater and had a good job until the Depression.

"What panels?" I asked, "and why are they beaten?"

"Car panels. All the posh car bodies were shaped by hand. Dad was a wonderful craftsman, known all over the north." A pause. "But he wasn't an easy man to live with. He had a violent temper." I laughed, said the Ruck Keenes were very explosive, but it didn't last, and asked Harry about his mother.

He said, "She died when I was six," adding with a frown, "No-one told me she was dead. Suddenly one day she was no longer around. They simply said she'd gone away and that she was a saint. I thought I'd been bad and that's why she'd gone, but I was very angry with her."

This situation seemed cruel and incomprehensible, but there was no point in dwelling on it, so I asked if he remembered the Depression.

"Very much so," he said. "I was ten, and Dad lost his job and went off to look for work. But I'd just won a scholarship to Birmingham

Grammar School, and was more interested in that. You probably don't know that grammar school for people like us is our one chance of going to university and getting a good job." He shrugged, went on, "Dad walked from the Midlands to the south coast before he found work. My sister and I were sent to join him, but there wasn't a grammar school for me, so I went to the local school and left when I was fourteen."

"What a shame, but did it matter all that much?" I asked. "Look where you've got to!" and added cheerfully, "No-one would know you were working-class, and people here say you've done a first-rate job."

"Thanks," Harry said drily, and I felt a stab of misgiving. But I'd not meant to patronize, and vexed by his being so prickly, did not take into account that my cool gentry voice might be irritating.

Only hindsight reveals that we were out of our elements in this ruined city. Though the military government had established a kind of order out of the chaotic aftermath of war, confusion lurked at the edge of everyday. People's minds were fractured by the truth of atrocities committed in their name, the old signposts were down, the old references blown sky high. As for the future, it was a wide open landscape without maps.

Yet there was a palpable exhilaration in the disarray - or was it just me? I'd been coasting along in neutral ever since David's death and now, in this city, and with this stranger, the changes David foresaw as imperative were no less unlikely than Essen becoming a neat city with everything working like clockwork. In fact chaos promised liberation, and the two of us were poised at the intersection of roads, leading anywhere.

But territories without maps tend to set reason at sixes and sevens. As Harry walked away down a long corridor there was no reason why I should feel such a rush of tenderness, simply because the back of his neck was vulnerable as a child's. And reason was overturned when he casually whistled a tune, the sound true and sweet as a bird's. And beyond reason I was alive again.

Even so, I was quite unprepared when, two days before leaving Essen, Harry said, "I must tell you something. I'm married. We married very young. One day we had a blazing row and she left with our son; he was just a few months old. I never bothered to divorce her. I don't know why. I was very angry."

I said nothing, wishing he'd told me this earlier. He went on, "I'm going to divorce her now. It's time we were free." Then he said, "Will you leave Sandy? I want you to be my wife."

Here I stick to facts. We must have talked, but I only recall inevitability. We agreed to meet again at greater leisure, and this we did. After the third meeting I told Sandy that I must leave him. He then asked me to give our marriage a year, without my seeing or communicating with Harry. I accepted: it seemed only fair.

So Sandy and I slipped back into having the cottage as a base, and I interspersed my time there with days in London at the Berkeley Square flat. At weekends we met with local friends, in London there were other friends, and at the cottage I was content to be alone, with Jess, for days on end - especially at first, when it was difficult to think or feel straight about anything. Which is why, one day on an impulse, I wrote to Abbie at Copford Green, said I'd love to come and see her, and suggested a date.

More than twenty years had passed since I'd cried, "Goodbye everyone, I'll see you all soon!" That was the last I saw of the 'everyone' of Copford. But Abbie lived in the cottage given her by the family. She replied briefly that she and Emma were looking forward to seeing me, and confirmed the date.

I didn't know then that Abbie deeply disapproved of my divorce from Arthur, and at first it seemed she was minded to give me 'whatfor' - that awful threat which always stopped me in my tracks. Then Emma said she bicycled over from Eight Ash Green most days to see that Abbie was getting on all right - and we laughed. It was a good joke because both of them were, except for white hair, unchanged. Abbie was still tall, slender and quite capable of being 'all right', while Emma was, as always, round, huggable and unavoidably in second place.

After much family talk I asked about the Rectory, and if it still looked the same. Abbie said, "You can see for yourself, Thelma. No-one's about, they're away on holiday. We'll have a cup of tea when you're back."

The front door of the Rectory was closed, the windows shut, and no voices called to one another. But the rooks were cawing. To this familiar music I went to the back of the house and walked straight across the lawn to the bordering row of elms. Then I turned - and stared at a house I didn't know. The grey stone walls were completely bare, and the beautiful wisteria, which had climbed right up to the boys' bedrooms, might never have been there at all.

I turned away and took the path to the old church. No-one was about, and I sat in the peace of the empty church, remembering how Oophats would howl when we sang hymns in a minor key, and had to be led away by Abbie. Dear Oophats, he'd been no trouble during cheerful hymns in a major key, and I hummed my favourite - *All things bright and beautiful*. I picked up a stray *Hymns Ancient and Modern* from the pew, and read all the verses, including one I'd quite forgotten:

The rich man in his castle,
The poor man at his gate.
God made them, high or lowly,
And gave each his estate.

'Well, I'll be blowed!' I thought, 'Everyone in their place, and no questions asked.'

Abbie had tea brewed and a plateful of my favourite sticky ginger biscuits. "You remembered!" I cried, and Abbie gave a little smile. Darling Abbie, her virtues were staunch and unchanging.

I complained about the destruction of the wisteria, but Abbie said practically, "Seems they had to. Eating the mortar it was." Emma agreed that it was a shame. But Abbie, of course, was right.

As I drove back to Albury I thought irritably about God divinely dispensing riches to the rich and poverty to the poor. It was abominable - yet, oh yet! there were elements of grace in the old gentry life. Abbie and Emma had been content to give unstinted service to the Ruck Keenes, who returned their service with love and care. But not all the gentry were like that, and even Birdie believed her handkerchief drawer distinctions were set in stone. It really wouldn't do; and come to think of it her 'Not out of the handkerchief drawer, darling', wasn't all that different from Hitler's boring nonsense about the purity of the Aryan race. And where did that lead? To gas chambers and concentration camps.

After these mental acrobatics I thought of David and his "Things must change." But the problem was *How?* And where to start? The answer escaped me, but by the time I was back at my cottage I knew one thing for sure: I had a hunger to find out how change came about. I wanted to know, and this was more demanding than what to do about Sandy, or Harry, or marriage.

I began sating my hunger with books. Voraciously and wildly I devoured books that ranged from Frazer's *Golden Bough* to a thesis on World Federalism. In Frazer I explored myth, ritual and religion; and the ideas behind World Federalism spun dreams of creating a system in which everyone worked together with a common purpose. It was heady stuff. I must have been a terrible bore as well as a poor bargain for Sandy. We tried to talk about what was thronging in my head, but it wasn't Sandy's way, and my project might well have foundered had I not read an article about Boimondau, a co-partnership experiment in Valence, France.

The idea had been born in 1940 when Barbu, a maker of watch-cases, offered to teach his trade to seven of his friends. All seven had different skills and were out of work. He set up a workshop in his garage, and while they worked they planned their ideal workplace - a co-partnership whose members would elect their director and executives, and profits would be equally shared. Their slogan was, "We make watch-cases to make men." In due course they managed to muster enough money to start production. Ten years later Boimondau had 350 members and annual sales equivalent to £150,000. By this time the system had become more sophisticated, and included something called 'total human pay', and a day-care centre in the factory itself, for Boimondau was not a live-in community.

This was real hands-on 'How'. I told Sandy about it and said I would love to visit Boimondau, and if possible work in the factory for a few weeks. With his usual kindness Sandy assented, and I left London for Valence in late October.

The French consul in London had warned me that Boimondau was a hotbed of communists. I thought this was silly, though there was a moment in Valence when I hesitated. The directions I'd been given led me down a dusty side-road lined with shuttered villas and straggly gardens until, at the end, I found Boimondau hidden behind a high, whitewashed wall. It was very quiet. Was it possible that this place was seething with bearded fanatics, and I was a fool to come? Then I pushed the door open and went into a neat courtyard with beds of brilliant scarlet dahlias. A few minutes later I was shaking hands with Mermoz, the director - a stocky man, bright eyes, a shock of grey hair, and no beard.

After we'd talked, Mermoz introduced me to one of the founding members, who took me on a tour of the factory. At one point I was amused when he patted a large machine, saying "We nearly made fools of ourselves over this one!"

'This one' was, oddly enough, one of Harry's reparation machines from Krupp's. The machine hadn't been a gift, and when the director proposed using profits for the purchase, there was strong opposition.

My guide said, "We argued that we were doing very well without the machine, and wanted to share the profits instead of wasting money on something we didn't need. But Mermoz wouldn't stand for that. He told us we'd elected him as director because we valued his advice. If we rejected his advice, he would resign." With a grin my guide concluded, "That made us think! Mermoz is a good *copain*. So we didn't make fools of ourselves, and the machine has nearly doubled our production."

For a month I worked every morning at a bench putting watch-cases together (I was good at this). I ate all my meals in the factory cafeteria where, stumbling along in rusty French, I asked questions about innovations like 'social pay' and the day care scheme. Social pay was given for attendance at study courses run by the university in Valence, or for useful community work. The day-care centre on the premise was not just for wives working in the factory, but for house-bound wives needing a few hours free.

Every Friday after work the director gave a report on current business to the workers and their families (and a dog or two). Questions and opinions were freely bandied about, but without acrimony. I also went to a Neighbourhood Group meeting. These groups met once a month in each other's houses to discuss a list of matters provided by the director - and discuss they did, vigorously, their opinions recorded for the director's reading.

The day I left Valence I told Mermoz that Boimondau was democracy in the making. But he said, "The test for us will be when we have 500 members, and we won't know everybody's name. Then we may forget our vision."

In England I got in touch with the writer of the article on Boimondau, hoping there might be one or two similar English experiments. "Nothing so sophisticated," he said. "The only co-operatives here are farm-based communities, but worth a visit." He noted three addresses, said they were all very different, and wished me luck.

I visited all three. The first had lost its momentum, and the second was badly run and an emotional shambles. I left after a week of listening to whispered complaints from, and about, everyone.

The third and last community was the *Brüderhof*, or Society of Brothers. Founded in Germany, it was dispersed when Nazi persecution threatened Jewish members. One group came to England and prospered until the outbreak of war, and the German members faced internment. Happily they were allowed to leave *en masse* and join another *Brüderhof* in Brazil. A handful of members stayed to tidy up affairs before joining the others in South America: but they never left. Though food was short and the farm lease was up, pacifists kept turning up, urging them to stay. Somehow money was raised for a modest down-payment on a derelict farm on the Welsh border. By the end of World War Two the farm was given a top government rating.

In 1950 I found a thriving community of people from diverse professions, education, race and religion. There was no pressure to stay, and no-one was ever refused. The result was a microscopic world community where old and young and a few crazies had tasks they could handle. Their aim, they said, was to witness that all kinds of people could live together peacefully if based on "...whatsoever ye would that men should do unto you, do ye even so unto them."

It was a busy, happy place, including a school with about one hundred children (their artwork was stunning), and a flourishing printing business. They were housed according to their needs as a family or a single person, and retained few personal possessions. The women all wore Austrian *dirndls* and the men were all bearded. I asked why the *dirndls* and beards, and was told that beards saved time and money, and the *dirndl* was comfortable and attractive without being provocative.

"Provocative?" The simple answer was that sex could disrupt a community and *dirndls* were charming, but not sexy.

I spent a week at the *Brüderhof* and a few days before leaving I walked into the Welsh foothills until I could look down on the well-tilled fields and neat kitchen gardens. The setting was beautiful and there was order and tolerance at work in the community. It was tempting. I knew my marriage with Sandy was at an end, and the future uncertain. But after a while I knew the *Brüderhof* was not for me.

In London I took the underground to Berkeley Square. After the *Brüderhof* the faces around me look blank and tired, and no-one spoke. But a voice in my head said flatly, 'This is our world. I must live in it, and get mud on my boots.'

When Sandy and I parted he said sadly, "You were not committed." I could not disagree and said I was sorry to have treated him so shabbily. Then I asked why he'd married me.

After a pause he said, "I wanted to possess you, like one wants to own a beautiful piece of porcelain."

Porcelain? That wasn't me at all. Then I remembered Alexis saying "Strange how we invent the people we live with." Yet Sandy loved this porcelain me, and was kind and generous. I hoped my leaving him meant he was free to live on his own terms - and he did. Before long he married a cousin, fathered a son and daughter, and became a director of his prestigious advertising firm.

And I, balanced precariously between exhilaration and fear, set off into uncharted territory with Harry, who was an oik, but as good as anyone with privilege and pedigree. As for change, there was only one way to start, and that was to live it.

✣ 44 ✣

"Of the greatest moment in human life, methinks,
is the departure upon a distant journey
into unknown lands."
Sir Richard Burton, 1862

Burton ends his statement with, "Afresh dawns the morn of life." Yes, that's it, though he doesn't mention fear. Maybe after many disasters and disappointments he didn't think fear was worth mentioning.

Hope, not fear, was paramount when Harry and I began our life together, though for a while it was a restless time. Harry, his job in Germany completed, was back in England with no immediate plans, other than our marriage when his divorce was final. I had no money, for Sandy owed me nothing, so I was in the process of selling my cottage. I loved the place as if it was an ancient family heritage, but old buildings, however stout, need constant upkeep. Whatever our future might be, Albury belonged to the past.

In 1937 I had paid £450 for two cottages combined into one on an acre of land. In 1950 the little property sold for £4,000. With this astonishing access of wealth I felt rich as Croesus, and talked with Harry about Boimondau and how we might use the money for some such purpose. We also considered visiting Albert Schweitzer in Africa, I'm not sure why, but suddenly I got cold feet. I was living on the capital, and we had to be practical. So we decided to spend a few days walking on the Sussex downs and think soberly about our future.

The future. Maybe I heard violins playing as we set off into the sunrise of a new world. Maybe not. What the weekend proved was that when you journey into unknown lands, expect nothing, and be ready for the unforeseen.

The weather was lovely and on the first day we set off for a long walk. On a high place we stopped to eat our picnic lunch, and sat peacefully with the rolling downs at our feet, the sky wide-open overhead. All of a sudden Harry asked, "How many lovers did you have during the war?"

Taken aback, and rather embarrassed by this crass question, I said, "That sounds as though you think they were a legion!" But he didn't laugh, and I hesitated. From my marriage with Sandy I had carried away one certainty, that honesty and trust were essential to loving. So I gave Harry a straight answer, and feeling I'd established a point, added, "Let's always be honest with one another."

Probably he agreed, for when he sprang the next question, I blithely said the first thing that came into my head. I'd just had a bath, and Harry asked, "Do you have a bath every day?"

"Of course," I said. Then, trying make a joke of it, added "otherwise I'd be a bit smelly."

Harry said drily, "Every day seems rather overdoing it."

The tone of his voice roused a little *afreet* of anxiety. For once I kept quiet, guessing I'd blundered into some reality of working-class life. I'd read about it, glimpsed it from the soldier clerks in Beirut, and even seen and smelt it on the surveys I made in Holborn and Liverpool. But I'd never lived in a house without a bathroom or running hot water (except for Copford Rectory, but that was overcome by the servants and jugs of hot water). So I didn't know that Friday night, for many working-class families, was bath night in the kitchen. Water would be heated on the stove, and the hip-bath put in place for everyone to take turns in getting clean. Every day would certainly have been overdoing it.

These two questions were the first of many which would come out of the blue and, surprised, I would answer quickly, without thinking, and wish I hadn't. This happened in London when, for a treat, Harry took me to the theatre. He bought tickets in the stalls, and I changed into a long evening dress. Harry put on a dinner jacket, but later asked, "Do you always dress up when you go to the theatre?"

I said, "Yes, everyone does. I'd feel out-of-place any other way." Then I realized this wasn't strictly true. Evening dress would have been eccentric in the sixpenny seats up 'in the gods' at the Old Vic. But when I was married and affluent we usually sat in the stalls or dress circle, and anything but evening dress would have been a social solecism. I probably tried to explain all this, but the little *afreet* gave me a prod of anxiety - or was it vexation? I didn't want to be forever on guard about what I was saying - or doing, for that matter.

One day we were waiting to go in to a movie when I got into conversation with a man in the queue. When I turned back to speak with Harry he was frowning, and obviously angry. After the movie I asked, "What upset you in the queue?" and was dumbfounded when he accused me of giving the stranger a come-on. I said that was nonsense, I was just being friendly. But Harry called me a bitch.

Nobody had ever spoken like that to me. What ailed this sensitive, loving man who could whistle, pure and sweet as a bird? Shocked, I couldn't stop the tears. Then Harry put his arms round me and said he was sorry, and in the happiness of trust I was sure such words would never be repeated.

But they were repeated.

Could it be jealousy that provoked these sudden moods, and I was to blame for unleashing them with my list of wartime lovers. In defence I began avoiding mention of Budapest, or Greece, or the Middle East. Then I'd forget when I was relaxed and cheerful, and suddenly Harry would be, not a person, but a black cloud. At last, frustrated after too many black cloud repetitions, I sought the advice of an unknown quantity - a German Freudian psychologist.

Someone must have recommended this kindly man who, on my first visit, said gravely, "Your man should not speak like that to you." This was a comfort, but I wanted to know why my man had to put me down, and what I could do about it. In his fatherly, guttural voice the psychologist expatiated on how the unexplained death of Harry's mother had left him not only desolate, but guilty, and angry.

"But that's the past," I exclaimed, and he attempted explanations; but I could only afford a few sessions. On the last visit I said, "So Harry needs to feel that I won't vanish, like his mother. Is that it?"

His reply was gentle. "Your man has a deep empty hole that demands to be filled with love, and it may never be."

I rejected this as a counsel of despair. But what could I do to help? For a start I could stick around and not vanish, and if he felt secure there'd be no cause for offensive, absurd accusations. What else? I couldn't do anything about his dead mother, or his father's temper - but what about the Depression, which threw his father out of work? It still bugged Harry that he had to give up his scholarship, because in the place his father found work, there was no grammar school. No scholarship meant no chance of university, and he had to do the normal working-class thing – a state school education, leave at fourteen, and go to work. All right - my money could give him another chance for university. He would have to study for the entrance exam, but with luck he would get a grant to see us through until he graduated. It was a brilliant idea.

It was a little disappointing that Harry didn't exactly jump at my idea, but he did agree to give it a try. The first step was to get through the entrance exam, and we rented a couple of rooms at Woking where there was a good community college. Harry went off to register for his courses, but when he came back he suggested that I also should take a course.

Astonished, I cried, "But I'm not clever enough!"

"Come on, love," he said, "you can do it."

This was proof positive that we really were looking together in the same direction. So it was my turn to have a try, and the next day I registered for a London University extension course in social studies.

"It sounds awfully interesting," I told Harry, "but I'll just go to the lectures. Written term papers and such will be beyond me."

Harry said that written work would be expected, and he was right. Nervously I gave in my first assignment - and it came back with a high mark. O my! Was it possible that I wasn't all that stupid? But it didn't matter - I was hooked, and settled down to study, away upon another journey into unknown lands.

But Harry dropped out a few weeks later. He'd worked with an aircraft development company during the war, and they wanted him back, offering to make a position specially for him. It was a great compliment. I could have stomached the blow to my brilliant idea had the company's emphasis not been essentially military.

I argued that war was murder, and never resolved conflicts, only produced new ones. To this Harry said, "So what would you do about Hitler?"

'Bother Hitler!' I thought, feeling the question was an evasion. I could only say that new ways of dealing with conflict had to be evolved, and went on about the Boimondau experiment and co-partnership. It was all rather wild and vague.

Harry sensibly pointed out that already some of my four thousand pounds was spent, and anyway it was his business to support me. I respected that, remembered his work had been developing Spitfires, and had to admit that aircraft development was Harry's *métier*. It wasn't fair to be critical, but I did have a nagging fear of what would happen to him if, day after day, he worked to refine instruments of death. I couldn't say this to him, but in October we would be married, and that would surely work miracles.

The only witness at our wedding was my cousin Muriel, Elizabeth's mother. Muriel was a stalwart family upholder, and I was grateful to her. My mother had not met Harry, and disliked the idea of him, and as she wasn't good at hiding her feelings, I was thankful she stayed away. In fact we had no parental blessing, for Harry didn't ask his father - nor did I ever meet either him or Harry's sister. There was no explanation, just a shrug and, "Maybe sometime."

So we got on with our lives, Harry to work, and I to my studies which from the very first lecture, plunged me into the excitement of free-for-all discussions on subjects I'd wrestled with on my own. The four-year programme covered social history, philosophy, psychology and social organization. It was a banquet, but Harry wasn't pleased when his supper wasn't ready on time because I was absorbed in writing or studying. Also I felt nervous about cooking, my one skill being limited to roasting the little pheasants and partridges Sandy had so distressfully shot. I took some cooking lessons which weren't much help: but I got a bit better at having meals on time.

Early in the new year of 1951 I wrote a paper which included a description of the Boimondau experiment. My professor returned it with the suggestion that I should circulate it to a few people who might be interested; he jotted down names and addresses, and wished me luck. His suggestion seemed ridiculous, but I sent the paper off and told myself to expect nothing. There was only one reply, but on opening it I cried, "Harry, listen to this! The BBC wants me to give a talk on Boimondau. But I've never given any kind of talk."

Harry said with a grin, "You're always giving talks, so why not on the BBC?"

Stung into bravado I said, "All right, I will."

And so, on a fine spring day, and almost witless with panic, I arrived at the BBC building on Great Portland Street. Here a pleasant young woman took me to a very small room, furnished with a table, a chair and a microphone. It looked like a cell.

"In here?" I asked.

"In here," she said.

I sat on the one chair while I was told how to position the microphone and recognize the signal to begin. I thanked her faintly, watched her go to the door - and then she turned, and with a smile said, "Enjoy your talk. If you don't, nobody else will," and shut the door.

It seemed impossible to talk to a microphone with no breathing soul in sight, but the signal came on and there was no time to fuss. I took a deep breath, thought wildly, 'All right, you lot out there, listen to me,' and began.

Afterwards my guide said, "So you took my advice!"

"Did it sound all right?"

"Of course. You enjoyed yourself. Remember that for future use." Future use? That was a joke. This was probably the only public talk I'd ever give.

But it wasn't a joke. Not long after the broadcast a letter arrived, postmarked Bristol and signed by someone called Crofton Gane. He wanted more information about Boimondau, and asked if he might call on me, suggesting a day he could arrange to be in Woking.

Harry said he was probably a crackpot. "Why?" I asked, and confirmed the date, secretly wondering what I was in for.

Crofton Gane arrived exactly on time. I opened the door to a tall, broad-shouldered, white-haired man with a pleasant, rugged face. He was dressed in comfortable tweeds, and when he smiled, and firmly grasped my hand, I knew he was a friend.

We talked for a couple of hours. I learnt that for years Crofton had run a family furniture business in Bristol which had been one of the first to introduce Scandinavian furniture to England. He talked about Scandinavia's excellent craftsmanship and the simple, clean lines of their furniture, and then told me about the Trust he had set up to fund young English furniture makers to attend workshops in Scandinavia. "That sort of interchange is invaluable to young craftsmen," he said.

All of this was new, and made so much sense. Without realizing it, but because it all made sense, everything he said about the importance of good craftsmanship and interchange of skills, took root and, twenty years later, was a ground base for new beginnings.

Naturally I asked Crofton why he was interested in Boimondau, and he said, "Connections between people are vital if we are to work fruitfully together in any field. We ran our business as a partnership with the employees, though not nearly so radically as Boimondau. Your broadcast interested me because I believe there's much to be learnt from their work community." He paused, looked at me kindly, and said, "I'd greatly appreciate it if you would be my guest in Bristol and speak about Boimondau at our Rotary Club lunch in December."

Daunted by a vision of unsmiling businessmen in dark suits, I asked, "Rotary Club? What is that?" He explained, and I said his invitation was a tall order for someone who'd only talked to a microphone, and that only once.

He took my ignorance about Rotary Clubs without flinching, and after reassuring me I'd have a friendly reception in Bristol, he said, "People in business are slow to change, but new ideas are like seeds; some fall by the wayside, others take root. They may grow slowly, but one day the business world will accept the necessity to treat workers like human beings." After that I could hardly refuse his invitation.

Over the next few months it was a relief to have the BBC script ready for the Rotary Club ordeal. But in December no relief was offered when I stood on a podium in a Bristol restaurant hoping I wouldn't make an ass of myself. Male faces were lined up on either side of long tables, each table covered with very white cloths dotted with little vases of flowers. There seemed a lot of tables. They fanned out lengthwise, the male faces like pink melons, silent and expectant. 'Enjoy yourself!' I thought, breathed deeply, and began.

The following week a letter from Crofton enclosed a cutting from the Western Daily Press which began:

> IT IS NOT often that Bristol Rotarians have a woman speaker after their weekly luncheons at the Berkeley Cafe; they had one yesterday whom they will remember for a very long time.

For a dizzy moment it seemed possible I'd changed the Bristol business world. Then I read the next part:

> Thelma Edge is not the typical woman speaker. Young, quiet and unassuming, with a face most actresses would envy (and probably spoil by make-up) she won attention for an unspectacular subject by sheer sincerity and mastery of the facts.

What had my face got to do with anything? At least the summary of what I'd said was to the point, and ruefully I couldn't quarrel with the writer's conclusions - especially as he wrapped them up so prettily:

> Rotarians, who include so many businessmen, are perhaps not intrinsically the most interested in an experiment in factory co-partnership...But before Mrs. Edge had finished they were wishing Great George's two o'clock closure was not so inexorable.

Obviously it was going to take more than my face, sincerity and mastery of the facts to start a revolution in business organization. But I had gained a friend. For the rest of Crofton's life we kept in touch about Boimondau and other French co-operatives - and above all, he applauded my studies.

In the new year of 1952 we began a course on social history, and I was cheered to learn how many other people had, over the centuries, wanted to change the world. But in the spring I reported joyously to Crofton that I was pregnant, and wrote, "This baby will surely change our lives - so for now, changing the world of business must wait."

At this time we moved to a farm near Maidenhead. The farmer's wife, Mrs. Marshallsay, made us delicious farm meals, which pleased Harry and gave me freedom to study as well as make baby clothes, do exercises, and walk in the lanes and fields around the farm. I felt wonderfully well, and these months were mostly blissful. Harry's moods were still volatile, but I kept my mind on the coming baby, and Mrs. Marshallsay who was happy to be a surrogate mother. She was from the north of England, a neat little person with as proverbial a heart of gold as ever walked and talked. She told me stories of her hard youth, and memorably of working as a 'pupil' teacher straight out of school.

"We were paid a pittance," she said, "but we weren't as badly off as many of the children's families. The poor little mites! Some of them came to school barefoot and a cotton shift, even in the depths of winter. Our problem was that they were hungry as well as bone cold, and they'd fall asleep, cold and hungry in the warm schoolroom. So us teachers pooled our few spare pennies to buy bread and feed the children. We had to: you can't teach children without something in their little bellies."

When Harry had one of his black moods I'd remember those children. I doubt he'd ever been in such straits, but in the working-class world destitution must have been only too real, and might strike any time. At least our baby was all right, already kicking lustily as if anxious to get out into the world. He/she was real, and we would be all right.

Our son Leo was born on December 20, 1952. Nothing could match the moment when he was laid on my thigh and I felt him – damp and warm and alive. That was a rapture beyond compare, whatever the future held.

Harry had stayed for a while as the labour pains came and went, on and on, but he left around suppertime. Leo finally arrived just after midnight, and Harry came in to see us later that morning. He was so delighted with his son, and it was good to feel I'd given him something he wanted. But after he'd gone, the nurse found me in tears.

"Whatever is the matter dear?" she asked. I mopped my eyes and said I was just being silly, it was nothing. The 'nothing' was indeed silly. I had asked Harry what he'd done while I was giving birth, and he said he'd played bridge with friends. Sounds reasonable - except I didn't know he liked playing bridge, and had never heard of the friends. All of a sudden I was engulfed by loneliness, and wept.

Later, with Leo feeding contentedly in my arms, I thought how this beautiful boy had been born of our loving, and whispered to him, "It will be all right, little love, it will be all right," and felt better. Wasn't there something in law that said women after childbirth were not in their right minds? "So push off!" I murmured to that pesky little *afreet*, the little demon of fear that sometimes pinched my heart. We were all right.

And we were all right. I gave thanks for Mrs. Marshallsay's help, for I knew nothing about babies, and for a while was afraid I might do some fatal act, or overlook a vital need. But what's wonderful about a baby is that you do what is necessary simply because the baby is there, crying, or mucky, or just needing a cuddle. Even so, I dreamt once that Leo's head fell off; I caught it, but woke before I could pop it back on, and crept out of bed to make sure he was in one piece.

I soon got into the routine, and he was a good baby. But it wasn't so easy to handle my mother's reaction to the news of his birth. Her reply began with a blunt refusal to see him, and then followed several pages full of anger and accusations. The one phrase which stuck in my head was, 'You always flap your eyes at Edward.' What was this about? Did she mean I *flirted* with Edward? With my *stepfather?* Feeling rather sick I stood with the letter in my hand until, unbidden, in my mind I heard my mother vehemently exclaim, 'You were so lucky Thelma! In Texas I always had you tagging along after me.' How odd – she'd said that when I stayed with her after David's death. I'd just described my visit to Jerusalem, and out came that exclamation like a slap. Now, holding her angry letter, up came a picture of her walking beside a tall young Texan in San Antonio. It was clear as a movie still – the two of them laughing, and me, trying to catch her hand. I know what's wrong – I feel left out. But how could that be, we were happy in Texas. Then as if in confirmation, I hear my mother murmuring, 'Dear peaceful Texas, how I loved you!'

I tore up the letter, knowing I must wait. Later I'd write again, and send a photograph of Leo. For now, we must get on with our lives: we had Leo, Harry was stimulated by his work, and I was looking forward to January when I would start a new course in psychology at a college in Guildford.

The college was about an hour's drive away, so I ate early and Harry came back with the car before six. All went well until the fogs began in February. The only way to see where I was going was to drive slowly, with my head hanging out of the window, so twice I was late home. The second time Harry said irritably "You shouldn't be driving in the fog, and I don't know why you bother to go on with these courses. They're a waste of time. You should be content to be a mother."

"I am being a mother," I said. "And I've been driving in fogs for years. As for the courses, I enjoy them - and don't you enjoy having Leo to yourself once a week?" I carried on with the course, the fogs cleared, and when Leo was crawling all over the place we moved from the farm to a rented house closer to Maidenhead.

It was a pleasant house with a big garden, but now I had to clean and cook as well as look after Leo. Sometimes supper was late, and the house in a mess, and Harry too ready to find fault, usually with my shortcomings as a mother. This began to get under my skin, and one day, feeling dispirited, I went to a local pediatrician and asked him if Leo was doing all right. His response was a gift: "If all the babies I see were in such good shape as yours, I'd have nothing to worry about."

I felt good about that, but not at all good when Harry called me a whore after I'd chatted with the milkman. Hurt and offended, I wept in frustration. But I was studying psychology, and began to brood on the reason for Harry's changeable moods. If it was jealousy, there was nothing to be jealous about - or did he imagine some cause? And then I remembered the war stories I'd written when I was on Dartmoor.

Two copies of the stories had been bound and tucked away for no special purpose - I just wanted to remember them. But maybe Harry couldn't forget them. All right - the stories must go. So I junked both copies - just like that, into the garbage. Then, while Leo had his afternoon nap, I made a bonfire in the garden and burned David's few letters. I watched the frail, blackened paper moths fly skywards, murmured to David, "Please understand. They're only bits of paper." But they felt like bits of me.

That evening I told Harry what I'd done and he didn't say much. But a few days later he gave me a hug and said, "Shall we buy a house?" My heart lifted: maybe I'd done the right thing.

❧ 45 ❧

Oh! Peter Pumpkin Eater.
O Canada!

1955. I write these figures in August of 2001, trying to feel the ground of this chapter under my feet. So far the past, with its players and surroundings, has sprung up real as yesterday. Now, in 1955, the past seems more diffuse, out of which thrust landmarks, some quite everyday, others not. But they are real enough.

For a start are two landmarks. The first is in the summer when I wrote the final exam for a Social Studies Diploma from London University. There is nothing diffuse about this top-of-the-hill moment ending four years of extra-mural courses in social history, philosophy, psychology and organization. For the first time in my life I had begun learning how to study, and I was ready for the exam, the date marked on my calendar. But then came a hitch - we were offered the use of a seaside cottage for the week which included my exam day.

"You could take it next year," Harry said. But I was damned if I'd cancel either the exam or the free holiday, and quick research disclosed that exams could be written anywhere if they were supervised by an approved invigilator. The vicar near our seaside cottage was such a one, and cheerfully offered to do the job. He was a gentle, kindly man and I wrote the exam in his study. Afterwards he praised my four-year diligence, and I walked back to Leo and Harry, feeling worthy and triumphant.

"How was it?" Harry asked.

Glowing, I said I thought I'd done all right. And I did. Harry was nice about it, maybe a little proud of me - as I was of him, for he was obviously doing well in his job. Not that I knew much about his work, any more than he knew what I'd been tackling in the last four years. But neither of us was turning out quite as expected.

One person who did know what I'd been up to was Crofton Gane. For the last six years, ever since the day I'd charmed, but failed to reform the Bristol Rotary Club members, Crofton had become a staunch friend. I sent him a card, saying simply, 'Whoopeee! I've done it!'

The second landmark of 1955 was when we bought a house. This was in October, Harry's fortieth birthday; Leo would be three in December, and I still thirty-nine. Harry found the house, and I suspected he hoped it would replace my old cottage, for it was thatched, and even had a roomy wood-sided building in the garden,, much like the studio at Albury. I was touched that Harry should want to make up for my selling the old cottage, but I wished he hadn't. That was the past. But I was touched.

We had £2,000 left from the sale of the Albury cottage, and this we used as down payment on the new house. It was a cosy house down a leafy, dead-end lane in the small Berkshire village of Cookham Dean. It had three bedrooms, a splendid Aga cooker in the kitchen, and everything in good shape except for the hideous colour of the dining-room walls, which we repainted. Harry had an ever-burning fireplace installed in the drawing-room, and in the spring he made a sand pit for Leo in the garden. He also devised an impressive construction of posts and wires for raspberry canes. The sand pit was a great success, and I grew vegetables alongside the raspberry canes, though don't remember picking raspberries: but blackberry bushes grew everywhere, and blackberry-picking expeditions were fun. We were also lucky in having just one neighbour whose young daughter, Lynn, was happy to spend hours playing with Leo, and in the nearby village of Cookham there was a good play-school which had a place for him in the new year.

Altogether we had the makings of a good life - but no sooner have I made this affirmation than up springs a scene, clear as a movie still. I am sitting alone at the dining-room table. It is December, 1955, the first Christmas in our own house. On the table are two piles of Christmas cards, one already enveloped and addressed, the other waiting for me to add snippets of jolly news to the Christmas greetings. But I don't feel jolly: in fact my heart feels like a lump of lead.

The scene yields no reason for gloom, so I can only guess I'm missing friends and family. We keep in touch, but inevitably they are no longer part my life. I am beginning to make friends in the village, but the family is scattered, and there's no centre to replace the ever-welcoming thirteen bedrooms of Copford Rectory. Of course not - that is long gone. Phil and Dick have a cottage on Dartmoor, but they are only there in the summer. In the winter they ski at Kitzbüül in Austria where Phil built a chalet after the war. Typically he refused to obey a post-war travel restriction which made it illegal to take more than £50 out of England in any one year. Phil said, "I've served this country all my life. I'm damned if any tom-fool politician can tell me what to do with my money."

This reminds me of Ray, an Irishman who married Phil's daughter June after the war. To Ray's formal request for June's hand in marriage, Phil replied warmly, "My dear chap, I'm delighted. The Ruck Keenes can do with some peasant blood." Ray told this story with gusto, and even Phil laughed at himself - but said it was best to say what you think, then everyone knew where they were.

One family person I miss is my cousin Elizabeth. She and George and their three children are now far away in Canada. I address their envelope to Kingston, Ontario. Kingston, a dot on a map. I wonder what it's like.

A last card goes to my mother, who is coming to visit us in the spring. I waited for nearly a year before answering the strange, angry letter she wrote after Leo was born. I enclosed a photograph of Leo with brief, hopeful letter and she answered by return, as if nothing untoward had happened. She is coming to see us in the spring. I hope she and Harry will like each other. Yes, these were probably how I got out of my gloom that first Christmas for the three of us in our own house.

By the new year we had settled into a routine that had the makings of a good life. Every weekday, after Harry drove off to work, I strapped Leo on the back of my bicycle and we whizzed down the hill to his play-school. Back home I quickly tidied the house, then did the things I enjoyed. I taught myself to bake bread, and did this regularly: if I shopped at the village store I maybe dropped in for a chat with a friend, for already I had begun making friends, though Harry made little effort on that score. I usually fitted in a bit of piano practice before fetching Leo from Cookham, though mostly I played marches and songs so he and next-door-Lynn could prance around, banging saucepan lids. That was a favourite winter pleasure; another was building a house, big enough to creep into, with large wooden blocks and pieces that fitted them together like outsize Lego). Harry was good at finding inventive toys, but he hated mess, so we had to clean up before he came home to avoid a black mood of disapproval.

And there were black moods. They often came without warning, a sudden shock that would have me in tears. A natural optimism was a disadvantage, for I never managed to be prepared, which is why they are landmarks. But also there were small landmarks of incidents with Leo, bright treasures, real as yesterday.

One treasure involved angels. Neither Harry nor I were churchgoers, so angels were not an everyday feature in our lives; but it was Christmas, and angels are a lovely part of the Christmas story. I should have stuck with Christmas and the music of angels in the heavens. But someone lent me a little book about angels, with illustrations, and one bedtime, that first Christmas, Leo and I looked at it together.

The first picture showed an open road on which stood a very large angel beside a rather small child. "What is that bird doing?" Leo asked.

At once I realized I was on shaky ground. Lamely I said it was an angel, and angels lived in the sky and loved children. On the next page the child was in bed, with an angel at each of its four corners. "What are the birds doing now?" asked Leo.

I repeated that angels loved children, and rashly said that angels were also round *his* bed. He made no comment until, after I kissed him goodnight, he said, with great firmness, "Goodnight, Mummy, and take those birds away."

I did better a year or two later when I began reading Bible stories from the St. James' version. One day, on reaching a chapter about who begat whom, I said, "We'll skip this one, it's a bit boring."

But Leo said, "Read it, Mummy. I like the sound of the words." I was grateful for this - and for the angel fiasco.

The book angel was a bore, solid as Boy Scout with fake wings, no touch of angelic transcendence. Leo, like all children, was a powerful lie-detector.

I remembered this when he asked me, in a matter-of-fact way, how babies were made (he was probably six). I took a deep breath and, without excessive detail, explained.

"That's right," he said. "That's what Paul told me." Paul was the son of good friends in the village who, unfortunately, Harry didn't like.

A different memory is of Leo and I walking through the woods to Marlow. These were the Wild Woods of *The Wind in the Willows*, for Kenneth Grahame spent much of his childhood near our village. Leo and I are on our way to see the film about *Polyanna*. It is a cold winter's day, the sun shines through the trees, and every twig and branch is covered with ice. On our way back the sun is going down, and we walk through woods hung with little glistening icicles.

My mother's visit in the spring of 1956 was a good landmark. Harry was pleasant to her, she seemed to like him, and during the day the two of us had a leisurely time together. We did not speak of her angry letter, so I never knew its cause, but that didn't matter. When we parted I felt closer to her than I had for many years - and her coming was a needed touch of parental blessing. I made occasional efforts to persuade Harry to get in touch with his father and sister, but nothing happened. I'd have liked to know my father-in-law; however crusty-tempered, he was a craftsman, and Leo would have enjoyed hearing all about panel-beating. But I had to accept that Harry had cut himself off from his roots, and that was not going to change.

Maybe my mother's visit left a kind of blessing, for not long afterwards Harry put his arms round me and said, "I'd like to give you something you really want."

I was so happy that I said without hesitation, "What I'd really love, now I have my piano again, would be a few lessons. I need someone to get me going." Then I wished I'd not been so quick, feeling too late that Harry would have liked me to ask for an expensive dress. But he smiled, and I promised to find a teacher who wasn't too expensive.

With no presentiment of disaster, I got in touch with Kathleen Long in London. She was a teacher as well as a concert pianist whose playing I liked, and she took me on. After the first lesson she said, "You could be a good little pianist." Did 'little' refer to size or quality? Never mind, it was praise.

Maidenhead is close to London with a frequent train service, so I didn't bother with train times. But after my second lesson I got on to a slow train by mistake, and was late home.

Leo was with Lynn's mother next door, and fast asleep. I carried him home, still sleeping, but the front door was locked and I had no key. Harry's car was in the drive, so I knew he was home. Finally he let me in.

He said nothing, but his anger was like an affront, and I went straight upstairs with Leo. When he was tucked up in bed I crossed the landing to our bedroom, and was undressing when Harry came up, shut the door, and turning on me demanded to know whom I'd been dallying with in London. I said quietly I wasn't dallying with anyone, and tried to explain about the slow train. But he cut me short, calling me a liar and a whore, and smashed my bedside lamp on the floor. I went out of the room, but he came after me and took me by the throat. We were at the top of the stairs, and knowing I must break into his rage I called out to Leo. He woke with a cry of "Mummy!" - and Harry let me go.

I took Leo into our bed and told him his favourite story of the Little Red Hen. Harry meanwhile banged around in the cupboard under the roof of our bedroom, muttering about leaving the house: but he didn't leave.

I consulted a solicitor about divorce, and through friends was offered a job as house-mother at Dartington Hall, a remarkable school where Leo would have free tuition. I came very close to accepting: but I had no experience in looking after a houseful of children. If I wasn't up to the job, Leo's life would again be disrupted. But more to the point, Harry was Leo's father and loved his son. I could not take him away.

If Harry was writing this story it would, of course, zero in on my failings, and not without cause. I was no patient Griselda and could be stung into anger and unkindness when Harry abused me, though more often his abuse reduced me to tears. That further exasperated me: tears were feeble, but the anguish was real, and the ugly abuse played havoc with trust - and sex. I guess this is so because sexual loving is a wholeness beyond lust, springing from the heart's core to engage everything from the whirlwind of rapture to the little lazy pleasures of pillow talk and jokes. So we had a problem, and though we so wanted to love and be beloved, neither of us was turning out quite as expected - or invented.

Either word will do. We'd both expected to jump the barrier of our different backgrounds, but instead of a wall there was a gulf requiring bridges, and our bridges kept falling down. Of course they did: I was gentry ('Out of the handkerchief drawer, darling'), and Harry was out of the working-class. From these states of mind had gown attitudes, behaviour and speech, all tangled up with personal pains and expectations (or inventions).

What did I invent? That's easy - a comrade in common purpose with whom I could talk about anything without fear of giving offence. Harry expected much the same. But I rattled him, just by being myself, and he couldn't trust me - like Peter in the nursery jingle:

Peter, Peter Pumpkin Eater,
Had a wife and couldn't keep her.
Put her in a pumpkin shell
And there he kept her very well.

It's not clear what the wife thought about the pumpkin shell - and I was content to look after Leo, and the house and garden, and try to cook edible meals. But I couldn't live with doors closed, either to keep me in, or shut life out. So we had a problem.

My cousin Elizabeth's visit to us in the summer of 1956 could have been a problem, but Harry made a real effort to welcome her and George and their three children. Leo loved having a steady supply of kids to play with, and though it was a bit of a squeeze, this was how families should be, even without Copford Rectory and thirteen bedrooms.

Not long after we had the house to ourselves again Harry drove up in an unfamiliar car, got out and said cheerfully, "It's for you." This was a wonderful gift that I was sure presaged something good. For a while it was good; but one day Harry drove the car away. I can't remember any reason, though it might have been linked to the choir I sang with in Cookham.

It was a good choir (all women) and I loved singing with them. One evening as I was about to leave for a practice, he said irritably, "You should be staying home with Leo. Surely he's more important than this choir you go to?"

"But you are here," I said. "Leo and I have sung a song, and I've read him a story. Do read him another, he'd love it." Harry said nothing, and I, half-laughing, half-exasperated, exclaimed, "Dammit, Harry, the choir isn't a blazing orgy." He didn't laugh, and I left, rather too near to tears. I minded being sniped at, and having something I enjoyed belittled, instead of shared.

To be fair, we seemed to share less and less. Harry never talked about his work, and probably couldn't, given the hush-hush nature of aircraft development. But he sees my abhorrence of war as personal disloyalty, whether I say nothing, or the wrong thing. This must have happened at a reception for aeronautical engineers and military technocrats that Harry took me to. In a big, crowded room Lord knows what I said, but Harry is staring at me. I am miserable, and between us yawns a great gulf.

This small incident gave rise to a recurrent dream I thought of as the 'Essen dream'. It always starts with a replay of my watching Harry walk away down a long corridor, just as I had done in Essen. The tenderness of that day is there, but with it is a new, unbearable anguish as I call, "Harry! Harry!" and he will not turn his head.

So began an emotional roller-coaster existence of soaring up and whooshing down, interspersed with sketches of everydayness. It was bearable because, like the weather, it happens, and you were there.

It also happened that our family contacts were rare, and we had no mutual friends. If Harry had friends at work, he never brought them home, and he usually found reasons for disliking the friends I made in the village. I was fond of Chris and Elizabeth Thornycroft, whose son Paul had told Leo how babies were made. Chris had fought in the Spanish Civil war, and every year the family marched in the Aldermaston protest against nuclear war. Harry damned them as Reds.

"Do you have to be so adamant about views you don't share?" I asked him. "Chris is a very clever engineer, and they aren't communist any more. I know you disapprove of the Aldermaston protests, but couldn't you discuss your differences?"

Harry simply said that his job would be compromised if I had anything to do with the Aldermaston march, and reiterated, "I'm not interested in your Red friends."

I didn't join the march, but one day, quite by chance, Leo and I saw in the distance a great mass of people approaching along the main road to Maidenhead. We were above the road and in silence watched the tide of men, women, and children flow below us. "They want to stop countries making atom bombs," I told Leo. Then, choked by my first sight of a citizen protest, I thought, 'One day I will be part of this.' The words were clear as a voice, but as though someone else was the thinker.

I had no doubts about who was the thinker the day Harry took Leo and me to the Farnborough Air Show. This was Harry's outing, and I was happy that the three of us were doing something together. Leo was eight and fascinated by all things mechanical, especially aircraft, and Harry was taking trouble to answer his questions.

Halfway through the show a single aircraft suddenly roared into the sky, and Harry said to Leo, "Isn't it beautiful? It's a new machine for the Air Force." A fighter? A bomber? He didn't say. As I stared up at the aircraft feeling sick, Harry asked abruptly, "What's the matter now?"

I said, "It's so powerful, and the pilot doesn't match the technology."

"What are you talking about? The pilots are very capable."

"You know what I mean. That mannikin can wipe out people and cities and countrysides, and never hear a scream or see a speck of blood. I think we've gone mad."

"You're being neurotic and spoiling Leo's day."

"I'm being human," I said, but Leo's troubled face was a reproof. Would I ever manage to stop saying exactly what I felt?

Several weeks after the air show something induced me to suggest inviting a couple of people to supper. Maybe it was an impulse to try and be a normal couple, and share a meal with friends. I knew Harry tolerated the couple, so when he said, "If you want to," my spirits rose.

I enjoyed making the table look pretty, and set out the beautiful glass goblets my mother had given me. The evening went reasonably well. Harry was polite, though a bit stiff, and after our guests left it was rather a relief to go into the kitchen, and do the uncomplicated job of washing up.

I had just put the last glass goblet on the draining board when Harry came into the kitchen. He didn't say anything, just stood there - and suddenly I was frightened. So I kept quiet, went on washing dishes, and for a moment nothing happened. Then without a word he bent forward, picked up a glass goblet, and dashed it to pieces on the floor. Then, as I hung on to the sanity of washing up, Harry smashed every goblet, one by one.

No word was said. I had nothing to say because I knew, absolutely, that I would no longer be a party to what was damaging all of us. The decision simply made itself, and the door closed on feeling. Now I would need every ounce of energy to plan how to leave Harry, take Leo with me, and earn a living.

The rest is briefly told. I had no money other than the equity of £2,000 in the house, and needed a profession which left me free in the school holidays. Teaching was the obvious choice, even though I found schools depressing.

There was a teacher training college near Reading, and I was accepted for the following year. Next I needed money to buy a car, and somebody put me on to selling Tupperware. At the end of three months I put a down payment on an old van. Meanwhile Leo needed a stable background while I studied at the college. My Red friends recommended a well-endowed old city school found by Edward VII. It had become co-educational and was only an hour's drive away. I tried to make sense of this plan to Leo, but it was hard for him; he was not quite ten when he went away for his first term as a boarder.

I don't know how I persuaded Harry to accept these changes, but I did. I'd taken possession of myself, and went ahead.

Halfway through the first college year my mother had a stroke, and died within a week. I joined Joy and Edward for her cremation, and as the coffin slid into the furnace I remembered the two blissful years in San Antonio with her and Willoughby, and gave her thanks for endowing me with some of her spirit.

I majored in music at the college. I chose folk song for my thesis (titled *Are the Beatles folk?*), and made good use of the months I'd spent exploring English folk song at my cottage after the war. I graduated, and picked up a vacancy at a school in Marlow for the mandatory year of teaching. It was a church school, poorly funded, and I had 42 seven-year-olds crammed into a classroom with minimal teaching materials. That year I probably learnt more than they did.

Throughout these three years Harry and I lived a strange, alienated existence. I continued to do my household tasks, but we spoke rarely. It was a miserable situation for Leo, and flush with my first salary from teaching I took Leo to Austria for two weeks' skiing. Perhaps having money of my own went to my head, and at the end of my year's teaching Leo and I flew to Canada for three weeks with Elizabeth and her family on an island in Lake Ontario.

One night before we left I stood on the lakeside and thought how the land went north, right to the Pole, and on the west coast the sea flowed all the way to Japan. I thought of the Indians and Eskimos who had been the first people in Canada, and were still here: of Quebec, where French was spoken: and of the people who had come from all over the world to make a home here in this country which was barely a hundred years old. Canada was still being made, it was amazing - and I fell in love with it.

In mid-July the following year, 1966, Leo flew alone to join his cousins on Garden Island. As I watched his sturdy, beloved figure walk off to take his seat on the aircraft I prayed to whatever gods might be that I'd not asked too much of him. Harry had signed a solicitor's letter, giving me permission to take Leo to Canada, but I was afraid he might try to stop us. We had no time to waste: I was fifty, and Leo nearly fifteen. It was a bad time for him to make such a break, but staying was worse, and I was sure I could join him before he started school.

The only money I had was the £2,000, from the house equity, so I sold all the furniture that was mine, keeping only books and a sturdy, Elizabethan family oak chest. Into this I packed grandmother Birdie Ruck Keene's two legacies - the blue-and-white Crescent Worcester china, and the miniature Victorian chest of drawers where Birdie had kept her handkerchiefs.

By mid-August I was ready to leave - but suddenly there was a problem about Leo's immigrant status, and I couldn't leave until it was sorted out in Canada. It was the worst thing that could happen, fearing that Leo might not understand. All I could do was trust Elizabeth to explain - but the delay dragged on until it was clear I couldn't leave England until late in October. John and Diana Murray said I could stay with them, but suddenly I wanted out of England. My cousin June and Ray asked me to join them in a chalet they'd rented above Lausanne - and I took off, first for a week in Venice (where I'd never been), and thence to Switzerland.

In Venice I stayed cheaply at a hostel run by monks, and it was wonderful - except I wished Leo was there, enjoying everything. But that visit to June and Ray turned into a nightmare.

After a few days at the chalet Ray left for England on a business trip, and not many days later a London hospital telephoned to say that Ray was very ill, and June should come at once. "They didn't explain why," she said, and asked me to go on ahead. "Here's the key to Ray's pad in London and I'll join you there in a couple of days." When she arrived I had to tell her that Ray had a brain tumour, and might not survive surgery.

But he survived splendidly. Early in November Leo's immigration problem was resolved and, for the third time I booked my passage on a ship to Canada. The day before leaving England I went to say goodbye to Ray at the hospital - and Harry was there. He took me aside and asked me not to leave, looking at me with a boy's face. But it was too late, the door had closed.

June came to see me off at Victoria station. The boat train was in, faces staring out of the carriage windows, and after taking stock of them June said glumly, "Not a very inspiring bunch, are they? Maybe they'll improve on acquaintance."

"Well," I said, "they probably feel terrified and exhilarated, like me." June raised an eyebrow, but I grew inspired and went on, "One thing's for sure, I won't look back. I'll be *there*, you see. That's what matters, really *being* where you are."

For the next twenty-five years I was too occupied to look back. Then, on and off for ten years, I did look back, right back, and wrote down how it was I came over here from back there.

అఖ్గ

Epilogue

*La plus grande chose du monde
c'est de savoir être à soi.*
(The greatest thing in the world
is to know you belong to yourself.)
Michel Montaigne, 1533-1592

As our ship sailed up the St. Lawrence to Montreal I went on deck to study our new country. The land was flat and dusted with snow, punctuated by leafless skeleton trees, black against a dour sky. Cold. After a while I was joined by a stranger, an elderly man, who asked if this was my first visit to Canada. I said that I was an immigrant, and my son had gone ahead to Ontario.

"Whereabouts?"

"Kingston."

"Ah yes! The bastion of Empire Loyalists. They'll love your accent." I was about to ask why, but he added, "Well, if you can stick out the first two years, you'll be all right."

This wasn't cheery advice, but even on that bleak November day it made good sense. 'So I'll not look back,' I thought, and when I was alone again I tried to imagine sticking out the next two years, what it would be like, what I would discover. What I did discover is another story. But I'll steal from it to answer a question, the one Birdie Ruck Keene asked my father in 1915: "Who are the Garsias, dear boy?"

Luckily she never knew that they were not only Spanish, but also Jews, though she might have found a speck of comfort in their status. Angela Garcia - a newfound cousin in Victoria, B.C. - agrees that they were probably members of the intellectual and commercial élite of educated Jews who flourished in Medieval Spain. But in 1492 the iniquitous Torquemada, Director General of the Spanish Inquisition, proclaimed that Infidels must convert to Catholicism. Refusal meant expulsion from Spain (or being burnt at the stake during a popular auto-da-fé).

Some 170,000 Jews fled Spain, many to the Caribbean, and our Garcias ('c', not yet the anglicised 's') settled in Jamaica. In the late 18th century, my great-grandfather, Aaron Garcia, left Jamaica to train as a doctor in London. Probably it was then he changed 'Aaron' to 'Adrian', and spelled Garsia with an 's'. The British were not partial to foreigners, and Jews were generally despised, and socially marginalized. Aaron returned to practise in Jamaica. His son, my grandfather Willoughby Marston Garsia, also trained as a doctor in London and practised awhile in South America. But finally, back in England, he met Minna, my grandmother, and settled in England - and kept silent about his Jewish ancestry.

Was it possible he never told Minna? Did my mother and her brothers not know? It is too late now to find out why, in the 20th century, my generation was robbed of knowing about this vital, interesting ancestry. But now, two lifetimes later, the silence suddenly speaks loud and clear. It speaks of social terrorism (or the Handkerchief Drawer Syndrome) which divides races and cultures, religions and classes into Us and Them, divides them because They are different, and We fear them - and vice versa.

In the new millennium technology is creating a global village in which ideas get about: failure to communicate, whatever the differences, simply won't do. Differences are expressions of ideas, which are one of the means by which we learn to belong to ourselves. Ideas are seeds, blowing in the wind.

You can't bomb a seed, if you try, all you get is collateral damage, which can turn ideas sour, or inflammatory. Besides, what example do governments provide their citizens? Hessler, a young war hero of Vietnam, has an answer which Tony Parker recorded in his book, *The Violence of our Lives*. Hessler, in jail for murdering his wife, describes how he was trained to kill Vietnamese villagers without thought or guilt, and that's how it was when he killed his wife. But he cries, "I'm not saying I'm not to blame. I am and always will be, like others they taught to think the same way. But it was them in the first place, they are the ones who put it into me, the violence of our lives."

'Them'? There is no 'them' that isn't 'us'. Interchange, not Intifada, is the better path. It's a matter of sticking it out, as emigrants do in an unfamiliar land. We've done it, so it's possible.

December, 2001

Bibliography

This story has relied upon memory. I never kept a diary, but after World War Two, people I had known wrote books about their war experiences. I did not plunder these books. They confirmed dates, and filled in my own memories. Often our accounts differed in detail, sometimes there was no avoiding using the same words. I admit to lifting a quote from Richard Usborne's *Clubland Heroes;* but he didn't mind.

The following lists title, author and publisher:

Special Operations Europe: scenes from the anti-Nazi war
by Basil Davidson.
Victor Gollancz, 1980.

A Long Row of Candles
by Cy Sulzberger
Macmillan (New York), 1969.

Marina
by Cy Sulzberger
Crown Publishers (New York), 1978.

Peter Fleming
by Duff Hart-Davis
Cape (London), 1974.

Foreign Body in the Eye
by Charles Mott-Radclyffe
Cooper (London), 1975.

Waiting for the Firing Squad
by Alexis Ladas
Harpers, 1964.

In Aleppo Once
by Taqui Altounyan
John Murray, 1969.

Clubland Heroes
The nostalgic study of the fiction of John Buchan, 'Sapper' and
Dornford Yates.
by Richard Usborne.
Hutchinson, (revised edition 1983).

Journey Down a Blind Alley
by Mary Borden (Lady Spears)
Harpers, 1946.

Note:
Under Two Flags:
the life of Major-General Sir Edward Louis Spears
by Max Egremont
Weidenfeld & Nicolson, 1997.
I did not read this book. It came out when I was writing about Spears as
he seemed to me in my mid-twenties. But when I read the review of
what was obviously a perceptive biography, I was glad to find my very
personal impressions confirmed.

ISBN 1553691350

9 781553 691358

Edwards Brothers Malloy
Oxnard, CA USA
September 16, 2014